XML
BY EXAMPLE

201 West 103rd Street
Indianapolis, Indiana 46290

Benoît Marchal

XML by Example

Copyright © 2000 by Que ®

International Standard Book Number: 0-7897-2242-9

Library of Congress Catalog Card Number: 99-66449

Printed in the United States of America

First Printing: December 1999

01 00   7 6 5

Trademarks

Warning and Disclaimer

Publisher
John Pierce

Acquisitions Editor
Todd Green

Development Editor
Susan Hobbs

Technical Editor
Karl Fast

Managing Editor
Thomas F. Hayes

Project Editor
Karen S. Shields

Copy Editor
Sossity Smith

Indexer
Tina Trettin

Proofreader
Maribeth Echard

Team Coordinator
Julie Otto

Media Developer
Jay Payne

Interior Designer
Karen Ruggles

Cover Designer
Rader Design

Copy Writer
Eric Borgert

Production
Louis Porter Jr.

Contents at a Glance

Table of Contents

Dedication

To Pascale for her never-failing trust and patience.

Acknowledgments

This book is an important station on a long journey. I would like to thank all the people who have helped me and trusted me along the way. In chronological order, Ph. Capelle, who helped a confused student; Ph. van Bastelaer and J. Berge, who were curious about SGML; H. Karunaratne and K. Kaur and the folks at Sitpro, who showed me London; S. Vincent, who suggested I get serious about writing; V. D'Haeyere, who taught me everything about the Internet; Ph. Vanhoolandt, who published my first article; M. Gonzalez, N. Hada, T. Nakamura, and the folks at Digital Cats, who published my first U.S. papers; S. McLoughlin, who helps with the newsletter; and T. Green, who trusted me with this book.

Thanks the XML/EDI Group and, in particular, M. Bryan, A. Kotok, B. Peat, and D. Webber.

Special thanks to my mother for making me curious.

Writing a book is a demanding task, both for a business and for a family. Thanks to my customers for understanding and patience when I was late. Special thanks to Pascale for not only showing understanding, but also for encouraging me!

About the Author

Benoît Marchal runs the consulting company, Pineapplesoft, which specializes in Internet applications, particularly e-commerce, XML, and Java. He has worked with major players in Internet development such as Netscape and EarthWeb, and is a regular contributor to `developer.com` and other Internet publications.

In 1997, he cofounded the XML/EDI Group, a think tank that promotes the use of XML in e-commerce applications. Benoît frequently leads corporate training on XML and other Internet technologies. You can reach him at `bmarchal@pineapplesoft.com`.

Tell Us What You Think!

As the reader of this book, you are our most important critic and commentator. We value your opinion and want to know what we're doing right, what we could do better, what areas you'd like to see us publish in, and any other words of wisdom you're willing to pass our way.

As a Publisher for Que, I welcome your comments. You can fax, email, or write me directly to let me know what you did or didn't like about this book—as well as what we can do to make our books stronger.

Please note that I cannot help you with technical problems related to the topic of this book, and that due to the high volume of mail I receive, I might not be able to reply to every message.

When you write, please be sure to include this book's title and author as well as your name and phone or fax number. I will carefully review your comments and share them with the author and editors who worked on the book.

Fax: 317-581-4666

Email: que.programming@macmillanusa.com

Mail: John Pierce
            Publisher
            Que-Programming
            201 West 103rd Street
            Indianapolis, IN 46290 USA

Introduction

The *by Example* Series

How does the *by Example* series make you a better programmer? The *by Example* series teaches programming using the best method possible. After a concept is introduced, you'll see one or more examples of that concept in use. The text acts as a mentor by figuratively looking over your shoulder and showing you new ways to use the concepts you just learned. The examples are numerous. While the material is still fresh, you see example after example demonstrating the way you use the material you just learned.

The philosophy of the *by Example* series is simple: The best way to teach computer programming is using multiple examples. Command descriptions, format syntax, and language references are not enough to teach a newcomer a programming language. Only by looking at many examples in which new commands are immediately used and by running sample programs can programming students get more than just a feel for the language.

Who Should Use This Book

XML by Example is intended for people with some basic HTML coding experience. If you can write a simple HTML page and if you know the main tags (such as <P>, <TITLE>, <H1>), you know enough HTML to understand this book. You don't need to be an expert, however.

Some advanced techniques introduced in the second half of the book (Chapter 7 and later) require experience with scripting and JavaScript. You need to understand loops, variables, functions, and objects for these chapters. Remember these are advanced techniques, so even if you are not yet a JavaScript wizard, you can pick up many valuable techniques in the book.

This book is for you if one of the following statements is true:

- You are an HTML whiz and want to move to the next level in Internet publishing.

- You publish a large or dynamic document base on the Web, on CD-ROM, in print, or by using a combination of these media, and you have heard XML can simplify your publishing efforts.

- You are a Web developer, so you know Java, JavaScript, or CGI inside out, and you have heard that XML is simple and enables you to do many cool things.

- You are active in electronic commerce or in EDI and you want to learn what XML has to offer to your specialty.

- You use software from Microsoft, IBM, Oracle, Corel, Sun, or any of the other hundreds of companies that have added XML to their products, and you need to understand how to make the best of it.

You don't need to know anything about SGML (a precursor to XML) to understand *XML by Example*. You don't need to limit yourself to publishing; *XML by Example* introduces you to all applications of XML, including publishing and nonpublishing applications.

This Book's Organization

This book teaches you about XML, the eXtensible Markup Language. XML is a new markup language developed to overcome limitations in HTML.

XML exists because HTML was successful. Therefore, XML incorporates many successful features of HTML. XML also exists because HTML could not live up to new demands. Therefore, XML breaks new ground when it is appropriate.

This book takes a hands-on approach to XML. Ideas and concepts are introduced through real-world examples so that you not only read about the concepts but also see them applied. With the examples, you immediately see the benefits and the costs associated with XML.

As you will see, there are two classes of applications for XML: publishing and data exchange. Data exchange applications include most electronic commerce applications. This book draws most of its examples from data exchange applications because they are currently the most popular. However, it also includes a very comprehensive example of Web site publishing.

I made some assumptions about you. I suppose you are familiar with the Web, insofar as you can read, understand, and write basic HMTL pages as well as read and understand a simple JavaScript application. You don't have to be a master at HTML to learn XML. Nor do you need to be a guru of JavaScript.

Most of the code in this book is based on XML and XML style sheets. When programming was required, I used JavaScript as often as possible. JavaScript, however, was not appropriate for the final example so I turned to Java.

You don't need to know Java to understand this book, however, because there is very little Java involved (again, most of the code in the final example is XML). Appendix A, "Crash Course on Java," will teach you just enough Java to understand the examples.

Conventions Used in This Book

EXAMPLE

Examples are identified by the icon shown at the left of this sentence:

Listing and code appears in monospace font, such as

`<?xml version="1.0"?>`

NOTE
Special notes augment the material you read in each chapter. These notes clarify concepts and procedures.

TIP
You'll find numerous tips offering shortcuts and solutions to common problems.

CAUTION
The cautions warn you about pitfalls that sometimes appear when programming in XML. Reading the caution sections will save you time and trouble.

What's Next

XML was introduced to overcome the limitations of HTML. Although the two will likely coexist in the foreseeable future, the importance of XML will only increase. It is important that you learn the benefits and limitations of XML so that you can prepare for the evolution.

Please visit the *by Example* Web site for code examples or additional material associated with this book:

`<http://www.quecorp.com/series/by_example/>`

Turn to the next page and begin learning XML by examples today!

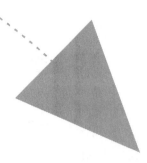

The XML Galaxy

This chapter introduces you to XML. It tells you the why and what: Why was XML developed and what is XML good at? Before we turn to how to use XML, we need to understand whether XML is an answer to your problems.

In this chapter, you will learn the essential concepts behind XML:

- which problems XML solves; in other words, what is XML good at;
- what is a markup language and what is the relationship between XML, HTML, and SGML;
- how and why XML was developed;
- typical applications of XML, with examples;
- the benefits of using XML when compared to HTML. Where is XML better than HTML?

Introduction

XML stands for the eXtensible Markup Language. It is a new markup language, developed by the W3C (World Wide Web Consortium), mainly to overcome limitations in HTML. The W3C is the organization in charge of the development and maintenance of most Web standards, most notably HTML. For more information on the W3C, visit its Web site at `www.w3.org`.

HTML is an immensely popular markup language. According to some studies there are 800 million Web pages, all based on HTML. HTML is supported by thousands of applications including browsers, editors, email software, databases, contact managers, and more.

Originally, the Web was a solution to publish scientific documents. Today it has grown into a full-fledged medium, equal to print and TV. More importantly, the Web is an interactive medium because it supports applications such as online shops, electronic banking, and trading and forums.

To accommodate this phenomenal popularity, HTML has been extended over the years. Many new tags have been introduced. The first version of HTML had a dozen tags; the latest version (HTML 4.0) is close to 100 tags (not counting browser-specific tags).

Furthermore, a large set of supporting technologies also has been introduced: JavaScript, Java, Flash, CGI, ASP, streaming media, MP3, and more. Some of these technologies were developed by the W3C whereas others were introduced by vendors.

However, everything is not rosy with HTML. It has grown into a complex language. At almost 100 tags, it is definitively not a small language. The combinations of tags are almost endless and the result of a particular combination of tags might be different from one browser to another.

Finally, despite all these tags already included in HTML, more are needed. Electronic commerce applications need tags for product references, prices, name, addresses, and more. Streaming needs tags to control the flow of images and sound. Search engines need more precise tags for keywords and description. Security needs tags for signing. The list of applications that need new HTML tags is almost endless.

However, adding even more tags to an overblown language is hardly a satisfactory solution. It appears that HTML is already on the verge of collapsing under its own weight, so why continue adding tags?

Worse, although many applications need more tags, some applications would greatly benefit if there were less, not more, tags in HTML. The W3C expects that by the year 2002, 75% of surfers won't be using a PC. Rather, they will access the Web from a personal digital assistant, such as the popular PalmPilot, or from so-called smart phones.

These machines are not as powerful as PCs. They cannot process a complex language like HTML, much less a version of HTML that would include more tags.

Another, but related, problem is that it takes many tags to format a page. It is not uncommon to see pages that have more markup than content! These pages are slow to download and to display.

In conclusion, even though HTML is a popular and successful markup language, it has some major shortcomings. XML was developed to address these shortcomings. It was not introduced for the sake of novelty.

XML exists because HTML was successful. Therefore, XML incorporates many successful features of HTML. XML also exists because HTML could not live up to new demands. Therefore, XML breaks new ground where it is appropriate.

It is difficult to change a successful technology like HTML so, not surprisingly, XML has raised some level of controversy.

Let's make it clear: XML is unlikely to replace HTML in the near or medium-term. XML does not threaten the Web but introduces new possibilities. Work is already under way to combine XML and HTML in XHTML, an XML version of HTML. At the time of this writing, XHTML version 1.0 is not finalized yet. However, it is expected that XHTML will soon be adopted by the W3C.

Some of the areas where XML will be useful in the near-term include:

- large Web site maintenance. XML would work behind the scene to simplify the creation of HTML documents

- exchange of information between organizations

- offloading and reloading of databases

- syndicated content, where content is being made available to different Web sites

- electronic commerce applications where different organizations collaborate to serve a customer

- scientific applications with new markup languages for mathematical and chemical formulas

- electronic books with new markup languages to express rights and ownership

- handheld devices and smart phones with new markup languages optimized for these "alternative" devices

This book takes a "hands-on" approach to XML. It will teach you how to deploy XML in your environment: how to decide where XML fits and how to best implement it. It is illustrated with many real-world examples.

As you will see, there are two classes of applications for XML: publishing and data exchange. This book draws most of its examples from data exchange applications because they are currently the most popular. However, it also includes a very comprehensive example of Web site publishing.

I make some assumptions about you. I assume you are familiar with the Web, insofar that you can read, understand, and write basic HMTL pages as well as read and understand a simple JavaScript application. You don't have to be a master at HTML to learn XML; nor do you need to be a guru of JavaScript.

Most of the code in this book is based on XML and its companion standards. When programming was required, I used JavaScript as often as possible. JavaScript, however, was not appropriate for the final example so I turned to Java.

You don't need to know Java to read this book. There is very little Java involved (again, most of the code in the final example is based on techniques that you will learn in this book) and Appendix A, "Crash Course on Java," will teach you just enough Java to understand the examples.

A First Look at XML

The idea behind XML is deceptively simple. It aims at answering the conflicting demands that arrive at the W3C for the future of HTML.

On one hand, people need more tags. And these new tags are increasingly specialized. For example, mathematicians want tags for formulas. Chemists also want tags for formulas but they are not the same.

On the other hand, authors and developers want fewer tags. HTML is already so complex! As handheld devices gain in popularity, the need for a simpler markup language also is apparent because small devices, like the PalmPilot, are not powerful enough to process HMTL pages.

How can you have both more tags and fewer tags in a single language? To resolve this dilemma, XML makes essentially two changes to HTML:

- It predefines no tags.

- It is stricter.

No Predefined Tags

Because there are no predefined tags in XML, you, the author, can create the tags that you need. Do you need a tag for price? Do you need a tag for a bold hyperlink that floats on the right side of the screen? Make them:

```
<price currency="usd">499.00</price>
<toc xlink:href="/newsletter">Pineapplesoft Link</toc>
```

The `<price>` tag has no equivalent in HTML although you could simulate the `<toc>` tag through a combination of table, hyperlink, and bold:

```
<TABLE>
    <TR>
        <TD><!-- main text here --></TD>
        <TD><A HREF="/newsletter"><B>Pineapplesoft Link</B></A></TD>
    </TR>
</TABLE>
```

This is the X in XML. XML is extensible because it predefines no tags but lets the author create tags that are needed for his or her application.

This is simple but it opens many questions such as

- How does the browser know that `<toc>` is equivalent to this combination of table, hyperlink, and bold?

- Can you compare different prices?

- What about the current generation of browsers?

- How does this simplify Web site maintenance?

We will address these and many other questions in detail in the following chapters of the book. Briefly the answers are

- The browsers use a style sheet: See Chapter 5, "XSL Transformation," and Chapter 6, "XSL Formatting Objects and Cascading Style Sheet."

- You can compare prices: See Chapter 7, "The Parser and DOM," and Chapter 8, "Alternative API: SAX."

- XML can be made compatible with the current generation of browsers: See Chapter 5.

- XML enables you to concentrate on more stable aspects of your document: See Chapter 5.

Stricter

HTML has a very forgiving syntax. This is great for authors who can be as lazy as they want, but it also makes Web browsers more complex. According to some estimates, more than 50% of the code in a browser handles errors or sloppiness on the author's part.

However, authors increasingly use HMTL editors so they don't really care how simple and forgiving the syntax is.

Yet, browsers are growing in size and are becoming generally slower. The speed factor is a problem for every surfer. The size factor is a problem for owners of handheld devices who cannot afford to download 10Mb browsers.

Therefore, it was decided that XML would adopt a very strict syntax. A strict syntax results in smaller, faster, and lighter browsers.

A First Look at Document Structure

XML is all about document structure. This section looks into the issue of structured documents.

CAUTION

Don't be confused by the vocabulary: XML is not just a solution to publishing Web pages.

XML clearly has its roots in publishing: technical documentation, books, letters, Web pages, and more.

The XML vocabulary dates back to publishing applications. For example, an XML file is referred to as an *XML document*. Likewise, to manipulate an XML document, you are likely to apply a *style sheet*, even though you might not be formatting the document. Relationships between documents are expressed through *links*, even though they might not be hyperlinks.

The vocabulary is the source of much confusion because it seems to restrict XML to publishing. This is unfortunate because it has turned off many people. So I urge you to keep an open mind, as you will see XML documents are more than what you would typically think of as documents.

EXAMPLE

To illustrate document structure, I will use the fictitious memo in Listing 1.1 as an example.

Listing 1.1: A Fictitious Memo

```
INTERNAL MEMO


From:      John Doe
To:        Jack Smith
Regarding: XML at WhizBang
```

```
Have you heard of this new technology, XML? It looks promising.
It is similar to HTML but it is extensible. All the big names
(Microsoft, IBM, Oracle) are backing it.

We could use XML to simplify our e-commerce and launch new
services. It is also useful for the Web site: You complained it
was a lot of work; apparently, XML can simplify the maintenance.

Check this Web site <http://www.w3.org/XML> for more information.
Also visit Que (<http://www.mcp.com>). It has just released
"XML by Example" with lots of useful information and some great
examples. I have already ordered two copies!

John
```

If we look at the structure of this memo, we see it is not a monolithic entity. The memo is made of at least three distinct elements:

- the title
- the header, which states the sender and recipient names as well as the subject
- the body text

These elements are organized in relation to one another, following a structure. For example, the title names the memo and it is followed with the header.

If we examine the memo more closely, we find that the body text itself consists of various elements, namely

- three paragraphs
- several URLs
- a signature

We could continue this decomposition process and recognize smaller elements like sentences, words, or even characters. However, these smaller elements usually add little information on the structure of the document.

EXAMPLE

The structure we have just identified is independent from the appearance of the memo. For example, the memo could have been written in HTML. It would have resulted in a nicer-looking document, as illustrated in Figure 1.1, but would have the same structure.

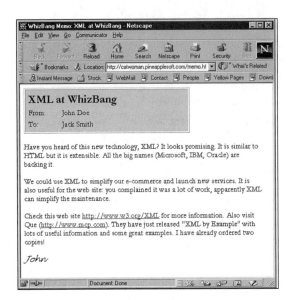

Figure 1.1: *The memo is nicely formatted in HTML.*

Figure 1.1 is just one possible formatting. The same memo could have been formatted completely differently, as illustrated by Figure 1.2.

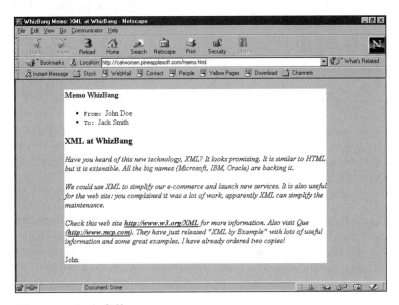

Figure 1.2: *A different appearance*

What is important to notice is that the memo can look completely different and yet it still follows the same structure: The appearance has no impact on the structure. In other words, whether the subject, sender, and recipient are enclosed in a frame or as a bulleted list does not impact the structure. In Listing 1.1, Figure 1.1, and Figure 1.2, the memo consists of

- a title
- a header containing
  - the sender
  - the recipient
  - a subject
- the body text containing
  - three paragraphs
  - several URLs
  - a signature

and the relationship between those elements remains unchanged.

Does it mean that structure and appearance are totally unrelated? Not at all! Ideally, a text is formatted to expose its structure to the reader because good formatting, when constantly applied, is a real help to the reader.

In our case, it is more pleasant to read the HTML versions of the memo rather than the text because the frame and bold characters make it easier to distinguish the header from the body.

For the same reasons, it is common practice to print chapter titles and other headings in bold. When we read, we come to rely on those typographic conventions: They help us build a mental image of the document structure. Also, they are particularly valuable when we leaf through a document.

Likewise, magazines and newspapers try to build a visual style. They select a set of fonts and apply them consistently over the years so that we should be able to recognize our favorite magazine only by its typesetting options.

It gives comfort to the regular reader and helps differentiate from the competition. For similar reasons, companies tend to enforce a corporate style with logos and common letterheads.

The moral of this section, and the key to understanding XML, is that the structure of a document is the foundation from which the appearance is deduced. Although I have illustrated it with only a memo, this holds true for all sorts of documents including technical documentation, books, letters, emails, reports, magazines, Web pages, and more.

Most document exchange standards concentrate on the actual appearance of a document. They take great pains to ensure almost identical display on various platforms.

XML uses a different approach and records the structure of documents from which the formatting is automatically deduced. The difference might seem trivial but we will see it has far reaching implications.

Markup Language History

HTML stands for Hypertext Markup Language; XML is the eXtensible Markup Language. There is another standard called SGML, which stands for the Standard Generalized Markup Language. Do you see the pattern here?

All three languages are markup languages. What exactly is a markup language? What problem does it solve?

The easiest way to understand markup languages in general, and XML in particular, is probably a historical study of electronic markup; that is, the progression from procedural markup to generalized markup through generic coding.

This requires a brief discussion of SGML, the internal standard underlying HTML and XML. I promise that I will limit references to SGML in this book. However, I cannot completely hide the relationship between XML and SGML.

Before we rush into the hows and whys, let me define markup. In an electronic document, the markup is the codes, embedded with the document text, which store the information required for electronic processing, like font name, boldness or, in the case of XML, the document structure. This is not specific to XML. Every electronic document standard uses some sort of markup.

Mark-Up

Mark-up originates in the publishing industry. In traditional publishing, the manuscript is annotated with layout instructions for the typesetter. These handwritten annotations are called mark-up.

Mark-up is a separate activity that takes place after writing and before typesetting.

Procedural Markup

Similarly, word processing requires the user to specify the appearance of the text. For example, the user selects a typeface and its boldness. The user also can place a piece of text at a given position on the page and more. This information is called markup and is stored as special codes with the text.

NOTE

Electronic markup is spelled as one word to distinguish it from traditional handwritten mark-up.

Practically, the user selects commands in menus to add formatting instructions to the text. The formatting instructions tell the printer whether to print in bold or when to use another typeface.

To select the formatting instructions, the user implicitly analyzes the structure of its document; that is, he identifies each separate meaningful element.

He then determines the commands that need to be applied to produce the format desired for that type of element and he selects the appropriate commands.

Please note that, once again, the document structure is the starting point from which actual formatting is deduced. However, this is an unconscious process.

This process is often referred to as procedural markup because the markup is effectively some procedure for the output device. It closely parallels the traditional mark-up activity. The main difference being that markup is stored electronically.

EXAMPLE

The Rich Text Format (RTF), developed by Microsoft but supported by most word processors, is a procedural markup. Listing 1.2 is the memo in RTF. You need not worry about all the codes used in this document but it is clear that instructions (markup) have been added to the text to describe how it should be formatted.

Listing 1.2: The Memo in RTF

```
{\rtf1\ansi\ansicpg1252\deff0\deflang1033\deflangfe1033{\fonttbl
{\f0\froman\fprq2\fcharset0 Garamond;}{\f1\froman\fprq2\fcharset0
Times New Roman;}{\f2\fscript\fprq2\fcharset0 Lucida Handwriting;}}
{\colortbl ;\red0\green0\blue255;}
\uc1\pard\sb100\sa100\nowidctlpar\lang3081\ulnone\b\f0\fs36 XML
at WhizBang\b0\fs24\par
From:\tab John Doe\line To:\tab Jack Smith\par
Have you heard of this new technology, XML? It looks promising.
It is similar to HTML but it is extensible. All the big names
(Microsoft, IBM, Oracle) are backing it.\f1\par
\f0 We could use XML to simplify our e-commerce and launch new
services. It is also useful for the web site: you complained it
was a lot of work, apparently XML can simplify the maintenance.
```

continues

Listing 1.2: continued

```
\f1\par
\f0 Check this web site <http://www.w3.org/XML> for more
information. Also visit Que (\cf1\ul <http://www.mcp.com>
\cf0\ulnone ). They have just released "XML by Example"
with lots of useful information and some great examples.
I have already ordered two copies!\f1\par
\i\f2 John\i0\f1\par
}
```

OUTPUT

Figure 1.3 shows the RTF memo loaded in a word processor.

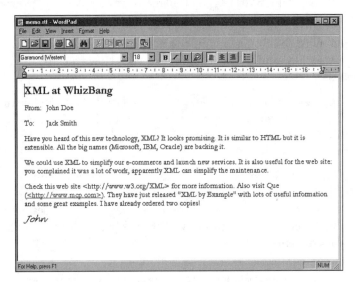

Figure 1.3: *The RTF memo in a word processor*

This approach has three major problems:

- It does not record the structure of the document. We see the user deduces the document appearance from its structure but it records only the result of the process. Therefore, information about the structure is lost.

- It is inflexible. Any change to the formatting rules implies manually changing the document. Also, the markup is more or less system dependent, which reduces portability. Relying on the availability of a particular typeface or on the output device being a certain printer reduces portability.

- It is an inherently slow process. It is also error-prone: It is easy to get confused and incorrectly format a document.

Generic Coding

Markup evolved into generic coding with the introduction of macros. Macros replace the controls with calls to external formatting procedures. A generic identifier (GI) or tag is attached to each text element and formatting rules are further associated with tags. A formatter processes the text and produces a document in the format of the output device.

EXAMPLE

T_eX is a good example of generic coding. Listing 1.3 is the memo in T_eX.

Listing 1.3: The Memo in T_eX

```
% memo.tex
\nopagenumbers


\noindent John Doe\par
\noindent Jack Smith\par
\noindent XML at WhizBang\par
\smallskip


Have you heard of this new technology, XML? It looks promising.
It is similar to HTML but it is extensible. All the big names
(Microsoft, IBM, Oracle) are backing it.\par
We could use XML to simplify our e-commerce and launch new
services. It is also useful for the web site: you complained it
was a lot of work, apparently XML can simplify the maintenance.
Check this web site {\url http://www.w3.org/XML} for more
information.
Also visit Que ({\url http://www.mcp.com}).\par
They have just released "XML by Example" with lots of useful
information and some great examples. I have already ordered
two copies!\par
John\par
\bye
```

The benefits of generic coding over procedural markup are twofold:

- It achieves higher portability and is more flexible. To change the appearance of the document it suffices to adapt the macro. By editing one macro, the change is automatically reported throughout the document. In particular, it does not require reencoding the markup, which is a time-consuming and error-prone activity.

- The markup is closer to describing the structure.

Users tend to give significant names to the tags—for example, 'Heading' is preferred to 'X12', clearly recognizing the predominance of the structure over the formatting.

The good news is that it is now possible to automatically process the document—for example, it would be possible to compile an index of URLs.

Standard Generalized Markup Language

The Standard Generalized Markup Language (SGML) extends generic coding. Furthermore, it is an international standard published by the ISO (International Standard Organization). It is based on the early work done by Dr. Charles Goldfarb from IBM.

Dr. Goldfarb was the inventor of the concepts behind SGML. He was a technical leader of the team that developed SGML.

SGML is similar to generic coding but with two additional characteristics:

- The markup describes the document's structure, not the document appearance.

- The markup conforms to a model, which is similar to a database schema. This means that it can be processed by software or stored in a database.

SGML is not a standard structure that every document needs to follow. In other words, it does not define what a title or a paragraph is. In fact, it is unrealistic to believe that a single document structure can satisfy the needs of all authors. Technical documentation, books, letters, dictionaries, Web pages, timetables, and memos, to name only a few, are too different to fit in a single canvas without putting unacceptable constraints on the authors.

The SGML approach is not to impose its own tag set but to propose a language for authors to describe the structure of their documents and mark them accordingly. This is the first difference between generic coding and SGML: The markup describes the structure of the document.

SGML is an enabling standard, not a complete document architecture. The strength of SGML is that it is a language to describe documents—in many respects similar to programming languages. It is therefore flexible and open to new applications.

The document structure is written in a *Document Type Definition* (DTD) sometimes also referred to as *SGML application*. A DTD specifies a set of elements, their relationships, and the tag set to mark the document. This is another difference between generic coding and SGML: The markup follows a model.

Listing 1.4 is the document in SGML. You will recognize the syntax but none of the tags. HTML is an application of SGML; therefore, the syntax is familiar. The tags, however, are specific to the structure of this document.

Listing 1.4: The Memo in SGML

```
<!DOCTYPE memo SYSTEM "memo.dtd">

<memo>

   <header>

      <from>John Doe

      <to>Jack Smith

      <subject>XML at WhizBang

   <body>

      <para>Have you heard of this new technology, XML? It looks
         promising. It is similar to HTML but it is extensible.
         All the big names (Microsoft, IBM, Oracle) are backing
         it.

      <para>We could use XML to simplify our e-commerce and launch
         new services.  It is also useful for the web site: you
         complained it was a lot of work, apparently XML can
         simplify the maintenance.

      <para>Check this web site <url>http://www.w3.org/XML</url>
         for more information. Also visit Que
         (<url>http://www.mcp.com</url>). They have just released
         "XML by Example" with lots of useful information and some
         great examples. I have already ordered two copies!

      <signature>John

</memo>
```

Although SGML does not impose a structure on documents, standard committees, industry groups, and others build on SGML and describe standard document structures as SGML applications. Some document structures are maintained as public standards in the form of SGML DTDs.

Some famous examples are

- HTML is the well-known markup language for Web documents. Although few HTML authors know about SGML, HTML has been defined as an SGML DTD.

- CALS standard MIL-M-28001B. CALS (Continuous Acquisition and Life-cycle Support) is a DoD (U.S. Department of Defense) initiative to promote electronic document interchange. MIL-M-28001B specifies

DTDs for technical manuals in the format required for submission to the DoD.

- DocBook and other DTDs designed by the AAP (Association of American Publishers) for books, articles, and serials. This was the first major application of SGML.

Hypertext Markup Language

Without a doubt, the most popular application of SGML is HTML. Formally, HTML is an application of SGML. In other words, HTML is one set of tags that follows the rules of SGML. The set of tags defined by HTML is adapted to the structure of hypertext documents.

EXAMPLE

1. Listing 1.5 is the memo in HTML.

Listing 1.5: The Memo in HTML

```
<!DOCTYPE html PUBLIC "-//W3C//DTD HTML 4.0 Transitional//EN">
<HTML>
    <HEAD><TITLE>WhizBang Memo: XML at WhizBang</TITLE></HEAD>
    <BODY>
        <TABLE bgcolor="LIGHTGREY" border="1" width="70%"><TR><TD>
            <TABLE>
                <TR>
                    <TD colspan="2"><FONT size="+2" face="Garamond">
                        <B>XML at WhizBang</B></FONT>
                    </TD>
                </TR>
                <TR>
                    <TD><FONT face="Garamond">From:</FONT></TD>
                    <TD><FONT face="Garamond">John Doe</FONT></TD>
                </TR>
                <TR>
                    <TD><FONT face="Garamond">To:</FONT></TD>
                    <TD><FONT face="Garamond">Jack Smith</FONT></TD>
                </TR>
            </TABLE>
        </TD></TR></TABLE>
        <P><FONT face="Garamond">Have you heard of this new
            technology, XML? It looks promising. It is similar
            to HTML but it is extensible. All the big names
            (Microsoft, IBM, Oracle) are backing it.</FONT></P>
```

```
  <P><FONT face="Garamond">We could use XML to simplify
     our e-commerce and launch new services.
     It is also useful for the web site: you complained
     it was a lot of work, apparently XML can simplify
     the maintenance.</FONT></P>
  <P><FONT face="Garamond">Check this web site
     <A href="http://www.w3.org/XML">http://www.w3.org/XML</A>
     for more information. Also visit Que
     (<A href="http://www.mcp.com">http://www.mcp.com</A>).
     They have just released "XML by Example" with lots of
     useful information and some great examples. I have
     already ordered two copies!</FONT></P>
  <P><FONT face="Lucida Handwriting"><I>John</I></FONT></P>
  </BODY>
</HTML>
```

As you can see in Listing 1.5, HTML does not enforce a strict structure; in fact, HTML enforces very little structure.

HTML has evolved in two contradictory directions. First, many formatting tags have been introduced so that HTML is now partly a procedural markup language.

Tags in this category include <CENTER> and <FONT>. Listing 1.5 clearly shows that the tags are used to express presentation, not only structure.

EXAMPLE

2. At the same time, the class attribute and style sheets were added to HTML. This turns HTML in a generic coding language! Listing 1.6 illustrates the use of class.

Listing 1.6: The Memo in HTML with class

```
<!DOCTYPE html PUBLIC "-//W3C//DTD HTML 4.0 Transitional//EN">
<HTML>
   <HEAD>
      <TITLE>WhizBang Memo: XML at WhizBang</TITLE>
      <STYLE>
         .header {
            background-color: lightgrey;
         }
         .subject {
            font-family: Garamond;
            font-weight: bold;
```

continues

Listing 1.6: continued

```
            font-size: larger;
        }
        .to, .from   {
            font-family: Garamond;
        }
        .para { font-family: Garamond; }
        .signature {
            font-family: "Lucida Handwriting";
            font-style: italic;
        }
    </STYLE>
</HEAD>
<BODY>
    <TABLE CLASS="header" WIDTH="70%" BORDER="1"><TR><TD>
        <TABLE>
            <TR>
                <TD colspan="2" CLASS="subject">
                    XML at WhizBang</FONT>
                </TD>
            </TR>
            <TR>
                <TD CLASS="from">From:</TD>
                <TD CLASS="from">John Doe</TD>
            </TR>
            <TR>
                <TD CLASS="to">To:</TD>
                <TD CLASS="to">Jack Smith</TD>
            </TR>
        </TABLE>
    </TD></TR></TABLE>
    <P CLASS="para">Have you heard of this new
        technology, XML? It looks promising. It is similar
        to HTML but it is extensible. All the big names
        (Microsoft, IBM, Oracle) are backing it.</P>
    <P CLASS="para">We could use XML to simplify
        our e-commerce and launch new services.
        It is also useful for the web site: you complained
        it was a lot of work, apparently XML can simplify
```

```
        the maintenance.</P>
     <P CLASS="para">Check this web site
        <A href="http://www.w3.org/XML">http://www.w3.org/XML</A>
        for more information. Also visit Que
        (<A href="http://www.mcp.com">http://www.mcp.com</A>).
        They have just released "XML by Example" with lots of
        useful information and some great examples. I have
        already ordered two copies!</P>
     <P CLASS="signature">John</FONT></P>
   </BODY>
</HTML>
```

OUTPUT

Figure 1.4 is the document loaded in a browser. Note that it looks exactly like Figure 1.1. Figure 1.1 was the document in Listing 1.5. So, procedural markup and generic coding achieve identical pages.

Figure 1.4: *A document with classes in a browser*

Without going into the details of Listing 1.6, the classes are associated with formatting instructions. For example, the class "para" is associated with

```
.para { font-family: Garamond; }
```

This says that the typeface must be "Garamond." In effect, it achieves the same result as:

```
<FONT FACE="Garamond">...</FONT>
```

However, the class is a generic coding, whereas the <FONT> tag is procedural coding. Practically, it means that it is possible to change the appearance of all the paragraphs by changing only the formatting instructions associated with the para. That's one line to change as opposed to many <FONT> tags to update with a procedural markup.

3. Listing 1.7 illustrates this. It associates different formatting instructions to the paragraph. Figure 1.5 shows the result in a browser.

Listing 1.7: The Memo in HTML with Different Formatting Instructions

EXAMPLE

```
<!DOCTYPE html PUBLIC "-//W3C//DTD HTML 4.0 Transitional//EN">
<HTML>
   <HEAD>
      <TITLE>WhizBang Memo: XML at WhizBang</TITLE>
      <STYLE>
         .header {
            background-color: lightgrey;
         }
         .subject {
            font-family: Garamond;
            font-weight: bold;
            font-size: larger;
         }
         .to, .from  {
            font-family: Garamond;
         }
         .para {
            font-family: "Letter Gothic MT";
            font-size: 16px;
          }
         .signature {
            font-family: "Lucida Handwriting";
            font-style: italic;
         }
      </STYLE>
   </HEAD>
   <BODY>
      <TABLE CLASS="header" WIDTH="70%" BORDER="1"><TR><TD>
         <TABLE>
```

```
                    <TR>
                        <TD colspan="2" CLASS="subject">
                            XML at WhizBang</FONT>
                        </TD>
                    </TR>
                    <TR>
                        <TD CLASS="from">From:</TD>
                        <TD CLASS="from">John Doe</TD>
                    </TR>
                    <TR>
                        <TD CLASS="to">To:</TD>
                        <TD CLASS="to">Jack Smith</TD>
                    </TR>
                </TABLE>
        </TD></TR></TABLE>
        <P CLASS="para">Have you heard of this new
            technology, XML? It looks promising. It is similar
            to HTML but it is extensible. All the big names
            (Microsoft, IBM, Oracle) are backing it.</P>
        <P CLASS="para">We could use XML to simplify
            our e-commerce and launch new services.
            It is also useful for the web site: you complained
            it was a lot of work, apparently XML can simplify
            the maintenance.</P>
        <P CLASS="para">Check this web site
            <A href="http://www.w3.org/XML">http://www.w3.org/XML</A>
            for more information. Also visit Que
            (<A href="http://www.mcp.com">http://www.mcp.com</A>).
            They have just released "XML by Example" with lots of
            useful information and some great examples. I have
            already ordered two copies!</P>
        <P CLASS="signature">John</FONT></P>
    </BODY>
</HTML>
```

OUTPUT

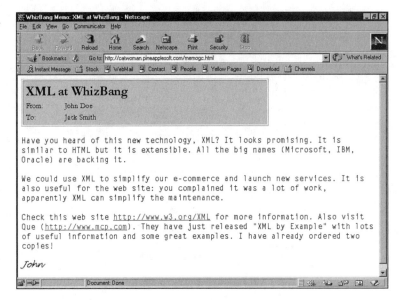

Figure 1.5: *The new style in a browser*

eXtensible Markup Language

This conflicting evolution of HTML, partly toward procedural markup and partly toward generic coding, is illustrative of the forces at play behind HTML.

On one hand, the Web has evolved into a media in its own right, similar to printed magazines and television. Therefore, people need lots of control over the formatting so they can produce visually appealing Web sites.

Yet Web sites also have grown in size and it is increasingly difficult to maintain them. For most organizations, building a Web site follows these steps:

- The first 20 pages are produced with enthusiasm.

- Somebody (usually from the marketing department) realizes that the Web site looks terrible.

- A design agency is contracted to redo the appearance of the site and it manually edits the 20 pages. The site is now three times slower but it looks great.

- Another 50 pages are added with enthusiasm. They more or less follow the new appearance. As time passes by, they tend to diverge from the original style.

- Another design agency is contracted to redo the site. It would be too expensive to edit the whole site so 30 pages are deleted. The remaining 40 pages are manually edited.

Hopefully, somebody realizes it is a very costly process before another 50 pages are added. If not, the process repeats.

Generic coding was added to HTML to help alleviate this problem. However, the class attribute is perceived as too limited and has generally not been very successful.

This problem also was one of the motivations for the development of XML. It was felt that HTML was increasingly inefficient and a more flexible mechanism was needed.

One option could have been to turn to SGML. In fact, it was envisioned at one point. However, it rapidly became evident that SGML was too complex for the Web. There are options in SGML that are useless in a Web environment.

Therefore, the solution was to simplify SGML. XML removes all the options that are not absolutely required in SGML. However, it retains the key principle that markup needs to describe the structure of the document.

The result is a simple standard that is almost as powerful as SGML while being as simple to use as HTML. In fact, simplicity was one of the criteria during the development of XML. Indeed, it was felt that the original simplicity of HTML had been a major element in its early success.

Today, of course, HTML is no longer simple and, in a way, XML is simpler than modern HTML.

As already stated, it is very unlikely that HTML will disappear in the predictable future. Rather, HTML will evolve toward XML. Work is already under way on an XML version of HTML dubbed XHTML.

Listing 1.8 is the memo in XML. You will notice that it is very similar to SGML but every element has an end tag. Do not worry about XML syntax now. We will cover the syntax in greater detail in the next two chapters.

EXAMPLE   **Listing 1.8:** The Memo in XML

```
<?xml version="1.0"?>
<!DOCTYPE memo SYSTEM "memo.dtd">
<memo>
  <header>
        <from>John Doe</from>
        <to>Jack Smith</to>
        <subject>XML at WhizBang</subject>
```

continues

Listing 1.8: continued

```
  </header>
  <body>
          <para>Have you heard of this new technology, XML? It looks
              promising. It is similar to HTML but it is extensible.
              All the big names (Microsoft, IBM, Oracle) are backing
              it.</para>
          <para>We could use XML to simplify our e-commerce and launch
              new services. It is also useful for the web site: you
              complained it was a lot of work, apparently XML can
              simplify the maintenance.</para>
          <para>Check this web site <url>http://www.w3.org/XML</url>
              for more information. Also visit Que
              (<url>http://www.mcp.com</url>). They have just
              released "XML by Example" with lots of useful
              information and some great examples. I have already
              ordered two copies!</para>
          <signature>John</signature>
  </body>
</memo>
```

Application of XML

Although I have mentioned in passing that XML is not just for Web site publishing, all the examples I have given so far are more or less related to Web publishing. In this section, I will present some of the most popular applications for XML.

Applications of XML are classified as being of one of the following two types:

- Document applications manipulate information that is primarily intended for human consumption.

- Data applications manipulate information that is primarily intended for software consumption.

The difference between the two types of application is a qualitative one. It is the same XML standard, it is implemented by using the same tools, but it serves different goals. This is important because it means you can reuse tools and experience across a large set of applications.

Document Applications

The first application of XML would be document publishing. The main advantage of XML in this arena is that XML concentrates on the structure of the document, and this makes it independent of the delivery medium (see Figure 1.6).

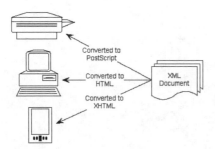

Figure 1.6: XML is independent from the medium.

Therefore, it is possible to edit and maintain documents in XML and automatically publish them on different media. The operative word here is automatically.

The ability to target multiple media is becoming increasingly important because many publications are available online and in print. Also, the Web is changing very rapidly. What is fashionable this year will be passé next year so one needs to reformat his site regularly.

Finally, some Web sites are optimized for specific viewers, such as Netscape or Internet Explorer. This often leads to the development of two or more versions of the same site: one generic version and one optimized for some users. If done manually, this is very costly.

For all these reasons, it makes sense to maintain a common version of the documentation in a media-independent format, such as XML, and to automatically convert it into publishing formats such as HTML, PostScript, PDF, RTF, and more.

Of course, the more media we need to support and the larger the document, the more important it is that publishing be automated.

Data Applications

One of the original goals of SGML was to give document management access to the software tools that had been used to manage data, such as databases.

With XML, the loop has come to a full circle because XML brings a publishing kind of distribution to data. This leads to the concept of "the application as the document" where, ultimately, there is no difference between documents and applications.

Indeed, if the structure of a document can be expressed in XML, as illustrated in Figure 1.7, so can the structure of a database, as illustrated in Figure 1.8.

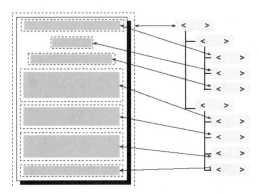

Figure 1.7: *The structure of a document in XML*

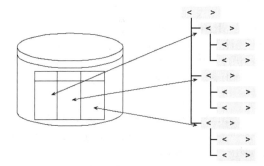

Figure 1.8: *The structure of a database in XML*

EXAMPLE

As an example, consider Table 1.1. which is a list of products and prices as they would be stored in a relational database. Listing 1.9 is the same list of products in XML.

Table 1.1: A list of products in a relational database

Identifier	Name	Price
p1	XML Editor	$499.00
p2	DTD Editor	$199.00
p3	XML Book	$19.99
p4	XML Training	$699.00

Listing 1.9: A List of Products in XML

```xml
<?xml version="1.0"?>
<products>
    <product id="p1">
        <name>XML Editor</name>
        <price>499.00</price>
    </product>
    <product id="p2">
        <name>DTD Editor</name>
        <price>199.00</price>
    </product>
    <product id="p3">
        <name>XML Book</name>
        <price>19.99</price>
    </product>
    <product id="p4">
        <name>XML Training</name>
        <price>699.00</price>
    </product>
</products>
```

In this context, XML is used to exchange information between organizations. The XML Web is a large database on which applications can tap (see Figure 1.9).

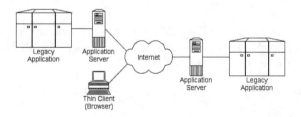

Figure 1.9: Applications exchanging data over the Web

This can be viewed as an extension for extranets. The idea behind an extranet is that one organization publishes some of its data on the Web for its partners.

For example, an organization will publish its price list on its Web site. In some industries, such as electronics, the price list is very dynamic. Prices can change several times during a month. If the information is available on a Web site, customers can always access the latest, most up-to-date information.

Currently, the price list is published in HTML—that is, intended for viewing by a human. This is acceptable if you have few providers with few products but as soon as you have many providers or many products, you want an automated solution.

With XML, software can automatically visit the price list, extract the price, and update the information in your own database. This is shown in the top half of Figure 1.9. It requires a markup language that does not concentrate on appearance but on structure.

Companion Standards

The value of XML is not that it is a markup language but that it is a standard markup language. It wouldn't be difficult to create your own markup language using your own convention. However, by adopting XML, you buy into a growing community supported by a large range of standards and products.

This means it will be easier to find support in the form of books, articles, and services, as well as software to create, manipulate, store, and exchange XML documents.

There is a sort of positive loop at play here: Because XML is standardized, more vendors are willing to support it. This leads more people to adopt it. A large market means that more vendors will propose XML tools. This, in turn, attracts more users, which, again, attracts new vendors. And so on, and so on.

The title for this chapter, "The XML Galaxy," reflects my view that XML is more than a markup language. It is a whole range of tools that you can put to work in your environment.

In particular, the W3C has developed a number of standards that complement XML. These standards are often referred to as "XML companion standards."

It is not my intention in this chapter to introduce these standards comprehensively, but I would like to give you a feeling for what they have to offer. Therefore, I will point to some of the major companion standards.

This is not a complete list. New standards are regularly being introduced.

XML Namespace

XML Namespace is often an overlooked companion standard although it is second to none in importance. Namespace associates an owner with elements.

This enables extensibility because it means an organization can add to existing elements and clearly label who is responsible for the extension. This prevents name conflicts and is the only way to enable reuse of standard structures.

✔ XML namespaces are covered in more detail in Chapter 4, "Namespaces," page 112.

Listing 1.10 is an address book in XML that uses namespaces to reuse a standard definition for addresses.

EXAMPLE

Listing 1.10: Using Namespaces to Reuse the Address

```
<?xml version="1.0"?>
<directory
    xmlns="http://catwoman.pineapplesoft.com/directory/1.0"
    xmlns:adr="http://catwoman.pineapplesoft.com/address/1.0">
    <adr:address>
        <adr:name>John Doe</adr:name>
        <adr:street>34 Fountain Square Plaza</adr:street>
        <adr:region>OH</adr:region>
        <adr:postal-code>45202</adr:postal-code>
        <adr:locality>Cincinnati</adr:locality>
        <adr:country>US</adr:country>
        <adr:tel>513-555-8889</adr:tel>
        <adr:email>jdoe@emailaholic.com</adr:email>
    </adr:address>
    <adr:address>
        <adr:name>Jack Smith</adr:name>
        <adr:tel>513-555-3465</adr:tel>
        <adr:email>jsmith@emailaholic.com</adr:email>
    </adr:address>
</directory>
```

Style Sheets

XML is supported by two style sheet languages: XSL (XML Stylesheet Language) and CSS (Cascading Style Sheet). Style sheets are probably the most widely discussed companion standards. They specify how XML documents should be rendered onscreen, on paper, or in an editor. XSL is more powerful but CSS is widely implemented.

> ✔ Listing 1.11 is an example of an XSL style sheet to render an XML article. Style sheets will be covered in more detail in Chapter 5, "XSL Transformation," page 125 and Chapter 6, "XSL Formatting Objects and Cascading Style Sheet," page 161.

EXAMPLE

Listing 1.11: A Simple XSL Style Sheet

```
<?xml version="1.0" encoding="ISO-8859-1"?>
<xsl:stylesheet
    xmlns:xsl="http://www.w3.org/1999/XSL/Transform/"
    xmlns="http://www.w3.org/TR/REC-html40">

<xsl:output method="html"/>

<xsl:template match="/">
    <HTML>
    <HEAD>
        <TITLE>Pineapplesoft Link</TITLE>
    </HEAD>
    <BODY>
        <xsl:apply-templates/>
    </BODY>
    </HTML>
</xsl:template>

<xsl:template match="section/title">
    <P><I><xsl:apply-templates/></I></P>
</xsl:template>

<xsl:template match="article/title">
    <P><B><xsl:apply-templates/></B></P>
</xsl:template>

<xsl:template match="url">
    <A TARGET="_blank">
        <xsl:attribute name="href">
            <xsl:apply-templates/>
        </xsl:attribute>
```

```
            <xsl:apply-templates/>
        </A>
    </xsl:template>


    <xsl:template match="url[@protocol='mailto']">
        <A>
            <xsl:attribute name="href">mailto:<xsl:apply-templates/>
            </xsl:attribute>
            <xsl:apply-templates/>
        </A>
    </xsl:template>


    <xsl:template match="p">
        <P><xsl:apply-templates/></P>
    </xsl:template>


    <xsl:template match="abstract ¦ date ¦ keywords ¦ copyright"/>


</xsl:stylesheet>
```

DOM and SAX

DOM (Document Object Model) and SAX (Simple API for XML) are APIs to access XML documents. They allow applications to read XML documents without having to worry about the syntax (not unlike translators). They are complementary: DOM is best suited for forms and editors, SAX is best with application-to-application exchange.

✔ DOM and SAX are covered in Chapter 7, "The Parser and DOM," page 191 and Chapter 8, "Alternative API: SAX," page 231. Chapter 9, "Writing XML," page 269 discusses how to create XML documents.

XLink and XPointer

XLink and XPointer are two parts of one standard currently under development to provide a mechanism to establish relationships between documents.

Listing 1.12 demonstrates how a set of links can be maintained in XML.

EXAMPLE

Listing 1.12: A Set of Links in XML

```
<?xml version="1.0" standalone="no"?>
<references xmlns:xlink="http://www.w3.org/XML/XLink/0.9">
    <link xlink:href="http://www.mcp.com">
```

continues

Listing 1.12: continued

```
    Macmillan
    </link>
    <link xlink:href="http://www.pineapplesoft.com/newsletter">
    Pineapplesoft Link
    </link>
    <link xlink:href="http://www.xml.com">
    XML.com
    </link>
    <link xlink:href="http://www.comics.com">
    Comics.com
    </link>
    <link xlink:href="http://www.fatbrain.com">
    Fatbrain.com
    </link>
    <link xlink:href="http://www.abcnews.com">
    ABC News
    </link>
</references>
```

✔ XLink is discussed in Chapter 10, "Modeling for Flexibility," page 307.

XML Software

As explained in the previous section, XML popularity means that many vendors are supporting it. This, in turn, means that many applications are available to manipulate XML documents.

This section lists some of the most commonly used XML applications. Again, this is not a complete list. We will discuss these products in more detail in the following chapters.

XML Browser

An XML browser is the first application you would think of because it is so close to the familiar HTML browser. An XML browser is used to view and print XML documents. At the time of this writing, there are not many high-quality XML browsers.

Microsoft Internet Explorer has supported XML since version 4.0. Internet Explorer 5.0 has greatly enhanced the XML support. Unfortunately, the support is based on early versions of the style sheet standards and is not complete. Yet Internet Explorer 5.0 is the closest thing to a largely deployed XML browser today.

Netscape Communicator currently has no support for XML except for Mozilla, the open-source version of Netscape Communicator. Mozilla has strong support for XML. However, because Mozilla is still a work-in-progress, it is not yet stable enough for practical usage.

Several other vendors have produced XML browsers. These browsers are at various stages of development. One of the most interesting is InDelv XML Browser, which has the most complete implementation of XSL at the time of writing.

✔ Browsers are discussed in Chapter 5, "XSL Transformation," and Chapter 6, "XSL Formatting Objects and Cascading Style Sheet."

XML Editors

To view documents, somebody must have written them. There is a surprisingly large range of XML editors available. Some of these editors, however, are scaled-down versions of SGML editors (such as Adobe Framemaker); others are entirely new products (such as XML Pro).

A new range of editors is appearing on the market, led by products such as XMetaL from SoftQuad. These editors offer the power of SGML editors but with the ease of use you would expect from an XML product.

✔ Editors are discussed in Chapter 6, "XSL Formatting Objects and Cascading Style Sheet."

XML Parsers

If you are writing your own XML applications, you probably don't want to fool around with the XML syntax. Parsers shield programmers from the XML syntax.

There are many XML parsers available on the Internet, such as IBM's XML for Java. Also an increasing number of applications include an XML parser, such as Oracle 8i.

✔ Parsers are discussed in Chapter 7, "The Parser and DOM," and Chapter 8, "Alternative API: SAX."

XSL Processor

In many cases, you want to use XML "behind the scene." You want to take advantage of XML internally but you don't want to force your users to upgrade to an XML-compliant browser.

In all these cases, you will use XSL. XSL enables you to produce classic HTML that works with current-generation browsers (and older, too) while enabling you to retain the advantages of XML internally.

To apply the magic of XSL, you will use an XSL processor. There also are many XSL processors available, such as LotusXSL.

✔ XSL processors are discussed in Chapter 5, "XSL Transformation."

What's Next

The book is organized as follows:

- Chapters 2 through 4 will teach you the XML syntax, including the syntax for DTDs and namespaces.

- Chapters 5 and 6 will teach you how to use style sheets to publish documents.

- Chapters 7, 8, and 9 will teach you how to manipulate XML documents from JavaScript applications.

- Chapter 10 will discuss the topic of modeling. You have seen in this introduction how structure is important for XML. Modeling is the process of creating the structure.

- Chapter 11, "N-Tiered Architecture and XML," and Chapter 12, "Putting It All Together: An e-Commerce Example," will wrap it up with a realistic electronic commerce application. This application exercises most if not all the techniques introduced in the previous chapters.

- Appendix A will teach you just enough Java to be able to follow the examples in Chapters 8 and 12. It also discusses when you should use JavaScript and when you should use Java.

The XML Syntax

In this chapter, you will learn the syntax used for XML documents. More specifically, you will learn

- how to write and read XML documents

- how XML structures documents

- how and where XML can be used

If you are curious, the latest version of the official recommendation is always available from www.w3.org/TR/REC-xml. XML version 1.0 (the version used in this book) is available from www.w3.org/TR/1998/REC-xml-19980210.

A First Look at the XML Syntax

If I had to summarize XML in one sentence, it would be something like "a set of standards to exchange and publish information in a structured manner." The emphasis on structure cannot be underestimated.

XML is a language used to describe and manipulate structured documents. XML documents are not limited to books and articles, or even Web sites, and can include objects in a client/server application.

However, XML offers the same tree-like structure across all these applications. XML does not dictate or enforce the specifics of this structure—it does not dictate how to populate the tree.

XML is a flexible mechanism that accommodates the structure of specific applications. It provides a mechanism to encode both the information manipulated by the application and its underlying structure.

XML also offers several mechanisms to manipulate the information—that is, to view it, to access it from an application, and so on. Manipulating documents is done through the structure. So we are back where we started: The structure is the key.

Getting Started with XML Markup

Listing 2.1 is a (small) address book in XML. It has only two entries: John Doe and Jack Smith. Study it because we will use it throughout most of this chapter and the next.

EXAMPLE **Listing 2.1:** An Address Book in XML

```xml
<?xml version="1.0"?>
<!-- loosely inspired by vCard 3.0 -->
<address-book>
    <entry>
        <name>John Doe</name>
        <address>
            <street>34 Fountain Square Plaza</street>
            <region>OH</region>
            <postal-code>45202</postal-code>
            <locality>Cincinnati</locality>
            <country>US</country>
        </address>
        <tel preferred="true">513-555-8889</tel>
        <tel>513-555-7098</tel>
        <email href="mailto:jdoe@emailaholic.com"/>
```

```
      </entry>
      <entry>
           <name><fname>Jack</fname><lname>Smith</lname></name>
           <tel>513-555-3465</tel>
           <email href="mailto:jsmith@emailaholic.com"/>
      </entry>
</address-book>
```

As you can see, an XML document is textual in nature. XML-wise, the document consists of *character data* and *markup*. Both are represented by text.

Ultimately, it's the character data we are interested in because that's the information. However, the markup is important because it records the structure of the document.

There are a variery of markup constructs in XML but it is easy to recognize the markup because it is always enclosed in angle brackets.

NOTE

vCard is a standard for electronic business cards. In the next chapter, you will learn where I used the vCard standard in preparing this example.

EXAMPLE

Obviously, it's the markup that differentiates the XML document from plain text. Listing 2.2 is the same address in plain text, with no markup and only character data.

Listing 2.2: The Address Book in Plain Text

```
John Doe
34 Fountain Square Plaza
Cincinnati, OH 45202
US
513-555-8889 (preferred)
513-555-7098
jdoe@emailaholic.com
Jack Smith
513-555-3465
jsmith@emailaholic.com
```

Listing 2.2 helps illustrate the benefits of a markup language. Listing 2.1 and 2.2 carry exactly the same information. Because Listing 2.2 has no markup, it does not record its own structure.

In both cases, it is easy to recognize the names, the phone numbers, the email addresses, and so on. If anything, Listing 2.2 is probably more readable.

For software, however, it's exactly the opposite. Software needs to be told which is what. It needs to be told what the name is, what the address is, and so on. That's what the markup is all about; it breaks the text into its constituents so software can process it.

Software does have one major advantage—speed. While it would take you a long time to sort through a long list of a thousand addresses, software will plunge through the same list in less than a minute.

However, before it can start, it needs to have the information in a predigested format. This chapter and the following two chapters will concentrate on XML as a predigested format.

The reward comes in Chapter 5, "XSL Transformation," and subsequent chapters where we will see how to tell the computer to do something useful with these documents.

Element's Start and End Tags

The building block of XML is the *element*, as that's what comprises XML documents. Each element has a name and a content.

```
<tel>513-555-7098</tel>
```

EXAMPLE

The content of an element is delimited by special markups known as *start tag* and *end tag*. The tagging mechanism is similar to HTML, which is logical because both HTML and XML inherited their tagging from SGML.

The start tag is the name of the element (tel in the example) in angle brackets; the end tag adds an extra slash character before the name.

Unlike HTML, both start and end tags are required. The following is not correct in XML:

```
<tel>513-555-7098
```

It can't be stressed enough that XML does not define elements. Nowhere in the XML recommendation will you find the address book of Listing 2.1 or the tel element. XML is an enabling standard that provides a common syntax to store information according to a structure.

In this respect, I liken XML to SQL. SQL is the language you use to program relational databases such as Oracle, SQL Server, or DB2. SQL provides a common language to create and manage relational databases. However, SQL does not specify what you should store in these database or which tables you should use.

Still, the availability of a common language has led to the development of a lively industry. SQL vendors provide databases, modeling and development tools, magazines, seminars, conferences, training, books, and more.

Admittedly, the XML industry is not as large as the SQL industry, but it's catching up fast. By moving your data to XML rather than an esoteric syntax, you can tap the growing XML industry for support.

Names in XML

Element names must follow certain rules. As we will see, there are other names in XML that follow the same rules.

Names in XML must start with either a letter or the underscore character ("_"). The rest of the name consists of letters, digits, the underscore character, the dot ("."), or a hyphen ("-"). Spaces are not allowed in names.

Finally, names cannot start with the string "xml", which is reserved for the XML specification itself.

NOTE

There is one more character you can use in names—the colon (:). However, the colon is reserved for namespaces; therefore, it will be introduced in Chapter 4, "Namespaces."

EXAMPLE

The following are examples of valid element names in XML:

```
<copyright-information>

<p>

<base64>

<décompte.client>

<firstname>
```

The following are examples of invalid element names. You could not use these names in XML:

```
<123>

<first name>

<tom&jerry>
```

Unlike HTML, names are case sensitive in XML. So, the following names are all different:

```
<address>

<ADDRESS>

<Address>
```

By convention, HTML elements in XML are always in uppercase. (And, yes, it is possible to include HTML elements in XML documents. In Chapter 5, you will see when it is useful.)

By convention, XML elements are frequently written in lowercase. When a name consists of several words, the words are usually separated by a hyphen, as in address-book.

Another popular convention is to capitalize the first letter of each word and use no separation character as in AddressBook.

EXAMPLE

There are other conventions but these two are the most popular. Choose the convention that works best for you but try to be consistent. It is difficult to work with documents that mix conventions, as Listing 2.3 illustrates.

Listing 2.3: A Document with a Mix of Conventions

```
<?xml version="1.0"?>

<address-book>

    <ENTRY>

        <name>John Doe</name>

        <Address>

            <street>34 Fountain Square Plaza</street>

            <Region>OH</Region>

            <PostalCode>45202</PostalCode>

            <locality>Cincinnati</locality>

            <country>US</country>

        </Address>

        <TEL PREFERRED="true">513-555-8889</TEL>

        <TEL>513-555-7098</TEL>

        <email href="mailto:jdoe@emailaholic.com"/>

    </ENTRY>

</address-book>
```

Although the document in Listing 2.3 is well-formed XML, it is difficult to work with it because you never know how to write the next element. Is it Address or address or ADDRESS? Mixing case is cumbersome and is considered a poor style.

> **NOTE**
>
> As we will see in the "Unicode" section, XML supports characters from most spoken languages. You can use letters from any alphabet in names, including letters from the Greek, Japanese, or Cyrillic alphabets.

Attributes

It is possible to attach additional information to elements in the form of *attributes*. Attributes have a name and a value. The names follow the same rules as element names.

Again, the syntax is similar to HTML. Elements can have one or more attributes in the start tag, and the name is separated from the value by the equal character. The value of the attribute is enclosed in double or single quotation marks.

For example, the `tel` element can have a `preferred` attribute:

```
<tel preferred="true">513-555-8889</tel>
```

Unlike HTML, XML insists on the quotation marks. The XML processor would reject the following:

```
<tel preferred=true>513-555-8889</tel>
```

The quotation marks can be either single or double quotes. This is convenient if you need to insert single or double quotation marks in an attribute value.

```
<confidentiality level="I don't know">
This document is not confidential.
</confidentiality>
```

or

```
<confidentiality level='approved "for your eyes only"'>
This document is top-secret
</confidentiality>
```

Empty Element

Elements that have no content are known as *empty elements*. Usually, they are enclosed in the document for the value of their attributes.

There is a shorthand notation for empty elements: The start and end tags merge and the slash from the end tag is added at the end of the opening tag.

For XML, the following two elements are identical:

```
<email href="mailto:jdoe@emailaholic.com"/>
<email href="mailto:jdoe@emailaholic.com"></email>
```

Nesting of Elements

As Listing 2.1 illustrates, element content is not limited to text; elements can contain other elements that in turn can contain text or elements and so on.

An XML document is a tree of elements. There is no limit to the depth of the tree, and elements can repeat. As you see in Listing 2.1, there are two `entry` elements in the `address-book` element. The `entry` for John Doe has two `tel` elements. Figure 2.1 is the tree of Listing 2.1.

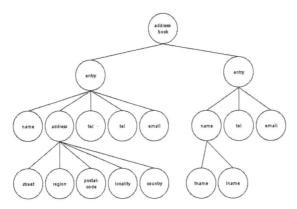

Figure 2.1: *Tree of the address book*

EXAMPLE

An element that is enclosed in another element is called a *child*. The element it is enclosed into is its *parent*. In the following example, the name element has two children: the fname and the lname elements. name is the parent of both elements.

```
<name>

    <fname>Jack</fname>

    <lname>Smith</lname>

</name>
```

Start and end tags must always be balanced and children are always completely enclosed in their parents. In other words, it is not possible that the end tag of a child appears after the end tag of its parent. So, the following is illegal:

```
<name><fname>Jack</fname><lname>Smith</name></lname>
```

NOTE

It is not an accident if XML documents are trees. Trees are flexible, simple, and powerful. In particular, trees can be used to serialize any data structure.

XML is particularly well adapted to serialize objects from object-oriented languages such as JavaScript, Java, or C++.

Root

EXAMPLE

At the root of the document there must be one and only one element. In other words, all the elements in the document must be the children of a single element. The following example is illegal because there are two entry elements that are not enclosed in a top-level element:

```
<?xml version="1.0"?>

<entry>

    <name>John Doe</name>
```

```
    <email href="mailto:jdoe@emailaholic.com"/>
</entry>
<entry>
    <name>JackSmith</name>
    <email href="mailto:jsmith@emailaholic.com"/>
</entry>
```

EXAMPLE

It is easy to fix the previous example. It suffices to introduce a new root, such as address-book.

```
<?xml version="1.0"?>
<address-book>
    <entry>
        <name>John Doe</name>
        <email href="mailto:jdoe@emailaholic.com"/>
    </entry>
    <entry>
        <name>JackSmith</name>
        <email href="mailto:jsmith@emailaholic.com"/>
    </entry>
</address-book>
```

EXAMPLE

There is no rule that says the top-level element must be address-book. If there is only one entry, then entry can act as the top-level element.

```
<?xml version="1.0"?>
<entry>
    <name>John Doe</name>
    <email href="mailto:jdoe@emailaholic.com"/>
</entry>
```

XML Declaration

EXAMPLE

The *XML declaration* is the first line of the document. The declaration identifies the document as an XML document. The declaration also lists the version of XML used in the document. For the time being, it's 1.0.

```
<?xml version="1.0"?>
```

An XML processor can reject documents that have another version number.

The declaration can contain other attributes to support other features such as character set encoding. The attributes are introduced with the feature they support in this chapter and the next chapter.

EXAMPLE

The XML declaration is optional. The following document is valid even though it doesn't have a declaration:

```
<address-book>
    <entry>
        <name>John Doe</name>
        <email href="mailto:jdoe@emailaholic.com"/>
    </entry>
    <entry>
        <name>JackSmith</name>
        <email href="mailto:jsmith@emailaholic.com"/>
    </entry>
</address-book>
```

If the declaration is included however, it must start on the first character of the first line of the document. The XML recommendation suggests you include the declaration in every XML document.

Advanced Topics

As you can see, the core of the XML syntax is not difficult. Furthermore, if you already know HTML, XML is familiar.

One of the design goals of XML was to develop a simple markup language that would be easy to use and would remain human-readable. I think it achieved that goal.

This section covers more advanced features of XML. You might not use them in every document, but they are often useful.

Comments

EXAMPLE

To insert comments in a document, enclose them between "<!--" and "-->". Comments are used for notes, indication of ownership, and more. They are intended for the human reader and they are ignored by the XML processor. In the following example, a comment is made that the document was inspired by vCard. The software does nothing with this comment but it helps us next time we open this document.

```
<!-- loosely inspired by vCard 3.0 -->
```

Comments cannot be inserted in the markup. They must appear before or after the markup.

Unicode

Characters in XML documents follow the Unicode standard. Unicode is a major extension to the familiar ASCII character set. The Unicode

Consortium (www.unicode.org) is responsible for publishing and maintaining the Unicode standard. The same standard is published by ISO as ISO/IEC 10646.

Unicode supports all spoken languages (on Earth) as well as mathematical and other symbols. It supports English, Western European languages, Cyrillic, Japanese, Chinese, and so on.

Support for Unicode is a major step forward in the internationalization of the Web. Unicode also is supported in Windows NT.

However, to accommodate all those characters, Unicode needs 16 bits per character. We are used to character sets, such as Latin-1 (Windows default character set), that use only 8 bits per character. However, 8 bits supports only 256 choices—not enough for Japanese, not to mention Japanese and Chinese and English and Greek and Norwegian and more.

Unicode characters are twice as large as their Latin-1 equivalent; logically, XML documents should be twice as large as normal text files. Fortunately, there is a workaround. In most cases, we don't need 16 bits and we can encode XML documents with an 8-bit character set.

XML processor must recognize the UTF-8 and UTF-16 encodings. As the name implies, UTF-8 uses 8 bits for English characters. Most processors support other encodings. In particular, for Western European languages, they support ISO 8859-1 (the official name for Latin-1).

Documents that use encoding other than UTF-8 or UTF-16 must start with an XML declaration. The declaration must have an attribute encoding to announce the encoding used.

EXAMPLE

For example, a document written in Latin-1 (such as with Windows Notepad) could use the following declaration:

```
<?xml version="1.0" encoding="ISO-8859-1"?>
<entrée>
    <nom>José Dupont<nom/>
    <email href="mailto:jdupont@emailaholic.com"/>
</entrée>
```

NOTE

You might wonder how the XML processor can read the encoding parameter. Indeed, to reach the encoding parameter, the processor must read the declaration. However, to read the declaration, the processor needs to know which encoding is being used.

This looks like a dog running after his tail until you realize that the first characters of an XML document always are <?xml. The XML processor can match these four characters against the encoding it supports and guess enough of the encoding (is it 8 or 16 bits?) to read the declaration.

continues

What about those documents that have no declaration (since the declaration is optional)? These documents must use one of the default encoding parameters (UTF-8 or UTF-16). Again, the XML processor can match the first character (which must be a <) against its encoding in UTF-8 or UTF-16.

Entities

The document in Listing 2.1 (page 42) is self-contained: The document is complete and it can be stored in just one file. Complex documents are often split over several files: the text, the accompanying graphics, and so on.

XML, however, does not reason in terms of files. Instead it organizes documents physically in *entities*. In some cases, entities are equivalent to files; in others, they are not.

XML entities is a complex topic that we will revisit in the next chapter, when we will see how to declare entities in the DTD. In this chapter, we will see how to use entities.

EXAMPLE

Entities are inserted in the document through *entity references* (the name of the entity between an ampersand character and a semicolon). For the application, the entity reference is replaced by the content of the entity. If we assume we have defined an entity "us," which has the value "United States," the following two lines are equivalent:

```
<country>&us;</country>
<country>United States</country>
```

XML predefines entities for the characters used in markup (angle brackets, quotes, and so on). The entities are used to escape the characters from element or attribute content. The entities are

- < left angle bracket "<" must be escaped with <

- & ampersand "&" must be escaped with &

- > right angle bracket ">" must be escaped with > in the combination]]> in CDATA sections (see the following)

- ' single quote "'" can be escaped with ' essentially in parameter value

- " double quote """ can be escaped with " essentially in parameter value

EXAMPLE

The following is not valid because the ampersand would confuse the XML processor:

```
<company>Mark & Spencer</company>
```

Instead, it must be rewritten to escape the ampersand bracket with an & entity:

```
<company>Mark &amp; Spencer</company>
```

XML also supports *character references* where a letter is replaced by its Unicode character code. For example, if your keyboard does not support accentuated letters, you can still write my name in XML as:

```
<name>Beno&#238;t Marchal</name>
```

Character references that start with &#x provides a hexadecimal representation of the character code. Character references that start with &# provide a decimal representation of the character code.

TIP

Under Windows, to find the character code of most characters, you can use the Character Map. The character code appears in the status bar (see Figure 2.2).

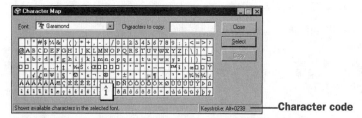
────────Character code

Figure 2.2: *The character code in Character Map*

Special Attributes

XML defines two attributes:

- xml:space for those applications that discard duplicate spaces (similar to Web browsers that discard unnecessary spaces in HTML). This attribute controls whether the application can discard spaces. If set to preserve, the application should preserve all spaces in this element and its children. If set to default, the application can use its default space handling.

EXAMPLE

- xml:lang in publishing, it is often desirable to know in which language the content is written. This attribute can be used to indicate the language of the element's content. For example:

```
<p xml:lang="en-GB">What colour is it?</p>
    <p xml:lang="en-US">What color is it?</p>
```

Processing Instructions

Processing instructions (abbreviated PI) is a mechanism to insert non-XML statements, such as scripts, in the document.

At first sight, processing instruction is at odds with the XML concept that processing is always derived from the structure. As we saw in the first chapter, with SGML and XML, processing is derived from the structure of the document. There should be no need to insert specific instructions in a document. This is one of the major improvements of SGML when compared to earlier markup languages.

That's the theory. In practice, there are cases where it is easier to insert processing instructions rather than define complex structure. Processing instructions are a concession to reality from the XML standard developers.

You already are familiar with processing instructions because the XML declaration is a processing instruction:

```
<?xml version="1.0" encoding="ISO-8859-1"?>
```

EXAMPLE

> ✔ In Chapter 5, "XSL Transformation," you will see how to use processing instructions to attach style sheets to documents (page 125).

```
<?xml-stylesheet href="simple-ie5.xsl" type="text/xsl"?>
```

Finally, processing instructions are used by specific applications. For example, XMetaL (an XML editor) uses them to create templates. This processing instruction is specific to XMetaL:

```
<?xm-replace_text {Click here to type the name}?>
```

The processing instruction is enclosed in <? and ?>. The first name is the *target*. It identifies the application or the device to which the instructions are directed. The rest of the processing instructions are in a format specific to the target. It does not have to be XML.

CDATA Sections

As you have seen, markup characters (left angle bracket and ampersand) that appear in the content of an element must be escaped with an entity.

For some applications, it is difficult to escape markup characters, if only because there are too many of them. Mathematical equations can use many left angle brackets. It is difficult to include a scripting language in a document and to escape the angle brackets and ampersands. Also, it is difficult to include an XML document in an XML document.

CDATA sections are intended for these cases. CDATA sections are delimited by "<[CDATA[" and "]]>". The XML processor ignores all markup except for]]> (which means it is not possible to include a CDATA section in another CDATA section).

EXAMPLE

The following example uses a CDATA section to insert an XML example into an XML document:

```
<?xml version="1.0"?>
<example>
<[CDATA[
<?xml version="1.0"?>
<entry>
   <name>John Doe</name>
   <email href="mailto:jdoe@emailaholic.com"/>
</entry>]]>
</example>
```

NOTE

CDATA stands for character data. In the next chapters you will see that text in an element is called PCDATA, parsed character data.

The difference between CDATA and PCDATA is that PCDATA cannot contain markup characters.

Frequently Asked Questions on XML

This completes our study of the XML syntax. The only aspect of the XML recommendation we haven't studied yet is the DTD. The DTD is discussed in Chapter 3, "XML Schemas."

Before moving to the DTD, however, I'd like to answer three common questions on XML documents.

Code Indenting

Listing 2.1 is indented to make the tree more apparent. Although it is not required for the XML processor, it makes the code more readable as we can see immediately where an element starts and ends.

This raises the question of what the processor does with the whitespaces used for indenting. Does it ignore it? The answer is a qualified yes.

EXAMPLE

Strictly speaking, the XML processor does not ignore whitespaces. In the following example, it sees the content of name as a line break, three spaces, fname, another line break, three spaces, lname, and a line break.

```
<name>
   <fname>Jack</fname>
   <lname>Smith</lname>
</name>
```

EXAMPLE

But in the following case, it sees the content of name as just fname and lname. No indenting.

```
<name><fname>Jack</fname><lname>Smith</lname></name>
```

It is easy to filter unwanted whitespaces and most applications do it. For example, XSL (XML Style Sheet Language) ignores what it recognizes as indenting.

Likewise, some XML editors give you the option of indenting source code automatically. If they indent the code, they will ignore indenting in the document.

If whitespaces are important for your document, then you should use the xml:space attribute that was introduced earlier.

Why the End Tag?

At first, the need to terminate each element with an end tag is annoying. It is required because XML does not have predefined elements.

An HTML browser can work out when an element has no closing tags because it knows the structure of the document, it knows which elements are allowed where, and it can deduce where each element should end.

EXAMPLE

Indeed, if the following is an HTML fragment, a browser does not need end tags for paragraphs, nor does it need an empty tag for the break (see Listing 2.4):

Listing 2.4: An HTML Document Needs No End Tags

```
<P><B>John Doe</B>
<P>34 Fountain Square Plaza<BR>
Cincinnati, OH 45202<BR>
US
<P>Tel: 513-555-8889
<P>Tel: 513-555-7098
<P>Email: jdoe@emailaholic.com
```

The browser can deduce where the paragraphs end because it knows that paragraphs cannot nest. Therefore, the beginning of a new paragraph must coincide with the end of the previous one. Likewise, the browser knows that the break is an empty element. Because of all this a priori knowledge, the browser can "fill in the blank" and know the document must be interpreted as

```
<P><B>John Doe</B></P>
<P>34 Fountain Square Plaza<BR></BR>
Cincinnati, OH 45202<BR></BR>
```

```
US</P>
<P>Tel: 513-555-8889</P>
<P>Tel: 513-555-7098</P>
<P>Email: jdoe@emailaholic.com</P>
```

However, an XML processor does not know the structure of the document because you define your own tags. So, an XML processor does not know that p elements (it does not know they are paragraphs, either) cannot nest. If Listing 2.4 was XML, the processor could interpret it as

```
<P><B>John Doe</B>
   <P>34 Fountain Square Plaza
      <BR>Cincinnati, OH 45202</BR>
      <BR>US</BR>
      <P>Tel: 513-555-8889
        <P>Tel: 513-555-7098
          <P>Email: jdoe@emailaholic.com</P>
        </P>
      </P>
   </P>
</P>
```

or as:

```
<P><B>John Doe</B></P>
<P>34 Fountain Square Plaza
  <BR>Cincinnati, OH 45202</BR>
  <BR/>US
  <P>Tel: 513-555-8889</P>
  <P>Tel: 513-555-7098</P>
</P>
<P>Email: jdoe@emailaholic.com</P>
```

There are many other possibilities and that's precisely the problem. The processor wouldn't know which one to pick so the markup has to be unambiguous.

TIP

In the next chapter, you will see how to declare the structure of documents with DTDs. Theoretically, the XML processor could use the DTD to resolve ambiguities in the markup. Indeed, that's how SGML processors work. However, you also will learn that a category of XML processors ignores DTDs.

XML and Semantic

It is important to realize that XML alone does not define the semantic (the meaning) of the document. The element names are meaningful only to humans. They are meaningless to the XML processor.

EXAMPLE

The processor does not know what a name is. And it does not know the difference between a name and an address, apart from the fact that an address has more children than a name. For the XML processor, Listing 2.5, where the element names are totally mixed up, is as good as Listing 2.1.

Listing 2.5: Meaningless Names

```
<?xml version="1.0"?>
<name>
    <tel>
        <street>John Doe</street>
        <country>
            <email>34 Fountain Square Plaza</email>
            <locality>OH</locality>
            <region>45202</region>
            <postal-code>Cincinnati</postal-code>
            <address>US</address>
        </country>
        <tel preferred="true">513-555-8889</tel>
        <tel>513-555-7098</tel>
        <address-book href="mailto:jdoe@emailaholic.com"/>
    </tel>
    <tel>
        <street>Jack Smith</street>
        <tel>513-555-3465</tel>
        <address-book href="mailto:jsmith@emailaholic.com"/>
    </tel>
</name>
```

The semantic of an XML document is provided by the application. As we will see in Chapter 5 and later, some XML companion standards deal with some aspects of semantic.

For example, XSL describes how to present information. It provides formatting semantic for a document. XLink and RDF (Resource Definition Framework) can be used to describe the relationships between documents.

Four Common Errors

As you have seen, the XML syntax is very strict: Elements must have both a start and end tag, or they must use the special empty element tag; attribute values must be fully quoted; there can be only one top-level element; and so on.

A strict syntax was a design goal for XML. The browser vendors asked for it. HTML is very lenient, and HTML browsers accept anything that looks vaguely like HTML. It might have helped with the early adoption of HTML but now it is a problem.

Studies estimate that more than 50% of the code in a browser deals with errors or the sloppiness of HTML authors. Consequently, an HTML browser is difficult to write, it has slowed competition, and it makes for mega-downloads.

It is expected that in the future, people will increasingly rely on PDAs (Personal Digital Assistants like the PalmPilot) or portable phones to access the Web. These devices don't have the resources to accommodate a complex syntax or megabyte browsers.

In short, making XML stricter meant simplifying the work of the programmers and that translates into more competition, more XML tools, smaller tools that fit in smaller devices, and, hopefully, faster tools.

Yet, it means that you have to be very careful about what you write. This is particularly true if you are used to writing HTML documents. In this section, I review the four most common errors in writing XML code.

Forget End Tags

EXAMPLE

For reasons explained previously, end tags are mandatory (except for empty elements). The XML processor would reject the following because street and country have no end tags:

```
<address>
    <street>34 Fountain Square Plaza
    <region>OH</region>
    <postal-code>45202</postal-code>
    <locality>Cincinnati</locality>
    <country>US
</address>
```

Forget That XML Is Case Sensitive

XML names are case sensitive. The following two elements are different for XML. The first one is a "tel" element whereas the second one is a "TEL" element:

```
<tel>513-555-7098</tel>
<TEL>513-555-7098</TEL>
```

A popular variation on this error is to use a different case in the opening and closing tag of an element:

```
<tel>513-555-7098</TEL>
```

Introduce Spaces in the Name of Element

It is illegal to introduce spaces in the name of elements. The XML processor interprets spaces as the beginning of an attribute. The following example is not valid because address book has a space in it:

```
<address book>
    <entry>
        <name>John Doe</name>
        <email href="mailto:jdoe@emailaholic.com"/>
    </entry>
</address book>
```

Forget the Quotes for Attribute Value

Unlike HTML, XML forces you to quote attribute values. The following is not acceptable:

```
<tel preferred=true>513-555-8889</tel>
```

A popular variation on this error is to forget the closing quote. The XML processor assumes that the content of the element is part of the attribute, which is guaranteed to produce funny results! The following is incorrect because the attribute has no closing quote:

```
<tel preferred="true>513-555-8889</tel>
```

XML Editors

If you are like me, you will soon hate writing XML by hand. It's not that the syntax is difficult, but it is annoying to remember to close every element and to escape left angle brackets.

Fortunately, there are several XML editors on the market that can help you with writing XML code. XML Notepad from Microsoft is a simple but effective editor. Notepad divides the screen into two panes. In the left pane, it shows the document tree (Structure); in the right pane, the content (Values). Figure 2.3 shows XML Notepad.

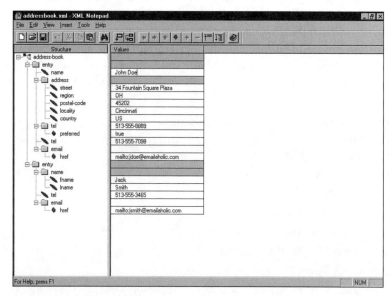

Figure 2.3: XML Notepad

Best of all, XML Notepad is free. You can download it from www.microsoft.com. Search for "XML Notepad." At the time of this writing, XML Notepad was still in beta. Take a moment to review the release notes to see how final the version you download is. Note XML Notepad works better if Internet Explorer 5.0 is installed. More specifically, if you are using Internet Explorer 4.0, all names are converted to uppercase! IBM also has useful tools at www.alphaworks.ibm.com.

If you are serious about XML editing, you will want to adopt a more powerful editor. Good editors use style sheets to present the information and they might hide the markup completely. It frees you to concentrate on what really matters—the text.

✔ For a more comprehensive discussion of what you should look for when shopping for an XML editor, turn to the section "CSS and XML Editors" in Chapter 6 (page 182).

Three Applications of XML

Another design goal for XML was to develop a language that could suit a wide variety of applications. In this respect, XML has probably exceeded its creators' wildest dreams.

In this section, I introduce you to some applications of XML. As you will see throughout this book, many applications can benefit from XML. This section gives you an introduction of what XML has been used for.

Publishing

Because XML roots are in publishing, it's no wonder the standard is well adapted to publishing. XML is being used by an increasing number of publishers as the format for documents. The XML standard itself was published with XML.

Listing 2.6 is an XML document for a monthly newsletter. As you can see, it uses elements for the title, abstract, paragraphs, and other concepts common in publishing.

EXAMPLE

Listing 2.6: A Newsletter in XML

```
<?xml version="1.0"?>

<article fname="19990101_xsl">

<title>XML Style Sheets</title>

<date>January 1999</date>

<copyright>1999, Benoit Marchal</copyright>

<abstract>Style sheets add flexibility to document viewing.</abstract>

<keywords>XML, XSL, style sheet, publishing, web</keywords>

<section>

<p>Send comments and suggestions to <url protocol="mailto">bmarchal
➥@pineapplesoft.com</url>.</p>

</section>

<section>

<title>Styling</title>

<p>Style sheets are inherited from SGML, an XML ancestor. Style sheets
➥originated in publishing and document management applications. XSL is XML's
➥ standard style sheet, see <url>http://www.w3.org/Style</url>.</p>

</section>

<section>

<title>How XSL Works</title>

<p>An XSL style sheet is a set of rules where each rule specifies how to format
➥certain elements in the document. To continue the example from the previous
➥section, the style sheets have rules for title, paragraphs, and keywords.</p>

<p>With XSL, these rules are powerful enough not only to format the document but
➥also to reorganize it, e.g., by moving the title to the front page or
➥extracting the list of keywords. This can lead to exciting applications of XSL
➥outside the realm of traditional publishing. For example, XSL can be used to
➥convert documents between the company-specific markup and a standard one.</p>

</section>

<section>

<title>The Added Flexibility of Style Sheets</title>
```

```
<p>Style sheets are separated from documents. Therefore, one document can have
➥more than one style sheet and, conversely, one style sheet can be shared
➥amongst several documents.</p>

<p>This means that a document can be rendered differently depending on the media
➥or the audience. For example, a "managerial" style sheet may present a summary
➥view of a document that highlights key elements but a "clerical" style sheet
➥may display more detailed information.</p>

</section>

</article>
```

The main advantages of using XML for publishing are

- the capability to convert XML documents to different media: the Web, print, and more

- for large document sets, the capability to enforce a common structure that simplifies editing

- the emphasis on structure means that XML documents are better equipped to withstand the test of time, because structure is more stable than formatting

✔ Turn to Chapter 5, "XSL Transformation," page 125 and Chapter 6, "XSL Formatting Objects and Cascading Style Sheet," page 161 for a more complete discussion of how to use XML for publishing.

Business Document Exchange

EXAMPLE

XML is not limited to publishing. It has been used successfully with business and commercial documents. In this case, the elements would be price, product names, and so on. Listing 2.7 is a book order in XML.

Listing 2.7: An Order in XML

```
<?xml version="1.0" encoding="ISO-8859-1"?>
<order>
    <date>19990727</date>
    <sender>
        <name>Playfield Software</name>
        <address>
            <street>38 Fountain Square Plaza</street>
            <region>OH</region>
            <postal-code>45263</postal-code>
            <locality>Cincinnati</locality>
            <country>US</country>
        </address>
    </sender>
```

```
<receiver>
    <name>Macmillan Publishing</name>
    <address>
        <street>201 West 103rd Street</street>
        <region>IN</region>
        <postal-code>46290</postal-code>
        <locality>Indianapolis</locality>
        <country>US</country>
    </address>
</receiver>
<lines>
    <reference href="urn:isbn:0-7897-2242-9"/>
    <description>XML By Example</description>
    <quantity>10</quantity>
    <price currency="usd">19.99</price>
</lines>
</order>
```

The main advantage of placing the order in XML rather than on paper is that software can process it. An application could read this order and automatically fulfill it.

For years, this was the realm of EDI technologies (EDI stands for Electronic Data Interchange). At the heart of EDI is a major effort to standardize the semantic of every commercial and administrative document (order, invoice, tax declaration, payment, catalog, and more).

There are many advantages to building a common semantic on a worldwide scale. In particular, it is possible to completely automate the flow of information between companies. However, one major inconvenience is the need to reach a consensus.

In practice, it is easy to agree on a few core elements, such as the quantity, the name, the address, and it is very easy to disagree on anything else. Imagine how complex an order can be when it must accommodate the regulations and business practice of every country.

In practice, organizations that use EDI have to simplify the standard. Unfortunately, they also might have to add specific applications that are not provided for in the standard.

In doing so, they often deviate from the standard. Unfortunately, nothing in the existing EDI standard supports that departure from the standard.

It is expected that XML will greatly simplify EDI because XML is a complete architecture for information exchange. It supports the common semantic where it makes sense, but it also supports extending and changing the documents where it makes sense.

Channel

Internet Explorer 4.0 introduced the concept of channels. Channels are Web sites to which you can subscribe. Figure 2.4 is the channel bar of Internet Explorer (if you are curious, the channels are the default channels for Belgium).

Figure 2.4: *Channel bar in Internet Explorer 4.0*

Behind each icon is an XML document. Indeed, the channels are described by using CDF, the Channel Definition Format. CDF is an application of XML.

EXAMPLE

Listing 2.8 is a CDF file for a channel. Again, the elements are specific to the application; in this case, they describe the channel, how often it must be updated, and which icon to use. However, the syntax is the familiar XML syntax.

Listing 2.8: A Channel Definition in XML

```
<?xml version="1.0"?>

<CHANNEL BASE="http://www.pineapplesoft.com/newsletter/" HREF="index.html"
➥PRECACHE="YES" LEVEL="0">

    <TITLE>Pineapplesoft Link</TITLE>

    <ABSTRACT>Free monthly newsletter</ABSTRACT>

    <LOGO HREF="pslnk.gif" STYLE="IMAGE"/>

    <SCHEDULE STARTDATE="1998-01-01">
```

continues

Listing 2.8: continued

```
        <INTERVALTIME DAY="14"/>
    </SCHEDULE>
</CHANNEL>
```

What's Next

In this chapter, you learned enough XML syntax to be able to read or write XML documents. You also learned that XML does not predefine elements, that it is up to the application to define elements that make sense.

In the next chapter, you will learn how to describe XML documents with a DTD. The DTD is an important modeling tool for XML developers, and it is used to better serve XML authors.

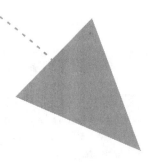

XML Schemas

In Chapter 2, "The XML Syntax," you learned how to write and read XML documents. More importantly, you learned that XML emphasizes the structure of documents.

This chapter further develops that theme by looking at the DTD, short for *Document Type Definition*, a mechanism to describe the structure of documents. Specifically, you will learn how to

- model XML documents
- express the model in a DTD
- validate a document against its model

The DTD is the original modeling language or schema for XML. However, for historical reasons, the DTD is somewhat limited and people are looking for solutions to overcome these limitations. The W3C is working on an alternative to DTD. We will review the current status of that effort.

This chapter is probably the most abstract chapter in this book. You might want to temporarily skip the second half (starting from the section "Entities and Notations") and revisit it after you have read through the book.

The DTD Syntax

EXAMPLE

The syntax for DTDs is different from the syntax for XML documents. Listing 3.1 is the address book introduced in Chapter 2 but with one difference: It has a new <!DOCTYPE> statement. The new statement is introduced in the section "Document Type Declaration." For now, it suffices to say that it links the document file to the DTD file. Listing 3.2 is its DTD.

Listing 3.1: An Address Book in XML

```
<?xml version="1.0"?>
<!DOCTYPE address-book SYSTEM "address-book.dtd">
<!-- loosely inspired by vCard 3.0 -->
<address-book>
    <entry>
        <name>John Doe</name>
        <address>
            <street>34 Fountain Square Plaza</street>
            <region>OH</region>
            <postal-code>45202</postal-code>
            <locality>Cincinnati</locality>
            <country>US</country>
        </address>
        <tel preferred="true">513-555-8889</tel>
        <tel>513-555-7098</tel>
        <email href="mailto:jdoe@emailaholic.com"/>
    </entry>
    <entry>
        <name><fname>Jack</fname><lname>Smith</lname></name>
        <tel>513-555-3465</tel>
        <email href="mailto:jsmith@emailaholic.com"/>
    </entry>
</address-book>
```

Listing 3.2: The DTD for the Address Book

```
<!-- top-level element, the address book
     is a list of entries                  -->
<!ELEMENT address-book  (entry+)>

<!-- an entry is a name followed by
     addresses, phone numbers, etc.         -->
```

```
<!ELEMENT entry   (name,address*,tel*,fax*,email*)>


<!-- name is made of string, first name
      and last name. This is a very flexible
          model to accommodate exotic name        -->
<!ELEMENT name    (#PCDATA ¦ fname ¦ lname)*>
<!ELEMENT fname   (#PCDATA)>
<!ELEMENT lname   (#PCDATA)>


<!-- definition of the address structure
      if several addresses, the preferred
          attribute signals the "default" one    -->
<!ELEMENT address       (street,region?,postal-code,locality,country)>
<!ATTLIST address       preferred (true ¦ false)  "false">
<!ELEMENT street        (#PCDATA)>
<!ELEMENT region        (#PCDATA)>
<!ELEMENT postal-code   (#PCDATA)>
<!ELEMENT locality      (#PCDATA)>
<!ELEMENT country       (#PCDATA)>


<!-- phone, fax and email, same preferred
      attribute as address                        -->
<!ELEMENT tel     (#PCDATA)>
<!ATTLIST tel     preferred (true ¦ false)  "false">
<!ELEMENT fax     (#PCDATA)>
<!ATTLIST fax     preferred (true ¦ false)  "false">
<!ELEMENT email   EMPTY>
<!ATTLIST email   href  CDATA              #REQUIRED
                  preferred (true ¦ false)  "false">
```

Element Declaration

EXAMPLE

1. DTD is a mechanism to describe every object (element, attribute, and so on) that can appear in the document, starting with elements. The following is an example of element declaration:

```
<!ELEMENT address-book  (entry+)>
```

After the <!ELEMENT markup comes the element name followed by its *content model*. The element declaration is terminated with a right angle bracket.

Element declarations are easy to read: The right side (the content model) defines the left side (the element name). In other words, the content model lists the children that are acceptable in the element.

The previous declaration means that an `address-book` element contains one or more `entry` elements. `address-book` is on the left side, `entry` on the right. The plus sign after `entry` means there can be more than one `entry` element.

EXAMPLE

2. Parentheses are used to group elements in the content model, as in the following example:

```
<!ELEMENT name (lname, (fname ¦ title))>
```

Element Name

As we saw in Chapter 2, XML names must follow certain rules. Specifically, names must start with either a letter or a limited set of punctuation characters ("_",":"). The rest of the name can consist of the same characters plus letters, digits and new punctuation characters (".", "-"). Spaces are not allowed in names.

Names cannot start with the string "xml," and as we will see in Chapter 4, "Namespaces," the colon plays a special role so it is advised you don't use it.

Special Keywords

For most elements, the content model is a list of elements. It also can be one of the following keywords:

- `#PCDATA` stands for parsed character data and means the element can contain text. `#PCDATA` is often (but not always) used for leaf elements. Leaf elements are elements that have no child elements.

- `EMPTY` means the element is an empty element. `EMPTY` always indicates a leaf element.

- `ANY` means the element can contain any other element declared in the DTD. This is seldom used because it carries almost no structure information. ANY is sometimes used during the development of a DTD, before a precise rule has been written. Note that the elements must be declared in the DTD.

Element contents that have `#PCDATA` are said to be *mixed content*. Element contents that contain only elements are said to be *element content*. In Listing 3.2, `tel` is a leaf element that contains only text while `email` is an empty element:

```
<!ELEMENT tel     (#PCDATA)>
<!ELEMENT email  EMPTY>
```

EXAMPLE   Note that CDATA sections appear anywhere #PCDATA appears.

The Secret of Plus, Star, and Question Mark

The plus ("+"), star ("*"), and question mark ("?") characters in the element content are *occurrence indicators*. They indicate whether and how elements in the child list can repeat.

- An element followed by no occurrence indicator must appear once and only once in the element being defined.

- An element followed by a "+" character must appear one or several times in the element being defined. The element can repeat.

- An element followed by a "*" character can appear zero or more times in the element being defined. The element is optional but, if it is included, it can repeat indefinitely.

- An element followed by a "?" character can appear once or not at all in the element being defined. It indicates the element is optional and, if included, cannot repeat.

EXAMPLE

The entry and name elements have content model that uses an occurrence indicator:

```
<!ELEMENT entry    (name,address*,tel*,fax*,email*)>
<!ELEMENT address  (street,region?,postal-code,locality,country)>
```

Acceptable children for the entry are name, address, tel, fax, and email. Except for name, these children are optional and can repeat.

Acceptable children for address are street, region, postal-code, locality, and country. None of the children can repeat but the region is optional.

The Secret of Comma and Vertical Bar

The comma (",") and vertical bar ("¦") characters are *connectors*. Connectors separate the children in the content model, they indicate the order in which the children can appear. The connectors are

- the "," character, which means both elements on the right and the left of the comma must appear in the same order in the document.

- the "¦" character, which means that only one of the elements on the left or the right of the vertical bar must appear in the document.

EXAMPLE

The name and address elements are good examples of connectors.

```
<!ELEMENT name     (#PCDATA ¦ fname ¦ lname)*>
<!ELEMENT address  (street,region?,postal-code,locality,country)>
```

Acceptable children for name are #PCDATA or a fname element or a lname element. Note that it is one or the other. However, the whole model can repeat thanks to the "*" occurrence indicator.

Acceptable children for address are street, region, postal-code, locality, and country, in exactly that order.

The various components of mixed content must always be separated by a "¦" and the model must repeat. The following definition is incorrect:

```
<!ELEMENT name  (#PCDATA, fname, lname)>
```

It must be

```
<!ELEMENT name (#PCDATA ¦ fname ¦ lname)*>
```

Element Content and Indenting

In the previous chapter, you learned that the XML application ignores indenting in most cases. Here again, a DTD can help.

If a DTD is associated with the document, then the XML processor knows that spaces in an element that has element content must indent (because the element has element content, it cannot contain any text). The XML processor can label the spaces as *ignorable whitespaces*. This is a very powerful hint to the application that the spaces are indenting.

Nonambiguous Model

The content model must be *deterministic* or unambiguous. In plain English, it means that it is possible to decide which part of the model applies to the current element by looking only at the current element.

EXAMPLE

For example, the following model is not acceptable:

```
<!ELEMENT cover  ((title, author) ¦ (title, subtitle))>
```

because when the XML processor is reading the element

```
<title>XML by Example</title>
```

in

```
<cover><title>XML by Example</title><author>Benoît Marchal</author></cover>
```

it cannot decide whether the title element is part of (title, author) or of (title, subtitle) by looking at title only. To decide that title is part of (title, author), it needs to look past title to the author element.

In most cases, however, it is possible to reorganize the document so that the model becomes acceptable:

```
<!ELEMENT cover  (title, (author ¦ subtitle))>
```

Now when the processor sees title, it knows where it fits in the model.

Attributes

EXAMPLE

Attributes also must be declared in the DTD. Element attributes are declared with the ATTLIST declaration, for example:

```
<!ATTLIST tel  preferred (true ¦ false)  "false">
```

The various components in this declaration are the markup (<!ATTLIST), the element name (tel), the attribute name (preferred), the attribute type ((true ¦ false)), a default value ("false"), and the right angle bracket.

EXAMPLE

For elements that have more than one attribute, you can group the declarations. For example, email has two attributes:

```
<!ATTLIST email  href      CDATA          #REQUIRED
                 preferred (true ¦ false) "false">
```

Attribute declaration can appear anywhere in the DTD. For readability, it is best to list attributes immediately after the element declaration.

CAUTION

If used in a valid document, the special attributes xml:space and xml:lang must be declared as

```
xml:space (default¦preserve) "preserve"

xml:lang  NMTOKEN  #IMPLIED
```

EXAMPLE

The DTD provides more control over the content of attributes than over the content of elements. Attributes are broadly divided into three categories:

- string attributes contain text, for example:

  ```
  <!ATTLIST email  href CDATA #REQUIRED>
  ```

- tokenized attributes have constraints on the content of the attribute, for example:

  ```
  <!ATTLIST entry id ID #IMPLIED>
  ```

- enumerated-type attributes accept one value in a list, for example:

  ```
  <!ATTLIST entry preferred (true ¦ false)  "false">
  ```

Attribute types can take any of the following values:

- CDATA for string attributes.

- ID for identifier. An identifier is a name that is unique in the document.

- IDREF must be the value of an ID used elsewhere in the same document. IDREF is used to create links within a document.

- IDREFS is a list of IDREF separated by spaces.

- ENTITY must be the name of an external entity; this is how you assign an external entity to an attribute.

- ENTITIES is a list of ENTITY separated by spaces.

- NMTOKEN is essentially a word without spaces.

- NMTOKENS is a list of NMTOKEN separated by spaces.

- Enumerated-type list is a closed list of nmtokens separated by |, the value has to be one of the nmtokens. The list of tokens can further be limited to NOTATIONS (introduced in the section "Notation," later in this chapter).

Optionally, the DTD can specify a default value for the attribute. If the document does not include the attribute, it is assumed to have the default value. The default value can take one of the four following values:

- #REQUIRED means that a value must be provided in the document

- #IMPLIED means that if no value is provided, the application must use its own default

- #FIXED followed by a value means that attribute value must be the value declared in the DTD

- A literal value means that the attribute will take this value if no value is given in the document.

EXAMPLE

NOTE
Information that remains constant between documents is an ideal candidate for #FIXED attributes. For example, if prices are always given in dollars, you could declare a price element as

```
<!ELEMENT price (#PCDATA)>
<!ATTLIST price currency NMTOKEN #FIXED "usd">
```

When the application reads

```
<price>19.99</price>
```

in a document, it appears as though it reads

```
<price currency="usd">19.99</price>
```

The application has received additional information but it didn't require additional markup in the document!

Document Type Declaration

EXAMPLE

The *document type declaration* attaches a DTD to a document. Don't confuse the document type declaration with the document type definition (DTD). The document type declaration has the form:

```
<!DOCTYPE address-book SYSTEM "address-book.dtd">
```

It consists of markup (`<!DOCTYPE`), the name of the top-level element (`address-book`), the DTD (`SYSTEM "address-book.dtd"`) and a right angle bracket. As Listing 3.1 illustrates, the document type declaration appears at the beginning of the XML document, after the XML declaration.

EXAMPLE

The top-level element of the document is selected in the declaration. Therefore, it is possible to create a document starting with any element in the DTD. Listing 3.3 has the same DTD as Listing 3.1, but its top-level element is an `entry`.

Listing 3.3: An Entry

```
<?xml version="1.0"?>
<!DOCTYPE entry SYSTEM "address-book.dtd">
<entry>
    <name>John Doe</name>
    <address>
        <street>34 Fountain Square Plaza</street>
        <region>OH</region>
        <postal-code>45202</postal-code>
        <locality>Cincinnati</locality>
        <country>US</country>
    </address>
    <tel preferred="true">513-555-8889</tel>
    <tel>513-555-7098</tel>
    <email href="mailto:jdoe@emailaholic.com"/>
</entry>
```

Internal and External Subsets

The DTD is divided into internal and external subsets. As the name implies, the internal subset is inserted in the document itself, whereas the external subset points to an external entity.

The internal and the external subsets have different rules for parameter entities. The differences are explained in the section "General and Parameter Entities," later in this chapter.

The internal subset of the DTD is included between brackets in the document type declaration. The external subset is stored in a separate entity and referenced from the document type declaration.

The internal subset of a DTD is stored in the document, specifically in the document type declaration, as in

```
<!DOCTYPE address [
<!ELEMENT address  (street,region?,postal-code,locality,country)>
<!ATTLIST address  preferred (true ¦ false)  "false">

<!ELEMENT street        (#PCDATA)>
<!ELEMENT region        (#PCDATA)>
<!ELEMENT postal-code  (#PCDATA)>
<!ELEMENT locality      (#PCDATA)>
<!ELEMENT country       (#PCDATA)>
]>
```

The external subset is not stored in the document. It is referenced from the document type declaration through an identifier as in the following examples:

```
<!DOCTYPE address-book SYSTEM "http://www.xmli.com/dtd/address-book.dtd">

<!DOCTYPE address-book PUBLIC "-//Pineapplesoft//Address Book//EN"
➥"http://catwoman.pineapplesoft.com/dtd/address-book.dtd">

<!DOCTYPE address-book SYSTEM "../dtds/address-book.dtd">
```

There are two types of identifiers: *system identifiers* and *public identifiers*. A keyword, respectively SYSTEM and PUBLIC, indicates the type of identifier.

- A system identifier is a *Universal Resource Identifier* (URI) pointing to the DTD. URI is a superset of URLs. For all practical purposes, a URI is a URL.

- In addition to the system identifier, the DTD identifier might include a public identifier. A public identifier points to a DTD recorded with the ISO according to the rules of ISO 9070. Note that a system identifier must follow the public identifier.

The system identifier is easy to understand. The XML processor must download the document from the URI.

Public identifiers are used to manage local copies of DTDs. The XML processor maintains a catalog file that lists public identifiers and their associated URIs. The processor will use these URIs instead of the system identifier.

Obviously, if the URIs in the catalog point to local copies of the DTD, the XML processor saves some downloads.

Listing 3.4 is an example of a catalog file.

Listing 3.4: A Catalog File

```
<XMLCatalog>
    <Base HRef="http://catwoman.pineapplesoft.com/dtd/"/>
    <Map PublicId="-//Pineapplesoft//Address Book//EN"
        HRef="address-book.dtd"/>
    <Map PublicId="-//Pineapplesoft//Article//EN"
        HRef="article.dtd"/>
    <Map PublicId="-//Pineapplesoft//Simple Order//EN"
        HRef="order.dtd"/>
    <Extend Href="http://www.w3.org/xcatalog/mastercat.xml"/>
</XMLCatalog>
```

EXAMPLE

Finally, note that a document can have both an internal and an external subset as in

```
<!DOCTYPE address SYSTEM "address-content.dtd" [
<!ELEMENT address  (street,region?,postal-code,locality,country)>
<!ATTLIST address  preferred (true ¦ false)  "false">
]>
```

Public Identifiers Format

EXAMPLE

The following public identifiers point to the address book:

```
"-//Pineapplesoft//Address Book//EN"
```

There are four parts, separated by "//":

- The first character is + if the organization is registered with ISO, - otherwise (most frequent).

- The second part is the owner of the DTD.

- The third part is the description of the DTD; spaces are allowed.

- The final part is the language (EN for English).

Standalone Documents

As you have seen, the DTD not only describes the document, but it can affect how the application reads the document. Specifically, default and fixed attribute values will add information to the document. Entities, which are also declared in the DTD, modify the document.

If all the entries that can influence the document are in the internal subset of the DTD, the document is said to be standalone. In other words, an XML processor does not need to download external entities to access all the information (it might have to download external entities to validate the document but that does not impact the content).

Conversely, if default attribute values or entities are declared in the external subset of the document, then the XML processor has to read the external subset, which might involve downloading more files.

EXAMPLE

Obviously, a standalone document is more efficient for communication over a network because only one file needs to be downloaded. The XML declaration has an attribute, standalone, that declares whether the document is a standalone document or not. It accepts only two values: yes and no. The default is no.

```
<?xml version="1.0" standalone="yes"?>
```

Note that a standalone document might have an external DTD subset but the external subset cannot modify how the application reads the document. Specifically, the external subset cannot

- declare entities

- declare default attribute values

- declare element content if the elements include spaces, such as for indenting. The last rule is the easiest to break but it is logical: If the DTD declares element content, then the processor reports indenting as ignorable whitespaces; otherwise, it reports as normal whitespaces.

Why Schemas?

Why do we need DTDs or schemas in XML? There is a potential conflict between flexibility and ease of use. As a rule, more flexible solutions are more difficult, if only because you have to work your way through the options. Specific solutions might also be optimized for certain tasks.

Let's compare a closed solution, HTML, with an open one such as XML. Both can be used to publish documents on the Web (XML serves many other purposes as well). HTML has a fixed set of elements and software can be highly optimized for it. For example, HTML editors offer templates, powerful visual editing, image editing, document preview, and more.

XML, on the other hand, is a flexible solution. It does not define elements but lets you, the developer, define the structure you need. Therefore, XML editors must accept any document structure. There are very little opportunities to optimize the XML editors because, by definition, they must be as generic as XML is. HTML, the close solution, has an edge here.

The DTD is an attempt to bridge that gap. DTD is a formal description of the document. Software tools can read it and learn about the document structure. Consequently, the tools can adapt themselves to better support the document structure.

For example, some XML editors use DTDs to populate their element lists as well as adopt default styling, based on the DTD. Finally, these XML editors will guide the author by making certain the structure is followed.

In other words, the editor is a generic tool that accepts any XML document, but it is configured for a specific application (read specific structure) through the DTD.

Figure 3.1 is a screenshot from a DTD-aware editor. Notice that the editor prompts for elements based on the structure.

EXAMPLE

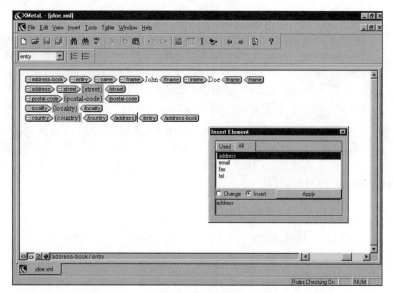

Figure 3.1: XML editor uses the DTD to guide the user.

Well-Formed and Valid Documents

XML recognizes two classes of documents: *well-formed* and *valid*. The documents in Chapter 2 were well-formed, which in XML jargon means they follow the XML syntax. Well-formed documents have the right mix of start and end tags, attributes are properly quoted, entities are acceptable, character sets are properly used, and so on.

Well-formed documents have no DTD, so the XML processor cannot check their structure. It only checks that they follow the syntax rules.

Valid documents are stricter. They not only follow the syntax rules, they also comply with a specific structure, as described in a DTD.

Valid documents have a DTD. The XML processor will check that the documents are syntactically correct but it also ensures they follow the structure described in the DTD.

Why two classes of documents? Why not have only valid documents? In practice, some applications don't need a DTD. Also, among those applications that do, they need the DTD only at specific steps in the process.

The DTD is useful during document creation, when it makes sense to enforce the document structure. However, it is less useful after the creation. For example, in most cases, it is useless to distribute the DTD with the document. Indeed, a reader cannot fix errors in the structure of a document (that's the role of the author and editor), so what is a reader to do with the DTD?

Relationship Between the DTD and the Document

Unless it's overlooked, let me stress the relationship between the DTD and the XML document. The role of the DTD is to specify which elements are allowed where in the document.

EXAMPLE

The documents in Listings 3.6 and 3.7 are valid and respect the DTD in Listing 3.5. The document in Listing 3.6 has a region element, whereas the one in Listing 3.7 has none. It works because region is a conditional element in the DTD.

Listing 3.5: The DTD

```
<!ELEMENT address  (street,region?,postal-code,locality,country)>
<!ATTLIST address  preferred (true ¦ false)  "false">


<!ELEMENT street       (#PCDATA)>
<!ELEMENT region       (#PCDATA)>
<!ELEMENT postal-code  (#PCDATA)>
<!ELEMENT locality     (#PCDATA)>
<!ELEMENT country      (#PCDATA)>
```

Listing 3.6: A Valid Document

```
<?xml version="1.0"?>
<!DOCTYPE address SYSTEM "address.dtd">
<address>
    <street>34 Fountain Square Plaza</street>
    <region>OH</region>
```

```
        <postal-code>45202</postal-code>
        <locality>Cincinnati</locality>
        <country>US</country>
</address>
```

Listing 3.7: Another Valid Document

```
<?xml version="1.0"?>
<!DOCTYPE address SYSTEM "address.dtd">
<address>
        <street>Rue du Lombard 345</street>
        <postal-code>5000</postal-code>
        <locality>Namur</locality>
        <country>Belgium</country>
</address>
```

However, Listings 3.8 and 3.9 are not valid documents. Listing 3.8 is missing a country element and country is not optional. In Listing 3.9, the region element has a code attribute that is not declared in the DTD.

Listing 3.8: An Invalid Document

```
<?xml version="1.0"?>
<!DOCTYPE address SYSTEM "address.dtd">
<address>
        <street>34 Fountain Square Plaza</street>
        <region>OH</region>
        <postal-code>45202</postal-code>
        <locality>Cincinnati</locality>
</address>
```

Listing 3.9: An Invalid Document

```
<?xml version="1.0"?>
<!DOCTYPE address SYSTEM "address.dtd">
<address>
        <street>34 Fountain Square Plaza</street>
        <region code="OH">Ohio</region>
        <postal-code>45202</postal-code>
        <locality>Cincinnati</locality>
        <country>US</country>
</address>
```

Another way to look at the relationship between DTD and document is to say that the DTD describes the tree that is acceptable for the document. Figure 3.2 shows the tree described by the DTD in Listing 3.5.

Figure 3.2: The tree for the address

Benefits of the DTD

The main benefits of using a DTD are

- The XML processor enforces the structure, as defined in the DTD.

- The application accesses the document structure, such as to populate an element list.

- The DTD gives hints to the XML processor—that is, it helps separate indenting from content.

- The DTD can declare default or fixed values for attributes. This might result in a smaller document.

Validating the Document

You can validate documents with an XML processor. I invite you to download XML for Java from the IBM Web site at www.alphaworks.ibm.com. There are other XML processors, but I will use the IBM one in Chapter 5, "XSL Transformation," and Chapter 8, "Alternative API: SAX."

XML for Java is a Java application. You don't need to be a Java programmer to use it, but you must have installed a Java runtime on your system. You can download a Java runtime from java.sun.com.

Tools are sometimes updated. If the status of XML for Java changes, we will post an update on the Macmillan Web site at www.quecorp.com/series/by_example. If you experience a problem finding the tool, visit www.quecorp.com/series/by_example.

EXAMPLE

The XML for Java comes with a command-line version that you can use to validate documents against their DTD. To validate the document in Listing 3.1, save it in a file called "abook.xml," save its DTD in the file called "address-book.dtd," and issue the command:

```
java -classpath c:\xml4j\xml4j.jar;c:\xml4j\xml4jsamples.jar
➥XJParse -p com.ibm.xml.parsers.ValidatingSAXParser abook.xml
```

This looks like a long and complex command line. If you are curious, Appendix A breaks it into smaller pieces.

OUTPUT

This command assumes XML for Java is installed in the c:\xml4j directory. You might have to update the classpath for your system. If everything goes well, the result is a message similar to

```
abook.xml: 1420 ms (24 elems, 9 attrs, 105 spaces, 97 chars)
```

If the document contains errors (either syntax errors or it does not respect the structure outlined in the DTD), you will have an error message.

CAUTION

The IBM for Java processor won't work unless you have installed a Java runtime.

If there is an error message similar to "Exception in thread "main" java.lang.NoClassDefFoundError," it means that either the `classpath` is incorrect (make sure it points to the right directory) or that you typed an incorrect class name for XML for Java (`XJParser` and `com.ibm.xml.parsers.ValidatingSAXParser`).

If there is an error message similar to "Exception in thread "main" java.io.FileNotFoundException: d:\xml\abook.xm", it means that the filename is incorrect (in this case, it points to "abook.xm" instead of "abook.xml").

TIP

You can save some typing with batch files (under Windows) or shell scripts (under UNIX). Adapt the path to your system, replace the filename (abook.xml) with "%1" and save in a file called "validate.bat". The file should contain the following command:

```
java -classpath c:\xml4j\xml4j.jar;c:\xml4j\xml4jsamples.jar
➥XJParse -p com.ibm.xml.parsers.ValidatingSAXParser %1
```

Now you can validate any XML file with the following (shorter) command:

```
validate abook.xml
```

Entities and Notations

As already mentioned in the previous chapter, XML doesn't work with files but with entities. Entities are the physical representation of XML documents. Although entities usually are stored as files, they need not be.

In XML the document, its DTD, and the various files it references (images, stock-phrases, and so on) are entities. The document itself is a special entity because it is the starting point for the XML processor. The entity of the document is known as the *document entity*.

XML does not dictate how to store and access entities. This is the task of the XML processor and it is system specific. The XML processor might have to download entities or it might use a local catalog file to retrieve the entities.

In Chapter 7, "The Parser and DOM," you'll see how SAX parsers (a SAX parser is one example of an XML processor) enable the application to retrieve entities from databases or other sources.

XML has many types of entities, classified according to three criteria: *general* or *parameter entities, internal* or *external entities*, and *parsed* or *unparsed entities.*

General and Parameter Entities

EXAMPLE

General entity references can appear anywhere in text or markup. In practice, general entities are often used as macros, or shorthand for a piece of text. External general entities can reference images, sound, and other documents in non-XML format. Listing 3.10 shows how to use a general entity to replace some text.

Listing 3.10: General Entity

```
<?xml version="1.0"?>
<!DOCTYPE address-book [
<!ENTITY jacksmith
'<entry>
    <name><fname>Jack</fname><lname>Smith</lname></name>
    <tel>513-555-3465</tel>
    <email href="mailto:jsmith@emailaholic.com"/>
 </entry>'>
]>
<address-book>
    &jacksmith;
</address-book>
```

General entities are declared with the markup <!ENTITY followed by the entity name, the entity definition, and the customary right angle bracket.

TIP

General entities also are often used to associate a mnemonic with character references as in

```
<!ENTITY icirc "&#238;">
```

As we saw in Chapter 2, "The XML Syntax," the following entities are predefined in XML: "<", "&", ">", "'", and """.

Parameter entity references can only appear in the DTD. There is an extra % character in the declaration before the entity name. Parameter entity references also replace the ampersand with a percent sign as in

```
<!ENTITY % boolean   "(true ¦ false) 'false'">
<!ELEMENT tel        (#PCDATA)>
<!ATTLIST tel        preferred %boolean;>
```

Parameter entities have many applications. You will learn how to use parameter entities in the following sections: "Internal and External Entities," "Conditional Sections," "Designing DTDs from an Object Model."

CAUTION

The previous example is valid only in the external subset of a DTD. In the internal subset, parameter entities can appear only where markup declaration can appear.

Internal and External Entities

XML also distinguishes between internal and external entities. Internal entities are stored in the document, whereas external entities point to a system or public identifier. Entity identifiers are identical to DTD identifiers (in fact, the DTD is a special entity).

The entities in the previous sections were internal entities because their value was declared in the entity definition. External entities, on the other hand, reference content that is not part of the current document.

TIP

External entities might start with an XML declaration—for example, to declare a special encoding.

```
<?xml version="1.0" encoding="ISO-8859-1"?>
```

External general entities can be parsed or unparsed. If parsed, the entity must contain valid XML text and markup. External parsed entities are used to share text across several documents, as illustrated by Listing 3.11.

In Listing 3.11, the various entries are stored in separate entities (separate files). The address book combines them in a document.

Listing 3.11: Using External Entities

EXAMPLE

```
<?xml version="1.0"?>
<!DOCTYPE address-book [
<!ENTITY johndoe   SYSTEM "johndoe.ent">
<!ENTITY jacksmith SYSTEM "jacksmith.ent">
]>
<address-book>
   &johndoe;
   &jacksmith;
</address-book>
```

Where the file "johndoe.ent" contains:

```
<entry>
   <name>John Doe</name>
```

```
<address>
    <street>34 Fountain Square Plaza</street>
    <region>OH</region>
    <postal-code>45202</postal-code>
    <locality>Cincinnati</locality>
    <country>US</country>
</address>
</entry>
```

And "jacksmith.ent" contains

```
<entry>
    <name><fname>Jack</fname><lname>Smith</lname></name>
    <tel>513-555-3465</tel>
    <email href="mailto:jsmith@emailaholic.com"/>
</entry>
```

EXAMPLE

However, unparsed entities are probably the most helpful external general entities. Unparsed entities are used for non-XML content, such as images, sound, movies, and so on. Unparsed entities provide a mechanism to load non-XML data into a document.

The XML processor treats the unparsed entity as an opaque block, of course. By definition, it does not attempt to recognize markup in unparsed entities.

A notation must be associated with unparsed entities. Notations are explained in more detail in the next section but, in a nutshell, they identify the type of a document, such as GIF, JPEG, or Windows bitmap for images. The notation is introduced by the NDATA keyword:

```
<!ENTITY logo SYSTEM "http://catwoman.pineapplesoft.com/logo.gif"
            NDATA GIF>
```

EXAMPLE

External parameter entities are similar to external general entities. However, because parameter entities appear in the DTD, they must contain valid XML markup.

External parameter entities are often used to insert the content of a file in the markup. Let's suppose we have created a list of general entities for every country, as in Listing 3.12 (saved in the file countries.ent).

Listing 3.12: A List of Entities for the Countries

```
<?xml version="1.0" encoding="ISO-8859-1"?>
<!ENTITY be "Belgium">
```

```
<!ENTITY ch "Switzerland">
<!ENTITY de "Germany">
<!ENTITY it "Italy">
<!ENTITY jp "Japan">
<!ENTITY uk "United Kingdom">
<!ENTITY us "United States">
<!-- and more -->
```

Creating such a list is a large effort. We would like to reuse it in all our documents. The construct illustrated in Listing 3.13 pulls the list of countries from countries.ent in the current document. It declares a parameter entity as an external entity and it immediately references the parameter entity. This effectively includes the external list of entities in the DTD of the current document.

Listing 3.13: Using External Parameter Entities

```
<?xml version="1.0"?>
<!DOCTYPE address SYSTEM "address.dtd" [
<!ENTITY % countries SYSTEM "countries.ent">
%countries;
]>
<address>
    <street>34 Fountain Square Plaza</street>
    <region>Ohio</region>
    <postal-code>45202</postal-code>
    <locality>Cincinnati</locality>
    <country>&us;</country>
</address>
```

CAUTION
Given the limitation on parameter entities in the internal subset of the DTD, this is the only sensible application of parameter entities in the internal subset.

Notation

Because the XML processor cannot process unparsed entities, it needs a mechanism to associate them with the proper tool. In the case of an image, it could be an image viewer.

Notation is simply a mechanism to declare the type of unparsed entities and associate them, through an identifier, with an application.

```
<!NOTATION GIF89a PUBLIC "-//CompuServe//NOTATION Graphics
➥ Interchange Format 89a//EN" "c:\windows\kodakprv.exe">
```

This declaration is unsafe because it points to a specific application. The application might not be available on another computer or it might be available but from another path. If your system has defined the appropriate file associations, you can get away with a declaration such as

```
<!NOTATION GIF89a SYSTEM "GIF">
<!NOTATION GIF89a SYSTEM "image/gif">
```

The first notation uses the filename, while the second uses the MIME type.

Managing Documents with Entities

External entities are helpful to modularize and help manage large DTDs and large document sets.

The idea is very simple: Try to divide your work into smaller pieces that are more manageable. Save each piece in a separate file and include them in your document with external entities.

Also try to identify pieces that you can reuse across several applications. It might be a list of entities (such as the list of countries) or a list of notations, or some text (such as a copyright notice that must appear on every document). Place them in separate files and include them in your documents through external entities.

Figure 3.3 shows how it works. Notice that some files are shared across several documents.

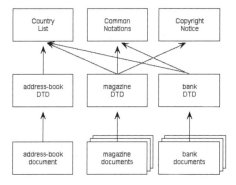

Figure 3.3: *Using external entities to manage large projects*

This is like eating a tough steak: You have to cut the meat into smaller pieces until you can chew it.

Conditional Sections

As your DTDs mature, you might have to change them in ways that are partly incompatible with previous usage. During the migration period, when you have new and old documents, it is difficult to maintain the DTD.

To help you manage migrations and other special cases, XML provides *conditional sections*. Conditional sections are included or excluded from the DTD depending on the value of a keyword. Therefore, you can include or exclude a large part of a DTD by simply changing one keyword.

EXAMPLE

Listing 3.13 shows how to use conditional sections. The `strict` parameter entity resolves to `INCLUDE`. The `lenient` parameter entity resolves to `IGNORE`. The application will use the definition of name in the `%strict;` section (`(fname, lname)`) and ignores the definition in the `%lenient;` section (`(#PCDATA ¦ fname ¦ lname)*`).

Listing 3.13: Using Conditional Sections

```
<!ENTITY % strict 'INCLUDE'>
<!ENTITY % lenient 'IGNORE'>


<![%strict;[
<!-- a name is a first name and a last name -->
<!ELEMENT name  (fname, lname)>
]]>
<![%lenient;[
<!-- name is made of string, first name
     and last name. This is a very flexible
     model to accommodate exotic name        -->
<!ELEMENT name  (#PCDATA ¦ fname ¦ lname)*>
]]>
```

However, to revert to the lenient definition of name, it suffices to invert the parameter entity declaration:

```
<!ENTITY % strict 'IGNORE'>
<!ENTITY % lenient 'INCLUDE'>
```

Designing DTDs

Now that you understand what DTDs are for and that you understand how to use them, it is time to look at how to create DTDs. DTD design is a creative and rewarding activity.

It is not possible, in this section, to cover every aspect of DTD design. Books have been devoted to that topic. Use this section as guidance and remember that practice makes proficient.

Yet, I would like to open this section with a plea to use existing DTDs when possible. Next, I will move into two examples of the practical design of practically designing DTDs.

Main Advantages of Using Existing DTDs

There are many XML DTDs available already and it seems more are being made available every day. With so many DTDs, you might wonder whether it's worth designing your own.

I would argue that, as much as possible, you should try to reuse existing DTDs. Reusing DTDs results in multiple savings. Not only do you not have to spend time designing the DTD, but also you don't have to maintain and update it.

However, designing an XML application is not limited to designing a DTD. As you will learn in Chapter 5, "XSL Transformation," and subsequent chapters, you might also have to design style sheets, customize tools such as editors, and/or write special code using a parser.

This adds up to a lot of work. And it follows the "uh, oh" rule of project planning: Uh, oh, it takes more work than I thought." If at all possible, it pays to reuse somebody else's DTD.

The first step in a new XML project should be to search the Internet for similar applications. I suggest you start at `www.oasis-open.org/sgml/ xml.html`. The site, maintained by Robin Cover, is the most comprehensive list of XML links.

In practice, you are likely to find DTDs that almost fit your needs but aren't exactly what you are looking for. It's not a problem because XML is extensible so it is easy to take the DTD developed by somebody else and adapt it to your needs.

Designing DTDs from an Object Model

I will take two examples of DTD design. In the first example, I will start from an object model. This is the easiest solution because you can reuse the objects defined in the model. In the second example, I will create a DTD from scratch.

EXAMPLE

Increasingly, object models are made available in UML. UML is the Unified Modeling Language (yes, there is an ML something that does not stand for markup language). UML is typically used for object-oriented applications such as Java or C++ but the same models can be used with XML.

An object model is often available when XML-enabling an existing Java or C++ application. Figure 3.4 is a (simplified) object model for bank accounts. It identifies the following objects:

- "Account" is an abstract class. It defines two properties: the balance and a list of transactions.

- "Savings" is a specialized "Account" that represents a savings account; interest is an additional property.

- "Checking" is a specialized "Account" that represents a checking account; rate is an additional property.

- "Owner" is the account owner. An "Account" can have more than one "Owner" and an "Owner" can own more than one "Account."

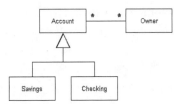

Figure 3.4: The object model

The application we are interested in is Web banking. A visitor would like to retrieve information about his or her various bank accounts (mainly his or her balance).

The first step to design the DTD is to decide on the root-element. The top-level element determines how easily we can navigate the document and access the information we are interested in. In the model, there are two potential top-level elements: Owner or Account.

Given we are doing a Web banking application, Owner is the logical choice as a top element. The customer wants his list of accounts.

Note that the choice of a top-level element depends heavily on the application. If the application were a financial application, examining accounts, it would have been more sensible to use account as the top-level element.

At this stage, it is time to draw a tree of the DTD under development. You can use a paper, a flipchart, a whiteboard, or whatever works for you (I prefer flipcharts).

In drawing the tree, I simply create an element for every object in the model. Element nesting is used to model object relationship.

Figure 3.5 is a first shot at converting the model into a tree. Every object in the original model is now an element. However, as it turns out, this tree is both incorrect and suboptimal.

Figure 3.5: *A first tree for the object model*

Upon closer examination, the tree in Figure 3.5 is incorrect because, in the object model, an account can have more than one owner. I simply cannot add the owner element into the account because this would lead to infinite recursion where an account includes its owner, which itself includes the account, which includes the owner, which... You get the picture.

The solution is to create a new element co-owner. To avoid confusion, I decided to rename the top-level element from owner to accounts. The new tree is in Figure 3.6.

Figure 3.6: *The corrected tree*

The solution in Figure 3.6 is a correct implementation of the object model. To evaluate how good it is, I like to create a few sample documents that follow the same structure. Listing 3.14 is a sample document I created.

Listing 3.14: Sample Document

```
<?xml version="1.0"?>
<accounts>
  <co-owner>John Doe</co-owner>
  <co-owner>Jack Smith</co-owner>
  <account>
    <checking>170.00</checking>
  </account>
  <co-owner>John Doe</co-owner>
  <account>
    <savings>5000.00</savings>
  </account>
</accounts>
```

This works but it is inefficient. The checking and savings elements are completely redundant with the account element. It is more efficient to treat account as a parameter entity that groups the commonality between the various accounts. Figure 3.7 shows the result. In this case, the parameter entity is used to represent a type.

Figure 3.7: *The tree, almost final*

We're almost there. Now we need to flesh out the tree by adding the object properties. I chose to create new elements for every property (see the following section "On Elements Versus Attributes").

Figure 3.8 is the final result. Listing 3.15 is a document that follows the structure. Again, it's useful to write a few sample documents to check whether the DTD makes sense. I can find no problems with this structure in Listing 3.15.

Figure 3.8: *The final tree*

Listing 3.15: A Sample Document

```
<?xml version="1.0"?>
<accounts>
  <co-owner>John Doe</co-owner>
  <co-owner>Jack Smith</co-owner>
  <checking>
        <balance>170.00</balance>
        <transaction>-100.00</transaction>
        <transaction>-500.00</transaction>
        <fee>4.00</fee>
  </checking>
  <co-owner>John Doe</co-owner>
  <savings>
        <balance>5000.00</balance>
        <interest>212.50</interest>
  </savings>
</accounts>
```

Having drawn the tree, it is trivial to turn it into a DTD. It suffices to list every element in the tree and declare their content model based on their children. The final DTD is in Listing 3.16.

Listing 3.16: The DTD for Banking

```
<!ENTITY % account     "(balance,transaction*)">
<!ELEMENT accounts     (co-owner+,(checking ¦ savings))+>
<!ELEMENT co-owner     (#PCDATA)>
<!ELEMENT checking     (%account;,fee)>
<!ELEMENT savings      (%account;,interest)>
<!ELEMENT fee          (#PCDATA)>
<!ELEMENT interest     (#PCDATA)>
<!ELEMENT balance      (#PCDATA)>
<!ELEMENT transaction  (#PCDATA)>
```

Now I have to publish this DTD under a URI. I like to place versioning information in the URI (version 1.0, and so on) because if there is a new version of the DTD, it gets a different URI with the new version. It means the two DTDs can coexist without problem.

It also means that the application can retrieve the URI to know which version is in use.

```
http://catwoman.pineapplesoft.com/dtd/accounts/1.0/accounts.dtd
```

If I ever update the DTD (it's a very simplified model so I can think of many missing elements), I'll create a different URI with a different version number:

```
http://catwoman.pineapplesoft.com/dtd/accounts/2.0/accounts.dtd
```

You can see how easy it is to create an XML DTD from an object model. This is because XML tree-based structure is a natural mapping for objects.

As more XML applications will be based on object-oriented technologies and will have to integrate with object-oriented systems written in Java, CORBA, or C++, I expect that modeling tools will eventually create DTDs automatically.

Already modeling tools such as Rational Rose or Together/J can create Java classes automatically. Creating DTDs seems like a logical next step.

On Elements Versus Attributes

As you have seen, there are many choices to make when designing a DTD. Choices include deciding what will become of an element, a parameter entity, an attribute, and so on.

Deciding what should be an element and what should be an attribute is a hot debate in the XML community. We will revisit this topic in Chapter 10, "Modeling for Flexibility," but here are some guidelines:

- The main argument in favor of using attributes is that the DTD offers more controls over the type of attributes; consequently, some people argue that object properties should be mapped to attributes.

- The main argument for elements is that it is easier to edit and view them in a document. XML editors and browsers in general have more intuitive handling of elements than of attributes.

I try to be pragmatic. In most cases, I use element for "major" properties of an object. What I define as major is all the properties that you manipulate regularly.

I reserve attributes for ancillary properties or properties that are related to a major property. For example, I might include a currency indicator as an attribute to the balance.

Creating the DTD from Scratch

Creating a DTD without having the benefit of an object model results in more work. The object model provides you with ready-made objects that you just have to convert in XML. It also has identified the properties of the objects and the relationships between objects.

However, if you create a DTD from scratch, you have to do that analysis as well.

A variant is to modify an existing DTD. Typically, the underlying DTD does not support all your content (you need to add new elements/attributes) or is too complex for your application (you need to remove elements/attributes).

This is somewhat similar to designing a DTD from scratch in the sense that you will have to create sample documents and analyze them to understand how to adapt the proposed DTD.

On Flexibility

When designing your own DTD, you want to prepare for evolution. We'll revisit this topic in Chapter 10 but it is important that you build a model that is flexible enough to accommodate extensions as new content becomes available.

The worst case is to develop a DTD, create a few hundred or a few thousand documents, and suddenly realize that you are missing a key piece of information but that you can't change your DTD to accommodate it. It's bad because it means you have to convert your existing documents.

To avoid that trap you want to provide as much structural information as possible but not too much. The difficulty, of course, is in striking the right balance between enough structural information and too much structural information.

You want to provide enough structural information because it is very easy to degrade information but difficult to clean degraded information.

Compare it with a clean, neatly sorted stack of cards on your desk. It takes half a minute to knock it down and shuffle it. Yet it will take the best part of one day to sort the cards again.

The same is true with electronic documents. It is easy to lose structural information when you create the document. And if you lose structural information, it will be very difficult to retrieve it later on.

EXAMPLE

Consider Listing 3.17, which is the address book in XML. The information is highly structured—the address is broken down into smaller components: street, region, and so on.

Listing 3.17: An Address Book in XML

```
<?xml version="1.0"?>
<!DOCTYPE address-book SYSTEM "address-book.dtd">
<!-- loosely inspired by vCard 3.0 -->
<address-book>
    <entry>
        <name>John Doe</name>
        <address>
            <street>34 Fountain Square Plaza</street>
            <region>OH</region>
            <postal-code>45202</postal-code>
            <locality>Cincinnati</locality>
            <country>US</country>
        </address>
        <tel preferred="true">513-555-8889</tel>
        <tel>513-555-7098</tel>
        <email href="mailto:jdoe@emailaholic.com"/>
    </entry>
    <entry>
        <name><fname>Jack</fname><lname>Smith</lname></name>
        <tel>513-555-3465</tel>
        <email href="mailto:jsmith@emailaholic.com"/>
    </entry>
</address-book>
```

Listing 3.18 is the same information as text. The structure is lost and, unfortunately, it will be difficult to restore the structure automatically. The software would have to be quite intelligent to go through Listing 3.18 and retrieve the entry boundaries as well as break the address in its components.

Listing 3.18: The Address Book in Plain Text

```
John Doe
34 Fountain Square Plaza
Cincinnati, OH 45202
US
513-555-8889 (preferred)
513-555-7098
jdoe@emailaholic.com
Jack Smith
513-555-3465
jsmith@emailaholic.com
```

However, as you design your structure, be careful that it remains usable. Structures that are too complex or too strict will actually lower the quality of your document because it encourages users to cheat.

Consider how many electronic commerce Web sites want a region, province, county, or state in the buyer address. Yet many countries don't have the notion of region, province, county, or state or, at least, don't use it for their addresses.

Forcing people to enter information they don't have is asking them to cheat. Keep in mind the number one rule of modeling: Changes will come from the unexpected. Chances are that, if your application is successful, people will want to include data you had never even considered. How often did I include for "future extensions" that were never used? Yet users came and asked for totally unexpected extensions.

There is no silver bullet in modeling. There is no foolproof solution to strike the right balance between extensibility, flexibility, and usability. As you grow more experienced with XML and DTDs, you also will improve your modeling skills.

My solution is to define a DTD that is large enough for all the content required by my application but not larger. Still, I leave hooks in the DTD—places where it would be easy to add a new element, if required.

Modeling an XML Document

The first step in modeling XML documents is to create documents. Because we are modeling an address book, I took a number of business cards and created documents with them. You can see some of the documents I created in Listing 3.20.

Listing 3.20: Examples of XML Documents

```
<address-book>
    <entry>
        <name><fname>John</fname><lname>Doe</lname></name>
        <address>
            <street>34 Fountain Square Plaza</street>
            <state>OH</state>
            <zip>45202</zip>
            <locality>Cincinnati</locality>
            <country>US</country>
        </address>
        <tel>513-555-8889</tel>
        <email href="mailto:jdoe@emailaholic.com"/>
    </entry>
    <entry>
        <name><fname>Jean</fname><lname>Dupont</lname></name>
        <address>
            <street>Rue du Lombard 345</street>
            <postal-code>5000</postal-code>
            <locality>Namur</locality>
            <country>Belgium</country>
        </address>
        <email href="mailto:jdupont@emailaholic.com"/>
    </entry>
    <entry>
        <name><fname>Olivier</fname><lname>Rame</lname></name>
        <email href="mailto:orame@emailaholic.com"/>
    </entry>
</address-book>
```

As you can see, I decided early on to break the address into smaller components. In making these documents, I tried to reuse elements over and over again. Very early in the project, it was clear there would be a name element, an address element, and more.

Also, I decided that addresses, phone numbers, and so on would be conditional. I have incomplete entries in my address book and the XML version must be able to handle it as well.

I looked at commonalties and I found I could group postal code and zip code under one element. Although they have different names, they are the same concepts.

This is the creative part of modeling when you list all possible elements, group them, and reorganize them until you achieve something that makes sense. Gradually, a structure appears.

Building the DTD from this example is easy. I first draw a tree with all the elements introduced in the document so far, as well as their relationship. It is clear that some elements such as state are optional. Figure 3.9 shows the tree.

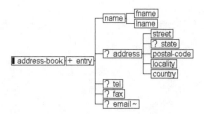

Figure 3.9: The updated tree

This was fast to develop because the underlying model is simple and well known. For a more complex application, you would want to spend more time drafting documents and trees.

At this stage, it is a good idea to compare my work with other similar works. In this case, I choose to compare with the vCard standard (RFC 2426). vCard (now in its third version) is a standard for electronic business cards.

vCard is a very extensive standard that lists all the fields required in an electronic business card. vCard, however, is too complicated for my needs so I don't want to simply duplicate that work.

By comparing the vCard structure with my structure, I realized that names are not always easily broken into first and last names, particularly foreign names. I therefore provided a more flexible content model for names.

I also realized that address, phone, fax number, and email address might repeat. Indeed, it didn't show up in my sample of business cards but there are people with several phone numbers or email addresses. I introduced a repetition for these as well as an attribute to mark the preferred address. The attribute has a default value of false.

In the process, I picked the name "region" for the state element. For some reason, I find region more appealing.

Comparing my model with vCard gave me the confidence that the simple address book can cope with most addresses used. Figure 3.10 is the result.

TIP

There is a group working on the XML-ization of the vCard standard. Its approach is different: It starts with vCard as its model, whereas this example starts from an existing document and uses vCard as a check.

Yet, it is interesting to compare the XML version of vCard (available from www.imc. org/ietf-vcard-xml) with the DTD in this chapter. It proves that there is more than one way to skin a cat.

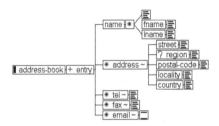

Figure 3.10: *The final tree*

Again converting the tree in a DTD is trivial. Listing 3.21 shows the result.

Listing 3.21: A DTD for the Address Book

```
<!ENTITY % boolean "(true | false) 'false'">


<!-- top-level element, the address book
     is a list of entries               -->
<!ELEMENT address-book  (entry+)>


<!-- an entry is a name followed by
     addresses, phone numbers, etc.      -->
<!ELEMENT entry  (name,address*,tel*,fax*,email*)>


<!-- name is made of string, first name
     and last name. This is a very flexible
        model to accommodate exotic name      -->
<!ELEMENT name    (#PCDATA | fname | lname)*>
<!ELEMENT fname   (#PCDATA)>
```

```
<!ELEMENT lname    (#PCDATA)>


<!-- definition of the address structure
     if several addresses, the preferred
         attribute signals the "default" one    -->
<!ELEMENT address       (street,region?,postal-code,locality,country)>
<!ATTLIST address       preferred (true ¦ false)  "false">
<!ELEMENT street        (#PCDATA)>
<!ELEMENT region        (#PCDATA)>
<!ELEMENT postal-code   (#PCDATA)>
<!ELEMENT locality      (#PCDATA)>
<!ELEMENT country       (#PCDATA)>


<!-- phone, fax and email, same preferred
     attribute as address                       -->
<!ELEMENT tel       (#PCDATA)>
<!ATTLIST tel       preferred (true ¦ false)  "false">
<!ELEMENT fax       (#PCDATA)>
<!ATTLIST fax       preferred (true ¦ false)  "false">
<!ELEMENT email     EMPTY>
<!ATTLIST email     href  CDATA               #REQUIRED
                    preferred (true ¦ false)  "false">
```

Naming of Elements

Again, modeling requires imagination. One needs to be imaginative and keep an open mind during the process. Modeling also implies making decisions on the name of elements and attributes.

As you can see, I like to use meaningful names. Others prefer to use meaningless names or acronyms. Again, as is so frequent in modeling, there are two schools of thought and both have very convincing arguments. Use what works better for you but try to be consistent.

In general, meaningful names

- are easier to debug

- provide some level of document for the DTD.

However, a case can be made for acronyms:

- Acronyms are shorter, and therefore more efficient.

- Acronyms are less language-dependent.

- Name choice should not be a substitute for proper documentation; meaningless tags and acronyms might encourage you to properly document the application.

A Tool to Help

I find drawing trees on a piece of paper an exercise in frustration. No matter how careful you are, after a few rounds of editing, the paper is unreadable and modeling often requires several rounds of editing!

Fortunately, there are very good tools on the market to assist you while you write DTDs. The trees in this book were produced by Near & Far from Microstar (www.microstar.com).

Near & Far is as intuitive as a piece of paper but, even after 1,000 changes, the tree still looks good. Furthermore, to convert the tree in a DTD, it suffices to save it. No need to remember the syntax, which is another big plus.

EXAMPLE

Figure 3.11 is a screenshot of Near & Far.

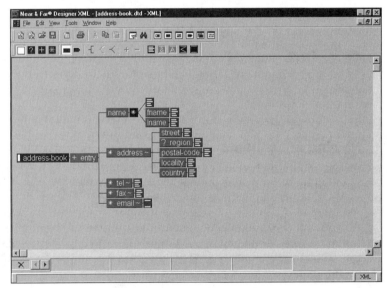

Figure 3.11: *Using a modeling tool*

New XML Schemas

The venerable DTD is very helpful. It provides valuable services to the application developer and the XML author. However, DTD originated in publishing and it shows.

For one thing, content is limited to textual content. Also, it is difficult to put in repetition constraints: You cannot say that an element can appear only four times. It's 0, 1, or infinite.

Furthermore, the DTD is based on a special syntax that is different from the syntax for XML documents. It means that it is not possible to use XML tools, such as editors or browsers, to process DTD!

These so-called limitations of the DTD are inherited directly from SGML. XML was originally designed as a subset of SGML and therefore it could not differ too much from the SGML DTD.

However, as XML takes a life of its own, people would like a new, more modern, replacement for the DTD. Various groups have made several proposals. Collectively, these proposals are known as schemas. The details of the proposals vary greatly but all:

- propose to use the same syntax as XML documents
- improve XML data typing to support not only strings but also numbers, dates, and so on
- introduce object-oriented concepts such as inheritance (an element could inherit from another)

The W3C has formed a working group to develop a new standard based on the existing proposals. At the time of this writing, the effort has just started and little is known about the final result.

You can find up-to-date information on new XML schemas on the W3C Web site at www.w3.org/XML.

The main proposals being considered are

- XML-Data, which offers types inspired from SQL types.
- DCD (Document Content Description), positioned as a simplified version of XML-Data.
- SOX (Schema for Object-oriented XML), as the name implies, is heavy on object-orientation aspects.
- DDML (Document Definition Markup Language), developed by the XML-Dev mailing list. It is intended as a simple solution to form a basis for future work.

What's Next

The next chapter is dedicated to the namespace proposal. Namespace is an often-overlooked but very useful standard that greatly enhances XML extensibility.

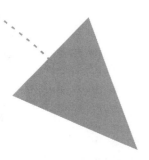

Namespaces

The previous two chapters introduced the XML recommendation as published by the W3C. You learned what an XML document is and what it can be used for. You also have seen how to write an XML document and you learned about modeling XML documents with DTDs.

This chapter complements the previous chapters with a discussion on *XML namespaces*. You will learn

- how namespaces complement XML extensibility
- how to use namespaces in documents
- how to use namespaces in DTD

The Problem Namespaces Solves

XML is extensible. So it says in the name: eXtensible Markup Language. The problem is that extensibility does not come free. In a distributed environment, extensibility must be managed to avoid conflicts. Namespaces is a solution to help manage XML extensibility.

Namespace can be defined as a mechanism to identify of XML elements. It places the name of the elements in a more global context: the namespace.

The namespace recommendation, published by the W3C, is available at `www.w3.org/TR/REC-xml-names`.

The namespace recommendation is relatively thin. The concepts are not difficult, either. Unfortunately, this means that namespaces are often overlooked! Don't make that mistake; namespaces are essential for many XML applications.

EXAMPLE

Let's suppose you decide to publish your bookmarks. (There is heavy competition from Yahoo! but let's ignore this for a moment.) Listing 4.1 shows what it might look like in XML. As a standalone document, Listing 4.1 works perfectly.

Listing 4.1: A List of Resources in XML

```
<?xml version="1.0"?>
<references>
    <name>Macmillan</name>
    <link href="http://www.mcp.com"/>
    <name>Pineapplesoft Link</name>
    <link href="http://www.pineapplesoft.com/newsletter"/>
    <name>XML.com</name>
    <link href="http://www.xml.com"/>
    <name>Comics.com</name>
    <link href="http://www.comics.com"/>
    <name>Fatbrain.com</name>
    <link href="http://www.fatbrain.com"/>
    <name>ABC News</name>
    <link href="http://www.abcnews.com"/>
</references>
```

✔ Chapter 5, "XSL Transformation," page 125 and Chapter 6, "XSL Formatting Objects and Cascading Style Sheet," page 161 will show you how to publish this document on a Web site.

EXAMPLE

In practice, however, documents are seldom standalone. In a collaborative environment like the Web, people build on one another's work. Somebody might take your list and rate it. The result would be Listing 4.2 (admittedly, I'm biased).

Listing 4.2: The References with Quality Ratings

```
<?xml version="1.0"?>

<references>

    <name>Macmillan</name>

    <link href="http://www.mcp.com"/>

    <rating>5 stars</rating>

    <name>Pineapplesoft Link</name>

    <link href="http://www.pineapplesoft.com/newsletter"/>

    <rating>5 stars</rating>

    <name>XML.com</name>

    <link href="http://www.xml.com"/>

    <rating>4 stars</rating>

    <name>Comics.com</name>

    <link href="http://www.comics.com"/>

    <rating>5 stars</rating>

    <name>Fatbrain.com</name>

    <link href="http://www.fatbrain.com"/>

    <rating>4 stars</rating>

    <name>ABC News</name>

    <link href="http://www.abcnews.com"/>

    <rating>3 stars</rating>

</references>
```

Listing 4.2 is the same document with one new element: rating. As we saw in the last chapter, it is often desirable to extend an existing document to convey new information instead of designing new schemas from scratch.

EXAMPLE

Problems occur, however, if the extension is not managed. Suppose somebody else decides to rate the list with parental advisory. Listing 4.3 shows the result (ABC News might report on violence, hence its PG rating).

Listing 4.3: Another Meaning for Rating

```
<?xml version="1.0"?>

<references>

    <name>Macmillan</name>

    <link href="http://www.mcp.com"/>

    <rating>G</rating>
```

continues

Listing 4.3: continued

```
    <name>Pineapplesoft Link</name>
    <link href="http://www.pineapplesoft.com/newsletter"/>
    <rating>G</rating>
    <name>XML.com</name>
    <link href="http://www.xml.com"/>
    <rating>G</rating>
    <name>Comics.com</name>
    <link href="http://www.comics.com"/>
    <rating>G</rating>
    <name>Fatbrain.com</name>
    <link href="http://www.fatbrain.com"/>
    <rating>G</rating>
    <name>ABC News</name>
    <link href="http://www.abcnews.com"/>
    <rating>PG</rating>
</references>
```

This is problematic. Listing 4.3 also is an extension to Listing 4.1 but the extension creates incompatibilities between Listing 4.2 and Listing 4.3. This is a very common problem: Two people extend the same document in incompatible ways.

Things get really out of hand when trying to combine both ratings in a listing. The result would look like Listing 4.4 where the two ratings conflict with each other.

EXAMPLE

Listing 4.4: The Combined Listing

```
<?xml version="1.0"?>
<references>
    <name>Macmillan</name>
    <link href="http://www.mcp.com"/>
    <rating>5 stars</rating>
    <rating>G</rating>
    <name>Pineapplesoft Link</name>
    <link href="http://www.pineapplesoft.com/newsletter"/>
    <rating>5 stars</rating>
    <rating>G</rating>
    <name>XML.com</name>
    <link href="http://www.xml.com"/>
    <rating>4 stars</rating>
```

```
    <rating>G</rating>

    <name>Comics.com</name>

    <link href="http://www.comics.com"/>

    <rating>5 stars</rating>

    <rating>G</rating>

    <name>Fatbrain.com</name>

    <link href="http://www.fatbrain.com"/>

    <rating>4 stars</rating>

    <rating>G</rating>

    <name>ABC News</name>

    <link href="http://www.abcnews.com"/>

    <rating>3 stars</rating>

    <rating>PG</rating>

</references>
```

The problem with Listing 4.4 is that software designed to operate with
Listing 4.3 and filter offensive links would be completely lost. It wouldn't
know what to do with the "4 stars" rating. The software should simply
ignore quality rating tags but how can it ignore quality rating tags if it cannot differentiate between the two rating tags?

EXAMPLE

The solution is obvious: Use different names for the two ratings. Listing 4.5
renames the "quality" element as qa-rating and the "parental" element as
pa-rating.

Listing 4.5: Using Different Names

```
<?xml version="1.0"?>

<references>

    <name>Macmillan</name>

    <link href="http://www.mcp.com"/>

    <qa-rating>5 stars</qa-rating>

    <pa-rating>G</pa-rating>

    <name>Pineapplesoft Link</name>

    <link href="http://www.pineapplesoft.com/newsletter"/>

    <qa-rating>5 stars</qa-rating>

    <pa-rating>G</pa-rating>

    <name>XML.com</name>

    <link href="http://www.xml.com"/>

    <qa-rating>4 stars</qa-rating>

    <pa-rating>G</pa-rating>

    <name>Comics.com</name>

    <link href="http://www.comics.com"/>
```

continues

Listing 4.5: continued

```
   <qa-rating>5 stars</qa-rating>

   <pa-rating>G</pa-rating>

   <name>Fatbrain.com</name>

   <link href="http://www.fatbrain.com"/>

   <qa-rating>4 stars</qa-rating>

   <pa-rating>G</pa-rating>

   <name>ABC News</name>

   <link href="http://www.abcnews.com"/>

   <qa-rating>3 stars</qa-rating>

   <pa-rating>PG</pa-rating>

</references>
```

Namespaces

The problem outlined in the previous example is... the extensible character of XML. There is no way to prevent somebody from extending a document in a way that is incompatible with other works. That's the nature of extensibility. Because anybody can create tags, there is a huge risk of conflicts.

One solution to prevent conflicts would be to establish a global registry of accepted tags and their associated definition. It would, however, severely limit XML's flexibility.

Nobody wants to limit XML's flexibility. Flexibility was a major goal in the design of XML. The namespaces proposal addresses this problem with a more elegant approach: It does not limit extensibility but it introduces mechanisms to manage it.

Listing 4.6 is equivalent to Listing 4.4 but it uses namespaces to prevent naming clashes.

EXAMPLE   **Listing 4.6:** Using Namespaces

```
<?xml version="1.0"?>
<references xmlns:qa="http://joker.playfield.com/star-rating/1.0"
            xmlns:pa="http://penguin.xmli.com/review/1.0"
            xmlns="http://catwoman.pineapplesoft.com/ref/1.5">
   <name>Macmillan</name>
   <link href="http://www.mcp.com"/>
   <qa:rating>5 stars</qa:rating>
   <pa:rating>G</pa:rating>
   <name>Pineapplesoft Link</name>
   <link href="http://www.pineapplesoft.com/newsletter"/>
   <qa:rating>5 stars</qa:rating>
```

```
     <pa:rating>G</pa:rating>
     <name>XML.com</name>
     <link href="http://www.xml.com"/>
     <qa:rating>4 stars</qa:rating>
     <pa:rating>G</pa:rating>
     <name>Comics.com</name>
     <link href="http://www.comics.com"/>
     <qa:rating>5 stars</qa:rating>
     <pa:rating>G</pa:rating>
     <name>Fatbrain.com</name>
     <link href="http://www.fatbrain.com"/>
     <qa:rating>4 stars</qa:rating>
     <pa:rating>G</pa:rating>
     <name>ABC News</name>
     <link href="http://www.abcnews.com"/>
     <qa:rating>3 stars</qa:rating>
     <pa:rating>PG</pa:rating>
</references>
```

At first sight, Listing 4.6 is similar to Listing 4.5: It declares two different names for the ratings.

The major difference is the form of the names. In Listing 4.6, a prefix is added before each element name. A colon separates the name and the prefix:

```
<qa:rating>5 stars</qa:rating>
```

The prefix unambiguously identifies the type of rating in this document. However, prefixes alone solve nothing because anybody can create prefixes. Therefore, different people can create incompatible prefixes and we are back to step one: We have moved the risk of conflicts from element names to prefixes. To avoid conflicts in prefixes, the prefixes must be declared:

```
<references xmlns:qa="http://joker.playfield.com/star-rating/1.0"
            xmlns:pa="http://penguin.xmli.com/review/1.0"
            xmlns="http://catwoman.pineapplesoft.com/ref/1.5">
```

The declaration associates a URI with a prefix. This is the crux of the namespaces proposal because URIs, unlike names, are unique. Namespaces piggyback on the registration mechanisms established for URIs.

For example, URLs are guaranteed to be unique because they are based on domain names. Domain names are registered to guarantee uniqueness.

Namespace declaration is done through attributes with the prefix xmlns followed by the prefix. In Listing 4.6, two prefixes are declared: qa and pa.

The attribute xmlns declares the default namespace—that is, the namespace for those elements that have no attributes.

In summary, XML namespaces is a mechanism to unambiguously identify who has developed which element. It's not much but it is an essential service.

The Namespace Name

The namespace name is the URI, not the prefix. When an XML application compares two elements, it uses the URI, not the prefix, to recognize their namespaces.

EXAMPLE

Therefore, in Listing 4.7 rff:name and ref:name are considered identical even though they have a different prefix. Both are in the namespace http://catwoman.pineapplesoft.com/ref/1.5.

Listing 4.7: One Namespace, Two Prefixes

```
<?xml version="1.0" standalone="yes"?>
<references>
    <rff:name
        xmlns:rff="http://catwoman.pineapplesoft.com/ref/1.5">
        Macmillan</rff:name>
    <link href="http://www.mcp.com"/>
    <ref:name
        xmlns:ref="http://catwoman.pineapplesoft.com/ref/1.5">
        Pineapplesoft Link</ref:name>
    <link href="http://www.pineapplesoft.com/newsletter"/>
</references>
```

URIs

The namespace declaration associates a global naming system (the URIs) to the name of the elements.

The URI is only used to ensure uniqueness of names. It might (but it need not) point to a description of the name. For example, there might be a document at http://penguin.xmli.com/review/1.0 that describes the rating or there might be nothing.

However, it is important that URIs are unique. The easiest solution is to create URLs based on your own domain name.

CAUTION

For namespaces, two URIs are identical only if they are identical character-by-character. According to this definition, the following two URLs are not identical, even though they point to the same document:

```
http://www.mcp.com
```

```
http://www.MCP.com
```

What's in a Name?

EXAMPLE

URLs are of the form:

```
http://www.mcp.com
http://www.pineapplesoft.com/newsletter
ftp://ftp.mcp.com
news://news.psol.com/comp.xml
mailto:bmarchal@pineapplesoft.com
```

The domain name is just a part of it: "mcp.com" and "pineapplesoft.com" in the examples.

The domain name is registered with a global authority to ensure there is no duplicate. Because of the global registration, one cannot do what one wants with domain names. For example, it is not possible to register names that are already in use.

Conversely, organizations control the URLs based on their domains. One is free to create any syntactically correct URL based on one's own domain name. For example, Pineapplesoft, my company, owns the pineapplesoft.com domain and it can create any URL derived from it.

The very last part of the domain name (".com" in this case) is known as the *Top Level Domain* (TLD in short). The TLD identifies the authority that assigned the domain name.

InterNIC (www.internic.net) is the authority for most so-called generic TLDs: ".com" (commercial), ".net" (ISPs), ".org" (nonprofit). They are generic because they are open to organizations (or individuals) worldwide.

There also are country-specific TLDs. Belgian organizations can register in the ".be" TLD, American ones in the ".us" TLD, Canadian ones in ".ca", Japanese ones in ".jp", and so on. Of course, Belgian, American, Canadian, and Japanese organizations also can register in the generic TLDs.

URLs provide a good balance of flexibility and control for namespaces. The control is derived from the domain names, which are guaranteed to be unique. The flexibility comes because organizations rule in their own domains.

Registering a Domain Name

If you are serious about XML development and you currently don't have a domain name, you might want to register one so you can identify your elements.

Indeed, because the URI identifies you as the owner of the namespace, you cannot use somebody else's domain unless they have agreed to it. It would not be appropriate, therefore, to use

```
http://www.mcp.com/myaddressbooks/1.0
```

as a URI (unless, of course, you work for Macmillan). Domain names are not really expensive so I would advise you to take one.

The cost varies depending on the TLD. At the time of writing, a ".com" domain costs $35 per year. Your ISP can register a domain name for you. For a monthly fee (in addition to the $35 per year), it will host the domain (provide a Web page).

If you just want to reserve the name for XML namespaces but don't need a Web page, you can turn to *domain parking*. The name is yours but you don't host it. Some ISPs offer domain parking for a nominal fee. You also can turn to Register.com (www.register.com), WorldNIC (www.worldnic.com), or MyDomain (www.mydomain.com).

After you register a domain name, it's yours. Just make sure you are listed as the administrative contact and that you are paying the yearly fee. You are free to move to another ISP of your choice and still retain your domain.

Some people (not surprisingly those who charge per registration) would want you to register in all possible TLDs. I doubt it's a good idea for at least two reasons:

- It defeats the purpose of having multiple TLDs. More TLDs should give more people a chance to find a sensible name.

- There are already more than 250 TLDs in operation and more TLDs will be added in the future. Unless you have very big pockets, it's a lost game.

TIP

If you register a domain name specifically for namespaces, opt for a short name such as an abbreviation. Over time, it will save you a lot of typing!

For example, in addition to pineapplesoft.com, Pineapplesoft also uses the domain psol.com (short for Pineapplesoft Object Library—it was originally registered for Java libraries).

Creating a Sensible URL

There are no rules on how to build URLs for namespaces. As long as it has the right format (as explained before), it works. Experience shows that URLs works best if they follow the following rules:

- Namespaces are identified by Web addresses. You might want to post a description of the namespace at a later point.

- The URL is reasonably short to save typing.

- The URL includes a readable description of the namespace.

- The URL includes a version number so you can update the namespace by changing the version number.

EXAMPLE

Some examples include

```
http://www.psol.com/xml/address/1.0
http://www.w3.org/XSL/Transform/1.0
http://www.w3.org/TR/REC-html40
```

CAUTION

Most importantly, write the URL down and make sure nobody else in your organization uses it. Remember the goal of the exercise is to avoid duplicates.

TIP

Large organizations should use subdomains to help manage unique URLs. For example, the namespace for finance department would be in the `finance.pineapplesoft.com` subdomain, whereas the sales department would use `sales.pineapplesoft.com`.

In this book, I pick URLs on the catwoman.pineapplesoft.com server. If you are curious, catwoman is Pineapplesoft's Intranet server.

URNs

Currently, most URIs are URLs. URLs are addresses. They point to a file on a machine, whereas an URN is a generic name for a resource. It means that if the document moves, the address is invalid. This is the dreadful "404 File not found" error message.

The IETF (Internet Engineering Task Force) is working on other forms of URIs, more specifically URN (*Uniform Resource Name*).

URNs are not addresses. They are independent of the location of the document. This should eliminate the "404" errors.

ISBN numbers (the number at the back of the book, on top of the bar code) are good candidates for URNs. An ISBN number identifies a book, irrespective of where the book is currently located. You can use the ISBN number to order the book from a bookstore or to borrow it from a library.

EXAMPLE

The URN for this book is

```
urn:ISBN:0-7897-2242-9
```

Another approach is to use PURLs (Permanent URLs). Unlike regular URLs, PURLs are registered to avoid "404" errors. The registration process is the key: If the document moves, it suffices to update the Registry. The PURL remains unchanged. You can find more information on PURLs (and create your first PURL) at `www.purl.org`.

Scoping

EXAMPLE

The namespace is valid for the element where it is declared and all the elements within its content, as illustrated in Listing 4.8.

Listing 4.8: Scoping of Namespaces

```xml
<?xml version="1.0"?>
<rff:references
    xmlns:rff="http://catwoman.pineapplesoft.com/ref/1.5">
    <rff:name>Macmillan</rff:name>
    <rff:link href="http://www.mcp.com"/>
    <pa:rating
        xmlns:pa="http://pinguin.xmli.com/review/1.0">G</pa:rating>
    <rff:name>Pineapplesoft Link</rff:name>
    <rff:link href="http://www.pineapplesoft.com/newsletter"/>
    <qa:rating
        xmlns:qa="http://joker.playfield.com/star-rating/1.0">
        5 stars</qa:rating>
</rff:references>
```

Again, there are three namespaces declared in Listing 4.7. rff is declared on the top-level element and is therefore valid for all the elements. pa is declared only for the first rating element and it is valid for that element only. qa is declared for the second rating element.

EXAMPLE

As Listing 4.9 illustrates, the namespace also can be associated with specific attributes. In Listing 4.9, a new attribute is added to the name element to convey the subscription fee.

Listing 4.9: Using Namespaces for Attributes

```xml
<?xml version="1.0"?>
<references
    xmlns="http://catwoman.pineapplesoft.com/ref/1.5"
```

```
    xmlns:sub="http://penguin.xmli.com/subscription/1.0">
    <name sub:subscription="$0.0">Pineapplesoft Link</name>
    <link href="http://www.pineapplesoft.com/newsletter"/>
</references>
```

Namespaces and DTD

EXAMPLE

If the document is a valid document, that is if it has a DTD, the prefix and the attributes for namespace declaration must be declared in the DTD. Listing 4.10 illustrates how it works.

Listing 4.10: Declaring the Namespace Prefix in the DTD

```
<?xml version="1.0" standalone="yes"?>
<!DOCTYPE rff:references [
<!ELEMENT rff:references (rff:name,rff:link)+>
<!ATTLIST rff:references xmlns:rff CDATA #REQUIRED>
<!ELEMENT rff:name        (#PCDATA)>
<!ELEMENT rff:link        EMPTY>
<!ATTLIST rff:link        href  CDATA #REQUIRED>
]>
<rff:references xmlns:rff="http://catwoman.pineapplesoft.com/ref/1.5">
    <rff:name>Macmillan</rff:name>
    <rff:link href="http://www.mcp.com"/>
    <rff:name>Pineapplesoft Link</rff:name>
    <rff:link href="http://www.pineapplesoft.com/newsletter"/>
    <rff:name>XML.com</rff:name>
    <rff:link href="http://www.xml.com"/>
    <rff:name>Comics.com</rff:name>
    <rff:link href="http://www.comics.com"/>
    <rff:name>Fatbrain.com</rff:name>
    <rff:link href="http://www.fatbrain.com"/>
    <rff:name>ABC News</rff:name>
    <rff:link href="http://www.abcnews.com"/>
</rff:references>
```

EXAMPLE

For valid documents, it is possible to declare the namespace as a fixed attribute in the DTD as shown in Listing 4.11.

Listing 4.11: Declaring the Namespace in the DTD

```
<?xml version="1.0" standalone="yes"?>
<!DOCTYPE rff:references [
```

continues

Listing 4.11: continued

```
<!ELEMENT rff:references (rff:name,rff:link)+>
<!ATTLIST rff:references xmlns:rff CDATA #FIXED
    "http://catwoman.pineapplesoft.com/ref/1.5">
<!ELEMENT rff:name       (#PCDATA)>
<!ELEMENT rff:link       EMPTY>
<!ATTLIST rff:link       href  CDATA #REQUIRED>
]>
<rff:references>
   <rff:name>Macmillan</rff:name>
   <rff:link href="http://www.mcp.com"/>
   <rff:name>Pineapplesoft Link</rff:name>
   <rff:link href="http://www.pineapplesoft.com/newsletter"/>
   <rff:name>XML.com</rff:name>
   <rff:link href="http://www.xml.com"/>
   <rff:name>Comics.com</rff:name>
   <rff:link href="http://www.comics.com"/>
   <rff:name>Fatbrain.com</rff:name>
   <rff:link href="http://www.fatbrain.com"/>
   <rff:name>ABC News</rff:name>
   <rff:link href="http://www.abcnews.com"/>
</rff:references>
```

CAUTION

It is dangerous to declare namespaces using this mechanism in an external DTD because a nonvalidating parser might skip external DTDs.

Using this mechanism, if the parser skips the external DTD, it also skips the namespace declaration. The rule of thumb is always declare the namespace in the document, either in the internal subset of the DTD or in the document itself.

✔ See the discussion on standalone documents in Chapter 3, "XML Schemas," page 69.

NOTE

DTDs are inherited from SGML and therefore are not namespace-aware. This is one of the arguments to replace DTDs with new XML schemas, as explained in Chapter 3, "XML Schemas."

Applications of Namespaces

Namespaces are a small extension to XML that associates an owner to specific XML elements. It's not much but it has led to new ways of creating XML documents.

Initially, XML documents were developed in isolation. One would develop a DTD for a specific application—that is a magazine, an order, or a channel—as we saw in Chapter 2, "The XML Syntax." The elements defined in the DTD would be specific to that application. There is little reuse of elements except, maybe, by cutting and pasting old DTDs into new ones.

Thanks to namespaces, it is possible to develop *reusable elements*—that is, elements that can be reused in multiple documents. This is a new approach for document development.

Increasingly, the W3C and other groups work on such reusable elements. Two examples are XML style sheets and digital signatures for XML.

XML Style Sheet

EXAMPLE

Listing 4.12 is an XML style sheet. As you can see, it combines elements from the style sheet language itself (in the namespace `http://www.w3.org/1999/XSL/Transform`) and elements from HTML (in the namespace `http://www.w3.org/TR/REC-html40`).

Listing 4.12: Using Namespaces with Style Sheets

```
<?xml version="1.0" encoding="ISO-8859-1"?>
<xsl:stylesheet
    xmlns:xsl="http://www.w3.org/1999/XSL/Transform"
    xmlns="http://www.w3.org/TR/REC-html40">

<xsl:output method="html"/>

<xsl:template match="/">
    <HTML>
    <HEAD>
        <TITLE>Article</TITLE>
    </HEAD>
    <BODY>
        <xsl:apply-templates/>
    </BODY>
    </HTML>
</xsl:template>

<xsl:template match="title">
    <P><B><xsl:apply-templates/></B></P>
</xsl:template>
```

Listing 4.12: continued

```
<xsl:template match="p">
   <P><xsl:apply-templates/></P>
</xsl:template>


</xsl:stylesheet>
```

> ✔ We will cover style sheets in more detail in Chapter 5, "XSL Transformation," page 125 and Chapter 6, "XSL Formatting Objects and Cascading Style Sheet," page 161.

Links

The XLink recommendation provides a standard set of elements to link between documents (links are similar, but more powerful, to HTML links). The elements and attributes defined in XLink can be included in any XML document. To differentiate XLink elements from the rest of the document, the recommendation uses namespaces, as illustrated by Listing 4.13.

Listing 4.13: Using Namespaces with XLink

```
<?xml version="1.0"?>

<info>

<para>XLink links XML documents. It supports simple

links, which are very similar to HTML links, but it

also supports more advanced links.</para>

<para>For more information on XLink, you can visit

<xlink:simple xmlns:xlink="http://www.w3.org/XML/XLink/0.9"

href="http://www.w3.org/TR/xlink" role="recommendation"

title="XML Linking Language (XLink)" show="replace"

actuate="user">the W3C site</xlink:simple></para>

</info>
```

What's Next

This chapter concludes the background introduction to XML. The next chapters will teach you how to use XML in your environment. We will start by looking at how XML can simplify Web site development.

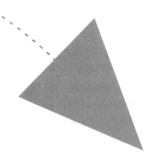

XSL Transformation

In the last three chapters, you learned the basics of XML. Specifically, you learned the XML syntax, how to read and write documents, how to organize and structure XML documents with schemas, and how to extend and reuse schemas through namespaces.

This chapter is more practical. It shows you how to manipulate XML documents. In this and the following chapter, we will look at *styling*—how to display a document with a browser or an editor.

In this chapter, you will learn how to use XSL, the XML Stylesheet Language, to

- convert XML documents in XML (with a different DTD), HTML, and other formats

- publish a large set of documents

- reorganize XML documents to create table of contents or other information

- extract information from XML documents

Why Styling?

XML concentrates on the structure of the information and not its appearance. However, to view XML documents we need to format or style them. Obviously, the styling instructions are directly related to and derived from the structure of the document.

In practice, styling instructions are organized in style sheets; to view a document, apply the appropriate style sheet to it.

The W3C has published two recommendations for style sheets: CSS, short for *Cascading Style Sheet,* and XSL, short for *XML Stylesheet Language.*

CSS

EXAMPLE

CSS was originally developed for HTML and browsers that support XML also largely support it. A CSS is a set of rules that tells the browser which font, style, and margin to use to display the text, as shown in the following example:

```
section.title

{

    font-family: Palatino, Garamond, "Times New Roman", serif;

    font-size: 10pt;

    margin: 5px;

    display: block;

    font-style: italic

}
```

✔ CSS is the topic of Chapter 6, "XSL Formatting and Cascading Style Sheet," page 161.

XSL

EXAMPLE

XSL is more ambitious than CSS because it supports transforming the document before display. XSL would typically be used for advanced styling such as creating a table of contents shown in the following example:

```
<P><B>Table of Contents</B></P>

<UL>

    <xsl:for-each select="article/section/title">

        <LI><A><xsl:value-of select="."/></A></LI>

    </xsl:for-each>

</UL>
```

XSL

XSL, the W3C recommendation, is organized into two parts: XSLT, short for *XSL Transformation*, and XSLFO, short for *XSL Formatting Objects*. This chapter concentrates on XSLT. The next chapter discusses both CSS and XSLFO. As we will see, CSS and XSLFO are very similar in scope.

NOTE

The similarity between CSS and XSLFO has led to some controversy. Given they are so similar, aren't they redundant? If CSS is already in use, why bother with the more complex XSL?

It turns out that we need both because XSL is more powerful than CSS. In particular, there is no equivalent for XSLT, the transformation part of XSL, in CSS.

In practice, most implementations of XSL today support only XSLT. For the time being, the consensus in the industry seems to be that XSLT is useful but CSS is preferred to XSLFO.

CAUTION

At the time of this writing, the XSL recommendation was not formally adopted. The content of this chapter is based on a Working Draft dated 21 April 1999 (www.w3.org/TR/1999/WD-xslt-19990421.html). It has been updated as changes to XSL were released.

The draft will be revised and enhanced. A situation that is particularly frustrating for an author: It is likely that, by the time you read this book, some changes will be introduced that are incompatible with the examples published in the chapter. Therefore, I invite you to check the Macmillan Web site at www.mcp.com where I will post updates to this chapter.

LotusXSL

To run the examples in this chapter, you need an *XSL processor*. An XSL processor is simply a software component that implements the XSL standard.

There are several XSL processors on the market including those from Microsoft (www.microsoft.com) and Lotus (www.alphaworks.ibm.com). James Clark, the editor of the XSLT standard, also has released an XSL processor (www.jclarck.com).

In this chapter, we'll use LotusXSL (version 0.19.1), which is available at no charge from www.alphaworks.ibm.com. Like most XML tools, LotusXSL is written in Java. Although you don't have to program in Java to use it, you must install either a *Java Runtime Environment* (JRE) or a *Java Development Kit* (JDK) on your computer. You can download a Java environment from Sun at java.sun.com.

✔ If you need help installing the Java Development Kit, turn to Appendix A, "Crash Course on Java," page 457.

Concepts of XSLT

XSLT is a language to specify transformation of XML documents. It takes an XML document and transforms it into another XML document, as illustrated by Figure 5.1.

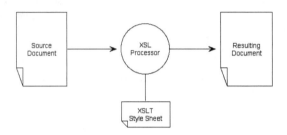

Figure 5.1: *Using XSL to transform an XML document*

XSLT is not limited to styling activities. Many applications require transforming documents. XSLT can be used to

- add elements specifically for viewing, such as add the logo or the address of the sender to an XML invoice

- create new content from an existing one, such as create the table of contents

- present information with the right level of details for the reader, such as using a style sheet to present high-level information to a managerial person while using another style sheet to present more detailed technical information to the rest of the staff

- convert between different DTDs or different versions of a DTD, such as convert a company specific DTD to an industry standard

- transform XML documents into HTML for backward compatibility with existing browsers

The last case is very common. The XSLT recommendation considers HTML conversion as a special case of XML transformation. This also is one of the solutions supported by Microsoft Internet Explorer 4.0 and 5.0.

Basic XSLT

I publish a monthly e-zine, Pineapplesoft Link. Every month, I email the e-zine to subscribers and I post a copy on my Web site. That's two formats to support: text and HTML.

XML and XSL can help because it enables me to write the document in one format (XML) and automatically create distribution copies in text and HTML.

Furthermore, because styling is applied automatically, it is easy to change the layout of the Web site: Just change the style sheet. As Web fashion keeps changing, this is a major advantage.

Viewing XML in a Browser

EXAMPLE

Listing 5.1 is an abbreviated version of the January 1999 article that discussed XML style sheets. The structure of the document is in Figure 5.2 (essentially an article is a set of sections). Figures 5.3 and 5.4 view the document in Internet Explorer 5.0.

Listing 5.1: An Article in XML

```
<?xml version="1.0"?>

<article fname="19990101_xsl">

<title>XML Style Sheets</title>

<date>January 1999</date>

<copyright>1999, Benoît Marchal</copyright>

<abstract>Style sheets add flexibility to document viewing.</abstract>

<keywords>XML, XSL, style sheet, publishing, web</keywords>

<section>

<p>Send comments and suggestions to <url protocol="mailto">bmarchal@
➥pineapplesoft.com</url>.</p>

</section>

<section>

<title>Styling</title>

<p>Style sheets are inherited from SGML, an XML ancestor. Style sheets
➥originated in publishing and document management applications. XSL is XML's
➥standard style sheet, see <url>http://www.w3.org/Style</url>.</p>

</section>

<section>

<title>How XSL Works</title>

<p>An XSL style sheet is a set of rules where each rule specifies how to format
➥certain elements in the document. To continue the example from the previous
➥section, the style sheets have rules for title, paragraphs and keywords.</p>

<p>With XSL, these rules are powerful enough not only to format the document
➥but also to reorganize it, e.g. by moving the title to the front page or
➥extracting the list of keywords. This can lead to exciting applications of XSL
➥outside the realm of traditional publishing. For example, XSL can be used to
➥convert documents between the company-specific markup and a standard one.</p>

</section>

<section>

<title>The Added Flexibility of Style Sheets</title>
```

continues

Listing 5.1: continued

```
<p>Style sheets are separated from documents. Therefore one document can have
➥more than one style sheet and, conversely, one style sheet can be shared
➥amongst several documents.</p>

<p>This means that a document can be rendered differently depending on the media
➥or the audience. For example, a "managerial" style sheet may present a summary
➥view of a document that highlights key elements but a "clerical" style sheet
➥may display more detailed information.</p>

</section>

</article>
```

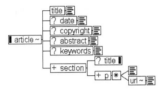

Figure 5.2: *The structure of the article*

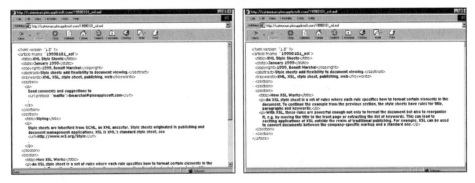

Figure 5.3: *The XML document in Internet Explorer 5.0*

Figure 5.4: *The same XML document with collapsed elements*

Internet Explorer 5.0 applies default formatting to XML documents. It is possible to override the default formatting with style sheets.

As you can see, by default, text is in bold. To make the structure more visible, each element is collapsible—clicking the minus or plus symbol next to an element will extend or collapse it. Figure 5.4 is the same document with some elements collapsed.

✔ Chapter 6, "XSL Formatting Objects and Cascading Style Sheet," discusses how browsers other than Internet Explorer 5.0 render XML.

A Simple Style Sheet

The first goal is to convert the XML document into HTML. The style sheet in Listing 5.2 is an example of how to do it.

Listing 5.2: XSLT Style Sheet to Convert the Article in HTML

```
<?xml version="1.0" encoding="ISO-8859-1"?>
<xsl:stylesheet
    xmlns:xsl="http://www.w3.org/1999/XSL/Transform"
    xmlns="http://www.w3.org/TR/REC-html40">

<xsl:output method="html"/>

<xsl:template match="/">
    <HTML>
    <HEAD>
        <TITLE>Pineapplesoft Link</TITLE>
    </HEAD>
    <BODY>
        <xsl:apply-templates/>
    </BODY>
    </HTML>
</xsl:template>

<xsl:template match="section/title">
    <P><I><xsl:apply-templates/></I></P>
</xsl:template>

<xsl:template match="article/title">
    <P><B><xsl:apply-templates/></B></P>
</xsl:template>

<xsl:template match="url">
    <A TARGET="_blank">
        <xsl:attribute name="HREF">
            <xsl:apply-templates/>
        </xsl:attribute>
        <xsl:apply-templates/>
    </A>
</xsl:template>
```

continues

Listing 5.2: continued

```
<xsl:template match="url[@protocol='mailto']">

    <A>

        <xsl:attribute name="HREF">mailto:<xsl:apply-templates/>

        </xsl:attribute>

        <xsl:apply-templates/>

    </A>

</xsl:template>


<xsl:template match="p">

    <P><xsl:apply-templates/></P>

</xsl:template>


<xsl:template match="abstract ¦ date ¦ keywords ¦ copyright"/>


</xsl:stylesheet>
```

The style sheet is applied with LotusXSL, as explained previously. From the DOS prompt, change to the document directory and type the following command:

```
java -classpath
➥c:\lotusxsl\xerces.jar;c:\lotusxsl\lotusxsl.jar
➥com.lotus.xsl.Process
➥-in 19990101_xsl.xml
➥-xsl simple.xsl -out 19990101_xsl.html
```

C A U T I O N

The LotusXSL processor won't work unless you have installed a Java runtime.

If there is an error message similar to "Exception in thread "main" java.lang. NoClassDefFoundError," either the `classpath` is incorrect (you might have to adapt it) or you typed an incorrect class name for LotusXSL (`com.lotus.xsl.xml4j. ProcessXSL`).

The parameters are self-explanatory: in is the document file (XML file), out is the result file (HTML file), xsl is the XSL file. The HTML parameter forces the processor to respect the HTML syntax (for example, <BR> instead of <BR/>).

If everything goes well, there is a new HTML file, 19990101_xsl.html, in the document directory. Listing 5.3 is 19990101_xsl.html. Figure 5.5 views it in a browser.

Listing 5.3: The HTML Document Generated by the XSL Style Sheet

```
<!DOCTYPE html PUBLIC "-//W3C//DTD HTML 4.0 Transitional//EN">

<HTML><HEAD><TITLE>Pineapplesoft Link</TITLE></HEAD><BODY>
```

EXAMPLE

continues

Listing 5.3: continued

```
<P><B>XML Style Sheets</B></P>

<P>Send comments and suggestions to <A
href="mailto:bmarchal@pineapplesoft.com">bmarchal@pineapplesoft.com</A>.</P>

<P><I>Styling</I></P>

<P>Style sheets are inherited from SGML, an XML ancestor. Style sheets
➥originated in publishing and document management applications. XSL is XML's
➥standard style sheet, see <A target="_blank"
➥href="http://www.w3.org/Style">http://www.w3.org/Style</A>.</P><P><I>How XSL
➥Works</I></P>

<P>An XSL style sheet is a set of rules where each rule specifies how to format
➥certain elements in the document. To continue the example from the previous
➥section, the style sheets have rules for title, paragraphs and keywords.</P>

<P>With XSL, these rules are powerful enough not only to format the document
➥but also to reorganize it, e.g. by moving the title to the front page or
➥extracting the list of keywords. This can lead to exciting applications of XSL
➥outside the realm of traditional publishing. For example, XSL can be used to
➥convert documents between the company-specific markup and a standard one.</P>

<P><I>The Added Flexibility of Style Sheets</I></P>

<P>Style sheets are separated from documents. Therefore one document can have
➥more than one style sheet and, conversely, one style sheet can be shared
➥amongst several documents.</P>

<P>This means that a document can be rendered differently depending on the media
➥or the audience. For example, a "managerial" style sheet may present a summary
➥view of a document that highlights key elements but a "clerical" style sheet
➥may display more detailed information.</P>

</BODY></HTML>
```

OUTPUT

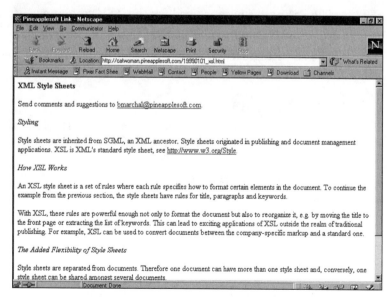

Figure 5.5: *Viewing the result with Netscape Communicator*

NOTE

The latest draft of XSLT available at the time of this writing has introduced a new element, xsl:output, that plays a role similar to the html command-line parameter of LotusXSL.

For example, the following element specifies that the transformation is from XML to HTML:

```
<xsl:output method="html"/>
```

The following sections examine the style sheet in more detail.

Stylesheet Element

EXAMPLE

The style sheet is a well-formed XML document (XSL designers thought that XML was the best syntax for a style sheet). It describes the tree of the source document, the tree of the resulting document, and how to transform one into the other. The top-level element is style sheet as shown in the example:

```
<xsl:stylesheet
    xmlns:xsl="http://www.w3.org/1999/XSL/Transform/"
    xmlns="http://www.w3.org/TR/REC-html40">
<xsl:output method="html"/>
```

Because the style sheet contains elements from different documents, namespaces are used to organize these elements:

- The xsl namespace is used for the XSL vocabulary. Its URI must be
  http://www.w3.org/1999/XSL/Transform/1.0.

- The resulting document has another namespace. In this case, the default namespace is attached to HTML 4.0.

Template Elements

EXAMPLE

The bulk of the style sheet is a list of *templates*. The following example transforms the title of a section in an HTML paragraph with the text in italic:

```
<xsl:template match="section/title">
    <P><I><xsl:apply-templates/></I></P>
</xsl:template>

<P><I>Styling</I></P>
```

OUTPUT

A template has two parts:

- The match parameter is a path to the element in the source tree to which the template applies.

- The content of the template lists the elements to insert in the resulting tree.

Paths

The syntax for XML paths is similar to file paths. XML paths start from the root of the document and list elements along the way. Elements are separated by the "/" character.

The root of the document is "/". The root is a node that sits before the top-level element. It represents the document as a whole.

EXAMPLE

The following four paths match respectively the title of the article (`<title>XML Style Sheets</title>`), the keywords of the article, the top-most article element, and all sections in the article. Note that the last path matches several elements in the source tree.

```
/article/title
/article/keywords
/article
/article/section
```

TIP

Note that "/" points to the immediate children of a node. Therefore, /article/title selects the main title of the article (XML Style Sheets), not all the titles below the article element. It won't select the section titles.

To select all the descendants from a node, use the "//" sequence. /article//title selects all the titles in the article. It selects the main title and the section titles.

In the style sheet, most paths don't start at the root. XSL has the notion of current element. Paths in the match attribute can be relative to the current element.

Again, this is similar to the file system. Double-clicking the accessories folder in the `c:\program files` folder moves to `c:\program files\accessories` folder, not to `c:\accessories`.

If the current element is an article, then `title` matches `/article/title` but if the current article is a section, `title` matches one of the `/article/section/titles`.

To match any element, use the wildcard character "*". The path `/article/*` matches any direct descendant from article, such as title, keywords, and so on.

It is possible to combine paths in a match with the "¦" character, such as `title ¦ p` matches title or p elements.

Matching on Attributes

EXAMPLE

Paths can match on attributes, too. The following template applies only to "mailto" URLs:

```
<xsl:template match="url[@protocol='mailto']">
    <A>
        <xsl:attribute name="HREF">mailto:<xsl:apply-templates/>
        </xsl:attribute>
        <xsl:apply-templates/>
    </A>
</xsl:template>
```

OUTPUT

```
<A href="mailto:bmarchal@pineapplesoft.com">
➥bmarchal@pineapplesoft.com</A>
```

It matches `<url protocol="mailto">bmarchal@pineapplesoft.com</url>` that has a protocol attribute with the value "mailto" but it does not match `<url>http://www.w3.org/Style</url>`. The more generic url path would match the later element.

`url[@protocol]` matches URL elements that have a protocol attribute, no matter what its value is. It would match the `<url protocol="http">www.w3.org/Style</url>` but it would not match `<url>http://www.w3.org/Style</url>`.

Matching Text and Functions

OUTPUT

Functions restrict paths to specific elements. The following two paths are identical and select the text of the title of the second section in the document (Styling).

```
/article/section[position()=2]/title/text()
/article/section[2]/title/text()
```

Most functions can also take a path as an argument. For example, `count(//title)` returns the number of title elements in the document. Table 5.1 lists some of the most common functions.

Table 5.1: Most common XSL functions

XSL Function	Description
position()	returns the position of the current node in the node set
text()	returns the text (the content) of an element

XSL Function	Description
last()	returns the position of the last node in the current node set
count()	returns the number of nodes in the current node set
not()	negates the argument
contains()	returns true if the first argument contains the second argument
starts-with()	returns true if the first argument starts with the second argument

EXAMPLE

New functions are declared in JavaScript, Java, C++, and so on, with the xsl:functions element.

```
<xsl:template match="/">
  <xsl:value-of select="psol:today()"/>
</xsl:template>

<xsl:functions ns="psol" type="text/javascript">
function today() {
  return Date().toString()
}
</xsl:functions>
```

CAUTION
Be aware that this element was still very much in flux in the draft we used to prepare this chapter.

Deeper in the Tree

After loading the style sheet, the XSL processor loads the source document. Next, it walks through the source document from root to leaf nodes. At each step it attempts to match the current node against a template.

If there is a match, the processor generates the nodes in the resulting tree. When it encounters xsl:apply-templates, it moves to the children of the current node and repeats the process; that is, it attempts to match them against a template.

In other words, xsl:apply-templates is a recursive call to the style sheet. A recursive approach is natural to manipulate trees. You might have recognized a deep-first search algorithm. Figure 5.6 illustrates how it works.

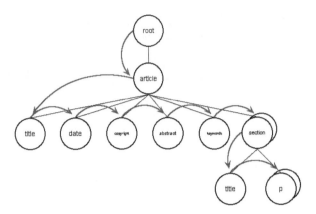

Figure 5.6: *Walking down the input tree*

Following the Processor

Let's follow the XSL processor for the first few templates in the style sheet. After loading the style sheet and the source document the processor positions itself at the root of the source document. It looks for a template that matches the root and it immediately finds

```
<xsl:template match="/">
    <HTML>
    <HEAD>
        <TITLE>Pineapplesoft Link</TITLE>
    </HEAD>
    <BODY>
        <xsl:apply-templates/>
    </BODY>
    </HTML>
</xsl:template>
```

Because the root sits before the top-level element, it is ideal to create the top-level element of the resulting tree. For HTML, it is the HTML element with HEAD and BODY elements.

When it encounters xsl:appy-templates, the processor moves to the first child of the current node. The first child of the root is the top-level element or the article element.

The style sheet defines no templates for the article but can match template against a *built-in template*. Built-in templates are not defined in the style sheet. They are predefined by the processor.

```
<xsl:template match="* ¦ /">

   <xsl:apply-templates/>

</xsl:template>
```

NOTE

The built-in template does not modify the resulting tree (it does not create elements) but it recursively calls the current element's children.

Without the default template, there would be no rules to trigger the recursive matching process and the processor would stop.

It is possible to override the built-in template, for example, to stop processing for elements not explicitly defined elsewhere:

```
<xsl:template match="* ¦ /"/>
```

The built-in template forces the processor to load the first children of article, that is, the title element. The following template matches

```
<xsl:template match="article/title">

   <P><B><xsl:apply-templates/></B></P>

</xsl:template>
```

Note that the processor matches on a relative path because the current node is article. It creates a paragraph in the HTML document. xsl:apply-templates loads title's children.

The first and only child of title is a text node. The style sheet has no rule to match text but there is another built-in template that copies the text in the resulting tree.

```
<xsl:template match="text()">

   <xsl:value-of select="."/>

</xsl:template>
```

The title's text has no children so the processor cannot go to the next level. It backtracks to the article element and moves to the next child: the date element. This element matches the last template.

```
<xsl:template match="abstract ¦ date ¦ keywords ¦ copyright"/>
```

This template generates no output in the resulting tree and stops processing for the current element.

The processor backtracks again to article and processes its other children: copyright, abstract, keywords, and section. Copyright, abstract, and keywords match the same rule as abstract and generate no output in the resulting tree.

The section element, however, matches the default template and the processor moves to its children, title, and p elements. The processor continues to match rules with nodes until it has exhausted all the nodes in the original document.

Creating Nodes in the Resulting Tree

EXAMPLE

Sometimes it is useful to compute the value or the name of new nodes. The following template creates an HTML anchor element that points to the URL. The anchor has two attributes. The first one, TARGET, is specified directly in the template. However, the processor computes the second attribute, HREF, when it applies the rule.

```
<xsl:template match="url">
    <A TARGET="_blank">
        <xsl:attribute name="HREF">
            <xsl:apply-templates/>
        </xsl:attribute>
        <xsl:apply-templates/>
    </A>
</xsl:template>
```

OUTPUT

```
<A target="_blank" href="http://www.w3.org/Style">
➥http://www.w3.org/Style</A>
```

Table 5.2 lists other XSL elements that compute nodes in the resulting tree.

Table 5.2: XSL elements to create new objects

XSL Element	Description
xsl:element	creates element with a computed name
xsl:attribute	creates attribute with a computed value
xsl:attribute-set	conveniently combines several xsl:attributes
xsl:text	creates a text node
xsl:processing-instruction	creates a processing instruction
xsl:comment	creates a comment
xsl:copy	copies the current node
xsl:value-of	computes text by extracting from the source tree or inserting a variable
xsl:if	instantiates its content if the expression is true
xsl:choose	selects elements to instantiate among possible alternatives
xsl:number	creates formatted number

PRIORITY

EXAMPLE

There are rules to prioritize templates. Without going into too many details, templates with more specific paths take precedence over less specific templates. In the following example, the first template has a higher priority than the second template because it matches an element with a specific attribute.

```
<xsl:template match="url[@protocol='mailto']">
    <A>
        <xsl:attribute name="HREF">mailto:<xsl:apply-templates/>
        </xsl:attribute>
        <xsl:apply-templates/>
    </A>
</xsl:template>

<xsl:template match="url">
    <A TARGET="_blank">
        <xsl:attribute name="HREF">
            <xsl:apply-templates/>
        </xsl:attribute>
        <xsl:apply-templates/>
    </A>
</xsl:template>
```

If there is a conflict between two templates of equivalent priority, then the XSL processor can either report an error or choose the template that appears last in the style sheet.

Supporting a Different Medium

Recall that my original problem is to provide both an HTML and a text version of the document. We have seen how to automatically create an HTML version document, now it's time to look at the text version.

Text Conversion

> **CAUTION**
> Text conversion stretches the concept of XML to XML conversion; therefore, you have to be careful in writing the style sheet.

EXAMPLE

Listing 5.4 is the text style sheet. It is very similar to the previous style sheet except that it inserts only text nodes, no XML elements, in the resulting tree.

Listing 5.4: A Style Sheet to Produce a Text File

```
<?xml version="1.0" encoding="ISO-8859-1"?>
<xsl:stylesheet
    xmlns:xsl="http://www.w3.org/1999/XSL/Transform/">

<xsl:output method="text"/>

<xsl:template match="article/title">
<xsl:text>=== </xsl:text>
<xsl:apply-templates/>
<xsl:text> ===</xsl:text>
</xsl:template>

<xsl:template match="section/title">
<xsl:text>*** </xsl:text>
<xsl:apply-templates/>
<xsl:text> ***</xsl:text>
</xsl:template>

<xsl:template match="url">
<xsl:text>[</xsl:text>
<xsl:apply-templates/>
<xsl:text>]</xsl:text>
</xsl:template>

<xsl:template match="p">
<xsl:text>
</xsl:text>
<xsl:apply-templates/>
</xsl:template>

<xsl:template match="abstract ¦ date ¦ keywords ¦ copyright"/>

</xsl:stylesheet>
```

Logically enough, the xsl:stylesheet element does not declare a name-space for the resulting tree. This style sheet also makes heavy use of text nodes.

```
<xsl:template match="section/title">
<xsl:text>*** </xsl:text>
<xsl:apply-templates/>
<xsl:text> ***</xsl:text>
</xsl:template>
```

The following command line creates the text in Listing 5.5.

```
java -classpath
➥c:\lotusxsl\xerces.jar;c:\lotusxs\lotusxsl.jar
➥com.lotus.xsl.Process
➥-in 19990101_xsl.xml
➥-xsl email.xsl -out 19990101_xsl.txt
```

Listing 5.5: The Resulting Text Document

```
=== XML Style Sheets ===
```

```
Send comments and suggestions to <bmarchal@pineapplesoft.com>.


*** Styling ***

Style sheets are inherited from SGML, an XML ancestor. Style sheets originated
➥in publishing and document management applications. XSL is XML's standard style
➥sheet, see [http://www.w3.org/Style].

*** How XSL Works ***

An XSL style sheet is a set of rules where each rule specifies how to format
➥certain elements in the document. To continue the example from the previous
➥section, the style sheets have rules for title, paragraphs and keywords.

With XSL, these rules are powerful enough not only to format the document
➥but also to reorganize it, e.g. by moving the title to the front page or
➥extracting the list of keywords. This can lead to exciting applications of XSL
➥outside the realm of traditional publishing. For example, XSL can be used to
➥convert documents between the company-specific markup and a standard one.

*** The Added Flexibility of Style Sheets ***

Style sheets are separated from documents. Therefore one document can have more
➥than one style sheet and, conversely, one style sheet can be shared amongst
➥several documents.

This means that a document can be rendered differently depending on the media or
➥the audience. For example, a "managerial" style sheet may present a summary
➥view of a document that highlights key elements but a "clerical" style sheet
➥may display more detailed information.
```

Customized Views

Currently, most people access the Web through a browser on a Windows PC. Some people use Macintoshes, others use UNIX workstations. This will change in the future as more people turn to specialized devices. Already WebTV has achieved some success with a browser in a TV set.

Mobile phones and PDAs, such as the popular PalmPilot, will be increasingly used for Web browsing. Ever tried surfing on a PalmPilot? It works surprisingly well but, on the small screen, many Web sites are not readable enough.

One solution to address the specific needs of smaller devices might be to use XHTML, an XML simplified version of HTML. XHTML is based on HTML but it has an XML syntax (as opposed to an SGML syntax). It is also designed to be modular as it is expected smaller devices will implement only a subset of the recommendation.

According to the W3C, these new platforms might account for up to 75% of Web viewing by the year 2002. What can you do about it? Will you have to maintain several versions of your Web site: one for existing Web browsers and one for each new device with its own subset?

XSL to the rescue! It will be easy to manage the diversity of browsers and platforms by maintaining the document source in XML and by converting to the appropriate XHTML subset with XSLT. In essence, this is how I manage the e-zine. Figure 5.7 illustrates how this works.

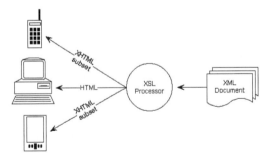

Figure 5.7: *Maintain one XML document and convert it to the appropriate markup language.*

Where to Apply the Style Sheet

So far, we have converted the XML documents before publishing them. The client never sees XML; it manipulates only HTML.

Today, this is the realistic option because few users have an XML-enabled browser such as Internet Explorer 5.0 or a beta version of *Mozilla* 5.0 (Mozilla is the open source version of Netscape Communicator). Furthermore, the XSL recommendation is not final yet so implementations of XSL processors are not always compatible with one another.

Yet, if your users have XML-enabled browsers, it is possible to send them raw XML documents and style sheets. The browser dynamically applies the style sheets and renders the documents. Figure 5.8 contrasts the two options.

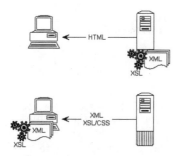

Figure 5.8: *Style sheets on the server or on the client*

Internet Explorer 5.0

CAUTION

Because XSL is still in draft, browser implementations are not compatible. The material in this section works with Internet Explorer 5.0, which implements an early draft of XSL and is not compatible with the current draft, much less with the future recommendation.

The processing instruction `xml-stylesheet` associates a style sheet with the current document. It takes two parameters, an href to the style sheet and the type of the style sheet (text/xsl, in this case).

```
<?xml-stylesheet href="simple-ie5.xsl" type="text/xsl"?>
```

Listing 5.6 is the XML document with the appropriate processing instruction for Internet Explorer 5.0.

Listing 5.6: The XML Document Prepared for Internet Explorer 5.0

EXAMPLE

```
<?xml version="1.0"?>

<?xml-stylesheet href="simple-ie5.xsl" type="text/xsl"?>
```

continues

Listing 5.6: continued

```
<article fname="19990101_xsl">

<title>XML Style Sheets</title>

<date>January 1999</date>

<copyright>1999, Benoît Marchal</copyright>

<abstract>Style sheets add flexibility to document viewing.</abstract>

<keywords>XML, XSL, style sheet, publishing, web</keywords>

<section>

<p>Send comments and suggestions to <url protocol="mailto">bmarchal@
➥pineapplesoft.com</url>.</p>

</section>

<section>

<title>Styling</title>

<p>Style sheets are inherited from SGML, an XML ancestor. Style sheets
➥originated in publishing and document management applications. XSL is XML's
➥standard style sheet, see <url>http://www.w3.org/Style</url>.</p>

</section>

<section>

<title>How XSL Works</title>

<p>An XSL style sheet is a set of rules where each rule specifies how to format
➥certain elements in the document. To continue the example from the previous
➥section, the style sheets have rules for title, paragraphs and keywords.</p>

<p>With XSL, these rules are powerful enough not only to format the document
➥but also to reorganize it, e.g. by moving the title to the front page or
➥extracting the list of keywords. This can lead to exciting applications of XSL
➥outside the realm of traditional publishing. For example, XSL can be used to
➥convert documents between the company-specific markup and a standard one.</p>

</section>

<section>

<title>The Added Flexibility of Style Sheets</title>

<p>Style sheets are separated from documents. Therefore one document can have
➥more than one style sheet and, conversely, one style sheet can be shared
➥amongst several documents.</p>

<p>This means that a document can be rendered differently depending on the media
➥or the audience. For example, a "managerial" style sheet may present a summary
➥view of a document that highlights key elements but a "clerical" style sheet
➥may display more detailed information.</p>

</section>

</article>
```

Furthermore, the style sheet must be adapted to the older version of XSL that Internet Explorer supports. Listing 5.7 is the adapted style sheet. Figure 5.9 shows the result in Internet Explorer.

Listing 5.7: XSLT Style Sheet for Internet Explorer 5.0

```
<?xml version="1.0" encoding="ISO-8859-1"?>
<xsl:stylesheet
    xmlns:xsl="http://www.w3.org/TR/WD-xsl"
    xmlns="http://www.w3.org/TR/REC-html40"
    >
<xsl:template match="*">
    <xsl:apply-templates/>
</xsl:template>
<xsl:template match="text()">
    <xsl:value-of select="."/>
</xsl:template>
<xsl:template match="/">
    <HTML>
    <HEAD>
        <TITLE>Pineapplesoft Link</TITLE>
    </HEAD>
    <BODY>
        <xsl:apply-templates/>
    </BODY>
    </HTML>
</xsl:template>
<xsl:template match="section/title">
    <P><I><xsl:apply-templates/></I></P>
</xsl:template>
<xsl:template match="article/title">
    <P><B><xsl:apply-templates/></B></P>
</xsl:template>
<xsl:template match="url">
    <A TARGET="_blank">
        <xsl:attribute name="href">
            <xsl:apply-templates/>
        </xsl:attribute>
        <xsl:apply-templates/>
    </A>
```

continues

Listing 5.7: continued

```
</xsl:template>

<xsl:template match="url[@protocol='mailto']">
   <A>
       <xsl:attribute name="href">mailto:<xsl:apply-templates/>
       </xsl:attribute>
       <xsl:apply-templates/>
   </A>
</xsl:template>

<xsl:template match="p">
   <P><xsl:apply-templates/></P>
</xsl:template>

<xsl:template match="abstract | date | keywords | copyright"/>

</xsl:stylesheet>
```

OUTPUT

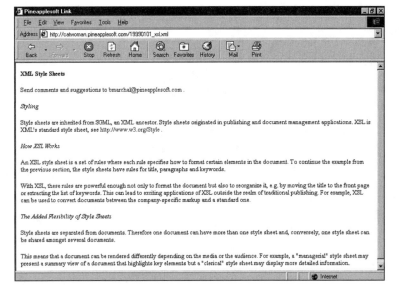

Figure 5.9: Internet Explorer 5.0 renders XML.

Changes to the Style Sheet

The style sheet has been adapted in two places. First, the XSL namespace points to an earlier version of XSL.

```
<xsl:stylesheet

   xmlns:xsl="http://www.w3.org/TR/WD-xsl"

   xmlns="http://www.w3.org/TR/REC-html40"

 >
```

Second, Internet Explorer has no built-in templates. They must be declared explicitly in the style sheet.

```
<xsl:template match="*">

   <xsl:apply-templates/>

</xsl:template>


<xsl:template match="text()">

   <xsl:value-of select="."/>

</xsl:template>
```

CAUTION

Internet Explorer 5.0 does not use the standard priority rules. Therefore, the default templates must be at the top of the style sheet; otherwise, they would have higher priority than our rules.

Advanced XSLT

XSLT is a powerful transformation mechanism. So far, we have only used a subset of it. Our resulting document follows a structure that is close to the original document. Elements might have been added or removed from the tree but they are not reorganized.

Yet, it is often useful to reorganize completely the source document. For example, we might want to create a table of contents at the beginning of the document.

This is possible with the xsl:value-of element. xsl:value-of inserts arbitrary elements from the source tree anywhere in the resulting tree.

EXAMPLE

Listing 5.8 is a more sophisticated style sheet that, among other things, creates a table of contents.

Listing 5.8: A More Powerful XSLT Style Sheet

```
<?xml version="1.0" encoding="ISO-8859-1"?>

<!DOCTYPE xsl:stylesheet [

<!ENTITY copy "&#0169;">

]>

<xsl:stylesheet

   xmlns:xsl="http://www.w3.org/1999/XSL/Transform/"
```

continues

Listing 5.8: continued

```
    xmlns="http://www.w3.org/TR/REC-html40">


<xsl:output method="html"/>


<xsl:template match="/">
    <HTML>
    <HEAD>
        <TITLE><xsl:call-template name="title"/></TITLE>
        <META NAME="keywords">
            <xsl:attribute name="CONTENT">
                <xsl:value-of select="article/keywords"/>,
            </xsl:attribute>
        </META>
    </HEAD>
    <BODY>
        <P><B><xsl:call-template name="title"/></B></P>
        <P><B>Table of Contents</B></P>
        <UL>
            <xsl:for-each select="article/section/title">
                <LI><A>
                    <xsl:attribute name="HREF">
                        ➡#<xsl:value-of select="generate-id()"/>
                    </xsl:attribute>
                    <xsl:value-of select="."/>
                </A></LI>
            </xsl:for-each>
        </UL>
        <xsl:apply-templates/>
        <P>Copyright &copy; <xsl:value-of select="article/copyright"/></P>
    </BODY>
    </HTML>
</xsl:template>


<xsl:template name="title">
    <xsl:value-of select="/article/title"/> (
    <xsl:value-of select="/article/date"/> )
</xsl:template>
```

```xsl
<xsl:template match="section/title">
   <P><I><A>
      <xsl:attribute name="NAME">
         <xsl:value-of select="generate-id()"/>
      </xsl:attribute>
      <xsl:apply-templates/>
   </A></I></P>
</xsl:template>


<xsl:template match="url">
   <A TARGET="_blank">
      <xsl:attribute name="href">
         <xsl:value-of select="."/>
      </xsl:attribute>
      <xsl:value-of select="."/>
   </A>
</xsl:template>


<xsl:template match="url[@protocol='mailto']">
   <A>
      <xsl:attribute name="href">mailto:<xsl:value-of select="."/>
      </xsl:attribute>
      <xsl:value-of select="."/>
   </A>
</xsl:template>


<xsl:template match="p">
   <P><xsl:apply-templates/></P>
</xsl:template>


<xsl:template match="article/title | abstract | date |
                     keywords | copyright"/>


</xsl:stylesheet>
```

You can use LotusXSL to apply this style sheet. It generates the HTML document in Listing 5.9. Figure 5.10 shows the result in a browser.

Listing 5.9: The Resulting HTML Document

```
<!DOCTYPE html PUBLIC "-//W3C//DTD HTML 4.0 Transitional//EN">

<HTML>

<HEAD>

<TITLE>XML Style Sheets ( January 1999 )</TITLE>

<META name="keywords" content="XML, XSL, style sheet, publishing, web">

</HEAD>

<BODY>

<P><B>XML Style Sheets ( January 1999 )</B></P>

<P><B>Table of Contents</B></P>

<UL>

   <LI><A href="#N-614609527">Styling</A></LI>

   <LI><A href="#N-634270327">How XSL Works</A></LI>

   <LI><A href="#N-653406839">The Added Flexibility of Style Sheets</A></LI>

</UL>

<P>Send comments and suggestions to <A
href="mailto:bmarchal@pineapplesoft.com">bmarchal@pineapplesoft.com</A>.</P>

<P><I><A name="N-614609527">Styling</A></I></P>

<P>Style sheets are inherited from SGML, an XML ancestor. Style sheets
➥originated in publishing and document management applications. XSL is XML's
➥standard style sheet, see <A target="_blank"
➥href="http://www.w3.org/Style">http://www.w3.org/Style</A>.</P><P><I><A name=
➥"N-634270327">How XSL Works</A></I></P>

<P>An XSL style sheet is a set of rules where each rule specifies how to format
➥certain elements in the document. To continue the example from the previous
➥section, the style sheets have rules for title, paragraphs and keywords.</P>

<P>With XSL, these rules are powerful enough not only to format the document
➥but also to reorganize it, e.g. by moving the title to the front page or
➥extracting the list of keywords. This can lead to exciting applications of XSL
➥outside the realm of traditional publishing. For example, XSL can be used to
➥convert documents between the company-specific markup and a standard one.</P>

<P><I><A name="N-653406839">The Added Flexibility of Style Sheets</A></I></P>

<P>Style sheets are separated from documents. Therefore one document can have
➥more than one style sheet and, conversely, one style sheet can be shared
➥amongst several documents.</P>

<P>This means that a document can be rendered differently depending on the media
➥or the audience. For example, a "managerial" style sheet may present a summary
➥view of a document that highlights key elements but a "clerical" style sheet
➥may display more detailed information.</P>

<P>Copyright ©1999, Benoît Marchal</P></BODY></HTML>
```

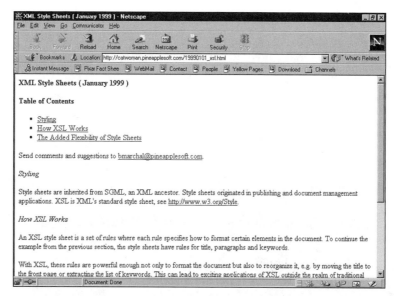

Figure 5.10: *The resulting HTML document in a browser*

Declaring HTML Entities in a Style Sheet

This style sheet has an internal DTD to declare the copy entity—an HTML entity. HTML has many entities that XML does not recognize.

```
<!DOCTYPE xsl:stylesheet [
<!ENTITY copy "&#0169;">
]>
```

Reorganizing the Source Tree

EXAMPLE

The list of keywords must appear in an HTML META element. The following example extracts the keywords from the source tree, with the xsl:value-of element.

```
<META NAME="keywords">
   <xsl:attribute name="CONTENT">
      <xsl:value-of select="article/keywords"/>,
   </xsl:attribute>
</META>
```

```
<META name="keywords" content="XML, XSL, style sheet, publishing, Web">
```

CAUTION

Because select points to any element in the source tree, paths tend to be longer than for the match attribute. It is common to spell out a path from root to element.

Calling a Template

EXAMPLE

When the same styling instructions are used at different places, group them in a named template. For example, titles appear in the HTML title and in the body of the document.

```
<xsl:template name="title">

    <xsl:value-of select="/article/title"/> (

    <xsl:value-of select="/article/date"/> )

</xsl:template>

<!-- ... -->

<P><B><xsl:call-template name="title"/></B></P>
```

This simplifies maintenance because changes to the title are localized in a single template.

EXAMPLE

xsl:include imports a style sheet into the current style sheet. The following imports the core.xsl style sheet:

```
<xsl:include href="core.xsl"/>
```

xsl:include must be a direct child of xsl:stylesheet, it cannot appear in xsl:template for example.

Repetitions

EXAMPLE

Sometimes a path points to several elements. For example, article/section/title points to the three section titles. To loop over the elements, use xsl:for-each. The following rule builds a table of contents with section titles:

```
<UL>

    <xsl:for-each select="article/section/title">

        <LI><A

            <xsl:attribute name="HREF">

            ➥#<xsl:value-of select="generate-id()"/>

            </xsl:attribute>

            <xsl:value-of select="."/>

        </A></LI>

    </xsl:for-each>

</UL>
```

OUTPUT

```
<UL>

    <LI><A href="#N-614609527">Styling</A></LI>

    <LI><A href="#N-634270327">How XSL Works</A></LI>

    <LI><A href="#N-653406839">The Added Flexibility of Style Sheets</A></LI>

</UL>
```

xsl:for-each has a select attribute so it needs a fully qualified path. However, within the loop, the current element is the selection that xsl:value-of retrieves through the "." path.

The template also introduces the generate-id() function. The function returns a unique identifier for the current node.

Using XSLT to Extract Information

As the various examples in this chapter illustrate, XSLT is a very powerful and flexible mechanism that serves many purposes.

Indeed XSLT is not limited to styling. It also can be used to extract information from XML documents.

Imagine I need to generate an index of articles. The XSLT solution is a two-step process. In the first step, a style sheet extracts useful information from the documents. Extracting information can be thought of as transforming a large XML document into a smaller one.

The first step creates as many extract documents as there are originals. The next step is to merge all the extracts in one listing. It is then a simple issue to convert the listing in HTML. Figure 5.11 illustrates the process.

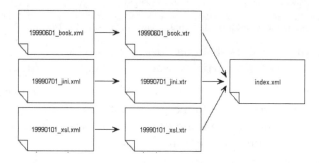

Figure 5.11: How using XSL can extract information from XML documents

A NEW STANDARD

The W3C works on a new standard XQL, the *XML Query Language*, that will offer a better solution to this problem. XQL can query multiple documents stored in an XML database.

XQL will use paths similar or identical to XSLT so it will be familiar. Because it works across several documents, XQL is really designed for XML databases. XML databases store documents in binary format to provide faster access.

To experiment with XQL without buying a database, you can download the GMD-IPSI XQL engine from xml.darmstadt.gmd.de/xml. The engine is written in Java but it has a command-line interface.

EXAMPLE

Listing 5.10 is a style sheet to extract the URL, the title, the abstract, and the date of an article document.

Listing 5.10: Style Sheet to Extract Data

```
<?xml version="1.0" encoding="ISO-8859-1"?>
<xsl:stylesheet
    xmlns:xsl="http://www.w3.org/1999/XSL/Transform/">

<xsl:template match="/article">
    <article>
        <url><xsl:value-of select="@fname"/>.html</url>
        <title><xsl:value-of select="title"/></title>
        <abstract><xsl:value-of select="abstract"/></abstract>
        <date><xsl:value-of select="date"/></date>
    </article>
</xsl:template>

</xsl:stylesheet>
```

EXAMPLE

Listing 5.11: An Extract from the Original Document

```
<article><url>19990101_xsl.html</url><title>XML Style
➥Sheets</title><abstract>Style sheets add flexibility to document
➥viewing.</abstract><date>January 1999</date></article>
```

By applying the style sheet against all my articles, I will create as many extract files as I have articles. Each file is similar to Listing 5.11.

EXAMPLE

The next step is to merge them in an XML listing. The trick to create a well-formed document is to merge two additional files with markup for the topmost element. I place the markup in two ASCII files, opening.tag and closing.tag. Opening.tag contains

```
<?xml version="1.0" encoding="ISO-8859-1"?>
<articles>
```

and closing.tag contains

```
</articles>
```

Listing 5.12 is the DOS batch that merges all the files. Running it creates index.xml (see Listing 5.13).

Listing 5.12: The DOS Batch to Compile the Index

```
set xslprocessor=java -classpath c:\lotusxsl\xerces.jar;
➥c:\lotusxsl\lotusxsl.jar com.lotus.xsl.Process
set files= 19990701_jini 19990601_book 19990101_xsl
➥for %%0 in (%files%) do %xslprocessor% -in %%0.xml -out %%0.xtr
```

```
-xsl extract.xsl

copy opening.tag index.xml

for %%0 in (%files%) do copy index.xml /a + %%0.xtr
➥/a index.xml /a

copy index.xml + closing.tag index.xml
```

TIP

Don't pass an xml, html, or text argument on the command-line so that LotusXSL generates a document without the XML declaration.

OUTPUT

Listing 5.13: The Compilation of All Small Extract Files

```
<?xml version="1.0" encoding="ISO-8859-1"?>

<articles>

<article><url>19990101_xsl.html</url><title>XML Style
➥Sheets</title><abstract>Style sheets add flexibility to document
➥viewing.</abstract><date>January 1999</date></article>

<article><url>19990701_jini.html</url><title>Jini</title><abstract>Jini is a new
➥offering from Sun. Jini extends Java towards distributed computing in novative
➥ways. In particular, Jini builds on the concept of "spontaneous
➥networking."</abstract><date>July 1999</date></article>

<article><url>19990601_book.html</url><title>Well Worth Reading</title><abstract>

This issue is atypical. It is not about technology, it is not about tools. It
➥is about a very interesting book: "The inmates are running the
➥asylum."</abstract><date>June 1999</date></article>

</articles>
```

The style sheet in listing 5.14 is used to convert index.xml in HTML. Figure 5.12 shows the result in a browser.

Listing 5.14: Styling the Index

EXAMPLE

```
<?xml version="1.0" encoding="ISO-8859-1"?>


<xsl:stylesheet
    xmlns:xsl="http://www.w3.org/1999/XSL/Transform/"
    xmlns="http://www.w3.org/TR/REC-html40">


<xsl:output method="html"/>


<xsl:template match="/">
    <HTML>
    <HEAD>
        <TITLE>Pineapplesoft Link: Archives</TITLE>
    </HEAD>
```

continues

Listing 5.14: continued

```
    <BODY>
        <UL>
            <xsl:for-each select="articles/article">
                <LI><A>
                        <xsl:attribute name="HREF">
                            <xsl:value-of select="url"/>
                        </xsl:attribute>
                        <xsl:value-of select="title"/>
                </A><BR/>
                <xsl:value-of select="date"/><BR/>
                <xsl:value-of select="abstract"/>
                </LI>
            </xsl:for-each>
        </UL>
    </BODY>
    </HTML>
</xsl:template>


</xsl:stylesheet>
```

OUTPUT

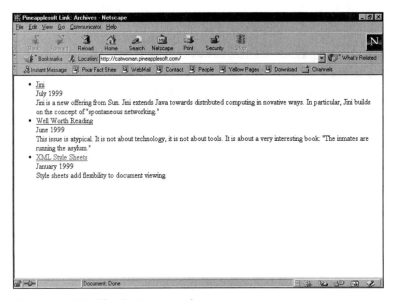

Figure 5.12: The listing in a browser

What's Next

In this chapter, you learned how to use the transformation half of XSL. The next chapter is dedicated to styling XML directly, no conversion required, with CSS and XSLFO.

The combination of XSLT and CSS gives you total control over how your document is displayed.

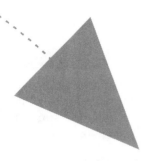

XSL Formatting Objects and Cascading Style Sheet

The previous chapter was a first look at styling XML documents. You learned how to use XSLT to convert XML documents to HTML and other formats.

This chapter picks up from there. It discusses Cascading Style Sheet (CSS) and XSLFO (XSL Formatting Objects). Conceptually, CSS and XSLFO are similar, but so far XSLFO has achieved limited market acceptance so I will concentrate on CSS and look only at how XSLFO differs.

Specifically, in this chapter, you will learn

- how to display XML without converting it to HTML

- how to customize XML editor for author comfort

Rendering XML Without HTML

HTML has a fixed set of elements and HTML browsers are hard-coded to render them onscreen. In other words, HTML browsers know that the title element will appear in the title bar; they know that hyperlinks are blue and underlined. They need not be told how to style elements.

XML, on the contrary, has no predefined set of elements. It is up to you, the author, to define elements. Consequently, an XML browser cannot be hard-coded. It needs to be told how to style each element you defined.

In the previous chapter, you worked around the difficulty by converting XML to HTML. Ultimately, the browser was a standard HTML browser rendering HTML documents. This is ideal for backward compatibility but it also limits what you can do with XML documents.

CSS (and XSLFO) have a different approach to the problem. CSS describes directly how to render documents onscreen or on paper. CSS is the mechanism you use to tell the browser how to style the elements. CSS deals with fonts, colors, text indentation, and so on. Figure 6.1 illustrates the difference between XSLT and CSS.

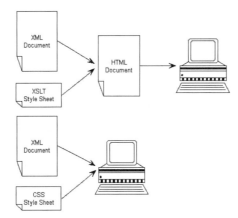

Figure 6.1: *How XSLT differs from CSS*

EXAMPLE

For example, to render a section title with XSLT, you used the following template:

```
<xsl:template match="section/title">
    <P><I><xsl:apply-templates/></I></P>
</xsl:template>
```

The equivalent in CSS would be

```
section>title
{
  display: block;
  font-style: italic;
}
```

The XSLT style sheet converts the XML title element in two HTML elements: paragraph and italicized text. The CSS style sheet retains the original elements but says how to display them. The title is an independent block of italicized text.

TIP

If we were to compare XML style sheets with word processor commands, XSLT is similar to the "Export" or the "Save As..." command that saves the current document in a different format. CSS is closer to commands in the "Format" menu.

The Basics of CSS

The CSS recommendation was originally drafted for HTML. Over the last few years, the complexity of HTML has grown dramatically. In particular, many elements have been added to HTML to support styling, such as <CENTER> or <FONT>.

Gradually, it appeared that adding even more elements to HTML was not a viable solution for the long term because it leads to very complex Web pages that are difficult to read and difficult to maintain as well as unnecessarily large.

The W3C responded with a style sheet language, CSS. CSS cleanly separates styling from the page content. Although it was originally designed for HTML, CSS also works with XML.

Two versions of CSS have been released so far: CSS1 and CSS2. CSS2 builds on CSS1 but it improves XML support, adds new styling options, and supports alternate media such as paper printing and aural rendering (for blind persons).

CAUTION

At the time of this writing, Internet Explorer 5.0 and Mozilla support CSS for XML documents. Other browsers support CSS but for HTML documents.

Currently, most browsers implement at least some support for CSS1. Unfortunately, they are not consistent in the features they support. Browsers that support a subset of CSS2 are appearing on the market.

Microsoft Internet Explorer supports CSS1. Mozilla, the open source version of Netscape Communicator, has a descent support for CSS 1 and CSS 2. Netscape Communicator 4.x supports CSS1 but it does not support XML.

EXAMPLE

If you are curious, Web Review tests the major browsers for CSS compatibility. The updated results are at `webreview.com/wr/pub/guides/style/lboard.html`.

Simple CSS

Listing 6.1 is an example of how to use a CSS style sheet to render the document you used throughout Chapter 5, "XSL Transformation."

Listing 6.1: A Simple CSS

```
/* a simple style sheet */
article
{
  font-family: Palatino, Garamond, "Times New Roman", serif;
  font-size: 10pt;
  margin: 5px;
}


article, p, title
{
  display: block;
  margin-bottom: 10px;
}

url
{
  text-decoration: underline;
  color: blue;
}

article title
{
  font-size: larger;
  font-weight: bold;
}

section title
{
  font-style: italic;
}

copyright, abstract, keywords, date
{
    display: none;
}
```

As you can see, the syntax is distinctively not XML. A CSS style sheet is a list of *rules* (similar to XSL templates). Each rule starts with a *selector* (similar to XSL path) to which *properties* are associated.

As the name implies, the selector selects to which element the properties apply.

To attach the style sheet to a document, use the familiar XML-stylesheet processing instruction. The type, however, must adapt to text/css. Unlike XSLT, there is no command-line processor for CSS. The browser is the processor. Figure 6.2 shows the document in Listing 6.2 loaded in Internet Explorer 5.0.

Listing 6.2: An XML Document Linking to a CSS Style Sheet

```
<?xml version="1.0"?>

<?xml-stylesheet href="article.css" type="text/css"?>

<article fname="19990101_xsl">

<title>XML Style Sheets</title>

<date>January 1999</date>

<copyright>1999, Benoît Marchal</copyright>

<abstract>Style sheets add flexibility to document viewing.</abstract>

<keywords>XML, XSL, style sheet, publishing, web</keywords>

<section>

<p>Send comments and suggestions to <url protocol="mailto">
➥bmarchal@pineapplesoft.com</url>.</p>

</section>

<section>

<title>Styling</title>

<p>Style sheets are inherited from SGML, an XML ancestor. Style sheets
➥originated in publishing and document management applications. XSL is XML's
➥standard style sheet, see <url>http://www.w3.org/Style</url>.</p>

</section>

<section>

<title>How XSL Works</title>

<p>An XSL style sheet is a set of rules where each rule specifies how to format
➥certain elements in the document. To continue the example from the previous
➥section, the style sheets have rules for title, paragraphs and keywords.</p>

<p>With XSL, these rules are powerful enough not only to format the document
➥but also to reorganize it, e.g. by moving the title to the front page or
➥extracting the list of keywords. This can lead to exciting applications of XSL
➥outside the realm of traditional publishing. For example, XSL can be used to
➥convert documents between the company-specific markup and a standard one.</p>

</section>

<section>

<title>The Added Flexibility of Style Sheets</title>
```

continues

Listing 6.2: continued

```
<p>Style sheets are separated from documents. Therefore one document can have
➡more than one style sheet and, conversely, one style sheet can be shared
➡amongst several documents.</p>

<p>This means that a document can be rendered differently depending on the media
➡or the audience. For example, a "managerial" style sheet may present a summary
➡view of a document that highlights key elements but a "clerical" style sheet
➡may display more detailed information.</p>

</section>

</article>
```

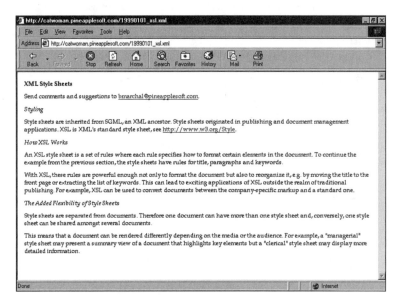

Figure 6.2: *The XML document loaded into a browser*

The next sections examine the style sheet in more detail.

Comments

Comments are enclosed in /* and */, like in C. Comments are ignored by the browser. For example, you could write

```
/* a simple style sheet */
```

EXAMPLE

Selector

CSS rules are associated with elements through selectors. Unfortunately, selectors have a different syntax than XSL paths!

To select an element, use its name. The following example applies a rule to all article elements:

```
article {
  font-family: Palatino, Garamond, "Times New Roman", serif;
```

EXAMPLE

```
    font-size: 10pt;
    margin: 5px;
}
```

EXAMPLE

To select several elements, separate them with commas. The following example applies to the `article`, `p`, and `title` elements. It is equivalent to `article ¦ p ¦ title` in XSL. The "*" character matches all elements.

```
article, p, title {
    display: block;
    margin-bottom: 10px;
}
```

EXAMPLE

To select an element depending on its ancestor, list the two elements separated by spaces. The following example selects every title with an article ancestor, not only a direct descendant from an article. In other words, it is equivalent to the `article//title` XSL path, not `article/title`.

```
article title {
    font-size: larger;
    font-weight: bold;
}
```

Priority

EXAMPLE

1. If two or more selectors point to the same element, then the rules are merged. Therefore, the following example

```
p {
    display: block;
}
p {
    font-size: 10pt;
}
```

is equivalent to

```
p {
    display: block;
    font-size: 10pt;
}
```

EXAMPLE

2. However, if the properties conflict with each other, then those rules with a more specific selector have a higher priority. Therefore, the following example

```
article section title {
    font-style: italic;
}
```

has a higher priority than

```
article title {
   font-style: normal;
}
```

EXAMPLE

3. Furthermore, rules that appear higher in the style sheet have a lower priority. So, in the following example, the second rule will preempt the first rule:

```
article title {
   font-style: normal;
}
section title {
   font-style: italic;
}
```

Properties

EXAMPLE

Properties are enclosed in curly brackets. Each property has a name followed by a colon and one or more values (separated by commas). A semicolon terminates the property.

```
article {
   font-family: Palatino, Garamond, "Times New Roman", serif;
   font-size: 10pt;
   margin: 5px;
}
```

Flow Objects and Boxes

The browser paints the document on what is known as the *canvas*. The canvas is simply the area onscreen or on paper where the browser paints. The CSS rules describe using flow objects to describe how to paint on the canvas.

Flow Objects

To render the screen or print a page, the browser uses *flow objects*. The concept is very simple: The document flows from the top to the bottom of the canvas. Anything in the flow (characters, words, paragraphs, images) is a flow object.

Style sheets associate properties to flow objects. CSS can address most flow objects from the element upwards. The recommendation even specifies how to associate properties to characters or words but browsers don't implement it, yet.

Properties Inheritance

Flow objects inherit most of their properties from their parents. In the example, section elements inherit their properties from the article element because sections are included in the article. Paragraph elements in turn inherit their properties from sections.

However, if a rule is attached to the paragraph element, it overrides some of the properties inherited from the section. The url element, which is included in a paragraph, in turn inherits its properties from the paragraph, including those properties overridden by the paragraph rule. Figure 6.3 illustrates the inheritance.

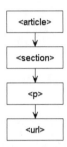

Figure 6.3: *Inheriting properties*

The inheritance works for most properties. Some properties, however, are not inherited. I will draw your attention to them in the following discussion.

Boxes

The simplest flow object is the box. As the name implies, a box is a rectangular area on the screen or on paper. Every element is rendered in a box.

Listing 6.3 illustrates how to make the boxes visible in a browser. Figure 6.4 shows the result.

Listing 6.3: A Style Sheet to Paint Titles in Boxes

EXAMPLE

```
article
{
  font-family: Palatino, Garamond, "Times New Roman", serif;
  font-size: 10pt;
  margin: 10px;
}


article, p, section, title
{
```

continues

Listing 6.3: continued

```
  display: block;
}

p, title
{
  border-style: solid;
  border-width: 1px;
}

url
{
  color: blue;
  background-color: silver;
}

article title
{
  font-size: larger;
  font-weight: bold;
  padding: 10px;
  margin: 25px;
}

section title
{
  font-style: italic;
  padding: 0px;
  margin: 10px;
}

copyright, abstract, keywords, date
{
    display: none;
}
```

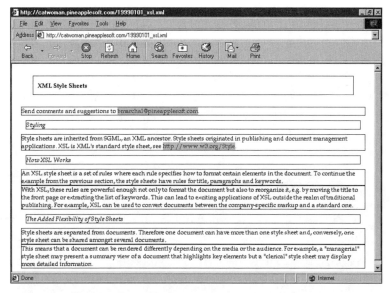

Figure 6.4: *Painting titles in boxes*

CSS supports several types of boxes. The important ones are

- block box, which has a line break before and after it. It is the most important element in organizing a document on the screen. In the example, you can see that paragraphs are rendered as a block box.

- inline box, which appears in a single line within a block box. There are no line breaks before or after it. In the example, the url element is rendered with an inline box.

- anonymous box, which is created automatically by the browser when needed. For example, the browser creates an anonymous box when a line spans several lines.

Figure 6.5 illustrates the major properties of boxes:

- margin, the space between the border and the edges

- box border, a rectangle around the box

- padding, the space between the text and the border

- element, the content

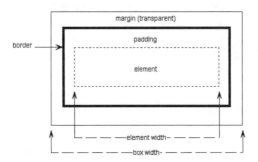

Figure 6.5: *Box properties*

In Figure 6.4, the large padding and large margins of the main title are visible. Compare with section titles that have no padding and a small margin.

Thanks to its silver background, you can see the box around the URL. This box is an inline box—you can see it's contained in the box of a paragraph.

CSS Property Values

Four values are commonly used by the properties: length, percentage, color, and URL. Before going into the specifics of properties, let's first review these values.

Length

EXAMPLE

Lengths are used for widths, heights, and sizes. A length is a number followed by a unit with no spaces between them. For example, the following two properties define a font size of 10 points and a margin of 5 pixels, respectively:

```
font-size: 10pt;
margin: 5px;
```

Units are represented by two-letter abbreviations:

- em: ems, the height of the element's font, this unit is relative to the element's font
- ex: x-height, the height of the "x" letter, this unit is relative to the element's font
- px: pixels
- in: inches
- cm: centimeters
- mm: millimeters

- pt: points, where a point is 1/72 inch

- pc: picas, where a pica is 12 points

Percentage

EXAMPLE

Percentages are used for width, height, and position. A percentage is a number followed by the percent sign "%". There are no spaces between the number and the sign. For example, the following rule defines a line height, which is twice the text:

```
line-height: 200%
```

Color

EXAMPLE

1. Many properties accept a color value. There are three solutions to re-present a color. The first one (borrowed from HTML) has the form: #00ffe1—that is, an RGB value in hexadecimal. This example selects a green background:

```
background-color: #00FF00
```

NOTE

With RGB, three numbers represent the proportion of red, green, and blue in the color. The three numbers are represented in hexadecimal and their value goes from 0 to 255 (or ff in hexadecimal).

Therefore, #FF0000 is pure red (maximum red, no green or blue) whereas #000022 is light blue (no red or green, some blue).

Shades of gray have the same amount of red, green, and blue. The following are all shades of gray: #222222, #555555, or #cccccc.

Most graphics programs can tell you the amount of red, green, and blue in a color.

EXAMPLE

2. The second solution is to define the RGB value with integers or percent-ages. This has the form rgb(0,15,128). Integer values go from 0 to 255, percentages from 0% to 100%. The following examples select blue text:

```
color: rgb(0,0,255)
```

```
color: rgb(0%,0%,100%)
```

EXAMPLE

3. Finally if, like me, you prefer readable colors to RGB values, then you will like keywords. Acceptable values for the keyword are black, maroon, green, navy, silver, red, lime, blue, gray, purple, olive, teal, white, fuchsia, yellow, and aqua. The following example paints the border in fuchsia: border-color: fuchsia

URL

EXAMPLE

URLs are used for images. They have the form url(image.gif). The following example uses the image logo.gif available from www.pineapplesoft.com/images as background:

```
background: url(http://www.pineapplesoft.com/images/logo.gif)
```

Box Properties

It is futile to try to cover every CSS property in this chapter. There are so many properties that I could write a book about it. Instead, I will concentrate on the most important properties—those properties that are frequently used. We will start with the properties associated with boxes.

For more information on specific properties, consult the recommendation at www.w3.org/TR/1998/REC-CSS2-19980512.

Display Property

EXAMPLE

The display property describes how an element is displayed. The following example selects the element as a block box:

```
display: block;
```

display accepts one of the four values: block, inline, list-item, and none. Lists are outside the scope of this chapter. block and inline create block boxes and inline boxes, respectively. none hides the element.

CAUTION

The display property is not inherited. Make sure to explicitly redefine display for each block.

Margin Properties

EXAMPLE

There are four properties to set the margin of a box. margin-top, margin-right, margin-bottom, and margin-left apply to each side of the margin as in the following example:

```
margin-top: 10px;
```

Acceptable values include an absolute length, a percentage relative to the parent's width, or the value auto. As the name implies, auto deduces the length from the size of the content.

EXAMPLE

The margin property sets the four sides in one pass. It accepts either one value if the four margins have the same length or four values in the order top, right, bottom, and left. The following example:

```
margin-top: 30%;
margin-right: 30px;
margin-bottom: 50%;
margin-left: auto;
```

is equivalent to

```
margin: 10px 30px 15px 50px;
```

The following example sets the margin to 10 pixels wide in every direction:

```
margin: 10px;
```

EXAMPLE

Padding Properties

Padding is defined exactly like margins with the properties `padding-top`, `padding-right`, `padding-bottom`, `padding-left`, and `padding` except that `auto` is not an acceptable value. The following example sets a padding of 0.2 inch:

EXAMPLE

```
padding: 0.2in;
```

Border-Style Properties

The `border-style` property sets the style of the border to `none`, `dotted`, `dashed`, `solid`, `double`, `groove`, `ridge`, `inset`, or `outset`. The following example paints a solid border around the box element:

EXAMPLE

```
border:solid;
```

It is possible to set a different style for the top, right, bottom, and left parts of the border by repeating the value as in

```
border: solid, dotted, double, inset;
```

EXAMPLE

TIP

The border of an element is not visible until the `border-style` property is set. By default, `border-style` is set to `none`.

Border-Width Properties

The `border-top-width`, `border-right-width`, `border-bottom-width`, and `border-left-width` properties control the width of each border independently. Acceptable values are `thin`, `medium`, `thick`, or an absolute length.

EXAMPLE

In most cases, it is easier to set the four values at once, with the `border-width` property, as in the following example:

```
border-width: thin;
```

Border Shorthand

The `border-top`, `border-right`, `border-bottom`, `border-left`, and `border` properties are shorthand for all previous properties. They list the width, style, and color of the border as in

EXAMPLE

```
border: thin solid silver;
```

Text and Font Properties

After boxes, text and font properties are the most widely used properties.

Font Name

EXAMPLE

The font-family property selects the name of the font. It is a good idea to list several font names in case the preferred font is not available to the browser. The following example attempts to select a serif font. The list goes from more specific font (Palatino) to more common ones (Times New Roman). The list ends with a generic family name for maximal safety:

```
font-family: Palatino, Garamond, "Times New Roman", serif;
```

Generic names (serif, sans-serif, cursive, fantasy, and monospace) select a typical font for the family.

Figure 6.6 shows the generic fonts on my computer.

serif

sans-serif

cursive

FANTASY

`monospace`

Figure 6.6: *Font samples on my machine*

Font Size

EXAMPLE

As the name implies, the font-size property selects the size of characters. The font-size value can be a length or xx-small, x-small, small, medium, large, x-large, and xx-large. Finally, it is possible to use values relative to the inherited size: larger and smaller.

The medium size font is around 10pt so the following two examples should be identical:

```
font-size: medium;
font-size: 10pt;
```

Font Style and Weight

The font-style and font-weight properties indicate whether the font is italicized or in bold, respectively. The following example sets the font to bold and italic:

```
font-weight: bold;
font-style: italic;
```

font-style accepts only three values: normal, italic, and oblique. Italic and oblique are similar but italic uses a special font drawn for italic whereas oblique is the original font bent.

font-weight accepts the following values: normal, bold, bolder, lighter, 100, 200, 300, 400, 500, 600, 700, 800, 900.

normal and bold are self-explanatory. bolder and lighter are relative to the inherited weight value. normal is equivalent to 400 and bold is 700.

Text Alignment

There are two properties to control text alignment: text-align controls alignment against the left and right margins, while vertical-align specifies vertical alignment. Use vertical alignment to write x^2. The following example prints the text in superscript justified against the right margin:

```
text-align: right;
vertical-align: super;
```

text-align accepts left, right, center, and justify. vertical-align accepts baseline, sub, super, top, text-top, middle, bottom, text-bottom, or a percentage. You will recognize values inherited from HTML.

Text Indent and Line Height

The text-indent and line-height properties define respectively the indentation of the first line and the spacing between adjacent lines. The following example indents the element by 0.5 inch. It also defines the line height as being 120% of the font size.

```
text-indent: 0.5in;
line-height: 120%;
```

text-ident accepts a percentage (relative to the parent's element) or a length. line-height defines the spacing between adjacent lines as normal, as a length, as a percentage (relative to the font size), or as a number. If the value is a number, the line height is equal to the font size times the number.

Font Shorthand

EXAMPLE

If you think there are too many font properties, you can group them all in one with the `font` property. It has the following format:

```
font: italic bold 12pt/14pt Palatino, serif
```

The order is significant: font style, variant, weight, size, line height (separated from the size by a "/"), and family names. The font weight and the line height are optional.

Color and Background Properties

CSS has several properties to set the color of texts, boxes, borders, or backgrounds.

Foreground Color

EXAMPLE

The simplest color property is the text foreground color. The `color` property controls it. The following examples all set the text color to blue:

```
color: blue;
color: rgb(0,0,100%);
color: #0000FF;
```

Background Color

EXAMPLE

The `background-color` controls the color of the background. It accepts a color value or the keyword `transparent` (what is behind a transparent background shines through). The following properties all set the background color to white:

```
background-color: white;
background-color: rgb(0,0,0);
background-color: #000000;
```

Border Color

EXAMPLE

The color of the box border is controlled by the `border-color` property, which accepts one or four colors as value. The four borders (top, right, bottom, and left) can be set independently, like margins. The following property draws an olive border:

```
border-color: olive;
```

Background Image

If you're unhappy with a plain background, then use an image, for example, a logo as background. `background-image` loads the image. It takes a URL as value or `none`. The following example sets a background image:

```
background-image: url(logo.gif);
```

Unlike HTML, a background image can be applied to any element such as a paragraph, a title, or any other element. Of course, if the element is the top element, then the background applies to the whole document, like HTML.

Some Advanced Features

EXAMPLE

The properties we looked at in the last section are the most commonly used ones. CSS has more advanced features and properties, most of which were introduced by CSS2.

Listing 6.4 illustrates some of the advanced features. Figure 6.7 shows how it looks with Mozilla, milestone 8. Mozilla supports more CSS2 properties than Internet Explorer 5.0.

Listing 6.4: An Advanced Style Sheet

```
article
{
  font-family: Palatino, Garamond, "Times New Roman", serif;
  font-size: 10pt;
  margin: 5px;
}
article, p, section, title, copyright
{
  display: block;
  margin-bottom: 10px;
}
p
{
   text-indent: 0.5in;
}
title + p
{
   text-indent: 0in;
}
url
{
  text-decoration: underline;
  color: blue;
```

continues

Listing 6.4: continued

```
}
url[protocol='mailto']
{
  text-decoration: none;
}

article title
{
  font-size: larger;
  font-weight: bold;
}

section > title
{
  font-style: italic;
}
copyright:before
{
   content: "Copyright © ";
}
abstract, keywords, date
{
   display: none;
}
```

EXAMPLE

Child Selector

CSS2 recognizes *child selectors*. A child selector points to an element that is a direct descendant from another element. The following rule illustrates a child select. The equivalent XSL is section/title.

```
section>title {
  font-style: italic;
}
```

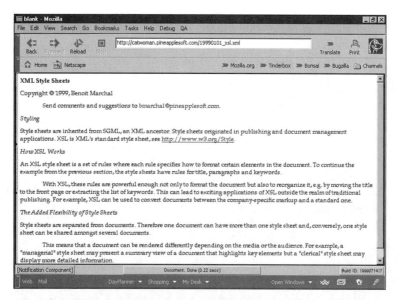

Figure 6.7: *Showing an advanced style sheet in a browser*

EXAMPLE

Sibling Selector

CSS2 also recognizes *sibling selectors*. A sibling selector points to an element only if it immediately follows another element. The following example states the first paragraph after a title has no indentation. Other paragraphs have normal indentation.

```
title + p {
    text-indent: 0in;
}
```

EXAMPLE

Attribute Selector

Like XSL paths, selectors can refer to the presence or the value of attributes. As the following example illustrates, the syntax is similar to XSL paths although it does not use the @ character:

```
url[protocol='mailto'] {
    text-decoration: none;
}
```

Attribute selectors were introduced in CSS1 and are supported by every browser.

EXAMPLE

Creating Content

It is possible to create content with the `content` property. The following rule inserts the text "Copyright © " before the element:

```
copyright:before {
   content: "Copyright © ";
}
```

Appending `:before` or `:after` to the selector places the text before or after the element.

EXAMPLE

Importing Style Sheets

Finally, it is possible to import style sheets through the `@import` keyword. Import takes a URL as value.

```
@import url(http://www.pineapplesoft.com/css/default.css);
```

Rules in the current style sheet take precedence over rules in the imported style sheet.

TIP

The name *cascading style sheet* is derived from how rules cascade from one style sheet to the other.

CSS and XML Editors

CSS is not only for browsers. XML editors can and, indeed, do use it. The HTML editor is faced with a similar problem as the browser: It must adapt to the DTD defined by the author.

Ideally, an XML editor should support the author. For one thing, it should validate the document against its DTD. But it also should guide the author by suggesting which elements are acceptable at any point.

The editor should be easy to use. Most users don't care about the structure of documents or markup or XML. They need to produce documents (articles, invoices, and so on) and they want a tool that looks and behaves like a word processor. The best editors also completely hide XML from the user.

There are three main classes of XML editors: text editors with syntax highlighting, tree-based editors, and pseudo-WYSIWYG editors.

Text Editor

EXAMPLE

A text editor is a programmer's editor with XML syntax highlighting. XML tags, attributes, and so on are painted in a different color so as to be easy to separate the markup from the content of the document.

Figure 6.8 is eNotepad, a text editor with XML syntax highlighting. Because text editors require intimate knowledge of XML, they are geared toward programmers and knowledgeable users.

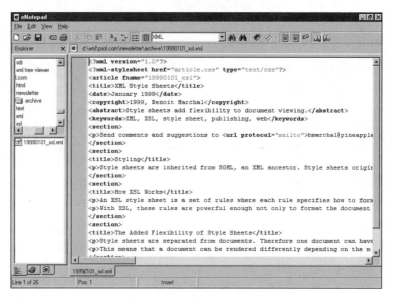

Figure 6.8: eNotepad has syntax highlighting.

Tree-Based Editor

EXAMPLE

When judged by the number of products, tree-based editors are the most popular XML editors. These tools use the XML tree as the centerpiece for document editing.

Figure 6.9 is the XML Notepad from Microsoft. You can see the document tree on the left side of the screen. Tools in this category are intended for experienced users. They expose too much XML for end-users' comfort.

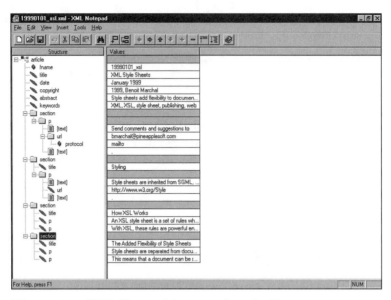

Figure 6.9: XML Notepad is a tree-based editor.

WYSIWYG Editors

WYSIWYG editors are geared toward end-users. They aim at making XML completely transparent and they should be as easy to use as a word processor.

However, tools in this category require customization. If you buy a tool in this category, you should be thinking in terms of a toolkit that has to be customized to your specific DTDs. Customization requires several steps:

- Prepare a DTD; with some editors it is necessary to compile the DTD before using it.

- Associate a style sheet with the DTD so the editor can render document onscreen in WYSIWYG mode.

- Make editors-specific customization such as create DTD-specific toolbars, and so on.

Some editors use their own style sheet language but the trend is toward using CSS. It means the same style sheet used to edit the document can be used to view it.

EXAMPLE

Figure 6.10 shows XMetaL, a pseudo-WYSIWYG editor. As you can see, it looks (and feels) like a word processor customized for a DTD.

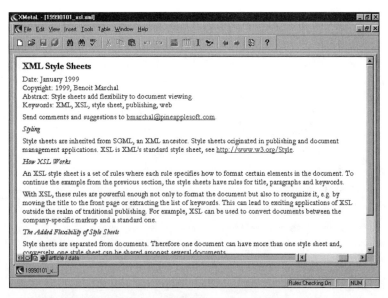

Figure 6.10: *XMetaL, a WYSIWYG editor*

XSLFO

CSS is a simple and efficient styling mechanism. However, it is limited to styling a document, it cannot reorganize or otherwise process them. CSS cannot build a table of contents or extract an index as XSLT.

XSLT and CSS

EXAMPLE

Nothing prevents you from combining XSLT with CSS. Listing 6.5 shows how an XSLT style sheet can attach a CSS style sheet to a document and create a table of contents in XML. Figure 6.11 shows the result in a browser.

Listing 6.5: XSLT Style Sheet

```
<?xml version="1.0" encoding="ISO-8859-1"?>
<xsl:stylesheet
    xmlns:xsl="http://www.w3.org/1999/XSL/Transform/">


<xsl:template match="/">
    <xsl:processing-instruction name="xml-stylesheet">
        href="article.css" type="text/css"
    </xsl:processing-instruction>
    <xsl:apply-templates/>
</xsl:template>
```

continues

Listing 6.5: continued

```
<xsl:template match="keywords">
    <keywords><xsl:apply-templates/></keywords>
    <section>
    <title>Table of Contents</title>
    <xsl:for-each select="/article/section/title">
        <p><xsl:value-of select="."/></p>
    </xsl:for-each>
    </section>
</xsl:template>


<xsl:template match="*">
    <xsl:copy><xsl:apply-templates/></xsl:copy>
</xsl:template>


</xsl:stylesheet>
```

OUTPUT

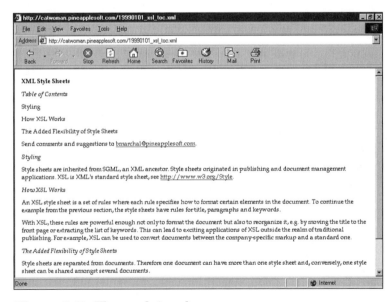

Figure 6.11: *The result in a browser*

Figure 6.12 shows how it works. First, you apply an XSLT style sheet to the document.

✔ Refer to Chapter 5, "XSL Transformation," for instructions on how to apply XSLT style sheets with LotusXSL.

This XSLT style sheet creates an XML document, not an HTML document. It reorganizes the document by creating a table of contents. The XSLT style sheet also inserts a processing instruction that links the XML document to a CSS style sheet.

The browser loads the XML document and the CSS style sheet to format it. The major advantage of this solution, when compared to using XSLT to create an HTML document, is that the final document is in XML. Therefore, the final document still contains structure-rich markup.

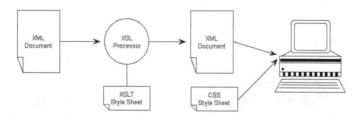

Figure 6.12: Combining XSLT and CSS

XSLFO

EXAMPLE

If using CSS in combination with XSLT makes sense, why not offer CSS features in XSLT? This is the reasoning behind XSLFO. XSLFO essentially ports the CSS properties to XSL.

Listing 6.6 is a simple XSLFO style sheet. Figure 6.13 shows the result in InDelv, currently the only browser on the market to support XSLFO.

Listing 6.6: A Simple XSLFO Style Sheet

```
<?xml version="1.0"?>

<xsl:stylesheet
    xmlns:xsl="http://www.w3.org/TR/WD-xsl"
    xmlns:fo="http://www.w3.org/TR/WD-xsl/FO">

<xsl:template match="/">
    <fo:display-sequence
        start-indent="5pt"
        end-indent="5pt"
        font-size="10pt"
        font-family="serif">
```

continues

Listing 6.5: continued

```
        <xsl:apply-templates/>
    </fo:display-sequence>
</xsl:template>

<xsl:template match="p">
    <fo:block>
        <xsl:apply-templates/>
    </fo:block>
</xsl:template>

<xsl:template match="title">
    <fo:block
        font-size="13pt"
        font-weight="bold">
        <xsl:apply-templates/>
    </fo:block>
</xsl:template>

<xsl:template match="url">
    <fo:inline-link
        destination="text()"
        color="blue">
        <xsl:apply-templates/>
    </fo:inline-link>
</xsl:template>

<xsl:template match="date"/>
<xsl:template match="keywords"/>
<xsl:template match="abstract"/>
<xsl:template match="copyright"/>

</xsl:stylesheet>
```

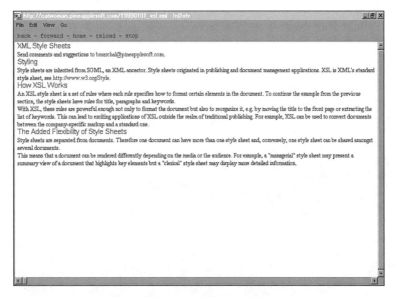

Figure 6.13: *An XSLFO style sheet in a browser*

An XSLFO style sheet is a list of XSL templates. The templates create formatting objects in the resulting tree. These formatting objects are equivalent to CSS' flow objects.

In Listing 6.6, you will recognize formatting objects for block boxes (for example, `fo:block`) and inline boxes (for example, `fo:inline-link`). The object properties are word for word taken from the CSS specification.

XLSFO also includes formatting objects specifically designed for XML; for example, `fo:inline-link` creates a hyperlink. It has no equivalent in CSS.

This section is a very brief look at XSLFO because, at the time of this writing, XSLFO has not achieved significant market acceptance. The concepts, however, are very close to CSS.

What's Next

Now that you know how to create and view XML documents, the next three chapters will take you one step further and teach you how to manipulate and create XML documents from a scripting or programming language.

The Parser and DOM

The previous chapters showed how to view and transform XML documents. Style sheet is a powerful technology but it is limited to viewing and transforming. When you have more specific needs, you need to turn to programming. This chapter introduces how to read XML documents from JavaScript or Java.

In this chapter, you learn

- what an XML parser is
- how to interface a parser with an application
- what DOM, the Document Object Model, is
- how to write JavaScript applications that use DOM
- how to write Java applications that use DOM
- which other applications use DOM

What Is a Parser?

A parser is the most basic yet most important XML tool. Every XML application is based on a parser.

A parser is a software component that sits between the application and the XML files. Its goal is to shield the developer from the intricacies of the XML syntax.

Parsers are confusing because they have received a lot of publicity: There are dozens of parsers freely available on the Internet. When Microsoft shipped Internet Explorer 4.0 as the first browser with XML support, they bundled two XML parsers with it.

Yet, if you ask for a demo of a parser, you won't see much. The parser is a low-level tool that is almost invisible to everybody but programmers. The confusion arises because the tool that has so much visibility in the marketplace turns out to be a very low-level device.

Parsers

Why do you need parsers? Imagine you are given an XML file with product descriptions, including prices. Your job is to write an application to convert the dollar prices to Euros.

It looks like a simple assignment: Loop through the price list and multiply each price by the exchange rate. Half a day's work, including tests.

Remember the prices are in an XML file. To loop through the prices means to read and interpret the XML syntax. It doesn't look difficult—basically elements are in angle brackets. Let's say the half-day assignment is now a one-day assignment.

Do you remember entities? The XML syntax is not just about angle brackets. There might be entities in the price list. The application must read and interpret the DTD to be able to resolve entities. While it's reading the DTD, it might as well read element definitions and validate the document.

> ✔ For more information on how the DTD influences the document, see the section "Standalone Documents" in Chapter 3 (page 79).

What about other XML features: character encodings, namespaces, parameter entities? And did you consider errors? How does your software recover from a missing closing tag?

The XML syntax is simple. Yet, it's an extensible syntax so XML applications have to be ready to cope with many options. As it turns out, writing a software library to read XML files is a one-month assignment. If you were to write such a library, you would be writing your own parser.

Is it productive to spend one month writing a parser library when you need only half a day's work to process the data? Of course not.

That's why developers download a parser from the Internet or use the one that ships with the development tool. This is the common definition of a parser: off-the-shelf components that isolate programmers from the specifics of the XML syntax.

If you are not convinced yet and if you'd rather write your own XML parser, consider this: No programmer in his/her right mind (except those working for Oracle, Sybase, Informix, and the like) would write low-level database drivers. It makes more sense to use the drivers that ship with the database.

Likewise, no programmer should spend time decoding XML files—it makes more sense to turn to existing parsers.

NOTE

The word *parser* comes from compilers. In a compiler, a parser is the module that reads and interprets the programming language.

In a compiler, the parser creates a parse tree, which is an in-memory representation of the source code.

The second half of the compiler, known as the *backend*, uses parse trees to generate object files (compiled modules).

Validating and Nonvalidating Parsers

XML documents can be either well-formed or valid. Well-formed documents respect the syntactic rules. Valid documents not only respect the syntactic rules but also conform to a structure as described in a DTD.

Likewise, there are validating and nonvalidating parsers. Both parsers enforce syntactic rules but only validating parsers know how to validate documents against their DTDs.

Lest there be any confusion, there is no direct mapping between well-formed and nonvalidating parsers. Nonvalidating parsers can read valid documents but won't validate them. To a nonvalidating parser, every document is a well-formed document.

Similarly, a validating parser accepts well-formed documents. Of course, when working on well-formed documents, it behaves as a nonvalidating parser.

As a programmer, you will like the combination of validating parsers and valid documents. The parser catches most of the structural errors for you. And you don't have to write a single line of code to benefit from the service: The parser figures it out by reading the DTD. In short, it means less work for you.

The Parser and the Application

This section shows you how to integrate the parser in your applications. It discusses the various interfaces available to the programmer.

The Architecture of an XML Program

Figure 7.1 illustrates the architecture of XML programs. As you can see, it is divided into two parts:

- The parser deals with the XML file.

- The application consumes the content of the file through the parser.

Figure 7.1: *Architecture of an XML program*

Note that the application can be very simple (such as printing information on the screen), or quite complex (such as a browser or an editor).

This chapter and the next one concentrate on the dotted line between the two elements. This is the interface, or the communication path, between the parser and the application.

The parser and the application must share a common model for XML data. In practice, the common model is always some variation on a tree in memory that matches the tree in the XML document.

The parser reads the XML document and populates the tree in memory. This tree built by the parser is an exact match of the tree in the XML document. The application manipulates it as if it were the XML document. In fact, for the application, it is the XML document.

Object-Based Interface

There are two basic ways to interface a parser with an application: using object-based interfaces and using event-based interfaces. In practice, the two approaches are more complementary than competitive.

Using an object-based interface, the parser explicitly builds a tree of objects that contains all the elements in the XML document.

This is probably the most natural interface for the application because it is handed a tree in memory that exactly matches the file on disk.

Obviously, it's more convenient for the application to work with the tree in memory, if only because it doesn't have to worry about the XML syntax. Furthermore, if using a validating parser, the tree may have been validated against the DTD.

EXAMPLE

Listing 7.1 is a list of products, with their prices in U.S. dollars, presented in an XML document. The structure for this document is shown in Figure 7.2.

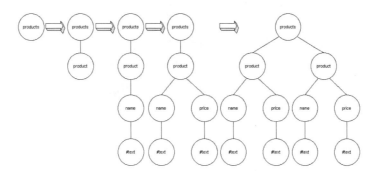

Figure 7.2: *The structure of the price list*

Listing 7.1: A Price List in XML

```xml
<?xml version="1.0"?>
<products>
    <product>
        <name>XML Editor</name>
        <price>499.00</price>
    </product>
    <product>
        <name>DTD Editor</name>
        <price>199.00</price>
    </product>
    <product>
        <name>XML Book</name>
        <price>19.99</price>
    </product>
    <product>
        <name>XML Training</name>
        <price>699.00</price>
    </product>
</products>
```

The parser reads this document and gradually builds a tree of objects that matches the document. Figure 7.3 illustrates how the tree is being built.

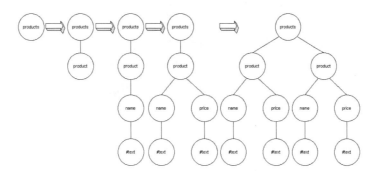

Figure 7.3: *Building the tree of objects*

When the XML parser reads the document in Listing 7.1, it recognizes that the top-level element is named products. Therefore, it constructs an object to represent the products element.

The next element is a product. The parser creates another object to represent the product element. Because this is a tree, it attaches the product object to the products object.

The next element is a name. Again, the parser creates an object for the name and adds it to the tree being built.

In the name, there is some text that the parser translates in another object in the tree.

After the name comes a price element, which also contains some text. The parser adds two new objects to the tree.

It then moves to another product element, which also contains a name and a price. This results in more objects in the tree.

The process continues until the document has been completely read. By the time the parser reaches the end of the document, it has built a tree of objects in memory that matches the tree of the document.

Event-Based Interface

The second approach to interfacing the parser and the application is through events. An event-based interface is natural for the parser but it is more complex for the application. Yet, with some practice, event-based interfaces prove very powerful. More programmers (and more parsers) are turning to event-based interfaces for this reason.

EXAMPLE

With an event-based interface, the parser does not explicitly build a tree of objects. Instead, it reads the file and generates events as it finds elements, attributes, or text in the file. There are events for element starts, element ends, attributes, text content, entities, and so on. Figure 7.4 illustrates how it works.

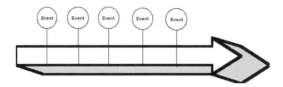

Figure 7.4: *An event-based API*

At first sight, this solution is less natural for the application because it is not given an explicit tree that matches the file. Instead, the application has to listen to events and determine which tree is being described.

In practice, both forms of interfaces are helpful but they serve different goals. Object-based interfaces are ideal for applications that manipulate XML documents such as browsers, editors, XSL processors, and so on.

Event-based interfaces are geared toward applications that maintain their own data structure in a non-XML format. For example, event-based interfaces are well adapted to applications that import XML documents in databases. The format of the application is the database schema, not the XML schema. These applications have their own data structure and they map from an XML structure to their internal structure.

An event-based interface is also more efficient because it does not explicitly build the XML tree in memory. Fewer objects are required and less memory is being used.

> ✔ Chapter 8 discusses event-based interfaces in greater detail ("Alternative API: SAX," page 231).

The Need for Standards

Ideally, the interface between the parser and the application should be a standard. A standard interface enables you to write software using one parser and to deploy the software with another parser.

Again, there is a similarity with databases. Relational databases use SQL as their standard interface. Because they all share the same interface, developers can write software with one database and later move to another database (for price reasons, availability, and so on) without changing the application.

That's the theory, at least. In practice, small differences, vendor extensions, and other issues mean that moving from one vendor to another requires more work than just recompiling the application. At the minimum, even if they follow the same standards, vendors tend to introduce different bugs.

But even if different vendors are not 100-percent compatible with one another, standards are a good thing.

For one thing, it is still easier to adapt an application from a vendor-tainted version of the standard to another vendor-tainted version of the same standard than to port the application between vendors that use completely different interfaces.

Furthermore, standards make it easier to learn new tools. It is easier to learn a new interface when 90 percent of it is similar to the interface of another product.

The two different approaches for interfaces translate into two different standards. The standard for object-based interfaces is DOM, Document Object Model, published by the W3C (www.w3.org/TR/REC-DOM-Level-1).

The standard for event-based interface is SAX, Simple API, developed collaboratively by the members of the XML-DEV mailing list and edited by David Megginson (www.megginson.com/SAX).

The two standards are not really in opposition because they serve different needs. Many parsers, such as IBM's XML for Java and Sun's ProjectX, support both interfaces.

This chapter concentrates on DOM. The next chapter discusses SAX. Chapter 9, "Writing XML," looks at how to create XML documents.

Document Object Model

Originally, the W3C developed DOM for browsers. DOM grew out of an attempt to unify the object models of Netscape Navigator 3 and Internet Explorer 3. The DOM recommendation supports both XML and HTML documents.

The current recommendation is DOM level 1. Level 1 means that it fully specifies well-formed documents. DOM level 2 is under development and it will support valid documents—that is, the DTDs.

DOM's status as the official recommendation from the W3C means that most parsers support it. DOM is also implemented in browsers, meaning that you can write DOM applications with a browser and JavaScript.

As you can imagine, DOM has defined classes of objects to represent every element in an XML file. There are objects for elements, attributes, entities, text, and so on. Figure 7.5 shows the DOM hierarchy.

Getting Started with DOM

Let's see, through examples, how to use a DOM parser. DOM is implemented in a Web browser so these examples run in a browser. At the time of this writing, Internet Explorer 5.0 is the only Web browser to support the standard DOM for XML. Therefore, make sure you use Internet Explorer 5.0.

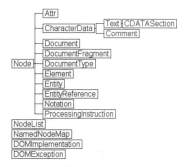

Figure 7.5: *The hierarchy in DOM*

A DOM Application

EXAMPLE

Listing 7.2 is the HTML page for a JavaScript application to convert prices from U.S. dollars to Euros. The price list is an XML document. The application demonstrates how to use DOM.

A slightly modified version of this page (essentially, putting up a better face) could be used on an electronic shop. International shoppers could access product prices in their local currency.

Listing 7.2: Currency Conversion HTML Page

```
<HTML>

    <HEAD>

        <TITLE>Currency Conversion</TITLE>

        <SCRIPT LANGUAGE="JavaScript" SRC="conversion.js"></SCRIPT>

    </HEAD>

    <BODY>

        <CENTER>

            <FORM ID="controls">

                File: <INPUT TYPE="TEXT" NAME="fname" VALUE="prices.xml">

                Rate: <INPUT TYPE="TEXT" NAME="rate" VALUE="0.95274" SIZE="4"><BR>

                <INPUT TYPE="BUTTON" VALUE="Convert"
ONCLICK="convert(controls,xml)">

                <INPUT TYPE="BUTTON" VALUE="Clear" ONCLICK="output.value=''"><BR>

                <!-- make sure there is one character in the text area -->

                <TEXTAREA NAME="output" ROWS="10" COLS="50" READONLY> </TEXTAREA>

            </FORM>

            <xml id="xml"></xml>

        </CENTER>
```

continues

Listing 7.2: continued
```
  </BODY>
</HTML>
```

The conversion routine is written in JavaScript. The script is stored in conversion.js, a JavaScript file that is loaded at the beginning of the HTML file. Listing 7.3 is conversion.js.

```
<SCRIPT LANGUAGE="JavaScript" SRC="conversion.js"></SCRIPT>
```

Listing 7.3: Conversion.js, the JavaScript File to Convert Prices

```javascript
function convert(form,xmldocument)
{
    var fname = form.fname.value,
        output = form.output,
        rate = form.rate.value;

    output.value = "";

    var document = parse(fname,xmldocument),
        topLevel = document.documentElement;
    searchPrice(topLevel,output,rate);
}


function parse(uri,xmldocument)
{
    xmldocument.async = false;
    xmldocument.load(uri);

    if(xmldocument.parseError.errorCode != 0)
        alert(xmldocument.parseError.reason);

    return xmldocument;
}


function searchPrice(node,output,rate)
{
    if(node.nodeType == 1)
    {
        if(node.nodeName == "price")
            output.value += (getText(node) * rate) + "\r";
```

Listing **7.2:** continued

```
    var children,
        i;
    children = node.childNodes;
    for(i = 0;i < children.length;i++)
        searchPrice(children.item(i),output,rate);
  }
}


function getText(node)
{
   return node.firstChild.data;
}
```

OUTPUT

Figure 7.6 shows the result in the browser. Be sure you copy the three files from Listings 7.1 (prices.xml), 7.2 (conversion.html), and 7.3 (conversion.js) in the same directory.

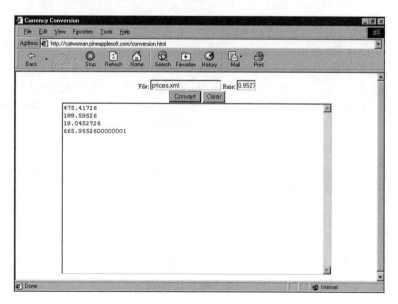

Figure 7.6: *Running the script in a browser*

The page defines a form with two fields: fname, the price list in XML, and rate, the exchange rate (you can find the current exchange rate on any financial Web site):

```
File: <INPUT TYPE="TEXT" NAME="fname" VALUE="prices.xml">
Rate: <INPUT TYPE="TEXT" NAME="rate" VALUE="0.95274" SIZE="4">
```

It also defines a read-only text area that serves as output:

```
<TEXTAREA NAME="output" ROWS="10" COLS="50" READONLY> </TEXTAREA>
```

Finally, it defines an XML island. XML islands are mechanisms used to insert XML in HTML documents. In this case, XML islands are used to access Internet Explorer's XML parser. The price list is loaded into the island.

Note that XML island is specific to Internet Explorer 5.0. It would not work with another browser. We will see why we have to use browser-specific code in a moment.

```
<xml id="xml"></xml>
```

The "Convert" button in the HTML file calls the JavaScript function convert(), which is the conversion routine. convert() accepts two parameters, the form and the XML island:

```
<INPUT TYPE="BUTTON" VALUE="Convert" ONCLICK="convert(controls,xml)">
```

The script retrieves the filename and exchange rate from the form. It communicates with the XML parser through the XML island.

DOM Node

The core object in DOM is the Node. Nodes are generic objects in the tree and most DOM objects are derived from nodes. There are specialized versions of nodes for elements, attributes, entities, text, and so on.

Node defines several properties to help you walk through the tree:

- nodeType is a code representing the type of the object; the list of code is in Table 7.1.
- parentNode is the parent (if any) of current Node object.
- childNode is the list of children for the current Node object.
- firstChild is the Node's first child.
- lastChild is the Node's last child.
- previousSibling is the Node immediately preceding the current one.
- nextSibling is the Node immediately following the current one.
- attributes is the list of attributes, if the current Node has any.

In addition, Node defines two properties to manipulate the underlying object:

- nodeName is the name of the Node (for an element, it's the tag name).
- nodeValue is the value of the Node (for a text node, it's the text).

Table 7.1: **nodeType** *code*

Type	Code
Element	1
Attribute	2
Text	3
CDATA section	4
Entity reference	5
Entity	6
Processing instruction	7
Comment	8
Document	9
Document type	10
Document fragment	11
Notation	12

EXAMPLE

In the example, the function searchPrice() tests whether the current node is an element:

```
if(node.nodeType == 1)
{
    if(node.nodeName == "price")
        output.value += (getText(node) * rate) + "\r";
    var children,
        i;
    children = node.childNodes;
    for(i = 0;i < children.length;i++)
        searchPrice(children.item(i),output,rate);
}
```

Document Object

The topmost element in a DOM tree is Document. Document inherits from Node so it can be inserted in a tree. Document inherits most properties from Node and adds only two new properties:

- documentElement is the topmost element in the document.

- doctype is the Document Type. DOM level 1 does not fully specify the document type. This will be done in DOM level 2.

Document is similar to the root in XSL path. It's an object one step before the topmost element.

To return a tree, the parser returns a Document object. From the Document object, it is possible to access the complete document tree.

CAUTION

Unfortunately, the DOM recommendation starts with the Document object, not with the parser itself. For the time being, there is no standard mechanism to access the parser. It is advisable to clearly isolate the call to the parser from the rest of the code.

EXAMPLE

The parse() function loads the price list in the XML island and returns its Document object. Most of the code in this function is Internet Explorer-specific because the DOM specification starts only at the Document object.

```
function parse(uri,xmldocument)
{
    xmldocument.async = false;
    xmldocument.load(uri);

    if(xmldocument.parseError.errorCode != 0)
        alert(xmldocument.parseError.reason);

    return xmldocument;
}
```

The function first sets the async property to false. async is specific to Internet Explorer 5.0—it enables or disables background download. Next, it calls load(), which is also specific to Internet Explorer 5.0. As the name implies, load() loads the document.

Finally, it checks for errors while parsing. The parseError property holds information about parsing errors.

Walking the Element Tree

To extract information or otherwise manipulate the document, the application walks the tree. You have already seen this happening with the XSL processor.

Essentially, you write an application that visits each element in the tree. This is easy with a recursive algorithm. To visit a node:

- Do any node-specific processing, such as printing data.

- Visit all its children.

Given children are nodes, to visit them means visiting their children, and the children of their children, and so on.

EXAMPLE

The function searchPrice() illustrates this process. It visits each node by recursively calling itself for all children of the current node. This is a deep-first search—as you saw with the XSL processor. Figure 7.7 illustrates how it works.

```
function searchPrice(node,output,rate)
{
    if(node.nodeType == 1)
    {
        if(node.nodeName == "price")
            output.value += (getText(node) * rate) + "\r";
        var children,
            i;
        children = node.childNodes;
        for(i = 0;i < children.length;i++)
            searchPrice(children.item(i),output,rate);
    }
}
```

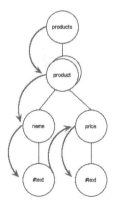

Figure 7.7: *Walking down the tree*

There is a major simplification in searchPrice(): the function examines nodes only of type Element. This is logical given that the function is looking for price elements so there is no point in examining other types of nodes such as text or entities. As you will see, more complex applications have to examine all the nodes.

At each step, the function tests whether the current node is a price. For each price element, it computes the price in Euros and prints it.

Next, the function turns to the node's children. It loops through all the children and recursively calls itself for each child.

To walk through the node's children, the function accesses the `childNodes` property. `childNodes` contains a `NodeList`. `NodeList` is a DOM object that contains a list of `Node` objects. It has two properties:

- `length`, the number of nodes in the list.

- `item(i)`, a method to access node i in the list.

Element Object

`Element` is the descendant of `Node` that is used specifically to represent XML elements. In addition to the properties inherited from `Node`, `Element` defines the `tagName` property for its tag name.

`Element` also defines specific methods (there are more methods but the other methods will be introduced in Chapter 9, "Writing XML"):

- `getElementsByTagName()` returns a `NodeList` of all descendants of the element with a given tag name.

- `normalize()` reorganizes the text nodes below the element so that they are separated only by markup.

Text Object

EXAMPLE

1. The function `getText()` returns the text of the current node. It assumes that node is an element.

```
function getText(node)
{
    return node.firstChild.data;
}
```

This is a simplification; the function assumes there is only one text object below the element. It is true in the example but it is not correct for arbitrary documents. The following <p> element contains two text objects and one element object (<img>).

```
<p>The element can contain text and other elements such as images
➥<img src="logo.gif"/> or other.</p>
```

The <img> element object splits the text into two text objects:

- the text before the <img> element "The element can contain text and other elements such as images"

- and the text after "or other."

EXAMPLE

2. In general, to retrieve the text of an element, it is safer to iterate over the element's children. Fortunately, because getText() is isolated in a separate function, it's easy to replace:

```
function getText(node)
{
   if(node.nodeType == 1)
   {
      var text = "",
          children = node.childNodes,
         i;
      for(i = 0;i < children.length;i++)
         if(children.item(i).nodeType == 3)
            text += children.item(i).data;
      return text
   }
   else
      return "";
}
```

Managing the State

The previous example is very simple. The script walks through the tree looking for a specific element. At each step, the script considers only the current node.

In many cases, the processing is more complicated. Specifically, it is common to collect information from several elements or to process elements only if they are children of other elements.

With XSL, you could write paths such as section/title and combine information from several elements with xsl:value-of.

To do the same thing with DOM, the script must maintain state information. In other words, as it examines a node, the script must remember where it's coming from or what children it is expecting.

A DOM Application That Maintains the State

EXAMPLE

As Listing 7.4 illustrates, this is very easy to do with special functions. Listing 7.4 is another version of conversion.js that prints the name of the product next to the converted price. The script does not only look for prices, but also for the combination of a price and a name. Figure 7.8 shows the result in a browser.

Listing 7.4: Walking Down the Tree While Retaining State Information

```
function convert(form,xmldocument)
{
    var fname = form.fname.value,
        output = form.output,
        rate = form.rate.value;

    output.value = "";

    var document = parse(fname,xmldocument),
        topLevel = document.documentElement;
    walkNode(topLevel,output,rate)
}


function parse(uri,xmldocument)
{
    xmldocument.async = false;
    xmldocument.load(uri);

    if(xmldocument.parseError.errorCode != 0)
        alert(xmldocument.parseError.reason);

    return xmldocument;
}

function walkNode(node,output,rate)
{
    if(node.nodeType == 1)
    {
        if(node.nodeName == "product")
                walkProduct(node,output,rate);
        else
            {
```

```
            var children,
                i;
            children = node.childNodes;
            for(i = 0;i < children.length;i++)
                walkNode(children.item(i),output,rate);
        }
    }
}


function walkProduct(node,output,rate)
{
    if(node.nodeType == 1 && node.nodeName == "product")
    {
        var name,
                price,
                    children,
            i;
        children = node.childNodes;
        for(i = 0;i < children.length;i++)
            {
                var child = children.item(i);
                if(child.nodeType == 1)
                    {
                        if(child.nodeName == "price")
                                price = getText(child) * rate;
                            else if(child.nodeName == "name")
                                name = getText(child);
                    }
            }
            output.value += name + ": " + price + "\r";
    }
}


function getText(node)
{
    return node.firstChild.data;
}
```

OUTPUT

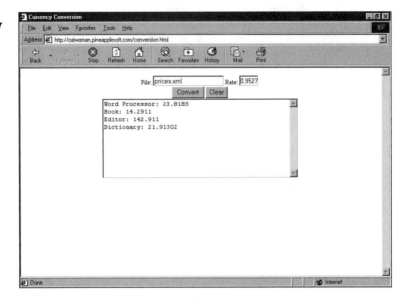

Figure 7.8: *Running the conversion utility*

You recognize many elements from the previous listing. The novelty is in functions walkNode() and walkProduct().

walkNode() is very similar to searchPrice(). It walks down the tree looking for product elements. When it finds a product, it calls walkProduct().

walkProduct() is a specialized function that processes only product elements. However, by virtue of being specialized, it knows that a product element contains a name element and a price element. It therefore extracts information from both the name and the price elements. This function maintains state information: It knows it is in a product element and it expects the product to contain specific elements.

Attributes

The previous two sections were interested only in elements. This section shows how to access attributes as well. Attributes are a very important part of XML documents.

EXAMPLE

Listing 7.5 is a different price list. This time, prices are expressed in several currencies (U.S. dollars, Canadian dollars, and Belgian francs). The currency attribute, attached to the price element, identifies the currency.

Listing 7.5: Price List in Different Currencies

```
<?xml version="1.0"?>
<products>
   <product>
      <name>XML Editor</name>
      <price currency="usd">499.00</price>
   </product>
   <product>
      <name>DTD Editor</name>
      <price currency="cad">299.00</price>
   </product>
   <product>
      <name>XML Book</name>
      <price currency="usd">19.99</price>
   </product>
   <product>
      <name>XML Training</name>
      <price currency="bef">28000</price>
   </product>
</products>
```

Because the prices are expressed in different currencies, exchange rates vary. Listing 7.6 is an XML file that lists the exchange rates for each currency. The structure of this document is shown in Figure 7.9.

Listing 7.6: Exchange Rates in XML

```
<?xml version="1.0"?>
<rates>
   <rate currency="bef" rate="0.02479"/>
   <rate currency="usd" rate="0.95274"/>
   <rate currency="cad" rate="0.63211"/>
</rates>
```

Listing 7.7 is an HTML file for a more sophisticated version of the price conversion utility. Now the exchange rates are read from an XML file instead of a field on the form. Also, the file uses attributes to recognize the price currency.

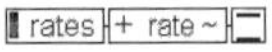

```
┃ rates ┣+  rate ~┫☐
```

Figure 7.9: *The structure of the exchange rate file*

To run the application, keep in mind it is split among four files:

- an HTML file that defines the interface
- an XML file with the exchange rates
- an XML file with products and prices
- a JavaScript file that does the conversions

Listing 7.7: The New Conversion Utility

```
<HTML>
    <HEAD>
        <TITLE>Currency Conversion</TITLE>
        <SCRIPT LANGUAGE="JavaScript" SRC="conversion.js"></SCRIPT>
    </HEAD>
    <BODY>
        <CENTER>
            <FORM ID="controls">
                Prices: <INPUT TYPE="TEXT" NAME="prices" VALUE="prices.xml">
                Rate: <INPUT TYPE="TEXT" NAME="rates" VALUE="rates.xml"><BR>
                <INPUT TYPE="BUTTON" VALUE="Convert"
ONCLICK="convert(controls,xml)">
                <INPUT TYPE="BUTTON" VALUE="Clear" ONCLICK="output.value=''"><BR>
                <!-- make sure there is one character in the text area -->
                <TEXTAREA NAME="output" ROWS="10" COLS="50" READONLY> </TEXTAREA>
            </FORM>
            <xml id="xml"></xml>
        </CENTER>
    </BODY>
</HTML>
```

Listing 7.8 is conversion.js, the JavaScript file that does the actual work. Figure 7.10 shows the result in a browser.

Listing 7.8: Converting with Attributes

```
// currency code
var BEF = 0,    // Belgian franc
    USD = 1,    // US dollars
    CAD = 2;    // Canadian dollars
```

```
// returns the code associated with a currency string
function getCurrencyCode(currency)
{
    if(currency == "bef")
            return BEF;
    else if(currency == "usd")
            return USD;
    else if(currency == "cad")
        return CAD;
    else
        return -1;
}

function convert(form,xmldocument)
{
    var pricesfname = form.prices.value,
        ratesfname = form.rates.value;
        output = form.output,
        rates = new Array(3);

    output.value = "";

    var document = parse(ratesfname,xmldocument),
        topLevel = document.documentElement;
    searchRate(topLevel,rates);

    document = parse(pricesfname,xmldocument);
    topLevel = document.documentElement;
    walkNode(topLevel,output,rates);
}

function parse(uri,xmldocument)
{
    xmldocument.async = false;
    xmldocument.load(uri);
```

continues

Listing 7.8: continued

```
    if(xmldocument.parseError.errorCode != 0)
        alert(xmldocument.parseError.reason);


    return xmldocument;
}


function searchRate(node,rates)
{
    if(node.nodeType == 1)
    {
        if(node.nodeName == "rate")
            walkRate(node,rates)
        var children,
            i;
        children = node.childNodes;
        for(i = 0;i < children.length;i++)
            searchRate(children.item(i),rates);
    }
}


function walkRate(node,rates)
{
    if(node.attributes != null)
    {
        var attr = node.attributes.getNamedItem("currency");
        var currency = getCurrencyCode(attr.value),
            rate = node.attributes.getNamedItem("rate");
        if(currency != -1)
            rates[currency] = rate.value;
    }
}


function walkNode(node,output,rates)
{
    if(node.nodeType == 1)
    {
        if(node.nodeName == "product")
```

```
            walkProduct(node,output,rates);
        else
            {
            var children,
                 i;
            children = node.childNodes;
            for(i = 0;i < children.length;i++)
                walkNode(children.item(i),output,rates);
            }
        }
    }

function walkProduct(node,output,rates)
{
    if(node.nodeType == 1 && node.nodeName == "product")
    {
        var price,
              name,
                children,
            i;
        children = node.childNodes;
        for(i = 0;i < children.length;i++)
            {
                var child = children.item(i);
                if(child.nodeType == 1)
                    {
                        if(child.nodeName == "price")
                                price = walkPrice(child,rates);
                            else if(child.nodeName == "name")
                                name = getText(child);
                    }
            }
            output.value += name + ": " + price + "\r";
    }
}

function walkPrice(node,rates)
```

continues

Listing 7.8: continued

```
{
    if(node.attributes != null)
    {
        var attr = node.attributes.getNamedItem("currency"),
                currency = getCurrencyCode(attr.value);
        if(currency != -1)
            return getText(node) * rates[currency];
    }
}


function getText(node)
{
    return node.firstChild.data;
}
```

OUTPUT

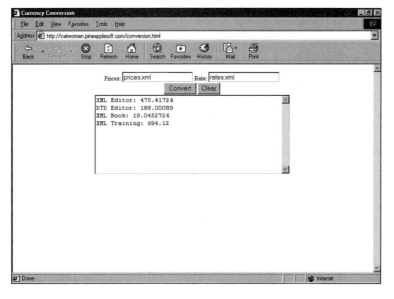

Figure 7.10: *Advanced conversion utility*

Most of the code in Listing 7.8 should be familiar. convert() parses two XML files: the price list and the rate list. It starts with the rate list. This is a simple walk down the DOM tree. It is very similar to the first example. Indeed, rates are self-contained objects so there is little need to retain state.

After it has collected the exchange rates, the application loads the price list and converts the prices. To do this, it needs to retain state information as it walks down the tree. Again, this is not new and it has been covered in the previous section.

CAUTION

This application does little error checking. Specifically it does not check whether the currency really exists. Also the currency code must be written in lowercase.

NamedNodeMap

Manipulating the attributes is done in the walkRate() function. Element objects have an attributes property. The attributes property is a NamedNodeMap object.

A NamedNodeMap is a list of nodes with a name attached to them. It supports the same properties and methods as NodeList—length and item(i)—but it also has special methods to access nodes by name:

- getNamedItem() returns the node with the given name.

- setNamedItem() sets the node with the given name.

- removeNamedItem() sremoves the node with the given name.

EXAMPLE

walkRate() illustrates how to use getNamedItem() to retrieve the currency attribute.

```
function walkRate(node,rates)
{
    if(node.attributes != null)
    {
        var attr = node.attributes.getNamedItem("currency");
        var currency = getCurrencyCode(attr.value),
            rate = node.attributes.getNamedItem("rate");
        if(currency != -1)
            rates[currency] = rate.value;
    }
}
```

Attr

Attr objects represent the attributes. Attr is a Node descendant. In addition to the properties it inherits from Node, Attr defines the following properties:

- name is the name of the attribute.

- value is the value of the attribute.

- `specified` is `true` if the attribute was given a value in the document; it is `false` if the attribute has taken a default value from the DTD.

TIP

The W3C decided to call the attribute object `Attr` to avoid confusion with object properties. In some languages, object properties are called object attributes. An `Attribute` object would have been very confusing.

A Note on Structure

If you compare Listing 7.5 and Listing 7.6, it appears that the structure of the two listings are different. The price listing has many elements and a hierarchy that goes three levels deep. Attributes convey *meta-information* (for example, information about the format of the data) only.

The rate listing has fewer elements. Data, and not meta-data, is stored in attributes.

✔ As you will see in Chapter 10 ("Modeling for Flexibility," page 307), there is raging debate between the element and the attribute supporters. In practice, applications often have to manipulate both types of files.

Listing 7.8 is interesting because it demonstrates walking the two documents side-by-side. As you can see, walking the rate listing is easier because there is no need to maintain state information. You will revisit this issue in Chapter 10.

TIP

One of the main reasons people place data in attributes is to avoid having to maintain state when walking down an XML file.

Common Errors and How to Solve Them

In this chapter, you have learned how to use XML parsers, particularly DOM parsers from JavaScript. A discussion of parsers would not be complete without a discussion of common parsing errors and how to solve them.

This section deals with debugging XML documents when the parser reports an error.

XML Parsers Are Strict

When debugging XML documents, it is important to remember that XML parsers are strict. They complain for errors that an HTML browser would silently ignore.

This was a design goal for the development of XML. It was decided that HTML had grown too difficult to implement because the browsers were too lenient. According to some estimate, more than 50 percent of the code in a browser deals with correcting errors.

That's a huge burden on the browser developers and it might explain why competition in the browser space is limited.

Furthermore, XML has been designed with a wide range of computing platforms in mind. This includes full-blown desktop but it also includes smaller devices (portable phones, PDAs like the PalmPilot, and so on). These devices lack the memory and power to recover from complex errors.

To minimize the risk of errors in XML documents, I suggest you adopt a validating XML editor. Such an editor validates your code as you write. Depending on the options, the validating editor might or might not enforce a DTD but it always enforces the XML syntax.

Error Messages

Parsers produce error messages that are often confusing. XML parsers are written with compiler technology. Consequently, error messages are similar to what you should expect from a compiler: helpful, but they rarely find the real error. Again, an XML editor might help. The best XML editors provide extra guidance about errors, which makes it easier to fix them.

EXAMPLE

1. In the best case, the error message points to the problem. For example, given the following fragment:

```
<p>Send comments and suggestions to <url protocol="mailto">
➥bmarchal@pineapplesoft.com.</p>
```

OUTPUT

The parser generates an error message similar to this (the exact message depends on your parser):

```
</url> expected
```

And it is right. The fragment misses an `</url>` closing tag.

EXAMPLE

2. Unfortunately, the error message can be very confusing. Given the following fragment

```
<p>Send comments and suggestions to <url protocol="mailto">
➥bmarchal@pineapplesoft.com.</url></p>
```

the parser generates two error messages:

```
attribute value must not contain '<'
"</p>" expected
```

OUTPUT

However, these error messages are incorrect. The real problem is that the attribute has no closing quote. The correct message should have been

`" expected.`

Instead, the parser thinks that the attribute continues until the end of the line. When it reaches the end of the line, the parser is confused and it misses the p closing tag.

As you can see, it's important to take error messages with a pinch of salt.

XSLT Common Errors

When writing XSLT style sheets, it is very common to forget to close HTML elements. However, in XML, a P element must have an opening and a closing tag.

The following line is guaranteed to confuse the parser:

EXAMPLE

```
<xsl:template match="p">
    <P><xsl:apply-templates/>
</xsl:template>
```

Fortunately, the error message (`"</P>" expected`) is clear.

Similarly, <BR> is an empty tag. In XML, empty tags have the format <BR/>. Again, the error message (`"</BR>" expected`) is useful to pinpoint the problem.

DOM and Java

DOM is not limited to browsers. Nor is it limited to JavaScript. DOM is a multiplatform, multilanguage interface.

DOM and IDL

There are versions of DOM for JavaScript, Java, and C++. In fact, there are versions of DOM for most languages because the W3C adopted a clever trick: It specified DOM using the OMG IDL.

The OMG IDL is a specification language for object interfaces. It is used to describe not what an object does but which methods and which properties it has. IDL, which stands for Interface Definition Language, was published by the OMG, the Object Management Group.

The good thing about IDL is that it has been mapped to many object-oriented programming languages. There are mappings of IDL for Java, C++, Smalltalk, Ada, and even Cobol. By writing the DOM recommendation in IDL, the W3C benefits from this cross-language support. Essentially, DOM is available in all these languages.

CAUTION

The fact that DOM is specified in IDL does not mean that parsers must be implemented as CORBA objects. In fact, to the best of my knowledge, **there are no XML parsers implemented as CORBA objects**. The W3C used only the multilanguage aspect of IDL and left out all the distribution aspects.

Java, like JavaScript, is a privileged language for XML development. In fact, most XML tools are written in Java and/or have a Java version. Indeed, there are probably more Java parsers than parsers written in all other languages. Most of these parsers support the DOM interface.

If you don't write Java software, feel free to skip this section.

✔ If you would like to learn how to write Java software for XML, read Appendix A, "Crash Course on Java," page 457.

A Java Version of the DOM Application

EXAMPLE

Listing 7.9 is the conversion utility in Java. As you can see, it uses the same objects as the JavaScript listing. The objects have the same properties and methods. That's because it's the same DOM underneath.

Listing 7.9: The Conversion Utility in Java

```java
import org.w3c.dom.*;

import com.ibm.xml.parsers.*;

import com.ibm.xml.framework.*;


public class Conversion
{
    public static void main(String[] args)
        throws Exception
    {
        if(args.length < 2)
        {
            System.out.println("java Conversion filename rate");
            return;
        }
        double rate = Double.valueOf(args[1]).doubleValue();

        Document document = parse(args[0]);
        Element topLevel = document.getDocumentElement();
        walkNode(topLevel,rate);
    }
```

continues

Listing 7.9: continued

```java
protected static Document parse(String uri)
    throws Exception
{
    NonValidatingDOMParser parser =
        new NonValidatingDOMParser();
    parser.parse(uri);
    return parser.getDocument();
}


protected static void walkNode(Node node,double rate)
{
    if(node.getNodeType() == Node.ELEMENT_NODE)
    {
        if(node.getNodeName().equals("product"))
            walkProduct((Element)node,rate);
        else
        {
            NodeList children = node.getChildNodes();
            for(int i = 0;i < children.getLength();i++)
                walkNode(children.item(i),rate);
        }
    }
}


protected static void walkProduct(Element element,double rate)
{
    if(element.getNodeName().equals("product"))
    {
        String name = null;
        double price = 0.0;
                NodeList children = element.getChildNodes();
        for(int i = 0;i < children.getLength();i++)
        {
            Node child = children.item(i);
            if(child.getNodeType() == Node.ELEMENT_NODE)
            {
```

```
            if(child.getNodeName().equals("price"))
            {
                String st = getText(child);
                price = Double.valueOf(st).doubleValue();
                price *= rate;
            }
            else if(child.getNodeName().equals("name"))
                name = getText(child);
        }
    }
        System.out.println(name + ": " + price);
    }
}


protected static String getText(Node node)
{
    Node child = node.getFirstChild();
    if(child != null && child.getNodeType() == Node.TEXT_NODE)
    {
        Text text = (Text)child;
        return text.getData();
    }
    else
        return null;
}
}
```

Two Major Differences

1.   The major difference between the Java and the JavaScript versions
      is that Java properties have the form getPropertyName().

Therefore, the following JavaScript code

```
if(node.nodeName == "product")
```

EXAMPLE

is slightly different in Java:

```
if(element.getNodeName().equals("product"))
```

EXAMPLE

2. The other difference is that Java is a strongly typed language. Typecasting between Node and Node descendants is very frequent, such as in the getText() method. In JavaScript, the typecasting was implicit.

```
protected static String getText(Node node)
{
    Node child = node.getFirstChild();
    if(child != null && child.getNodeType() == Node.TEXT_NODE)
    {
        Text text = (Text)child;    // typecasting from Node to Text
        return text.getData();
    }
    else
        return null;
}
```

The Parser

Listing 7.10 was written using the IBM parser for Java available from www.alphaworks.ibm.com. The IBM parser is popular because it was one of the first Java parsers to support both DOM and SAX (the event-based interface).

As always, updated instructions will be posted on the Macmillan Web site at www.mcp.com. Don't forget to visit Macmillan if you have a problem with XML for Java.

Other Java parsers are available from Microsoft (www.microsoft.com) and Oracle (www.oracle.com), as well as Sun (java.sun.com). The Sun parser is known as ProjectX.

You will remember that the DOM recommendation starts with the Document object. There is no standard on how to call the parser. Consequently, it is best to isolate this nonportable code in a separate function.

EXAMPLE

In the example, the parse() method isolates nonportable aspects:

```
protected static Document parse(String uri)
    throws Exception
{
    NonValidatingDOMParser parser = new NonValidatingDOMParser();
    parser.parse(uri);
    return parser.getDocument();
}
```

If you are using a different parser (such as a Microsoft parser), you will have to adapt this method.

In this particular case, the method creates a nonvalidating parser. IBM ships both validating and nonvalidating parsers.

DOM in Applications

Many applications, which you wouldn't think of as parsers, also rely on the DOM interface.

Browsers

Obviously, the browser uses the DOM interface everywhere. DOM is not limited to an XML island; any document loaded in a browser is accessible through DOM.

EXAMPLE

Listings 7.11, 7.12, 7.13, and 7.14 show yet another version of the conversion utility. This version loads the XML document in one frame (so it's not an XML island; it's an XML document loaded in the browser) and loads the bulk of the utility in another frame.

Listing 7.11 shows the HTML file that creates the frames.

Listing 7.11: An HTML File to Create the Frames

```
<HTML>
<HEAD>
    <TITLE>Currency Conversion</TITLE>
</HEAD>
<FRAMESET COLS="40%,60%">
    <FRAME SRC="conversion.html" NAME="conversion">
    <FRAME SRC="prices.xml"      NAME="xml">
</FRAMESET>
</HTML>
```

Listing 7.12 is conversion.html, the file that implements the conversion utility.

Listing 7.12: The Conversion Utility

```
<HTML>
<HEAD>
    <TITLE>Conversion</TITLE>
<SCRIPT LANGUAGE="JavaScript">
function convert(form,xmldocument)
{
    var output = form.output,
```

continues

Listing 7.12: continued

```
        rate = form.rate.value;


    output.value = "";


    var topLevel = xmldocument.documentElement;
    searchPrice(topLevel,output,rate)
}


function searchPrice(node,output,rate)
{
    if(node.nodeType == 1)
    {
        if(node.nodeName == "price")
            output.value += (getText(node) * rate) + "\r";
        var children,
            i;
        children = node.childNodes;
        for(i = 0;i < children.length;i++)
            searchPrice(children.item(i),output,rate);
    }
}


function getText(node)
{
    if(node.nodeType == 1)
    {
        var text = "",
                children = node.childNodes,
            i;
        for(i = 0;i < children.length;i++)
            if(children.item(i).nodeType == 3)
                    text += children.item(i).data;
        return text
    }
    else
        return "";
}
```

```
</SCRIPT>
</HEAD>
<BODY>
   <CENTER>
      <FORM ID="controls">
         Rate: <INPUT TYPE="TEXT" NAME="rate" VALUE="0.95274"
                  SIZE="4"><BR>
         <INPUT TYPE="BUTTON"
            ONCLICK="convert(controls,parent.xml.document)"
            VALUE="Convert">
         <INPUT TYPE="BUTTON" VALUE="Clear"
            ONCLICK="output.value=''"><BR>
         <!-- there must be one character in the text area -->
         <TEXTAREA NAME="output" ROWS="10" COLS="30" READONLY>
         </TEXTAREA>
      </FORM>
   </CENTER>
</BODY>
</HTML>
```

Listing 7.13 is prices.xml, the price list in XML. It is identical to Listing 7.1 except that it applies a CSS style sheet.

Listing 7.13: The Price List with a CSS Style Sheet

```
<?xml version="1.0"?>
<?xml-stylesheet href="prices.css" type="text/css"?>
<products>
   <product>
      <name>XML Editor</name>
      <price>499.00</price>
   </product>
   <product>
      <name>DTD Editor</name>
      <price>199.00</price>
   </product>
   <product>
      <name>XML Book</name>
      <price>19.99</price>
```

Listing 7.13: continued

```
   </product>
   <product>
      <name>XML Training</name>
      <price>699.00</price>
   </product>
</products>
```

Listing 7.14 is prices.css, the CSS style sheet. Figure 7.11 shows the result in a browser.

Listing 7.14: The CSS Style Sheet

```
product
{
    display: block;
    font-family: Palatino, Garamond, "Times New Roman", serif;
}


name
{
    font-weight: bold;
}
```

OUTPUT

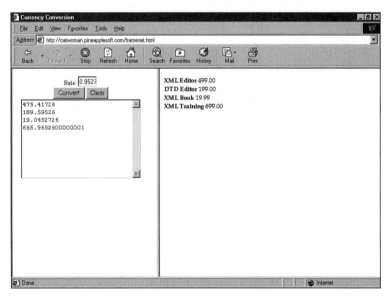

Figure 7.11: *The result in a browser*

The code is familiar; for the most part it's copied verbatim from Listing 7.3. Note, however, that it does not explicitly parse the document (there is no parse() function). Instead, the content of the XML frame is accessed directly through the DOM interface.

```
<INPUT TYPE="BUTTON"
    ONCLICK="convert(controls,parent.xml.document)"
    VALUE="Convert">
```

Editors

XML editors also use DOM. For example, XMetaL from SoftQuad exposes the current document through DOM.

For example, macros can access the document to create tables of contents, indeXEs, and so on. Using macros and DOM, you can customize the editor to suit your needs.

Databases

An XML database stores XML documents in binary format. It is therefore faster to load and manipulate documents.

The database exposes its documents to applications using DOM. The application does not even know it is working against a database. Through DOM, it makes no difference whether the document is in a database or in an XML file.

If you would like to experiment with this feature, you can download the GMD-IPSI PDOM engine from xml.darmstadt.gmd.de/xml. The engine implements Persistent DOM (PDOM), which is an interface that stores XML documents in binary format. The interface to access the binary document is familiar DOM, which means that any application that works with XML files can be upgraded to binary files with little or no work.

What's Next

This chapter looked at an object-based interface for XML parsers. In the next chapter, you will look at an event-based interface: SAX. It is interesting to compare SAX and DOM.

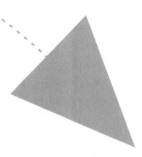

8

Alternative API: SAX

In the previous chapter, you learned how to use DOM, an object-based API for XML parsers. This chapter complements the discussion on XML parsers with an introduction to an event-based interface, SAX.

In this chapter, you learn how to use event-based interfaces. You will see that these interfaces

- operate at a lower level than object-based interfaces

- give you more control than object-based interfaces

- are more efficient than object-based interfaces

- require more work than object-based interfaces

Why Another API?

✔ The "What Is a Parser?" section in Chapter 7, "The Parser and DOM" (page 191), introduced you to XML parsers.

Parsers are software components that decode XML files on behalf of the application. Parsers effectively shield developers from the intricacies of the XML syntax.

You also learned how to integrate a parser with an application. Figure 8.1 shows the two components of a typical XML program:

- the *parser*, which deals exclusively with the XML file and makes its content available to the application

- the *application*, which consumes the file content

Obviously, the application can be simple, such as the process of printing information onscreen, or very complex, such as a distributed application to order goods over the Internet.

The previous chapter and this chapter concentrate on the dotted line, the interface or API (Application Programming Interface) between the parser and the application.

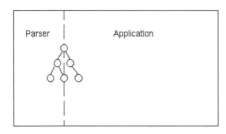

Figure 8.1: *Architecture of an XML program*

Object-Based and Event-Based Interfaces

In Chapter 7, "The Parser and DOM," you learned that there are two classes of interfaces for parsers: object-based and event-based interfaces.

> ✔ The section "Getting Started with DOM" in Chapter 7 introduced DOM as an example of object-based parser. DOM was developed and published by the W3C.

DOM is an object-based interface: It communicates with the application by explicitly creating a tree of objects in memory. The tree in memory is an exact map of the tree of elements in the XML file.

Object-based interfaces, like DOM, are simple because they offer a view that closely matches the underlying document. They are also ideal for those applications whose goal is to manipulate XML for the sake of manipulating XML documents (such as a browser or an editor).

DOM benefits from being the official interface endorsed by the W3C. Internet Explorer implements some support for DOM. Netscape will do so in the next version. XML editors and XML databases are also adopting DOM as their preferred interface.

However, for applications that are not so XML-centric, an object-based interface is less appealing. Indeed, those applications have their own data structure and their own objects, which are not based on XML.

For these applications, it is more sensible not to build the DOM tree, but to directly load the document in their data structure.

Otherwise, the application has to maintain two copies of the data in memory (one in the DOM tree and one in the application's own structure), which is inefficient. This might not be a problem for desktop applications, but can bring a server down to its knees.

Figure 8.2 illustrates how an application can map between an XML tree and its own data structure.

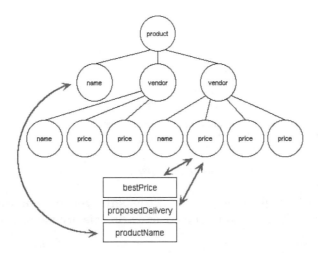

Figure 8.2: *Mapping the XML structure to the application structure*

In these cases, an event-based interface is more sensible. The major difference between an object-based interface and an event-based one is that the event-based interface does not explicitly build the tree. Rather, it builds it implicitly.

Event-Based Interfaces

As the name implies, an event-based parser sends events as it reads through an XML documents. Parser events are similar to user-interface events such as ONCLICK (in a browser) or AWT events (in Java).

Events alert the application that something happened and the application might want to react. Applications register *event handlers,* which are functions that process the events.

In a browser, events are typically generated in response to user actions: The user clicks on a button, the button fires an ONCLICK event.

With an XML parser, events are not related to user actions, but to elements in the XML document being read. There are events for

- element opening tags
- element closing tags
- content of elements
- entities
- parsing errors

Figure 8.3 shows how the parser generates events as it progresses along the document.

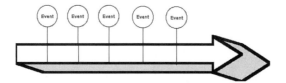

Figure 8.3: *The parser generates events.*

Listing 8.1 is a price list in XML. It lists the vendors and the prices they charge for XML training. The structure of this document is shown in Figure 8.4.

Listing 8.1: A Price List in XML

```
<?xml version="1.0"?>
<product>
<name>XML Training</name>
<price price="999.00"  vendor="Playfield Training"/>
<price price="699.00"  vendor="XMLi"/>
<price price="799.00"  vendor="WriteIT"/>
<price price="1999.00" vendor="Emailaholic"/>
</product>
```

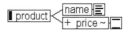

Figure 8.4: *The structure of the price list*

The XML parser reads this document and interprets it. Whenever it recognizes something in the document, it generates an event. The parser reads the XML declaration. It generates an event corresponding to the declaration.

When it encounters the first opening tag, <product>, the parser generates its second event. The event notifies the application that a product element is starting.

Next, the parser sees the opening tag for the name element and it generates its third event.

After the opening tag, the parser sees the content of the name element: XML Training. It generates an event by passing the application the content as a parameter.

The next event indicates the closing tag for the name element. The parser has completely parsed the name element. It has fired five events so far: three events for the name element, one event for the declaration, and one for product opening tag.

The parser now moves to the first price element. It generates two events for each price element: one event for the opening tag and one event for the closing tag.

Even though the closing tag is reduced to the / character in the opening tag, the parser generates an event for it. The parser passes the element's parameters to the application in the event for the opening tag.

There are four price elements, so the parser generates eight events as it parses them. Finally, the parser meets product's closing tag and it generates its last event.

As Figure 8.5 illustrates, taken together, the events describe the document tree to the application. An opening tag event means "going one level down in the tree," whereas a closing tag element means "going one level up in the tree."

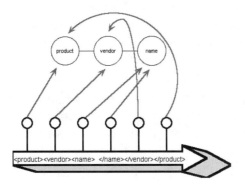

Figure 8.5: How the parser builds the tree implicitly

An event-based interface is the most natural interface for a parser. Indeed, the parser simply has to report what it sees.

Note that the parser passes enough information to build the document tree of the XML documents but, unlike an object-based parser, it does not explicitly build the tree.

NOTE

If needed, the application can build a DOM tree from the events it receives from the parser. In fact, several object-based parsers are built around an event-based parser. Internally, they use an event-based parser and they create objects in response to the events the parser generates.

Why Use Event-Based Interfaces?

Which type of interface do you use? An object-based or an event-based interface? Unfortunately, there is no clean-cut answer to this question. Neither of the two interfaces is intrinsically better; they serve different needs.

The main reason people prefer event-based interfaces is efficiency. Event-based interfaces are lower level than object-based interfaces. On the positive side, they give you more control over parsing and enable you to optimize your application. On the downside, it means more work for you.

As already discussed, an event-based interface consumes fewer resources than an object-based one, simply because it does not need to build the document tree.

Furthermore, with an event-based interface, the application can start processing the document as the parser is reading it. With an object-based interface, the application must wait until the document has been completely read.

Therefore, event-based interfaces are particularly popular with applications that process large files (which would take a lot of time to read and create a document tree) and for servers (which process many documents simultaneously).

The major limitation of event-based interfaces is that it is not possible to navigate through the document as you can with a DOM tree. Indeed, after firing an event, the parser forgets about it. As you will see, the application must explicitly buffer those events it is interested in. It might also have more work in managing the state.

Of course, whether it uses an event-based or an object-based interface, the parser does a lot of useful work: It reads the document, enforces the XML syntax, and resolves entities. When using a validating parser, it might validate the document against its DTD. So, there are many reasons to use a parser.

SAX: The Alternative API

By definition, the DOM recommendation does not apply to event-based parsers. The members of the XML-DEV mailing list have developed a standard API for event-based parsers called SAX, short for the Simple API for XML.

SAX is defined for the Java language. There is a version of SAX for Python and Perl but currently none for JavaScript or C++. Furthermore, SAX is not implemented in browsers; it is available only for standalone parsers.

Obviously, the examples in this chapter are written in Java. If you want to learn how to write Java applications, refer to Appendix A, "Crash Course on Java."

SAX is edited by David Megginson and published at www.megginson.com/ SAX. Unlike DOM, SAX is not endorsed by an official standardization body but it is widely used and is considered a de facto standard.

In particular, Sun has included SAX in ProjectX—an ongoing effort to add an XML parser to the Java platform. ProjectX also supports DOM so the parser offers both event-based and object-based interfaces. It is available from java.sun.com.

The IBM parser, XML for Java (available from www.alphaworks.ibm.com), and the DataChannel parser, XJParse (available from www.datachannel.com), are other parsers that support both the DOM and SAX interfaces.

Microstar's Ælfred (www.microstar.com) and James Clark's XP (www.jclark.com) support only the SAX interface.

Getting Started with SAX

EXAMPLE

Listing 8.2 is a Java application that finds the cheapest price from the list of prices in Listing 8.1. The application prints the best price as well as the name of the vendor.

Listing 8.2: Simple SAX Application

```
/*
 * XML By Example, chapter 8: SAX
 */


package com.psol.xbe;


import org.xml.sax.*;
import org.xml.sax.helpers.ParserFactory;
```

continues

Listing 8.2: continued

```java
/**
 * SAX event handler to find the cheapest offering
 * in a list of prices.
 * @author bmarchal@pineapplesoft.com
 */

public class Cheapest
   extends HandlerBase
{
   /*
    * event handler
    */

   /**
    * properties we are collecting: cheapest price
    */
   protected double min = Double.MAX_VALUE;

   /**
    * properties we are collecting: cheapest vendor
    */
   protected String vendor = null;

   /**
    * startElement event: the price list is stored as price
    * elements with price and vendor attributes
    * @param name element's name
    * @param attributes element's attributes
    */
   public void startElement(String name,AttributeList attributes)
   {
      if(name.equals("price"))
      {
         String attribute = attributes.getValue("price");
         if(null != attribute)
         {
```

```
            double price = toDouble(attribute);
            if(min > price)
            {
                min = price;
                vendor = attributes.getValue("vendor");
            }
        }
    }
}


/**
 * helper method: turn a string in a double
 * @param string number as a string
 * @return the number as a double, or 0.0 if it cannot convert
 * the number
 */
protected double toDouble(String string)
{
    Double stringDouble = Double.valueOf(string);
    if(null != stringDouble)
        return stringDouble.doubleValue();
    else
        return 0.0;
}


/**
 * property accessor: vendor name
 * @return the vendor with the cheapest offer so far
 */
public String getVendor()
{
    return vendor;
}


/**
 * property accessor: best price
 * @return the best price so far
```

continues

Listing 8.2: continued

```java
     */
    public double getMinimum()
    {
        return min;
    }


    /*
     * main() method and properties
     */


    /**
     * the parser class (IBM's XML for Java)
     */
    protected static final String
        PARSER_NAME = "com.ibm.xml.parsers.SAXParser";


    /**
     * main() method
     * decodes command-line parameters and invokes the parser
     * @param args command-line argument
     * @throw Exception catch-all for underlying exceptions
     */
    public static void main(String[] args)
        throws Exception
    {
        // command-line arguments
        if(args.length < 1)
        {
            System.out.println("java com.psol.xbe.CheapestCL
➥filename");
            return;
        }


        // creates the event handler
        Cheapest cheapest = new Cheapest();


        // creates the parser
```

```
Parser parser = ParserFactory.makeParser(PARSER_NAME);
parser.setDocumentHandler(cheapest);


// invokes the parser against the price list
parser.parse(args[0]);


// prints the results
System.out.println("The cheapest offer is " +
                   cheapest.getVendor() +
                   " ($" + cheapest.getMinimum() + ')');
   }
}
```

Compiling the Example

To compile this application, you need a Java Development Kit (JDK) for your platform. For this example, the Java Runtime is not enough. You can download the JDK from java.sun.com. Furthermore, you have to download the IBM parser, XML for Java, from www.alphaworks.ibm.com.

As always, I will post updates on www.mcp.com. So, if you have problems downloading a component, visit www.mcp.com.

Save Listing 8.2 in a file called Cheapest.java. Go to the DOS prompt, change to the directory where you saved Cheapest.java, and create an empty directory called classes. The compile will place the Java program in the classes directory. Finally, compile the Java source with

```
javac -classpath c:\xml4j\xml4j.jar -d classes Cheapest.java
```

This command assumes you have installed the IBM parser in c:\xml4j; you might have to adapt the classpath if you installed the parser in a different directory.

To run the application against the price list, issue the following command:

```
java -classpath c:\xml4j\xml4j.jar;classes
➥com.psol.xbe.Cheapest prices.xml
```

This command assumes that the XML price list from Listing 8.1 is in a file called prices.xml.

CAUTION

The programs in this chapter do essentially no error checking. The programs minimize errors; however, if you type parameters incorrectly, the programs can crash.

Running this program against the price list in Listing 8.1 gives the result:

```
The cheapest offer is XMLi ($699.0)
```

Note that the classpath points to the parser and to the classes directory. The fully qualified name of the file is `com.psol.xbe.Cheapest`.

CAUTION

This example won't work unless you have installed a Java Development Kit.

If there is an error message similar to "Exception in thread "main" java.lang.NoClassDefFoundError", it means that either the classpath is incorrect (be sure it points to the right directories) or that you typed an incorrect class name (com.psol.xbe.Cheapest).

SAX Interfaces and Objects

Events in SAX are defined as methods attached to specific Java interfaces. An application implements some of these methods and registers as an event-handler with the parser.

Main SAX Events

SAX groups its events in a few interfaces:

- `DocumentHandler` defines events related to the document itself (such as opening and closing tags). Most applications register for these events.

- `DTDHandler` defines events related to the DTD. Few applications register for these events. Moreover, SAX does not define enough events to completely report on the DTD (SAX-validating parsers read and use the DTD but they cannot pass all the information to the application).

- `EntityResolver` defines events related to loading entities. Few applications register for these events. They are required to load entities from special sources such as a database.

- `ErrorHandler` defines error events. Applications register for these events if they need to report errors in a special way.

To simplify work, SAX provides a default implementation for all these interfaces in the `HandlerBase` class. It is easier to extend `HandlerBase` and override the methods that are relevant for the application rather than to implement an interface directly.

Parser

To register event handlers and to start parsing, the application uses the `Parser` interface. To start parsing, the application calls `parse()`, a method of `Parser`:

```
parser.parse(args[0]);
```

Parser defines the following methods:

- parse() starts parsing an XML document. There are two versions of parse()—one accepts a filename or a URL, the other an InputSource object (see section "InputSource").

- setDocumentHandler(), setDTDHandler(), setEntityResolver(), and setErrorHandler() allow the application to register event handlers.

- setLocale() requests error messages in a specific Locale.

ParserFactory

ParserFactory creates the parser object. It takes the class name for the parser. For XML for Java, it is com.ibm.xml.parsers.SAXParser. To switch to another parser, you can change one line and recompile:

EXAMPLE

```
protected static final String
        PARSER_NAME = "com.ibm.xml.parsers.SAXParser";
// ...
Parser parser = ParserFactory.makeParser(PARSER_NAME);
```

For more flexibility, the application can read the class name from the command line or from a configuration file. In this case, it is even possible to change the parser without recompiling.

InputSource

InputSource controls how the parser reads files, including XML documents and entities.

In most cases, documents are loaded from the local file system or from a URL. The default implementation of InputSource knows how to load them. However, if an application has special needs, such as loading documents from a database, it can override InputSource.

The parse() method is available in two versions—one takes a string, the other an InputSource. The string version uses the default InputSource to load the document from a file or a URL.

DocumentHandler

Listing 8.2 is simple because it needs to handle only the startElement message. As the name implies, the message is sent when the parser sees the opening tag of an element.

EXAMPLE

The event is defined by the DocumentHandler interface. The application creates a new class, Cheapest, which overrides the startElement() method. The application registers Cheapest as an event handler with the parser.

```
// creates the event handler
```

```
Cheapest cheapest = new Cheapest();
// ...
parser.setDocumentHandler(cheapest);
```

DocumentHandler declares events related to the document. The following events are available:

- startDocument()/endDocument() notify the application of the document's beginning or ending.

- startElement()/endElement() notify the application that an element starts or ends (which corresponds to the opening and closing tags of the element). Attributes are passed as an AttributeList; see the section "AttributeList" that follows. Empty elements (<img href="logo.gif"/>) generate both startElement and endElement events even though there is only one tag.

- characters()/ignorableWhitespace() notify the application when the parser finds content (text) in an element. The parser can break a piece of text in several events or pass it all at once as it sees fit. However, one event is always attached to a single element. The ignorableWhitespace event is used for ignorable spaces as defined by the XML specs.

- processingInstruction() notifies the application of processing instructions.

- setDocumentLocator() passes a Locator object to the application; see the section "Locator" that follows. Note that the SAX parser is *not* required to supply a Locator, but if it does, it must fire this event before any other event.

AttributeList

EXAMPLE

In the event, the application receives the element name and the list of attributes in an AttributeList.

In this example, the application waits until a price element is found. It then extracts the vendor name and the price from the list of attributes. Armed with this information, finding the cheapest product requires a simple comparison:

```
public void startElement(String name,AttributeList attributes)
{
    if(name.equals("price"))
    {
        String attribute = attributes.getValue("price");
```

```
        if(null != attribute)
        {
            double price = toDouble(attribute);
            if(min > price)
            {
                min = price;
                vendor = attributes.getValue("vendor");
            }
        }
    }
}
```

The parser uses `AttributeList` in the `startElement` event. As the name implies, an `AttributeList` encapsulates a list of attributes. It defines the following methods:

- `getLength()` returns the length of the attribute list.

- `getName(i)` returns the name of the *i*th attribute (where i is an integer).

- `getType(i)/getType(name)` return the type of the ith attribute or the type of the attribute whose name is given. The first method accepts an integer, the second a string. The type is a string, as used in the DTD: `"CDATA"`, `"ID"`, `"IDREF"`, `"IDREFS"`, `"NMTOKEN"`, `"NMTOKENS"`, `"ENTITY"`, `"ENTITIES"`, or `"NOTATION"`.

- `getValue(i)/getValue(name)` return the value of the ith attribute or the value of an attribute whose name is given.

Locator

A `Locator` enables the application to retrieve line and column positions. The parser may provide a `Locator` object. If the application is interested in line information, it must retain the reference to the `Locator`.

`Locator` defines the following methods:

- `getColumnNumber()` returns the column where the current event ends. In an `endElement` event, it would return the last column of the end tag.

- `getLineNumber()` returns the line where the current event ends. In an `endElement` event, it would return the last line of the end tag.

- `getPublicId()` returns the public identifier for the current document event.

- `getSystemId()` returns the system identifier for the current document event.

DTDHandler

DTDHandler declares two events related to parsing the DTD:

- notationDecl() notifies the application that a notation has been declared.

- unparsedEntityDecl() notifies the application that an unparsed entity declaration has been found.

EntityResolver

> ✔ The EntityResolver interface defines only one event, resolveEntity(). The method returns an InputSource, which was introduced in the section "InputSource" on page 243.

Few applications need to implement EntityResolver because the SAX parser can resolve filenames and most URLs already.

ErrorHandler

The ErrorHandler interface defines several events in case of errors. Applications that handle these events can provide custom error processing.

After a custom error handler is installed, the parser doesn't throw exceptions anymore. Throwing exceptions is the responsibility of the event handlers.

There are three methods in this interface that correspond to three levels or gravity of errors:

- warning() signals problems that are not errors as defined by the XML specification. For example, some parsers issue a warning when there is no XML declaration. It is not an error (because the declaration is optional), but it is worth noting.

- error() signals errors as defined by the XML specification.

- fatalError() signals fatal errors, as defined by the XML specification.

SAXException

Most methods defined by the SAX standard can throw a SAXException. A SAXException signals an error while parsing the XML document.

The error can either be a parsing error or an error in an event handler. To report errors from the event handler, it is possible to wrap exceptions in SAXException.

EXAMPLE

Suppose an event handler catches an IndexOutOfBoundsException while processing the startElement event. The event handler wraps the IndexOutOfBoundsException in a SAXException:

```
public void startElement(String name,AttributeList attributes)
{
    try
    {
        // the code may throw an IndexOutOfBoundsException
    }
    catch(IndexOutOfBounds e)
    {
        throw new SAXException;
    }
}
```

The SAXException flows all the way up to the parse() method where it is caught and interpreted:

```
try
{
    parser.parse(uri);
}
catch(SAXException e)
{
    Exception x = e.getException();
    if(null != x)
        if(x instanceof IndexOutOfBoundsException)
            // process the IndexOutOfBoundsException
}
```

Maintaining the State

Listing 8.1 on page 234 is convenient for a SAX parser because the information is stored as attributes of price elements. The application has to register only for elementStart.

EXAMPLE

Listing 8.3 is more complex because the information is scattered across several elements. Specifically, vendors have different prices depending on the urgency of the delivery. Therefore, finding the lowest price is more difficult. If the user waits longer, he or she might get a better price. Figure 8.6 illustrates the structure of the document.

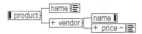

Figure 8.6: Price list structure

Listing 8.3: Price List with Delivery Information

```
<?xml version="1.0"?>
<product>
  <name>XML Training</name>
  <vendor>
      <name>Playfield Training</name>
      <price delivery="5">999.00</price>
      <price delivery="15">899.00</price>
  </vendor>
  <vendor>
      <name>XMLi</name>
      <price delivery="3">2999.00</price>
    <price delivery="30">1499.00</price>
      <price delivery="45">699.00</price>
  </vendor>
  <vendor>
      <name>WriteIT</name>
      <price delivery="5">799.00</price>
      <price delivery="15">899.00</price>
  </vendor>
  <vendor>
      <name>Emailaholic</name>
      <price delivery="2">1999.00</price>
  </vendor>
</product>
```

To find the best deal, the application must collect information from several elements. However, the parser may generate up to three events for each element (start, character, and end). The application must somehow relate events and elements by managing the state.

✔ See the section "Managing the State" in Chapter 7 for a discussion of state (page 207). The example in this section achieves the same result but for a SAX parser.

Listing 8.4 is a new Java application that looks for the best deal in the price list. When looking for the best deal, it takes the urgency in consideration. Indeed, the cheapest vendor (XMLi) is also the slowest one to deliver. On the other hand, Emailaholic is expensive but it delivers in two days.

Listing 8.4: Improved Best Deal Looker

```
/*
 * XML By Example, chapter 8: SAX
 */


package com.psol.xbe;

import java.util.*;
import org.xml.sax.*;
import org.xml.sax.helpers.ParserFactory;

/**
 * Starting point class: initializes the parser, creates the
 * various objects, etc.
 * @author bmarchal@pineapplesoft.com
 */

public class BestDeal
{
    /**
     * the parser class (IBM's XML for Java)
     */
    private static final String
        PARSER_NAME = "com.ibm.xml.parsers.SAXParser";

    /**
     * main() method
     * decodes command-line parameters and invokes the parser
     * @param args command-line argument
     * @throw Exception catch-all for underlying exceptions
     */
    public static void main(String[] args)
        throws Exception
    {
```

Listing 8.4: continued

```java
        if(args.length < 2)
        {
            System.out.println("java com.psol.xbe.BestDeal filename delivery");
            return;
        }

        ComparingMachine comparingMachine =
            new ComparingMachine(Integer.parseInt(args[1]));
        SAX2Internal sax2Internal =
            new SAX2Internal(comparingMachine);

        try
        {
            Parser parser = ParserFactory.makeParser(PARSER_NAME);
            parser.setDocumentHandler(sax2Internal);
            parser.parse(args[0]);
        }
        catch(SAXException e)
        {
            Exception x = e.getException();
            if(null != x)
                throw x;
            else
                throw e;
        }

        System.out.println("The best deal is proposed by " +
                            comparingMachine.getVendor());
        System.out.println("a " +
                            comparingMachine.getProductName() +
                            " at " + comparingMachine.getPrice() +
                            " delivered in " +
                            comparingMachine.getDelivery() +
                            " days");
    }
}
```

```
/**
 * This class receives events from the SAX2Internal adapter
 * and does the comparison required.
 * This class holds the "business logic."
 */

class ComparingMachine
{
    /**
     * properties we are collecting: best price
     */
    protected double bestPrice = Double.MAX_VALUE;

    /**
     * properties we are collecting: delivery time
     */
    protected int proposedDelivery = Integer.MAX_VALUE;

    /**
     * properties we are collecting: product and vendor names
     */
    protected String productName = null,
                     vendorName = null;

    /**
     * target delivery value (we refuse elements above this target)
     */
    protected int targetDelivery;

    /**
     * creates a ComparingMachine
     * @param td the target for delivery
     */
    public ComparingMachine(int td)
    {
        targetDelivery = td;
    }
```

continues

Listing 8.4: continued

```java
/**
 * called by SAX2Internal when it has found the product name
 * @param name the product name
 */
public void setProductName(String name)
{
    productName = name;
}


/**
 * called by SAX2Internal when it has found a price
 * @param vendor vendor's name
 * @param price price proposal
 * @param delivery delivery time proposal
 */
public void compare(String vendor,double price,int delivery)
{
    if(delivery <= targetDelivery)
    {
        if(bestPrice > price)
        {
            bestPrice = price;
            vendorName = vendor;
            proposedDelivery = delivery;
        }
    }
}


/**
 * property accessor: vendor's name
 * @return the vendor with the cheapest offer so far
 */
public String getVendor()
{
    return vendorName;
}
```

```
    /**
     * property accessor: best price
     * @return the best price so far
     */
    public double getPrice()
    {
        return bestPrice;
    }


    /**
     * property accessor: proposed delivery
     * @return the proposed delivery time
     */
    public int getDelivery()
    {
        return proposedDelivery;
    }


    /**
     * property accessor: product name
     * @return the product name
     */
    public String getProductName()
    {
        return productName;
    }
}

/**
 * SAX event handler to adapt from the SAX interface to
 * whatever the application uses internally.
 */
class SAX2Internal
    extends HandlerBase
{
    /**
```

continues

Listing 8.4: continued

```
       * state constants
       */
      final protected int START = 0,
                            PRODUCT = 1,
                            PRODUCT_NAME = 2,
                            VENDOR = 3,
                            VENDOR_NAME = 4,
                            VENDOR_PRICE = 5;


      /**
       * the current state
       */
      protected int state = START;


      /**
       * current leaf element and current vendor
       */
      protected LeafElement currentElement = null,
                            currentVendor = null;


      /**
       * BestDeal object this event handler interfaces with
       */
      protected ComparingMachine comparingMachine;


      /**
       * creates a SAX2Internal
       * @param cm the ComparingMachine to interface with
       */
      public SAX2Internal(ComparingMachine cm)
      {
         comparingMachine = cm;
      }


      /**
       * startElement event
       * @param name element's name
```

```
 * @param attributes element's attributes
 */
public void startElement(String name,AttributeList attributes)
{
    // this accepts many combinations of elements
    // it would work if new elements where being added, etc.
    // this ensures maximal flexibility: if the document
    // has to be validated, a validating parser does it
    switch(state)
    {
        case START:
            if(name.equals("product"))
                state = PRODUCT;
            break;
        case PRODUCT:
            if(name.equals("name"))
            {
                state = PRODUCT_NAME;
                currentElement = new LeafElement(name,attributes);
            }
            if(name.equals("vendor"))
                state = VENDOR;
            break;
        case VENDOR:
            if(name.equals("name"))
            {
                state = VENDOR_NAME;
                currentElement = new LeafElement(name,attributes);
            }
            if(name.equals("price"))
            {
                state = VENDOR_PRICE;
                currentElement = new LeafElement(name,attributes);
            }
            break;
    }
}
```

continues

Listing 8.4: continued

```
/**
 * content of the element
 * @param chars documents characters
 * @param start first character in the content
 * @param length last character in the content
 */
public void characters(char[] chars,int start,int length)
{
    switch(state)
    {
        case PRODUCT_NAME:
        case VENDOR_NAME:
        case VENDOR_PRICE:
            currentElement.append(chars,start,length);
            break;
    }
}


/**
 * endElement event
 * @param name element's name
 */
public void endElement(String name)
{
    switch(state)
    {
        case PRODUCT_NAME:
            if(name.equals("name"))
            {
                state = PRODUCT;
                comparingMachine.setProductName(
                    currentElement.getText());
            }
            break;
        case VENDOR:
            if(name.equals("vendor"))
```

```
                    state = PRODUCT;
                break;
            case VENDOR_NAME:
                if(name.equals("name"))
                {
                    state = VENDOR;
                    currentVendor = currentElement;
                }
                break;
            case VENDOR_PRICE:
                if(name.equals("price"))
                {
                    state = VENDOR;
                    double price = toDouble(currentElement.getText());
                    Dictionary attributes =
                        currentElement.getAttributes();
                    String stringDelivery =
                        (String)attributes.get("delivery");
                    int delivery = Integer.parseInt(stringDelivery);
                    comparingMachine.compare(currentVendor.getText(),
                                        price,
                                        delivery);
                }
                break;
        }
}


/**
 * helper method: turn a string in a double
 * @param string number as a string
 * @return the number as a double, or 0.0 if it cannot convert
 * the number
 */
protected double toDouble(String string)
{
    Double stringDouble = Double.valueOf(string);
    if(null != stringDouble)
```

continues

Listing 8.4: continued

```
            return stringDouble.doubleValue();
        else
            return 0.0;
    }
}


/*
 * helper class: used to store a leaf element content
 */
class LeafElement
{
    /**
     * property: element's name
     */
    protected String name;

    /**
     * property: element's attributes
     */
    protected Dictionary attributes;

    /**
     * property: element's text
     */
    protected StringBuffer text = new StringBuffer();

    /**
     * creates a new element
     * @param n element's name
     * @param a element's attributes
     */
    public LeafElement(String n,AttributeList al)
    {
        name = n;
        attributes = new Hashtable();
        for(int i = 0;i < al.getLength();i++)
            attributes.put(al.getName(i),al.getValue(i));
```

```
    }

    /**
     * append to the current text
     * @param chars array of characters
     * @param start where to start in chars
     * @param length how many characters to consider in chars
     */
    public void append(char[] chars,int start,int length)
    {
        text.append(chars,start,length);
    }

    /**
     * property accessor: text
     */
    public String getText()
    {
        return text.toString();
    }

    /**
     * property accessor: name
     */
    public String getName()
    {
        return name;
    }

    /**
     * property accessor: attributes
     */
    public Dictionary getAttributes()
    {
        return attributes;
    }
}
```

You compile and run this application just like the "Cheapest" application introduced previously. The results depend on the urgency of the delivery. You will notice that this program takes two parameters: the filename and the longest delay.

```
java -classpath c:\xml4j\xml4j.jar;classes com.psol.xbe.BestDeal
➥product.xml 60
```

returns

```
The best deal is proposed by XMLi

a XML Training at 699.0 delivered in 45 days
```

whereas

```
java -classpath c:\xml4j\xml4j.jar;classes com.psol.xbe.BestDeal
➥product.xml 3
```

returns

```
The best deal is proposed by Emailaholic

a XML Training at 1999.0 delivered in 2 days
```

A Layered Architecture

Listing 8.4 is the most complex application you have seen so far. It's logical: The SAX parser is very low level so the application has to take over a lot of the work.

The application is organized around two classes: SAX2Internal and ComparisonMachine. SAX2Internal manages the interface with the SAX parser. It manages the state and groups several elements in a coherent way. For that purpose, it uses the LeafElement class as temporary storage.

ComparisonMachine has the logic to perform price comparison. It also maintains information in a structure that is optimized for the application, not XML. The architecture for this application is illustrated in Figure 8.7.

SAX2Internal handles several events from DocumentHandler. It registers the startElement, endElement, and character events.

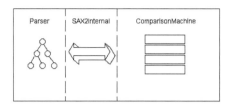

Figure 8.7: *The architecture for the application*

When processing these events, SAX2Internal needs to know where it is in the document tree. When handling a character event, for example, it needs to know whether the text is attached to a name or to a price element. It also needs to know whether the name is the product name or the vendor name.

States

A SAX parser, unlike a DOM parser, does not provide context information. Therefore, the application has to track its location within the document.

First, you have to identify all possible states and determine how to transition from one state to the next. It's easy to derive states from the document structure in Figure 8.6.

It is obvious that the application will first encounter a product tag. The first state should therefore be "within a product element." From there, the application will reach a product name. The second state is therefore "within a name element in the product element."

The next element has to be a vendor, so the third state is "within a vendor element in the product element." The fourth state is "within a name element in a vendor element in a product element" because a name follows the vendor.

The name is followed by a price element and the corresponding state is "within a price element in a vendor element in a product element." Afterward, the parser will encounter either a price element or another vendor element. You already have state for these two cases.

It's easier to visualize this concept on a graph with state and state transitions, such as the one shown in Figure 8.8. Note that there are two different states related to two different name elements depending on whether you are dealing with the product/name or product/vendor/name.

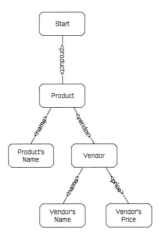

Figure 8.8: *State transition diagram*

EXAMPLE

In the example, the `state` variable is the current state:

```
/**
 * state constants
 */
final protected int START = 0,
                    PRODUCT = 1,
                    PRODUCT_NAME = 2,
                    VENDOR = 3,
                    VENDOR_NAME = 4,
                    VENDOR_PRICE = 5;


/**
 * the current state
 */
protected int state = START;
```

Transitions

EXAMPLE

1. The value of state changes in response to events. Specifically, in the example, `elementStart` and `elementEnd` cause the state to transition:

```
switch(state)
{
    case START:
        if(name.equals("product"))
```

```
            state = PRODUCT;
            break;
    case PRODUCT:
        if(name.equals("name"))
        {
            state = PRODUCT_NAME;
            currentElement = new LeafElement(name,attributes);
        }
        if(name.equals("vendor"))
            state = VENDOR;
        break;
    case VENDOR:
        if(name.equals("name"))
        {
            state = VENDOR_NAME;
            currentElement = new LeafElement(name,attributes);
        }
        if(name.equals("price"))
        {
            state = VENDOR_PRICE;
            currentElement = new LeafElement(name,attributes);
        }
        break;
    }
}
```

SAX2Internal creates instances of LeafElement to temporarily store the content of the name and price elements. At any time, SAX2Internal maintains a small subset of the tree in memory. Note that, unlike DOM, it never builds the complete tree but builds only small subsets. It also discards the subset as the application consumes them.

CAUTION
The values in AttributeList are available only during the startElement event. Consequently, LeafElement copies them to a Dictionary.

EXAMPLE

2. The character event is used to record the content of an element. It makes sense to record text only in the name and price elements, so the event handler uses the state.

```
switch(state)

{

    case PRODUCT_NAME:

    case VENDOR_NAME:

    case VENDOR_PRICE:

        currentElement.append(chars,start,length);

        break;

}
```

3. The event handler for the endElement event updates the state and
   calls ComparisonMachine. ComparisonMachine consumes the data

```
switch(state)

{

    case PRODUCT_NAME:

        if(name.equals("name"))

        {

            state = PRODUCT;

            comparingMachine.setProductName(

                currentElement.getText());

        }

        break;

    case VENDOR:

        if(name.equals("vendor"))

            state = PRODUCT;

        break;

    case VENDOR_NAME:

        if(name.equals("name"))

        {

            state = VENDOR;

            currentVendor = currentElement;

        }

        break;

    case VENDOR_PRICE:

        if(name.equals("price"))

        {

            state = VENDOR;

            double price = toDouble(currentElement.getText());

            Dictionary attributes =

                currentElement.getAttributes();
```

```
        String stringDelivery =
            (String)attributes.get("delivery");
        int delivery = Integer.parseInt(stringDelivery);
        comparingMachine.compare(currentVendor.getText(),
                                 price,
                                 delivery);
    }
    break;
}
```

Lessons Learned

Listing 8.4 is typical for a SAX application. The SAX event handler packages the data in the format most appropriate for the application. It might have to build a partial tree (in this case, using LeafElement) in the process.

The application logic (in ComparisonMachine) is totally unaware of XML. As far as it is concerned, the data could be coming from a database or a comma-delimited file.

Because of this clean-cut separation between the application logic and the parsing, it is a good idea to adopt a layered approach and use a separate class for the event handler.

The example also clearly illustrates that SAX is more efficient than DOM but it requires more work from the programmer. With a SAX parser, the programmer has to explicitly manage states and transitions between states.

With DOM, the state was implicit in the recursive walk of the tree.

Flexibility

XML is a very flexible standard. However, in practice, XML applications are only as flexible as you, the programmer, make them. In this section, we will look at some tips to ensure your applications exploit XML flexibility.

Build for Flexibility

EXAMPLE

This application puts very few constraints on the structure of the underlying document. It simply ignores new elements. For example, it would accept the following vendor element:

```
<vendor>
    <name>Playfield Training</name>
    <contact>John Doe</contact>
```

```
<price delivery="5">999.00</price>
<price delivery="15">899.00</price>
</vendor>
```

but it would ignore the contact information. In general, it's a good idea to simply ignore unknown elements. Doing so provides more flexibility when the document evolves.

Enforce a Structure

It's not difficult to enforce a specific structure. The following code snippet checks the structure and throws a SAXException if a vendor element contains anything but name or price elements.

EXAMPLE

```
case VENDOR:
    if(name.equals("name"))
    {
        state = VENDOR_NAME;
        currentElement = new LeafElement(name,attributes);
    }
    else if(name.equals("price"))
    {
        state = VENDOR_PRICE;
        currentElement = new LeafElement(name,attributes);
    }
    else
        throw new SAXException("<name> or <price> expected");
    break;
```

In practice, if the application is really dependent on the structure of the document, it is easier to write a DTD and use a validating parser.

What's Next

In the previous chapter and in this chapter, you learned how to read XML documents. In the next chapter, you learn how to write documents, thereby closing the loop.

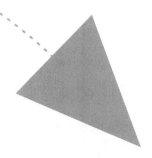

Writing XML

In the last four chapters, you learned how to use XML documents in your applications. You studied style sheets and how to convert XML documents in HTML. You also learned how to read XML documents from JavaScript or Java applications with a parser.

This chapter looks at the mirror problem: how to write XML documents from an application. The mirror component for the parser is called a *generator*. Whereas the parser reads XML documents, the generator writes them.

In this chapter, you learn how to write documents

- through DOM, which is ideal for modifying XML documents.

- through your own generator, which is more efficient.

The Parser Mirror

In practice, some parsers integrate a generator. They can read and write XML documents. Consequently, the term *parser* is often used to symbolize the combination of the parser and the generator.

There are two schools of thought when it comes to generators:

- The first school argues that you need packaged generators for the same reason you need packaged parsers: to shield the programmer from the XML syntax.

- The other school argues that writing XML documents is simple and can easily be done with ad hoc code.

As usual, I'm a pragmatist and I choose one option or the other depending on the needs of the application at hand. In general, however, it is dramatically easier to generate XML documents than to read them. This is because you control what you write but the author controls what you read.

Indeed, when reading a document, you may have to deal not only with tags but also with entities, exotic character sets, and notations—not to mention errors and DTD validation.

However, when writing the document, you decide. If your applications don't need entities, don't use them. If you are happy with ASCII, stick to it. Most applications need few of the features of XML besides the tagging mechanism.

Therefore, although a typical XML parser is a thousand lines of code, a simple but effective generator can be written in a dozen lines.

This chapter looks at both approaches. You'll start by using a DOM parser to generate XML documents and then you'll see how to write your own generator. Finally, you will see how to support different DTDs.

The techniques are illustrated with JavaScript but port easily in to Java.

Modifying a Document with DOM

In Chapter 7, "The Parser and DOM," you saw how DOM parsers read documents. That is only one half of DOM. The other half is writing XML documents. DOM objects have methods to support creating or modifying XML documents.

EXAMPLE

Listing 9.1 is the XML price list used in Chapter 7.

✔ The example in the section "A DOM Application" in Chapter 7 (page 199) converted the prices into Euros and printed the result.

With small changes to the original application, you can record the new prices in the original document.

Listing 9.1: XML Price List

```
<?xml version="1.0"?>
<products>
    <product>
        <name>XML Editor</name>
        <price>499.00</price>
    </product>
    <product>
        <name>DTD Editor</name>
        <price>199.00</price>
    </product>
    <product>
        <name>XML Book</name>
        <price>19.99</price>
    </product>
    <product>
```

```
        <name>XML Training</name>
        <price>699.00</price>
    </product>
</products>
```

Listing 9.2 is the HTML form for a new version of the currency conversion that will modify the XML file.

Listing 9.2: HTML Form for the Currency Converter

```
<HTML>
    <HEAD>
        <TITLE>Currency Conversion</TITLE>
        <SCRIPT LANGUAGE="JavaScript" SRC="conversion.js"></SCRIPT>
    </HEAD>
    <BODY>
        <CENTER>
            <FORM ID="controls">
                File: <INPUT TYPE="TEXT" NAME="fname"
                        VALUE="prices.xml">
                Rate: <INPUT TYPE="TEXT" NAME="rate"
                        VALUE="0.95274" SIZE="4"><BR>
                <INPUT TYPE="BUTTON" VALUE="Convert"
                 ONCLICK="convert(controls,xml)">
                <INPUT TYPE="BUTTON" VALUE="Clear"
                 ONCLICK="output.value=''"><BR>
                <!-- need one character in the text area -->
                <TEXTAREA NAME="output" ROWS="22" COLS="70" READONLY>
                </TEXTAREA>
            </FORM>
            <xml id="xml"></xml>
        </CENTER>
    </BODY>
</HTML>
```

Listing 9.2 is familiar from Chapter 7. Listing 9.3 is the JavaScript file, conversion.js, where the real action takes place. Figure 9.1 shows the result in a browser.

Listing 9.3: JavaScript Code

```
function convert(form,xmldocument)
{
    var fname = form.fname.value,
        output = form.output,
        rate = form.rate.value;

    output.value = "";

    var document = parse(fname,xmldocument),
        topLevel = document.documentElement;
    walkNode(topLevel,document,rate);

    addHeader(document,rate);

    output.value = document.xml;
}

function parse(uri,xmldocument)
{
    xmldocument.async = false;
    xmldocument.load(uri);

    if(xmldocument.parseError.errorCode != 0)
        alert(xmldocument.parseError.reason);

    return xmldocument;
}

function walkNode(node,document,rate)
{
    if(node.nodeType == 1)
    {
        if(node.nodeName == "product")
            walkProduct(node,document,rate);
        else
        {
            var children,
                i;
```

```
            children = node.childNodes;
            for(i = 0;i < children.length;i++)
                walkNode(children.item(i),document,rate);
        }
    }
}


function walkProduct(node,document,rate)
{
    if(node.nodeType == 1 && node.nodeName == "product")
    {
        var price,
            children,
            i;
        children = node.childNodes;
        for(i = 0;i < children.length;i++)
        {
            var child = children.item(i);
            if(child.nodeType == 1)
                if(child.nodeName == "price")
                    price = child;
        }
        // append the new child after looping to avoid infinite loop
        var element = document.createElement("price"),
            text = document.createTextNode(getText(price) * rate);
        element.setAttribute("currency","eur");
            element.appendChild(text);
        node.appendChild(element);
            price.setAttribute("currency","usd");
    }
}


function addHeader(document,rate)
{
    var comment = document.createComment(
                    "Rate used for this conversion: " + rate),
        stylesheet = document.createProcessingInstruction(
                    "xml-stylesheet",
```

continues

Listing 9.3: continued

```
                              "href=\"prices.css\" type=\"text/css\""),
        topLevel = document.documentElement;
    document.insertBefore(comment,topLevel);
    document.insertBefore(stylesheet,comment);
}


function getText(node)
{
    return node.firstChild.data;
}
```

OUTPUT

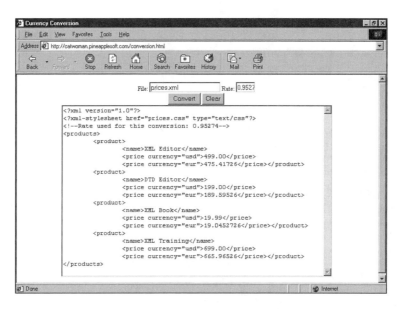

Figure 9.1: *Result in a browser*

This example displays the XML document in a form. The section "Doing Something with the XML Documents" explains how to save it.

Inserting Nodes

EXAMPLE

1. Most of Listing 9.3 is familiar. It walks through the price list and converts prices from American dollars to Euros. The novelty is that it inserts a new price element in the price list with the price in Euros. It also adds a `currency` attribute to every price element.

```
function walkProduct(node,document,rate)
{
    if(node.nodeType == 1 && node.nodeName == "product")
    {
        var price,
            children,
            i;
        children = node.childNodes;
        for(i = 0;i < children.length;i++)
        {
            var child = children.item(i);
            if(child.nodeType == 1)
                if(child.nodeName == "price")
                    price = child;
        }
        // append the new child after looping to avoid infinite loop
        var element = document.createElement("price"),
            text = document.createTextNode(getText(price) * rate);
        element.setAttribute("currency","eur");
            element.appendChild(text);
        node.appendChild(element);
            price.setAttribute("currency","usd");
    }
}
```

The DOM Document object has methods to create elements, comments, text nodes, processing instruction, and so on. The walkProduct() function uses both createElement() and createTextNode().

The DOM Node object has methods for adding and removing objects from the document tree. Because most DOM objects are derived from Node, they inherit these methods. The walkProduct() function uses appendChild() to insert the new nodes.

Finally, Element has a setAttribute() method that creates new attributes.

CAUTION
Don't add children to a node while looping through them, or you will create an infinite loop.

EXAMPLE

2. While modifying the document, it is easy to attach a style sheet to it. The addHeader() function appends a small header at the beginning of the document with a style sheet and a comment.

```
function addHeader(document,rate)
{
    var comment = document.createComment(
                        "Rate used for this conversion: " + rate),
        stylesheet = document.createProcessingInstruction(
                        "xml-stylesheet",
                        "href=\"prices.css\" type=\"text/css\""),
        topLevel = document.documentElement;
    document.insertBefore(comment,topLevel);
    document.insertBefore(stylesheet,comment);
}
```

To attach a style sheet, you can simply create a processing instruction. addHeader() uses insertBefore() to control where the new nodes are being added.

Saving As XML

EXAMPLE

Unfortunately, the current DOM recommendation does not specify how to retrieve the actual XML markup from the XML island. In the Microsoft implementation, the Document object has an xml property.

```
var document = parse(fname,xmldocument),
    topLevel = document.documentElement;
walkNode(topLevel,document,rate);


addHeader(document,rate);


output.value = document.xml;
```

CAUTION

Theoretically, it should be possible to modify an XML document that is being displayed by the browser. However, in practice, the support for DOM is not strong enough.

With Internet Explorer, true support for DOM is limited to XML islands. As you saw in Chapter 7, documents being displayed are also available as DOM objects. However, it is not possible to manipulate these DOM trees. This limitation will probably be fixed in future versions of the browsers.

DOM Methods to Create and Modify Documents

This section defines properties and methods of DOM that are related to document manipulation. These methods and properties are in addition to the properties introduced in Chapter 7.

✔ You will find the original list of methods and properties in the section "Getting Started with DOM" in Chapter 7 (page 198).

Document

In addition to the properties introduced in Chapter 7, Document defines the following methods:

- createAttribute(name) creates an Attr object called name.
- createCDATASection(data) creates a CDATASection object with the data.
- createComment(data) creates a Comment object.
- createDocumentFragment() creates an empty DocumentFragment object.
- createElement(name) creates an Element object.
- createEntityReference(name) creates an EntityReference object called name.
- createProcessingInstruction(target,data) creates a ProcessingInstruction object for the target.
- createTextNode(data) creates a TextNode object.

Node

Node defines the following methods for adding and removing objects to or from the document tree. Because many DOM objects are derived from Node, they inherit these methods:

- appendChild(child) appends child to the end of the list of the children.
- insertBefore(child,before) appends child before before. before must be a child of the node.
- replaceChild(child,toReplace) replaces toReplace with child; toReplace must be a child of the node.
- removeChild(child) removes child from the node's children.
- cloneNode(deep) creates a copy of the node. If deep is true, it also clones all the children of the node recursively.

- hasChildNodes() returns true if the node has children; false otherwise.

CharacterData

CharacterData defines the following methods. These methods are inherited by Text, Comment, and CDATASection:

- appendData(data) appends data at the end of the text.
- insertData(offset,data) inserts data in the current text starting at offset.
- deleteData(offset,length) deletes length characters starting at offset.
- replaceData(offset,length,data) inserts data in place of the characters at offset for a length.
- substringData(offset,length) returns the characters starting at offset for a length.

Element

Element has the following methods for manipulating the XML document:

- setAttribute(name,value) creates an attribute called name with the value.
- setAttribute(attr) adds an Attr object to the element.
- getAttribute(name) returns the value of the attribute called name.
- removeAttribute(name) removes the attribute called name from the element.
- setAttributeNode(attr)/getAttributeNode(name)/ removeAttributeNode(attr) are similar to setAttribute(), getAttribute(), and removeAttribute() except that they accept or return Attr objects.

NOTE

There are two solutions for creating attributes:

- Create the attribute with Document.createAttribute() and attach it to the element with setAttribute().
- Create the element and attach it to the element in one step with Element.setAttribute().

Text

Text inherits its properties and methods from CharacterData. It defines one new method for manipulating the XML document:

> splitText(offset) splits the Text object in two Text objects. The new objects replace the existing one in the tree.

Creating a New Document with DOM

EXAMPLE

In most cases, applications use DOM to modify existing documents. However, DOM can also create documents from scratch as Listings 9.4 and 9.5 illustrate.

Listing 9.4: HTML for Price List Creation

```
<HTML>
    <HEAD>
        <TITLE>Price List Editor</TITLE>
        <SCRIPT LANGUAGE="JavaScript" SRC="createlist.js"></SCRIPT>
    </HEAD>
    <BODY>
        <CENTER>
            <FORM ID="controls">
                Product name: <INPUT TYPE="TEXT" NAME="name">
                Price: <INPUT TYPE="TEXT" NAME="price" SIZE="7">
                <SELECT NAME="currency">
                    <OPTION VALUE="eur">Euros</OPTION>
                    <OPTION VALUE="usd" SELECTED>Dollars</OPTION>
                </SELECT><BR>
                <INPUT TYPE="BUTTON" VALUE="Create"
                 ONCLICK="create(controls,xml)">
                <INPUT TYPE="BUTTON" VALUE="Clear"
                 ONCLICK="resetAll(controls,xml)"><BR>
                <!-- there must be one character in the text area -->
                <TEXTAREA NAME="output" ROWS="22" COLS="70" READONLY>
                </TEXTAREA>
            </FORM>
            <xml id="xml"></xml>
        </CENTER>
    </BODY>
</HTML>
```

Listing 9.5: JavaScript to Create a Document

```
function create(form,document)
{
    var name = form.name.value,
        price = form.price.value,
        currency = form.currency.value,
        output = form.output;


    var topLevel = getTopLevel(document);


    var elementProduct = document.createElement("product");
        elementName = document.createElement("name"),
        elementPrice = document.createElement("price");


    elementPrice.setAttribute("currency",currency);


    var text = document.createTextNode(name);
    elementName.appendChild(text);


    text = document.createTextNode(price);
    elementPrice.appendChild(text);


    elementProduct.appendChild(elementName);
    elementProduct.appendChild(elementPrice);


    topLevel.appendChild(elementProduct);


    output.value = "";
    output.value = document.xml;
}


function getTopLevel(document)
{
    var topLevel = document.documentElement;
    if(topLevel == null)
    {
        topLevel = document.createElement("products");
        document.appendChild(topLevel);
```

```
   }
   return topLevel;
}

function resetAll(form,document)
{
   var topLevel = document.documentElement;
   document.removeChild(topLevel);
   var output = form.output;
   output.value = "";
}
```

To create a new element in the XML document, the user enters the product name and prices in dollars and in Euros and presses the Create button. The result is available in the text area. Figure 9.2 shows the result in a browser.

OUTPUT

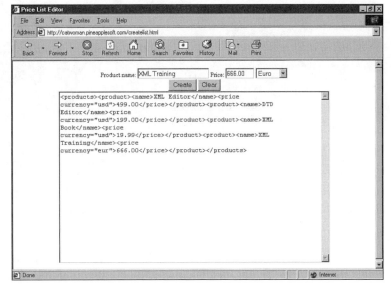

Figure 9.2: *The application in a browser*

EXAMPLE

Creating Nodes

The following application simply creates new DOM objects and inserts them in the document tree. It takes care to insert the new elements in the appropriate order. Except that there are more elements to create, this process is very similar to modifying an existing document.

```
function create(form,document)
{
    var name = form.name.value,
        price = form.price.value,
        currency = form.currency.value,
        output = form.output;

    var topLevel = getTopLevel(document);

    var elementProduct = document.createElement("product");
        elementName = document.createElement("name"),
        elementPrice = document.createElement("price");

    elementPrice.setAttribute("currency",currency);

    var text = document.createTextNode(name);
    elementName.appendChild(text);

    text = document.createTextNode(price);
    elementPrice.appendChild(text);

    elementProduct.appendChild(elementName);
    elementProduct.appendChild(elementPrice);

    topLevel.appendChild(elementProduct);

    output.value = "";
    output.value = document.xml;
}
```

Creating the Top-Level Element

EXAMPLE

Initially the Document is empty. The application must create the top-level element in the getTopLevel() function. Upon first call, it creates a top-level element. On subsequent invocations, it returns the top-level element.

```
function getTopLevel(document)
{
    var topLevel = document.documentElement;
    if(topLevel == null)
```

```
    {
        topLevel = document.createElement("products");
        document.appendChild(topLevel);
    }
    return topLevel;
}
```

Note that the top-level element is a child of the Document so it is added to the document tree with appendChild(). The only difference is that there is only one document element. Calling appendChild() with two different Elements results in an error.

Using DOM to Create Documents

It is very easy to create or modify XML documents with DOM. The parser creates a Document object and you can use it to add (or modify) objects to the document tree.

The main advantage to using DOM is the same reason you use a parser in the first place: It shields the application from the XML syntax.

The parser also enforces syntactical rules: It accepts only one element at the top level. Unfortunately, DOM level 1 does not support DTDs; therefore, it is not possible to force the parser to validate a document as it is being created. Hopefully, DOM level 2 will make this possible.

On the downside, the application has to explicitly create the DOM tree for the document. As always, it is inefficient if the application already has its own data structure. In this case, it might be more efficient to skip DOM and write the XML document directly from the application's own data structure.

Creating Documents Without DOM

EXAMPLE

It is not difficult to write XML documents without the help of a parser/generator. The core syntax (which is what most applications use) is not complex.

Listings 9.6 and 9.7 show an application that manages a list of products in an HTML form. Users can add or remove products from the list. The application has its own data structure, but it can export the list in XML.

Listing 9.6: The HTML Form

```
<HTML>
    <HEAD>
        <TITLE>Price List Editor</TITLE>
        <SCRIPT LANGUAGE="JavaScript" SRC="createlist.js"></SCRIPT>
    </HEAD>
    <BODY>
        <CENTER>
            <!-- NAME works with Netscape & IE -->
            <FORM NAME="controls">
                Product name: <INPUT TYPE="TEXT" NAME="name">
                Price (Dollars): <INPUT TYPE="TEXT"
                                    NAME="dollarsamount" SIZE="7">
                Price (Euros): <INPUT TYPE="TEXT"
                                    NAME="eurosamount" SIZE="7"><BR>
                <SELECT NAME="productlist" SIZE="5" WIDTH="250">
                </SELECT><BR>
                <INPUT TYPE="BUTTON" VALUE="Add"
                 ONCLICK="addProduct(controls)">
                <INPUT TYPE="BUTTON" VALUE="Delete"
                 ONCLICK="deleteProduct(controls)">
                <INPUT TYPE="BUTTON" VALUE="Export to XML"
                 ONCLICK="exportProduct(controls)">
                <INPUT TYPE="BUTTON" VALUE="Clear"
                 ONCLICK="output.value=''"><BR>
                <!-- there must be one character in the text area -->
                <TEXTAREA NAME="output" ROWS="12" COLS="50" READONLY>
                </TEXTAREA>
            </FORM>
        </CENTER>
    </BODY>
</HTML>
```

Listing 9.7: The JavaScript Code

```
var products = new Array();

function addProduct(form)
{
    // collects data from the form
```

```
    var name = form.name.value,
        dollars = form.dollarsamount.value,
        euros = form.eurosamount.value,
        productList = form.productlist;

    // creates the various objects required
    var dollarsPrice = new Price(dollars,"usd"),
        eurosPrice = new Price(euros,"eur"),
        prices = new Array(dollarsPrice,eurosPrice),
        product = new Product(name,prices);

    // arrays are zero-based so products.length points
    // to one past the latest product
    // JavaScript automatically allocates memory
    var pos = products.length;
    products[pos] = product;

    var option = new Option(name,pos);

    productList.options[productList.length] = option;
}

function deleteProduct(form)
{
    var productList = form.productlist,
        pos = productList.selectedIndex;

    if(pos != -1)
    {
        var product = productList.options[pos].value;
        productList.options[pos] = null;
        products[product] = null;
    }
}

function exportProduct(form)
{
```

continues

Listing 9.6: continued

```
    form.output.value = makeXML();
}


function send()
{
    var http = new ActiveXObject("Microsoft.XMLHTTP");
    http.open("POST","http://catwoman.pineapplesoft.com/Dump",false);
    http.setRequestHeader("Content-type","application/xml");
    http.send("value=" + makeXML());
    document.open();
    document.write(http.responseText);
}


function makeXML()
{
    var xmlCode = "";

    var i;
    for(i = 0;i < products.length;i++)
        if(products[i] != null)
            xmlCode += products[i].toXML();

    return element("products","",xmlCode);
}


function resetAll(form,document)
{
    priceList = null;
    form.output.value = "";
}


function element(name,attributes,content)
{
    var result = "<" + name;
    if(attributes != "")
        result += " " + attributes;
    result += ">";
```

```
        result += content;
        result += "</" + name + ">\r";
        return result;
}


function escapeXML(string)
{
    var result = "",
        i,
        c;
    for(i = 0;i < string.length;i++)
    {
        c = string.charAt(i);
        if(c == '<')
            result += "&lt;";
        else if(c == '&')
            result += "&amp;";
        else
            result += c;
    }
    return result;
}


// declares two JavaScript objects

// product object

function Product(name,prices)
{
    this.name = name;
    this.prices = prices;
    this.toXML = product_toXML;
}


function product_toXML()
{
    var result = element("name","",escapeXML(this.name)),
```

continues

Listing 9.6: continued
```
      i;
   for(i = 0;i < this.prices.length;i++)
      result += this.prices[i].toXML();
   return element("product","",result);
}


// price object

function Price(amount,currency)
{
   this.amount = amount;
   this.currency = currency;
   this.toXML = price_toXML;
}


function price_toXML()
{
   return element("price",
                  "currency=\"" + this.currency + "\"",
                  escapeXML(this.amount));
}
```

OUTPUT

Because this application does not use DOM, it works with browsers that have no XML support (obviously, they need to support JavaScript), such as Netscape 4. Figure 9.3 shows the result in Netscape.

A Non-DOM Data Structure

This application is radically different from the other applications introduced in this chapter. Internally, the application does not use XML, but uses its own data structure instead. In other words, it does not create Element objects; it creates Product and Price JavaScript objects.

In JavaScript, an object constructor is simply a function that sets the object properties. A method is a property that is assigned a function.

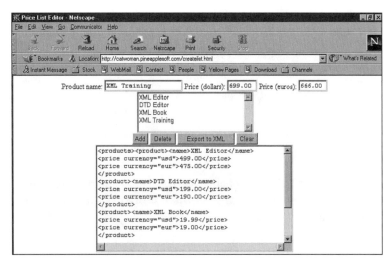

Figure 9.3: *The result in Netscape*

In this example, the constructor for Product declares two properties (name and prices) and one method (toXML).

```
function Product(name,prices)
{
    this.name = name;
    this.prices = prices;
    this.toXML = product_toXML;
}
```

These objects are created with the new operator like built-in JavaScript objects:

```
var product = new Product(name,prices);
```

JavaScript objects are used like built-in objects:

```
xmlCode += products[i].toXML();
```

Writing XML

EXAMPLE

The Product and Price objects are XML-aware because they know how to save (serialize) themselves as XML objects through the toXML() function. The makeXML() function is trivial: It iterates over the list of products calling the toXML() function. It wraps the result in a products element:

```
function makeXML()
{
    var xmlCode = "";
```

```
   var i;
   for(i = 0;i < products.length;i++)
      if(products[i] != null)
         xmlCode += products[i].toXML();


   return element("products","",xmlCode);
}
```

Notice that this approach is recursive. Product implements its toXML() method partly by serializing the list of Price and wrapping it in a product element.

```
function product_toXML()
{
   var result = element("name","",escapeXML(this.name)),
       i;
   for(i = 0;i < this.prices.length;i++)
      result += this.prices[i].toXML();
   return element("product","",result);
}

function price_toXML()
{
   return element("price",
                  "currency=\"" + this.currency + "\"",
                  escapeXML(this.amount));
}
```

XML is a convenient format because elements can nest in a way that is very similar to how objects are referenced by other objects.

Hiding the Syntax

This application needs to know very little about the XML syntax. Its knowledge is completely encapsulated in two functions—element() and escapeXML().

EXAMPLE

1. element() is in charge of the tagging. Again, the core XML syntax function is simple and it shows in this function.

```
function element(name,attributes,content)
{
   var result = "<" + name;
```

```
    if(attributes != "")
        result += " " + attributes;
    result += ">";
    result += content;
    result += "</" + name + ">\r";
    return result;
}
```

EXAMPLE

2. escapeXML() ensures that the angle bracket and ampersand characters are escaped. These characters are not allowed in the text of an element.

```
function escapeXML(string)
{
    var result = "",
        i,
        c;
    for(i = 0;i < string.length;i++)
    {
        c = string.charAt(i);
        if(c == '<')
            result += "&lt;";
        else if(c == '&')
            result += "&amp;";
        else
            result += c;
    }
    return result;
}
```

Creating Documents from Non-XML Data Structures

For most applications, it is easy to write an XML generator. Indeed, the core XML syntax (essentially composed of tags) is not complex. Furthermore, XML elements nest in a way that is very convenient for object-oriented applications.

Typically, creating documents from non-XML data structures is more efficient than the DOM-based approach because the application doesn't have to duplicate its data structure. Figure 9.4 compares the two approaches.

TIP

So, when do you use DOM and when do you write your own generator? I find that DOM is ideal for modifying existing documents. In most other cases, I prefer my own generator.

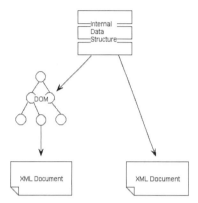

Figure 9.4: *Comparing DOM with an ad hoc generator*

Doing Something with the XML Documents

Now that you can create XML documents, you probably want to do something more involved than display the XML code in an HTML form. In most cases, the application can either save the document to a file or send it to a server.

> ✔ This section looks briefly at your options to save the document or send it to the server. We will revisit this topic in Chapter 12, "Putting It All Together: An e-Commerce Example," (page 381).

Sending the Document to the Server

There are two options to send the document to the server. You can place the XML document in an HTML form and have it sent along with the form, you can use a JavaBean or an ActiveX control to post the XML document to the Web server.

1. Sending the XML document in a form is the most portable approach. Because you already create the XML document in a form, this is easy to do. The FORM tag needs an ACTION attribute and the INPUT field must be changed from BUTTON to SUBMIT. You might also want to change the TEXTAREA in a HIDDEN field so XML does not appear onscreen:

Listing 9.8: HTML Form to Send the Document

```
<FORM NAME="controls" ACTION="/Dump" METHOD="POST">
    Product name: <INPUT TYPE="TEXT" NAME="name">
    Price (Dollars): <INPUT TYPE="TEXT"
                            NAME="dollarsamount" SIZE="7">
    Price (Euros): <INPUT TYPE="TEXT"
                        NAME="eurosamount" SIZE="7"><BR>
    <SELECT NAME="productlist" SIZE="5" WIDTH="250">
    </SELECT><BR>
    <INPUT TYPE="BUTTON" VALUE="Add"
            ONCLICK="addProduct(controls)">
    <INPUT TYPE="BUTTON" VALUE="Delete"
            ONCLICK="deleteProduct(controls)">
    <INPUT TYPE="SUBMIT" VALUE="Send in XML"
            ONCLICK="exportProduct(controls)">
    <INPUT TYPE="BUTTON" VALUE="Clear"
            ONCLICK="output.value=''"><BR>
    <!-- there must be one character in the text area -->
    <INPUT TYPE="HIDDEN" NAME="output" VALUE="">
</FORM>
```

The Web server will receive the XML document in a parameter called "output." You would have to write a servlet or a CGI script to retrieve the document on the Web server. The beauty of this approach is that the document is returned in a form so the servlet simply accesses form parameters to retrieve the XML document.

✔ The section "Viewer and Editor" in Chapter 12 (page 444) shows such a servlet.

CAUTION

This example uses the Dump service that comes standard with Jetty, the Web server. Dump replies with a document that contains whatever it originally received. It is convenient for testing.

If you don't use Jetty, you will need to write your own servlet to accept the XML document.

✔ The section "Servlet Engine" in Appendix A explains how to install Jetty (page 460).

Alternatively, you can post the data directly to the Web server, without going through a form. This method has the added benefit of not changing the current page. However, you have to go through an ActiveX object

(Internet Explorer), a plug-in (all browsers), or a JavaBean (all browsers, all platforms).

EXAMPLE

2. Internet Explorer 5.0 ships with XMLHTTP, an ActiveX control that can send XML documents from JavaScript. Listing 9.9 shows how to use XMLHTTP.

Listing 9.9: Posting the Result on a Web Site

```
function send()
{
    var http = new ActiveXObject("Microsoft.XMLHTTP");
    http.open("POST","http://catwoman.pineapplesoft.com/Dump",false);
    http.setRequestHeader("Content-type","application/xml");
    http.send(makeXML());
    document.open();
    document.write(http.responseText);
}
```

The ActiveX object has the following methods:

- open(protocol,url,asynchronous) connects to a url. Set the protocol to POST. Set asynchronous to false to send synchronously.

- setRequestHeader(keyword,value) adds a new keyword in the header of the document; you must use this function to set the content-type.

- send(data) posts the data to the server.

You need to change the "Send in XML" button in Listing 9.9 to call this function:

```
<INPUT TYPE="SUBMIT" VALUE="Send in XML" ONCLICK="send()">
```

Again, you need a servlet or CGI script on the server to receive the XML document.

OUTPUT

The URL http://catwoman.pineapplesoft.com/Dump points the Dump service on my machine. You will need to change this URL to your Web server. Listing 9.10 is a typical response from the server.

TIP

Jetty's Dump returns an HTML document that contains the POST parameters. Choose "View Source" in your browser options to see the XML document.

Listing 9.10: XML Document Returned by the Server

```
<products><product><name>XML Editor</name>
<price currency="usd">499.00</price>
<price currency="eur">475.00</price>
```

```
</product>

<product><name>DTD Editor</name>

<price currency="usd">199.00</price>

<price currency="eur">190</price>

</product>

<product><name>XML Book</name>

<price currency="usd">19.99</price>

<price currency="eur">19.00</price>

</product>

<product><name>XML Training</name>

<price currency="usd">699.00</price>

<price currency="eur">666.00</price>

</product>

</products>
```

Saving the Document

JavaScript applications cannot access the local hard disk unless they have been signed. Therefore, it is not common to save the XML in a file on a browser.

However, on the server, you often want to save XML documents. If you created the file with your own generator, you save it like any other file.

When creating a document with a Microsoft DOM parser, you use a Microsoft-specific extension to save the document. Microsoft parser supports the save() function.

However, as I have just explained, this extension does not work on the browser. It is therefore only useful when writing CGI scripts or ASP pages. The example in Listing 9.11 shows how to save a file from JavaScript in an ASP server.

Listing 9.11: Saving the XML Document

```
<%
  var xmldoc = new ActiveXObject("Microsoft.XMLDOM");
  // creates the XML document here
  // ...
  xmldoc.save(Server.MapPath("request.xml"));
%>
```

NOTE

To create an XML parser from ASP, you cannot use an XML island. Instead create the XML parser directly as an ActiveXObject as in

```
var xmldoc = new ActiveXObject("Microsoft.XMLDOM");
```

This is equivalent to creating an XML island on a browser.

Writing with Flexibility in Mind

One of the major advantages of XML is that it is extensible. Anyone can create a tagging language with tags specific to the application.

On the other hand, it means applications must be able to support different DTDs. For example, your company can have its own DTDs for internal exchange. However, when exchanging documents with other companies, you may have to use another DTD.

There are also so-called standard DTDs developed by various standardization committees. In fact, developing DTDs has become a favorite activity in standard bodies lately, so expect more in the future. Unfortunately, so many committees are actively developing standards that you may have to support several incompatible standards.

There are essentially two solutions to this problem. Either you define several toXML() functions, one for each DTD that you want to support, or you turn to XSLT.

In most cases, I would advocate using XSLT. It is a waste of time to write as many functions as there are DTDs. XSLT is also more flexible because you don't have to write code to add new DTDs or when a DTD changes (and it happens more often than you might think).

Supporting Several DTDs with XSLT

EXAMPLE

Listings 9.12 and 9.13 show how to use XSLT to support several DTDs. The user chooses the DTD from a list box. Unlike the previous version, this version uses the XSL processor of Internet Explorer. It will not run on Netscape.

TIP

If you need to support both browsers, you can replace the Internet Explorer XSL processor with LotusXSL.

LotusXSL comes with several examples that show how to use it in a browser. However, it is not as stable as using the built-in XSL processor. If at all possible, stick to Internet Explorer.

Listing 9.12: The HTML Code

```html
<HTML>
    <HEAD>
        <TITLE>Price List Editor</TITLE>
        <SCRIPT LANGUAGE="JavaScript" SRC="createlist.js"></SCRIPT>
    </HEAD>
    <BODY>
        <CENTER>
            <FORM NAME="controls">
                Product name: <INPUT TYPE="TEXT" NAME="name">
                Price (Dollars): <INPUT TYPE="TEXT"
                                    NAME="dollarsamount" SIZE="7">
                Price (Euros): <INPUT TYPE="TEXT"
                                    NAME="eurosamount" SIZE="7"><BR>
                <SELECT NAME="productlist" SIZE="5" WIDTH="250">
                </SELECT><BR>
                <INPUT TYPE="BUTTON" VALUE="Add"
                 ONCLICK="addProduct(controls)">
                <INPUT TYPE="BUTTON" VALUE="Delete"
                 ONCLICK="deleteProduct(controls)">
                <INPUT TYPE="BUTTON" VALUE="Export to XML"
                 ONCLICK="exportProduct(controls,xml,xslt)">
                <SELECT NAME="format">
                    <OPTION VALUE="default" SELECTED>products</OPTION>
                    <OPTION VALUE="external">price-list</OPTION>
                </SELECT>
                <INPUT TYPE="BUTTON" VALUE="Clear"
                 ONCLICK="output.value=''"><BR>
                <!-- there must be one character in the text area -->
                <TEXTAREA NAME="output" ROWS="12" COLS="50" READONLY>
                </TEXTAREA>
            </FORM>
        </CE_TER>
        <xml id="xml"></xml>
        <xml id="xslt" src="convert.xsl"></xml>
    </BODY>
</HTML>
```

Listing 9.13: The JavaScript Code

```
var products = new Array();

function addProduct(form)
{
   // collects data from the form
   var name = form.name.value,
       dollars = form.dollarsamount.value,
       euros = form.eurosamount.value,
       productList = form.productlist;

   // creates the various objects required
   var dollarsPrice = new Price(dollars,"usd"),
       eurosPrice = new Price(euros,"eur"),
       prices = new Array(dollarsPrice,eurosPrice),
       product = new Product(name,prices);

   // arrays are zero-based so products.length points
   // to one past the latest product
   // JavaScript automatically allocates memory
   var pos = products.length;
   products[pos] = product;

   var option = new Option(name,pos);

   productList.options[productList.length] = option;
}

function deleteProduct(form)
{
   var productList = form.productlist,
       pos = productList.selectedIndex;

   if(pos != -1)
   {
      var product = productList.options[pos].value;
      productList.options[pos] = null;
      products[product] = null;
```

```
      }
  }


  function exportProduct(form,xml,xslt)
  {
     var selected = form.format.selectedIndex,
         format = form.format.options[selected].value;

     if(format == "default")
        form.output.value = makeXML();
     else
     {
        var xmlDoc = makeXML();
        xml.async = false;
        // passes an XML string to the parser
        xml.loadXML(xmlDoc);
        form.output.value = xml.transformNode(xslt.XMLDocument);
     }
  }


  function send()
  {
     var http = new ActiveXObject("Microsoft.XMLHTTP");
     http.open("POST","http://catwoman.pineapplesoft.com/Dump",false);
     http.setRequestHeader("Content-type","application/xml");
     http.send("value=" + makeXML());
     document.open();
     document.write(http.responseText);
  }


  function makeXML()
  {
     var xmlCode = "";

     var i;
     for(i = 0;i < products.length;i++)
        if(products[i] != null)
```

continues

Listing 9.13: continued

```
            xmlCode += products[i].toXML();


  return element("products","",xmlCode);
}


function resetAll(form,document)
{
   priceList = null;
   form.output.value = "";
}


function element(name,attributes,content)
{
   var result = "<" + name;
   if(attributes != "")
       result += " " + attributes;
   result += ">";
   result += content;
   result += "</" + name + ">\r";
   return result;
}


function escapeXML(string)
{
   var result = "",
       i,
       c;
   for(i = 0;i < string.length;i++)
   {
      c = string.charAt(i);
      if(c == '<')
          result += "&lt;";
      else if(c == '&')
          result += "&amp;";
      else
          result += c;
   }
```

```
      return result;
}


// declares two JavaScript objects
// product object

function Product(name,prices)
{
   this.name = name;
   this.prices = prices;
   this.toXML = product_toXML;
}


function product_toXML()
{
   var result = element("name","",escapeXML(this.name)),
       i;
   for(i = 0;i < this.prices.length;i++)
      result += this.prices[i].toXML();
   return element("product","",result);
}


// price object

function Price(amount,currency)
{
   this.amount = amount;
   this.currency = currency;
   this.toXML = price_toXML;
}


function price_toXML()
{
   return element("price",
                  "currency=\"" + this.currency + "\"",
                  this.amount);
}
```

The application outputs a default XML format. The style sheet in Listing 9.14 does the conversion. Obviously, it is an Internet Explorer style sheet. As explained in Chapter 5, "XSL Transformation," this style sheet is not strictly compliant with the standard but it would not take too much work to adapt it.

Listing 9.14: The Style Sheet

```
<?xml version="1.0" encoding="ISO-8859-1"?>


<!-- I.E. 5.0 style sheet: no built-in rule and old URI-->


<xsl:stylesheet xmlns:xsl="http://www.w3.org/TR/WD-xsl">


<xsl:template match="/">
   <xsl:apply-templates/>
</xsl:template>


<xsl:template match="products">
   <price-list>
      <xsl:apply-templates/>
   </price-list>
</xsl:template>


<xsl:template match="product">
   <xsl:apply-templates/>
</xsl:template>


<xsl:template match="price">
   <line>
      <xsl:attribute name="name"><xsl:value-of select="../name"/>
➥</xsl:attribute>
      <xsl:attribute name="price"><xsl:value-of select="."/>
➥</xsl:attribute>
      <xsl:attribute name="currency">
➥<xsl:value-of select="@currency"/></xsl:attribute>
   </line>
</xsl:template>


</xsl:stylesheet>
```

Figures 9.5 and 9.6 illustrate the difference between the two DTDs. Figure 9.5 is the structure created so far—it is a complex structure with several levels of nesting. Figure 9.6, on the other hand, has a flat structure.

Figure 9.5: The default structure *Figure 9.6: The new structure*

Figures 9.7 and 9.8 show the difference when selecting one or the other output format in the browser.

OUTPUT

Figure 9.7: Default output format *Figure 9.8: New output format*

Calling XSLT

EXAMPLE

The major difference between this application and the previous one is the `exportProduct()` function. `exportProduct()` calls `makeXML()` to generate the XML document. Depending on the user choice, it may apply an XSLT style sheet to the result.

```
function exportProduct(form,xml,xslt)

{
    var selected = form.format.selectedIndex,
        format = form.format.options[selected].value;

    if(format == "default")
        form.output.value = makeXML();
```

```
        else
        {
            var xmlDoc = makeXML();
            xml.async = false;
            // passes an XML string to the parser
            xml.loadXML(xmlDoc);
            form.output.value = xml.transformNode(xslt.XMLDocument);
        }
}
```

Unfortunately, the DOM standard does not specify how to apply an XSLT style sheet to a document. Again, you can use a browser-specific extension. For Internet Explorer, the XSL processor is called by the `transformNode()` method.

The XSLT style sheet was loaded in a separate XML island.

```
<xml id="xml"></xml>
<xml id="xslt" src="convert.xsl"></xml>
```

Which Structure for the Document?

If your application supports several DTDs, you may wonder which one to use as the default DTD. Experience shows that it pays to be dumb when designing this default DTD.

I like to define a DTD that is very similar to my object structure. So, if the application has `Product` and `Price` objects, I create two elements: `product` and `price`.

There are two main advantages to designing a DTD that is close to the internal data structure:

- It is easy to generate the XML document.

- The resulting document is as expressive as the internal data structure.

XSLT Versus Custom Functions

XSLT has been designed specifically to convert XML documents. It offers a simple solution to cleanly separate the DTD from the application code. This separation of roles offers many advantages:

- If the format changes, you don't have to change your application, only the style sheet.

- Somebody else can write and maintain the style sheet while you concentrate on the application; this is a simple solution for separating work in a team.

- After the system is in place, it's easy to provide 5, 10, or 100 style sheets.

- Conversely, you can deploy the application with only those few style sheets the users really need. Therefore, the application loads faster.

NOTE

Work is underway to automate the development of the XSLT style sheet. See, for example, XTransGen from IBM at www.alphaworks.ibm.com. This tool automatically generates the transformation between two documents following different DTDs.

What's Next

The next chapter returns to modeling. Armed with a better understanding of how to manipulate XML documents, you see how to create simple and effective DTDs.

## 10

Modeling for Flexibility

You are reaching the end of your tour of XML. In the previous chapters, you learned not only the XML syntax but also how to manipulate XML. The next two chapters are devoted to a real-life e-commerce application based on XML.

In this chapter, you review some aspects of XML flexibility. In particular, you revisit some concepts related to modeling documents. I hope the previous chapters have convinced you that XML is a flexible solution for many applications.

You have already learned some of these topics in other chapters. This discussion consolidates previous discussions. More specifically, you learn

- how to take advantage of XML extensibility through XSL and other standards

- about some standards under development by the W3C

- about warning signs that may point to problems in an XML document

- about the raging debate in the XML community: to attribute or to element?

Structured and Extensible

As you learned in Chapter 1 and as you saw demonstrated in Chapters 2 through 9, XML focuses on the structure of documents. Unlike HTML, XML encourages you to focus on the structure of the information. How you eventually use the document is derived from the structure. For example, presentation is derived from the structure.

To support the structure, XML is extensible. In practice, it means that you can define your own elements, tags, and attributes and decide how to combine them.

The challenge of making a successful XML application is to channel XML extensibility in a positive way. There are two approaches to this challenge, each with its own advantages and disadvantages:

- Limit XML extensibility.

- Build on XML extensibility as an essential part of the application.

This is the first choice to make when considering a new application. Where should you limit XML extensibility or should you build it as an essential part of the application? This chapter illustrates both cases.

Limiting XML Extensibility

EXAMPLE

1. One of the first popular applications on intranets was the address book, and for a good reason. In a large organization, people change jobs very often, or they simply move to another office.

Therefore, the phone list is rarely up-to-date. In some organizations, it would require printing a new list every morning, which might not be an option when the list is large.

By putting the information on an intranet, the maintenance and the distribution of the list are simplified dramatically. To update the list, one simply publishes a new version. And because it is Web-based, the new list is instantaneously available to everybody.

To build such a list with XML, you can create a document similar to Listing 10.1.

Listing 10.1: A Phone List in XML

```
<?xml version="1.0"?>
<phonelist>
    <person>
        <fname>Bill</fname><lname>Allen</lname>
        <extension>103</extension>
        <email>ballen@emailaholic.com</email>
    </person>
    <person>
        <fname>John</fname><lname>Doe</lname>
        <extension>101</extension>
        <email>jdoe@emailaholic.com</email>
    </person>
    <person>
        <fname>Peter</fname><lname>Fill</lname>
        <extension>105</extension>
```

```
      <email>pfill@emailaholic.com</email>
   </person>
   <person>
      <fname>Tim</fname><lname>Martin</lname>
      <extension>104</extension>
      <email>tmartin@emailaholic.com</email>
   </person>
   <person>
      <fname>Jack</fname><lname>Smith</lname>
      <extension>102</extension>
      <email>jsmith@emailaholic.com</email>
   </person>
</phonelist>
```

You publish the list using the same techniques used in Chapter 5, "XSL Transformation," to publish the newsletter. Listing 10.2 illustrates what the style sheet might look like.

Listing 10.2: The Style Sheet for the Phone List

```
<?xml version="1.0"?>
<xsl:stylesheet
    xmlns:xsl="http://www.w3.org/1999/XSL/Transform/"
    xmlns="http://www.w3.org/TR/REC-html40">


<xsl:output method="html"/>


<xsl:template match="/">
    <HTML><HEAD><TITLE>Phone List</TITLE></HEAD>
       <H1>Phone List:</H1>
       <UL><xsl:for-each select="phonelist/person">
          <LI><A><xsl:attribute
             name="HREF">mailto:<xsl:value-of select="email"/>
          </xsl:attribute><FONT SIZE="+1">
          <xsl:value-of select="fname"/><xsl:text> </xsl:text>
          <xsl:value-of select="lname"/></FONT></A><BR/>
          Extension: <xsl:value-of select="extension"/></LI>
       </xsl:for-each></UL>
       <P>Please help us maintain the list,
       <A HREF="mailto:jdoe@emailaholic.com">email me</A>
       if you move!</P>
```

continues

Listing 10.2: continued
```
      </HTML>
   </xsl:template>

</xsl:stylesheet>
```

EXAMPLE

You invoke LotusXSL as in Chapter 5 with the command:
```
java -classpath
➥c:\lotusxsl\xerces.jar;c:\lotusxsl\lotusxsl.jar
➥com.lotus.xsl.Process
➥-in phonelist.xml
➥-xsl phonelist.xsl -out phonelist.html -html
```

The result, in a browser, is shown in Figure 10.1.

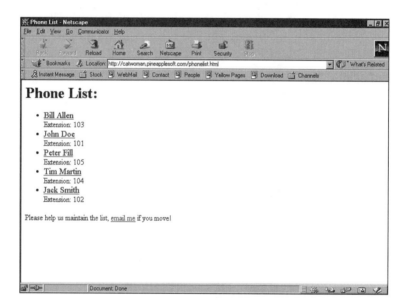

Figure 10.1: *The phone list in a browser*

EXAMPLE

2. You might want to publish the same list on your organization's Web site. The list is not only available internally but also externally. However, to limit attacks by spammers, many organizations choose not to publish email addresses. Therefore, you would use a different style sheet, such as the one shown in Listing 10.3.

Listing 10.3: Alternate Style Sheet
```
<?xml version="1.0"?>

<xsl:stylesheet
```

```
      xmlns:xsl="http://www.w3.org/1999/XSL/Transform/"
      xmlns="http://www.w3.org/TR/REC-html40">

<xsl:output method="html"/>

<xsl:template match="/">
    <HTML><HEAD><TITLE>Phone List</TITLE></HEAD>
        <H1>Phone List</H1>
        <P>Here are the direct numbers of our collaborators:</P>
        <UL><xsl:for-each select="phonelist/person">
           <LI><FONT SIZE="+1">
           <xsl:value-of select="fname"/><xsl:text> </xsl:text>
           <xsl:value-of select="lname"/></FONT><BR/>
           Tel.: 513-744-8<xsl:value-of select="extension"/></LI>
        </xsl:for-each></UL>
    </HTML>
</xsl:template>

</xsl:stylesheet>
```

Figure 10.2 shows the result of applying this style sheet.

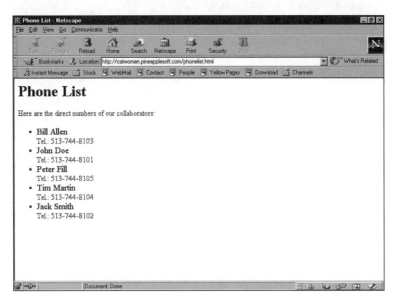

Figure 10.2: *The new list in a browser*

This simple example shows some of the benefits of maintaining the phone list in XML:

- The same document can be reused in different contexts; in this case, internal and external phone lists are produced with minimal effort.

- It is easy to change the presentation—just update the style sheet.

- Although not illustrated in the example, it is easy to maintain the list using an off-the-shelf XML editor.

- As the list grows and special needs arise, it is possible to write specialized software (using DOM or SAX) to further manipulate the list.

- If the list grows dramatically, it is possible to move to an XML database for better performance.

In other words, XML offers a high-quality off-the-shelf software application that you can use to solve a problem quickly and inexpensively.

The phone list is a perfect example of an application that does not need XML extensibility. The application is built around a specific DTD and the structure is not expected to change much for the life of the application.

The phone list is typical of most XML applications. To work, it greatly limits XML flexibility: A DTD is defined and data is made to fit it. It would not make sense for somebody to extend the list in any way.

Building on XML Extensibility

EXAMPLE

1. Some applications need a more flexible solution than used in the previous example. In particular, it might be impossible (or very difficult) to create one DTD for all the data. This is particularly true when several organizations exchange information.

Let's revisit the price comparison application from Chapter 8, "Alternative API: SAX." You will remember that the application finds the best price in an XML document such as the one shown in Listing 10.4.

Listing 10.4: A Price List in XML

```
<?xml version="1.0"?>
<product>
    <name>XML Training</name>
    <vendor>
        <name>Playfield Training</name>
        <price delivery="5">999.00</price>
        <price delivery="15">899.00</price>
    </vendor>
    <vendor>
```

```
      <name>XMLi</name>
      <price delivery="3">2999.00</price>
      <price delivery="30">1499.00</price>
      <price delivery="45">699.00</price>
   </vendor>
   <vendor>
      <name>WriteIT</name>
      <price delivery="5">799.00</price>
      <price delivery="15">899.00</price>
   </vendor>
   <vendor>
      <name>Emailaholic</name>
      <price delivery="1">1999.00</price>
   </vendor>
</product>
```

> ✔ The BestDeal application introduced in Chapter 8 compares prices and finds that XMLi
> delivers the cheapest training available in fewer than five days (page 231).

A price comparison agent such as BestDeal is really interesting when it is made available through the Internet.

The agent collects pricing information from various merchants and instantaneously computes the best deal for specific users. However, it is unlikely that merchants will want to contribute their price lists unless they receive some sort of promotion for doing so.

EXAMPLE

2. It would therefore make sense, at the minimum, to publish the list of merchants with links or additional information on the Web site.

Traditionally (without XML), this would require a fixed template that the merchants would need to fill in. For example, they could include their address or other useful information. The fixed template would look like Listing 10.5. However, you can do better thanks to XML's flexibility.

Listing 10.5: Price List with Merchant Information

```
<?xml version="1.0"?>
<product>
   <name>XML Training</name>
   <vendor>
      <name>Playfield Training</name>
      <price delivery="5">999.00</price>
```

Listing 10.5: continued

```
      <price delivery="15">899.00</price>
      <info>For more information call John Doe.</info>
   </vendor>
   <vendor>
      <name>XMLi</name>
      <price delivery="3">2999.00</price>
      <price delivery="30">1499.00</price>
      <price delivery="45">699.00</price>
      <info>XMLi is a specialist for XML training.
      Our staff has extensive practical experience.</info>
   </vendor>
   <vendor>
      <name>WriteIT</name>
      <price delivery="5">799.00</price>
      <price delivery="15">899.00</price>
      <info>We have been rated top-class by
      independent studies.</info>
   </vendor>
   <vendor>
      <name>Emailaholic</name>
      <price delivery="1">1999.00</price>
      <info>We are the fastest on the market!</info>
   </vendor>
</product>
```

EXAMPLE

3. The main limitation in Listing 10.5 is that merchants have to fit their data into the common mold. But this need not be the case. XML stands for extensible markup language so why not take advantage of its extensibility?

Listing 10.6 shows a document that a merchant might submit. To describe its services, the merchant has introduced new elements. The merchant can therefore create elements specifically to describe its products. To differentiate its elements from the common elements, the merchant uses a *namespace*.

Listing 10.6: Playfield Training Price List

```
<vendor>
   <name>Playfield Training</name>
   <price delivery="5">999.00</price>
   <price delivery="15">899.00</price>
```

```
<pt:contact
    xmlns:pt="http://www.playfield.com/product/1.0">
    <pt:name>John Doe</pt:name>
    <pt:tel>513-744-8889</pt:tel>
    <pt:email>jdoe@playfield.com</pt:email>
</pt:contact>
</vendor>
```

Each merchant submits a price list similar to Listing 10.6 and the various price lists are combined into a larger document (see Listing 10.7). Each merchant has extended the list with its own tags, in its own namespace.

Listing 10.7: Price List with Merchant-Specific Information

```
<?xml version="1.0"?>
<product>
    <name>XML Training</name>
    <vendor>
        <name>Playfield Training</name>
            <price delivery="5">999.00</price>
            <price delivery="15">899.00</price>
            <pt:contact
                xmlns:pt="http://www.playfield.com/product/1.0">
                <pt:name>John Doe</pt:name>
                <pt:tel>513-744-8889</pt:tel>
                <pt:email>jdoe@playfield.com</pt:email>
            </pt:contact>
    </vendor>
    <vendor>
        <name>XMLi</name>
        <price delivery="3">2999.00</price>
        <price delivery="30">1499.00</price>
        <price delivery="45">699.00</price>
        <xi:description xmlns:xi="http://www.xmli.com/vendor/1.5">
            XMLi is a specialist for XML training.
            Our staff has extensive practical experience.
        </xi:description>
    </vendor>
    <vendor>
        <name>WriteIT</name>
```

continues

Listing 10.7: continued

```
      <price delivery="5">799.00</price>

      <price delivery="15">899.00</price>

      <wi:rating xmlns:wi="http://www.writeit.com/r/4.5">

         <wi:p><wi:img

            href="http://www.psol.com/images/writeit.gif"/>

            We have been rated <wi:b>top-class</wi:b> by

            independent studies.</wi:p>

      </wi:rating>

   </vendor>

   <vendor>

      <name>Emailaholic</name>

      <price delivery="1">1999.00</price>

      <em:description

         xmlns:em="http://www.emailaholic.com/description/1.5">

         <em:p>We are the fastest on the market!</em:p>

         <em:p>Learn XML today!</em:p>

         <em:url>http://www.emailaholic.com</em:url>

      </em:description>

   </vendor>

</product>
```

There are two things remarkable about Listing 10.7:

- It still works with the BestDeal application from Chapter 8, "Alternative API: SAX," because it includes all the information required in the appropriate format.

- It includes additional information in the format that the merchants chose.

EXAMPLE

4. To publish this list, you need an XSLT style sheet. However, the style sheet must cope with vendor-specific tags. The easiest solution is to break the style sheet into vendor-specific style sheets and ask each vendor to contribute a style sheet for its own tags.

Listing 10.8 is the style sheet for the first vendor, *Playfield Training*. It is concerned only with Playfield's elements.

Listing 10.8: Playfield Style Sheet

```
<?xml version="1.0"?>

<xsl:stylesheet

   xmlns:pt="http://www.playfield.com/product/1.0"

   xmlns:xsl="http://www.w3.org/1999/XSL/Transform/"
```

```
        xmlns="http://www.w3.org/TR/REC-html40"
>


<xsl:template match="pt:contact">
    <P>Contact: <xsl:value-of select="pt:name"/>,
    <I><xsl:value-of select="pt:tel"/></I>,
    <A><xsl:attribute name="HREF">mailto:<xsl:value-of
    select="pt:email"/></xsl:attribute>
    <xsl:value-of select="pt:email"/></A></P>
</xsl:template>


</xsl:stylesheet>
```

Similarly, the other vendors will supply style sheets for their elements. The style sheets are shown in Listings 10.9, 10.10, and 10.11. Again, these style sheets only support the merchant-specific elements.

Listing 10.9: XMLi Style Sheet

```
<?xml version="1.0"?>
<xsl:stylesheet
    xmlns:xi="http://www.xmli.com/vendor/1.5"
    xmlns:xsl="http://www.w3.org/1999/XSL/Transform/"
    xmlns="http://www.w3.org/TR/REC-html40"
>


<xsl:template match="xi:description">
    <P><B><xsl:apply-templates/></B></P>
</xsl:template>


</xsl:stylesheet>
```

Listing 10.10: WriteIT Style Sheet

```
<?xml version="1.0"?>
<xsl:stylesheet
    xmlns:xsl="http://www.w3.org/1999/XSL/Transform/"
    xmlns="http://www.w3.org/TR/REC-html40"
    xmlns:wi="http://www.writeit.com/r/4.5"
>
```

continues

Listing 10.10: continued

```
<xsl:template match="wi:p">
    <P><xsl:apply-templates/></P>
</xsl:template>


<xsl:template match="wi:b">
    <STRONG><xsl:apply-templates/></STRONG>
</xsl:template>


<xsl:template match="wi:img">
    <IMG><xsl:attribute name="SRC"><xsl:value-of
    select="@href"/></xsl:attribute></IMG>
</xsl:template>


</xsl:stylesheet>
```

Listing 10.11: Emailaholic Style Sheet

```
<?xml version="1.0"?>
<xsl:stylesheet
    xmlns:xsl="http://www.w3.org/1999/XSL/Transform/"
    xmlns="http://www.w3.org/TR/REC-html40"
    xmlns:em="http://www.emailaholic.com/description/1.5"
>


<xsl:template match="em:description">
    <P>
        <xsl:for-each select="em:p">
            <xsl:value-of select="."/><BR/>
        </xsl:for-each>
        <A>
            <xsl:attribute name="HREF">
                <xsl:value-of select="em:url"/>
            </xsl:attribute>
            <xsl:value-of select="em:url"/>
        </A>
    </P>
</xsl:template>


</xsl:stylesheet>
```

Likewise, you also have a style sheet for the common elements. The merchants need not provide this style sheet because, by definition, it is common to all the vendors.

Listing 10.12 is the style sheet for common elements. Note that it includes an `<xsl:apply-templates/>` to start recursive processing of the subelements. This is required to ensure the subelements of `product/vendor` are being processed according to the merchant style sheets.

Listing 10.12: Style Sheet for Common Elements

```
<?xml version="1.0"?>
<xsl:stylesheet
    xmlns:xsl="http://www.w3.org/1999/XSL/Transform/"
    xmlns="http://www.w3.org/TR/REC-html40"
>

<xsl:template match="/">
    <HTML>
        <HEAD><TITLE>
            <xsl:value-of select="product/name"/>
        </TITLE></HEAD>
        <BODY>
        <xsl:for-each select="product/vendor">
            <P><xsl:value-of select="name"/></P>
            <UL><xsl:for-each select="price">
                <LI><xsl:value-of select="."/> (<xsl:value-of select="@delivery"/>
➥days)</LI>
            </xsl:for-each></UL>
            <xsl:apply-templates/>
            <HR/>
        </xsl:for-each>
        </BODY>
    </HTML>
</xsl:template>

<xsl:template match="name | price"/>

</xsl:stylesheet>
```

The final style sheet combines all these elements into one, as illustrated in Listing 10.13.

Listing 10.13: Combining All the Style Sheets

```
<?xml version="1.0"?>
<xsl:stylesheet
    xmlns:xsl="http://www.w3.org/1999/XSL/Transform/"
    xmlns="http://www.w3.org/TR/REC-html40">

<xsl:output method="html"/>

<xsl:include href="basic-product.xsl"/>
<xsl:include href="playfield.xsl"/>
<xsl:include href="xmli.xsl"/>
<xsl:include href="writeit.xsl"/>
<xsl:include href="emailaholic.xsl"/>

</xsl:stylesheet>
```

OUTPUT

Copy the XML file from Listing 10.7 in a folder along with the various vendor style sheets (Listing 10.8 to 10.13 inclusive). Use the following filenames for the style sheets: playfield.xsl, xmli.xsl, writeit.xsl, emaila-holic.xsl, basic-product.xsl and extended-product.xsl.

Use LotusXSL to apply extended-product.xsl to the XML document; extended-product.xsl automatically loads the other style sheets. The result from applying this combination of style sheets is shown in Figure 10.3.

Figure 10.4 illustrates how this application takes advantage of XML extensibility. The price list contains common elements that are required by the BestDeal application. The common elements are extended by the merchant to include merchant-specific information.

Each party has total control over its extensions and can specify how the extensions should be viewed—in this case, through a style sheet. In the next two sections, you will see other examples of applications that are being built with the same model.

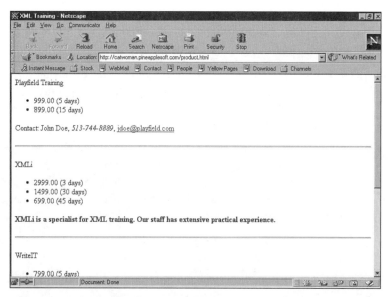

Figure 10.3: *The result in a browser*

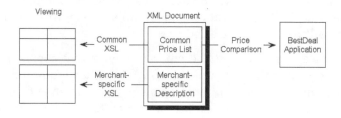

Figure 10.4: *Application architecture*

Lessons Learned

Most XML applications are similar to the phone list: There is one DTD that fully specifies the document. There are one or more style sheets and potentially other applications to process the document. The document is not extended.

However, if the document is shared by different organizations, it may be easier to adopt a more extensible approach, as illustrated by the price list application.

Theoretically, it would have been possible to devise a common DTD to accommodate the needs of all the merchants. In practice, however, this is a difficult exercise because the common DTD must take into account differences in culture between the organizations.

Furthermore, the merchants are competitors. In practice, trying to reach agreement on anything but the most basic elements might degenerate into a political fight.

Electronic Data Interchange (EDI) shows the limits of trying to build a universal data structure. The idea behind EDI is a promising one: A large number of paper documents printed by computers are rekeyed at the receiving site. Why not skip the paper?

In other words, your organization's accounting package prints invoices. The invoices are mailed to your customer, who reenters the information in his or her accounting package. Likewise for orders, delivery instructions, tax declarations, and checks. It would be more efficient to exchange the information electronically.

EDI tried to remove the paper from the equation. To that effect, a number of standards (X.12, UN/EDIFACT, Odette) were developed. These standards specified a universal electronic format for administrative and business documents.

The only problem is the universality. To accommodate the business practices of all the companies in various countries is an immense task. Remember that we are talking about different countries with radically different cultures and legislation.

In practice, the documents become so complex that people have to first simplify them before they can use them. Worse, they often find that, despite all the options, there are still missing elements. It is an endless fight for the standard to keep up with evolution. It results in too much complexity.

As you can imagine, XML has raised considerable interest in relation to EDI. One approach would be to publish simplified standards that would include only the most common subset of elements. The documents could be extended, using XML, to accommodate special needs.

In practice, this is exactly what you have just done with price lists, but on a larger scale. There is a common core of information that is small enough so it is easy to agree on the commonality. However, each party can extend the core with elements in its own namespace.

XML combines the best of both worlds: commonality where it is practical and extension or customization where it is required.

This raises many interesting questions. If each party can create its own elements, then how do you read them? One solution is to use a style sheet, as we have just done, to describe how to render the new elements.

Another solution is to use the DTD to describe the new elements and their structure. Several companies, including Microsoft, are working on mapper software. These mappers help you convert the DTD you received from a partner in a format that makes sense for you.

There are many other aspects to XML/EDI. However, it is clear that XML and EDI have a long way to go together. In 1997, I helped cofounding the XML/EDI Group. If you are interested in this topic, I encourage you to visit our Web site at www.xmledi.com.

XLink

Previous chapters have looked at some of the so-called companion XML standards such as XSL, CSS, DOM, and SAX. There are others including XLink and XPointer. XLink and XPointer are standards to express links between XML documents.

This section introduces the basics of XLink. The goals are as follows:

- to illustrate how standards can be built on the basis of extensibility

- to give you an introduction to XLink, should you need to introduce linking into your own documents

This section is not intended as a complete discussion of XLink.

CAUTION

At the time of this writing, the XLink standard is not final. Although the concepts seem stable, it is possible that the published standard will differ significantly from the material presented in this section.

The latest version of XLink is available from www.w3.org/TR/xlink.

XLink enables you to specify links between documents. It recognizes two types of links:

- *Simple links* are similar to HTML links such as the anchor tag (<A>).

- *Extended links* make it possible to link several documents.

Simple Links

1. The simple link is familiar because it closely mimics the features of HTML links. At its simplest, an XLink looks like

```
<xlink:simple xmlns:xlink="http://www.w3.org/XML/XLink/0.9"
              href="http://www.pineapplesoft.com/newsletter"
              role="newsletter"
              title="Pineapplesoft Link"
              show="replace"
              actuate="user">
   Pineapplesoft Link, free newsletter
</xlink:simple>
```

EXAMPLE

As the example illustrates, the simple link is a specific element in the XLink namespace. Browsers and other software recognize the `xlink:simple` element.

XLink needs many attributes to offer the same richness as HTML links. Some of these attributes are self-explanatory such as `href`, which is a URI. `title` is equally easy—it is a description of the link. `role` is a generic string that describes the function of the link's content.

`show` and `actuate` are not so intuitive. In HTML, there are several types of links. Take, for example:

```
<A HREF="http://www.pineapplesoft.com">Pineapplesoft</A>
<IMG SRC="http://www.pineapplesoft.com/images/logo.gif>
```

To activate the anchor element, the user must click it. When clicked, the link will replace the current document with the link content (assuming that frames are not used).

Conversely, the link in the image tag is immediately activated: The browser downloads the image when it loads the page. Furthermore, the image is integrated into the current document—it does not replace it.

`show` and `actuate` control the same behavior for XLink. The `show` attribute can have the values `new`, `parsed`, and `replace`. `new` means the browser should open a new window to display the link's content. `parsed` means the link's content should be parsed and integrated in the current document. `replace` means the browser should replace the current document with the content of the link. `replace` is the default behavior for an HTML anchor.

The `actuate` attribute can take the value `user` or `auto`. `user` means that the user must actively traverse the link whereas `auto` means the browser should automatically traverse the link when the document is being loaded.

2. There is another form of the simple link whereby the link is integrated into an existing element. Such a link is recognizable through its attributes, which are part of the XLink namespace, as in

EXAMPLE

```
<resource xmlns:xlink="http://www.w3.org/XML/XLink/0.9"
          xlink:type="simple"
          xlink:href="http://www.pineapplesoft.com/newsletter"
          xlink:role="newsletter"
          xlink:title="Pineapplesoft Link"
          xlink:show="replace"
          xlink:actuate="user">
    Pineapplesoft Link, free newsletter
</resource>
```

This link also needs the type attribute to identify whether the link is a simple link or an extended link.

TIP

To save typing, it is possible to associate default or fixed values with the attributes in the DTD of the document. As you saw in the section "Standalone Documents" in Chapter 3, using fixed attributes is not without problems. The following example illustrates how it works:

```
<?xml version="1.0"?>

<!DOCTYPE references [

<!ELEMENT references (name,link)+>

<!ELEMENT name       (#PCDATA)>

<!ELEMENT link       EMPTY>

<!ATTLIST link

    xmlns:xlink    CDATA #FIXED "http://www.w3.org/XML/XLink/0.9"

    xlink:type     (simple) #FIXED "simple"

    xlink:href     CDATA #REQUIRED

    xlink:role     CDATA #IMPLIED

    xlink:title    CDATA #IMPLIED

    xlink:show     (new¦parsed¦replace) "replace"

    xlink:actuate (user¦auto) "user">

]>

<references>

    <name>Macmillan</name>

    <link xlink:href="http://www.mcp.com"/>

    <name>Pineapplesoft Link</name>

    <link xlink:href="http://www.pineapplesoft.com/newsletter"/>

    <name>XML.com</name>

    <link xlink:href="http://www.xml.com"/>

    <name>Comics.com</name>

    <link xlink:href="http://www.comics.com"/>

    <name>Fatbrain.com</name>

    <link xlink:href="http://www.fatbrain.com"/>

    <name>ABC News</name>

    <link xlink:href="http://www.abcnews.com"/>

</references>
```

Beware that Internet Explorer 5.0 currently does not accept this notation. This is a problem specific to Internet Explorer and it will probably be fixed in a future version.

Extended Links

Extended links are more powerful. Some of the most exciting features of extended links include the capability to establish links between more than two resources and the capability to establish links that do not reside in the document.

The latter means that it is possible to maintain the links in a different document. This is useful in at least two cases:

- It is possible to store all the links from a Web site in a single, central document. This should simplify maintenance of the links (because there is only one document to search when a link must be updated) and might help reduce broken links.

- It is possible to add links to documents that cannot be modified, such as documents residing on another server or a document in non-XML format.

EXAMPLE

The following is an example of an extended link:

```
<xlink:extended xmlns:xlink="http://www.w3.org/XML/XLink/0.9"
                role="resources"
                title="Web Resources"
                showdefault="replace"
                actuatedefault="user">
    <xlink:locator href="http://www.mcp.com"
            role="resource"
            title="Macmillan"/>
    <xlink:locator href="http://www.pineapplesoft.com/newsletter"
            role="resource"
            title="Pineapplesoft Link"/>
    <xlink:locator href="http://www.xml.com"
            role="resource"
            title="XML.com"/>
    <xlink:locator href="http://www.comics.com"
            role="resource"
            title="Comics.com"/>
    <xlink:locator href="http://www.fatbrain.com"
            role="resource"
            title="Fatbrain.com"/>
    <xlink:locator href="http://www.abcnews.com"
            role="resource"
            title="ABC News"/>
</xlink:extended>
```

OUTPUT

The current generation of browsers do not support XLink, if only because the standard is not final yet. However, to render an extended link, the browser will need to offer a menu when the user clicks on the link.

Because Internet Explorer does not recognize XLink, Figures 10.5 and 10.6 simulate this behavior through an XSLT style sheet. The style sheet inserts JavaScript code that opens a new window when the user clicks the link.

Figure 10.5: *The extended link before the user clicks*

Figure 10.6: *The extended link after the user has clicked*

XLink and Browsers

XLink support will probably be added to browsers when the standard is complete. At that time, the browsers will be able to view and render the links automatically.

This feature is very similar to the price list example: A minimalist core is agreed upon (essentially, how to specify a link), just enough for the software (the browser) to process the document. This minimalist amount of standardization does not prevent the creation of other elements. Indeed, most documents will include many elements in addition to the links.

In the example of the price list, the BestDeal application picks the elements it needs for comparison, like a browser singles out links in a document. However, the document contains many other elements that are ignored by the application.

Signature

Expect more standards similar to XLink where the W3C defines elements and attributes for commonly used features. Over time, the W3C (and other groups) will build a toolbox of elements that you can use in your documents.

The signature standard currently being developed by the W3C and the IETF (Internet Engineering Task Force) is another example of this approach. Although it has nothing to do with links or product prices, it is based on the same idea of standardizing a few elements required for some application. The application is cryptographic software in this case.

Increasingly, you will need digitally signed documents. A digital signature guarantees that the document was written (or approved) by the signer.

For example, electronic prescriptions would have to be signed. If you receive a prescription from your doctor via email (don't laugh, some people are seriously considering this), you want to be sure it really originated from your doctor: You don't want anybody else to prescribe your medicine.

The same holds true for commercial and administrative documents such as orders, payments, passports, or even concert tickets. You want to be sure your tickets are valid. So does the show manager.

The xmldsig working group aims at developing a set of elements and attributes to represent digital signatures in XML documents.

The benefit of a standard set of elements and attributes is always the same: The software (such as a browser) can recognize it and automatically process it.

EXAMPLE

The work on the XML signature is still at a very preliminary stage. There is not even a draft standard, but the following example shows how XML signatures might look. This example is taken from *Digital Signatures for XML* by Richard D. Brown.

Listing 10.14: Digital Signature in an XML Document

```
<?xml version='1.0'?>
<!-- no URI has been agreed upon so far -->
<Ticket xmlns:dsig="...">
    <Body number='120456789'>
        <Event desc='concert in Austin'
               date='1999-04-12T20:30-0500'/>
        <Beneficiary name='John smith'
                     ssno='435-56-4023'/>
    </Body>
    <dsig:Signature>
        <dsig:Manifest>
            <dsig:Resources>
                <dsig:Resource>
                    <dsig:Locator href='120456789'/>
```

```
                    <dsig:Digest>
                        <dsig:Algorithm type='urn:com-globeset:xhash'/>
                        <dsig:Value encoding='base64'>
                            bndWGryrt245u6t1dgURTIrr4ir5=
                        </dsig:Value>
                    </dsig:Digest>
                </dsig:Resource>
            </dsig:Resources>
            <dsig:OriginatorInfo>
                <dsig:IssuerAndSerialNumber
                    issuer='o=GlobeSet Inc., c=US'
                    number='123456789102356'/>
            </dsig:OriginatorInfo>
            <dsig:SignatureAlgorithm>
                <dsig:Algorithm type='urn:rsasdi-com:rsa-encryption'>
                    <dsig:Parameter type='digest-algorithm'>
                        <dsig:Algorithm type='urn:globeset-com:xhash'/>
                    </dsig:Parameter>
                </dsig:Algorithm>
            </dsig:SignatureAlgorithm>
        </dsig:Manifest>
        <dsig:Value>
            xsqsfasDys2h44u4ehJDe54he5j4dJYTJ=
        </dsig:Value>
    </dsig:Signature>
    <dsig:Certificate type='urn:X500:X509v3'>
        <dsig:IssuerAndSerialNumber
            issuer='o=GlobeSet Inc., c=US'
            number='123456789102356'/>
        <dsig:Value>
            xsqsfasDys2h44u4ehJDe54he5j4dJYTJ=
        </dsig:Value>
    </dsig:Certificate>
</Ticket>
```

As you can see, the digital signature is included in the document in the form of elements in the dsig namespace. Other elements, such as Ticker and Body, are specific to the current document.

The Right Level of Abstraction

When designing XML applications and, more specifically, XML DTDs, it is not always easy to decide what to include in the markup and what to leave out. This section provides some guidance.

Destructive and Nondestructive Transformations

It takes very little effort to turn an office into a mess: just start piling old files and let documents accumulate in the inbox. In no time, the mess gets out of control. It requires continuous effort to keep the office tidy.

Unfortunately, the same is true for XML documents. It is very easy to turn an XML document in to a mess, but it is very difficult to keep it tidy. Also, it takes a lot of effort to clean up documents that have been degraded.

EXAMPLE

1. In particular, it is easy to lose information when transforming an XML document. The list of products in Listing 10.15 helps illustrate this point.

Listing 10.15: A List of Products in XML

```xml
<?xml version="1.0"?>

<products>
    <product>
        <name>XML Editor</name>
        <price>499.00</price>
    </product>
    <product>
        <name>DTD Editor</name>
        <price>199.00</price>
    </product>
    <product>
        <name>XML Book</name>
        <price>19.99</price>
    </product>
    <product>
        <name>XML Training</name>
        <price>699.00</price>
    </product>
</products>
```

Listing 10.16 is an XSLT style sheet that transforms this document into another XML document.

Listing 10.16: Style Sheet to Transform the Document

```xml
<?xml version="1.0"?>
<xsl:stylesheet xmlns:xsl="http://www.w3.org/XSL/Transform/1.0">

<xsl:template match="products">
   <products>
      <xsl:apply-templates/>
   </products>
</xsl:template>

<xsl:template match="product">
   <product>
      <xsl:attribute name="name">
         <xsl:value-of select="name"/>
      </xsl:attribute>
      <xsl:attribute name="price">
         <xsl:value-of select="price"/>
      </xsl:attribute>
   </product>
</xsl:template>

</xsl:stylesheet>
```

Listing 10.17 shows the result of applying the style sheet to the product list.

Listing 10.17: The XML Document Created by the Style Sheet

OUTPUT

```xml
<?xml version="1.0"?>
<products>
   <product name="XML Editor"
            price="499.00"/>
   <product name="DTD Editor"
            price="199.00"/>
   <product name="XML Book"
            price="19.99"/>
   <product name="XML Training"
            price="699.00"/>
</products>
```

This transformation has not degraded the original document because Listing 10.17 carries as much information as Listing 10.15. Furthermore, the information has the same structure as the information in Listing 10.15. This transformation is nondestructive—it does not lose any information.

EXAMPLE

2. To prove that the transformation is nondestructive, Listing 10.18 shows another style sheet that does the reverse operation. Applying Listing 10.18 to Listing 10.17 results in Listing 10.15.

Listing 10.18: The Reverse Style Sheet

```
<?xml version="1.0"?>

<xsl:stylesheet xmlns:xsl="http://www.w3.org/1999/XSL/Transform/">


<xsl:output method="xml"/>


<xsl:template match="products">
   <products>
      <xsl:apply-templates/>
   </products>
</xsl:template>


<xsl:template match="product">
   <product>
     <name>
        <xsl:value-of select="@name"/>
     </name>
     <price>
        <xsl:value-of select="@price"/>
     </price>
   </product>
</xsl:template>


</xsl:stylesheet>
```

From a data-management point of view, nondestructive transformations are ideal because they preserve the quality of the information.

EXAMPLE

3. On the other hand, destructive transformations are very useful in practice, if only because publishing is often a destructive transformation. Listing 10.19 converts the price list to HTML.

Listing 10.19: Converting to HTML

```
<?xml version="1.0"?>

<xsl:stylesheet
```

```
    xmlns:xsl="http://www.w3.org/1999/XSL/Transform/"
    xmlns="http://www.w3.org/TR/REC-html40">

<xsl:output method="html"/>

<xsl:template match="/">
    <HTML>
        <HEAD><TITLE>Product List</TITLE></HEAD><BODY>
            <P>Product List</P>
            <xsl:apply-templates/>
        </BODY>
    </HTML>
</xsl:template>

<xsl:template match="name">
    <P><xsl:apply-templates/></P>
</xsl:template>

<xsl:template match="price">
    <P><xsl:apply-templates/></P>
</xsl:template>

</xsl:stylesheet>
```

Unfortunately, this is also a destructive conversion. The result of applying Listing 10.19 to Listing 10.15 is shown in Listing 10.20.

Listing 10.20: HTML Result

OUTPUT

```
<!DOCTYPE html PUBLIC "-//W3C//DTD HTML 4.0 Transitional//EN">
<HTML>
    <HEAD>
        <TITLE>Product List</TITLE>
    </HEAD>
    <BODY>
        <P>Product List</P>
        <P>XML Editor</P>
        <P>499.00</P>
        <P>DTD Editor</P>
        <P>199.00</P>
        <P>XML Book</P>
```

continues

Listing 10.20: continued

```
        <P>19.99</P>
        <P>XML Training</P>
        <P>699.00</P>
    </BODY>
</HTML>
```

The tags in the HMTL version are meaningless. They do not reflect the structure and it is not possible to perform further conversions from the HTML tags alone. The <P> tag is ambiguous because it is used both for the price and product name. No style sheet could transform this document back in to XML.

Mark It Up!

The previous section reinforces the importance of structure and proper markup. In XML, everything is derived from the structure and it is therefore important that the structure be sound.

Figure 10.7 illustrates the optimal situation. The information is maintained in a highly structured format. To create new documents, transformations are applied to the highly structured document. Some transformations will be nondestructive but most are destructive transformations.

Most of these destructive transformations are for presentation purposes, such as converting XML to HTML. Ultimately, as browsers implement more XML companion standards like XLink or XSLFO, less destructive conversions will be required.

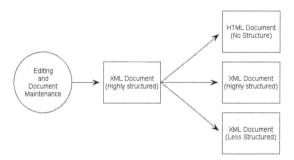

Figure 10.7: *How to best use XML*

The logical conclusion is to introduce as much structure as possible in your document. You should mark up all the major components of the document with either tags or attributes. It is not always easy to decide how far to go. Obviously, you wouldn't want to mark up every letter of every word:

```
<l>J</l><l>o</l><l>h</l><l>n</l>
```

Similarly, you need to easily recognize high-level structures. In the following document, it is easy to recognize that there is a name, an address, and a phone number.

```
John Doe
34 Fountain Square Plaza
Cincinnati, OH 45202
US
513-555-8889
```

This structure results in the following markup:

```
<entry>
    <name>John Doe</name>
    <address>34 Fountain Square Plaza
    Cincinnati, OH 45202
    US</address>
    <tel>513-555-8889</tel>
</entry>
```

The difficulty is finding the appropriate granularity. Is the previous example enough? Unlikely. It is probably best to mark more. For example:

```
<entry>
    <name>John Doe</name>
    <address>
        <street>34 Fountain Square Plaza</street>
        <region>OH</region>
        <postal-code>45202</postal-code>
        <locality>Cincinnati</locality>
        <country>US</country>
    </address>
    <tel>513-555-8889</tel>
</entry>
```

Is this enough or do you need to further break some of the elements, such as

```
<name>
    <fname>John</fname>
    <lname>Doe</lname>
</name>
```

The question is: "Where do you stop?" What is the correct granularity for an XML document? Unfortunately, there are no strict criteria. Your experience will guide you. It is, however, a good idea to mark up as much as is convenient.

The end user's convenience is the best guideline to use when deciding where to stop breaking a document into smaller pieces.

Indeed, if the DTD is too detailed and requires the user to identify details, it won't work. The document may be highly structured but, upon closer analysis, most of the markup will prove to be incorrect. This problem is often experienced by database administrators who have very good data schemas but very poor information in the database.

For example, if you were to ask users to break the street into further components such as

```
<street>
    <nr>34</nr>
    <name>Fountain Square</name>
    <type>Plaza</type>
</street>
```

It probably wouldn't work. Realistically, few people would know where to insert the markup. Is it <type>Plaza</type> or

```
<street>
    <nr>34</nr>
    <name>Fountain</name>
    <type>Square Plaza</type>
</street>
```

The only way to know when to stop breaking a document into smaller pieces is to write sample documents or even small prototypes as you design the DTD. As you gain experience with XML, this will become easier.

Use the sample documents or the prototype to test the usability of the DTD. Does it accurately capture all the information? Does it capture enough details? Is it nonobtrusive? You don't want to capture too many details and alienate the users.

Avoiding Too Many Options

As you finalize your DTD, you should proofread it to check against excessive use of options.

A warning bell should ring in your head if the DTD leaves too many options open. This is usually a sign that you need to be stricter in the markup.

The DTD in Listing 10.21 leaves too many options open. Figure 10.8 is a graphical view of the DTD.

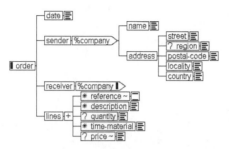

Figure 10.8: *A graphical view of the DTD*

Listing 10.21: A DTD for an Order

```
<!ENTITY % company      "(name,address)">
<!ELEMENT order         (date,sender,receiver,lines)>
<!ELEMENT date          (#PCDATA)>
<!ELEMENT sender        %company;>
<!ELEMENT receiver      %company;>
<!ELEMENT lines         (reference*,description*,quantity?,
                            time-material*,price?)+>
<!ELEMENT reference     EMPTY>
<!ATTLIST reference     href CDATA #IMPLIED>
<!ELEMENT description   (#PCDATA)>
<!ELEMENT quantity      (#PCDATA)>
<!ELEMENT time-material (#PCDATA)>
<!ELEMENT price         (#PCDATA)>
<!ATTLIST price         currency (usd ¦ eur) #IMPLIED>
<!ELEMENT name          (#PCDATA)>
<!ELEMENT address       (street,region?,postal-code,
                            locality,country)>
<!ELEMENT street        (#PCDATA)>
<!ELEMENT region        (#PCDATA)>
<!ELEMENT postal-code   (#PCDATA)>
<!ELEMENT locality      (#PCDATA)>
<!ELEMENT country       (#PCDATA)>
```

The problem with this DTD is the content model for lines:

```
<!ELEMENT lines (reference*,description*,quantity?,
                 time-material*,price?)+>
```

This model has so many options that the document in Listing 10.22 is valid, even though the lines element has no content. This is probably not what the DTD designer intended because it makes no sense to issue an order that contains only names and addresses.

Listing 10.22: A Valid Invoice

```
<?xml version="1.0" encoding="ISO-8859-1"?>
<!DOCTYPE order SYSTEM "order.dtd">
<order>
    <date>19990727</date>
    <sender>
        <name>Playfield Software</name>
        <address>
            <street>38 Fountain Square Plaza</street>
            <region>OH</region>
            <postal-code>45263</postal-code>
            <locality>Cincinnati</locality>
            <country>US</country>
        </address>
    </sender>
    <receiver>
        <name>Macmillan Publishing</name>
        <address>
            <street>201 West 103rd Street</street>
            <region>IN</region>
            <postal-code>46290</postal-code>
            <locality>Indianapolis</locality>
            <country>US</country>
        </address>
    </receiver>
    <lines/>
</order>
```

This creates a hole in the document. The solution is to use the or connector more often. A more realistic content model might be

```
<!ELEMENT lines ((reference ¦ description)+,
                 (quantity ¦ time-material+),price?)+>
```

This model states that there is at least one reference or one description for each product (there may be several references or several descriptions). Also the order is either for a certain quantity or on a time and material basis, one of the two elements must be present. Figure 10.9 illustrates this structure.

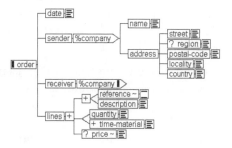

Figure 10.9: *The structure of the new DTD*

When resolving these problems, it is important to avoid introducing ambiguities in the DTD. The following model would have been ambiguous:

```
<!ELEMENT lines ((reference+ ¦ (reference+, description+) ¦
                 description+),
                 (quantity ¦ time-material+),price?)+>
```

It says that a line has either references or descriptions or both. Unfortunately, it is ambiguous. To remove the ambiguity, you can introduce a new element such as

```
<!ELEMENT line      ((ref-desc ¦ reference+ ¦ description+),
                     (quantity ¦ time-material+ ¦ price?))+>
<!ELEMENT ref-desc (reference+,description+)>
```

Attributes Versus Elements

As you have seen in the earlier section "The Right Level of Abstraction," you can use elements or attributes interchangeably to record the information in a DTD.

This has lead to heated debates in the XML community between the proponents of attributes and the proponents of elements. Specifically, the debate is whether it is best to store content in attributes or in elements.

Both sides have very convincing arguments and support their claims with good examples that clearly demonstrate the superiority of attributes over elements, or elements over attributes. The only problem is that both sides are right.

This debate is similar to the debate between inheritance and aggregation in object-oriented modeling. There are some clear arguments for and against each approach. And yet, when you have a blank sheet of paper in front of you, the solution is sometimes obvious, sometimes not.

I don't believe one approach is intrinsically better than the other. I try to keep an open mind and to adapt to the needs of the application at hand. For some applications, attributes just seem to work better, for others, elements are the clear winner. I always keep in mind that conversion is an option provided the structure is good enough.

Your experience will guide you as well. The next two sections present some of the reasons you might use attributes or elements.

Using Attributes

EXAMPLE

1. A major advantage of attributes is that they establish a strong relationship with their parent element. This makes it easy to process all the attributes attached to an element. This is particularly true for SAX parsers, as illustrated by the following code excerpt:

```
public void startElement(String name,AttributeList attributes)
{
    if(name.equals("price"))
    {
        String attribute = attributes.getValue("price");
        if(null != attribute)
        {
            double price = toDouble(attribute);
            if(min > price)
            {
                min = price;
                vendor = attributes.getValue("vendor");
            }
        }
    }
}
```

In contrast, it is more difficult to walk down the element tree and collect information from the children of an element.

EXAMPLE

2. Elements are naturally organized in a hierarchy, whereas attributes cannot nest.

This provides a clean-cut separation between elements and attributes that has led some to argue that elements should be used to express the structure (the relationship between elements) and attributes to hold the content.

This approach suggests that leaf elements should be turned into attributes:

```
<entry>
    <name name="John Doe"/>
    <address street="34 Fountain Square Plaza"
            region="OH"
            postal-code="45202"
            locality="Cincinnati"
            country="US"/>
    <tel tel="513-555-8889"/>
</entry>
```

EXAMPLE

3. Finally, attributes are also popular because the DTD gives you more control over the type and value of attributes than over the type and value of elements.

You can restrict an attribute to a list of values whereas the type of an element is essentially text.

```
<!ATTLIST price currency (usd ¦ eur) #IMPLIED>
```

This argument however will soon disappear. The new XML schema will offer better data typing for elements.

Using Elements

EXAMPLE

1. If attributes are easier to manipulate for the programmer, elements are typically easier to work with in XML editors or browsers. For one thing, it is impossible to display attributes with CSS.

This would suggest that attributes are great for abstract data and elements are ideal for human data.

```
url[protocol='mailto'] {
  text-decoration: none;
}
```

EXAMPLE

2. Elements can be repeated through the + and * occurrence indicators; attributes cannot.

```
<?xml version="1.0"?>
<entry>
    <name>John Doe</name>
```

```
<tel preferred="true">513-555-8889</tel>
<tel>513-555-7098</tel>
</entry>
```

EXAMPLE

3. Generally speaking, elements offer more room for extension and reuse than attributes because elements are highly structured.

For example, in Listing 10.22, the address element is reused in the sender and receiver elements. It is reused with its complete structure.

Lessons Learned

It is clear that elements and attributes have different characteristics. Unfortunately, nobody seems to agree on how to exploit them best.

Over time, you will develop your own set of rules of when to use an attribute and when to use an element. My set of rules, as I have already explained, is to use elements for the essential property of an object and attributes for ancillary properties.

This rule reflects my emphasis on structure over content. It is also very similar to the popular rule that originated in the SGML community that suggests using attributes for abstract concepts and elements for concrete ones.

EXAMPLE

Note that this is not a hard rule but one that depends on the application being considered. For example, in the price-comparison application, the currency is second in importance to the price:

```
<price currency="usd">499.00</price>
```

However in a financial application, the currency may be an element in its own right:

```
<currency>usd</currency>
```

TIP

Gray areas like this, where there are no clear rules, are unavoidable in XML. XML wouldn't be so powerful and flexible if it didn't offer several solutions for each problem.

Don't waste too much time trying to find the best rule because there probably is no one best rule. Pick one approach, document it in as nonambiguous terms as possible, and try to be consistent.

What's Next

The next two chapters put all the knowledge of XML you have acquired to the test because they help you build a realistic e-commerce application based on XML.

The application demonstrates many of the techniques you have studied in a real-life context. It also shows how to use XML for distributed applications.

## 11

N-Tiered Architecture and XML

You are now familiar with every aspect of XML. This chapter and the next one demonstrate how to put these techniques to use in a medium-sized example. There are no new techniques introduced in these chapters, but they illustrate how to apply what you have learned to a real-world application. In particular, you learn

- how to use XML for interapplication communication
- how to use XML for electronic commerce
- how to take advantage of XML tools

Throughout these two chapters, you'll develop a multimerchant Web shop or a Web mall, dubbed XCommerce (XML Commerce), as an example.

This chapter must be read in conjunction with the next chapter. This chapter introduces many of the ideas underlying the XCommerce application. It includes many code snippets and partial listings that are used to illustrate a point. The complete source code is in the next chapter. The concept of an electronic mall is increasingly popular; the largest sites such as Yahoo! and AOL are rushing to offer such services. The idea is to group several merchants on one Web site. The mall offers additional services, such as a single shopping cart, joint promotion, and, hopefully, more traffic.

However, a mall implementation needs to balance the need for common features among the various merchants, such as a shopping cart, with the need for the merchants to differentiate themselves and their products. XML helps in this respect.

What Is an N-Tiered Application?

Most medium- and large-scale XML applications are *distributed applications*, meaning that they involve several computers linked over a network (typically the Internet or a LAN).

Most of these applications are called *n-tiered* applications. XCommerce is an n-tier application. Essentially, n-tiered applications are a specialized form of client/server application.

Client/Server Applications

EXAMPLE

As Figure 11.1 illustrates, the Web is a good example of a client/server application, so you are already familiar with the idea. On the left side is the Web client also known as the *browser*. On the right side is the Web server.

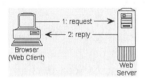

Figure 11.1: *The Web is a client/server application.*

At the user initiative, the browser requests Web pages from the server. The server delivers the pages and the client displays them. In effect, the client is a tool for the user to interact with the server.

Client/server applications have two essential characteristics:

- They are distributed applications, meaning that two or more computers are connected over a network.

- The two computers have specific roles.

The second point differentiates client/server applications from other forms of distributed applications (such as peer-to-peer ones). It means that there is a client and server and that their roles differ.

The server provides *services* to the client. The server is the producer and the client is the consumer. However, the server provides services only at the client's request. This is a sort of master/slave relationship where the master (the client) requests services from the slave (the server).

EXAMPLE

The Web is but one example of client/server. Other examples include

- Internet mail, where the mail client (such as Eudora or Outlook) interacts with the mail server to deliver and receive email

- Novell print and file servers, where the stations on a LAN can store files or print documents on a server

- PowerBuilder and other 4GL applications, where a local client interacts with a database server for administrative applications

Generally speaking, the server has access to resources that the client does not have access to or that are too difficult for the client to manage. In the case of the Web, the resources are HTML files. It would not be realistic to keep a local copy of every Web page. It makes more sense to request those pages you want to see at a particular time.

For email, the resource is a 24/7 Internet connection. A client could send emails directly but it makes more sense to pass the burden to a dedicated server that handles errors and retries.

Novell servers have printers and plenty of hard disks. In most setups, it is not cost-effective to give every user a fast printer and it is safer and more efficient to store files on a central location. Among other things, it simplifies backups.

Database servers provide a central storage for the data in the organization. Therefore, a database server has more information than is available to a given PC.

3-Tiered Applications

EXAMPLE

As we enter an increasingly wired world, the server itself needs to rely on other servers. Webmail is a good example of an n-tiered application. Webmail are those applications that let you read and compose emails through a Web site. Popular Webmails include Hotmail (www.hotmail.com) and Startmail (www.startmail.com).

As Figure 11.2 illustrates, in this setup, a server can also act as a client to another server. Indeed, the browser is a client. The email server is a server. But the Web server is both a client and a server: It is a server when talking to the browser and it is a client when talking to the email server.

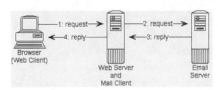

Figure 11.2: *The Web server plays both roles.*

This application consists of two client/server applications chained together. This is known as a three-tiered application. There are three tiers because there are three parties involved.

To differentiate between the various clients and servers, the leftmost client is often called the *presentation tier* because it is the interface for the end user. The machine in the middle, the one that plays both client and server, is often referred to as a *middle tier*.

In most cases, but not in this example, the rightmost server is a database server and is therefore often called the *data tier*.

N-Tiers

EXAMPLE

It's possible to add more parties to the application by chaining together more client/server applications. For example, some email servers depend on a database. The Webmail application would look like Figure 11.3 where there are four parties or tiers.

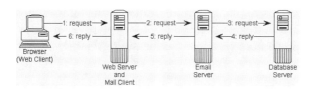

Figure 11.3: Adding one more tier

As you add more tiers, you can build 5-tiered or 6-tiered applications, or even more (although having more than four tiers is uncommon). The term *n-tiers* is a generic term for client/servers with three or more tiers.

The XCommerce Application

Chapter 12, "Putting It All Together: An e-Commerce Example," contains the source code with comments for the XCommerce application. As explained earlier, this is a shopping mall that allows several merchants to work together.

Figure 11.4 is a breakdown of XCommerce. The main components are the middle tier, or the shop, and the data tier, which can be either an XML server or a file.

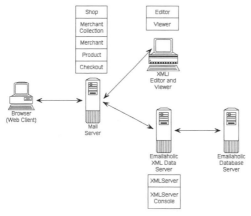

Figure 11.4: The main components of XCommerce

Simplifications

XCommerce is representative of a real Web mall. However, because this is a book about XML, I have made a few simplifications. These simplifications are not related to the use of XML in any way:

- There is no provision for payments. Processing payments typically requires credit card processing and a merchant account and is clearly outside the scope of this book.

- The buyer cannot shop for more than one product at a time. This saves writing a *shopping cart* (a small database that stores the items bought so far).

- Presentation is minimalist. You would want to include more graphics and better layout in a real shop.

Additionally, security has been kept simple. It is possible to add encryption but it is outside the scope of this book.

Shop

The middle tier is not very complex. Essentially, it manages a number of XML documents: one for the list of merchants, one for the list of products, and one for each product. The middle tier applies style sheets to these documents in response to user requests.

EXAMPLE

The shop is one servlet. It uses the URL to decide which document to use. The URL has the form /shop/merchant/product. Possible URLs include

```
/shop
/shop/xmli
/shop/xmli/1
/shop/emailaholic/0
```

Each level in the URL corresponds to a different XML document. The /shop URL is the list of merchants. The /shop/xmli URL is the list of products for the XMLi merchant. The /shop/xmli/1 is product number 1 from the XMLi merchant.

EXAMPLE

There is a different Java class for each level in the URL. These classes are responsible for downloading the appropriate XML document and for applying the style sheet. The following example shows how to download the list of products for a merchant:

```
protected Document getDocument()
    throws ServletException
{
    if(null == productsDocument ||
```

```
        expire < System.currentTimeMillis())
    {

    Element productsElement =
        XMLUtil.extractFirst(merchantElement,"products");
    if(null != productsElement)
    {

        String fname =
            productsElement.getAttribute("href");
        String update =
            productsElement.getAttribute("update");
        if(!XMLUtil.isEmpty(fname))
        {
            productsDocument = XMLUtil.parse(fname);
            freshened();
            productXSL = null;
            productsXSL = null;
        }
        if(!XMLUtil.isEmpty(update))
        {
            long u = Long.parseLong(update) * 1000;
            expire = System.currentTimeMillis() + u;
        }
    }
    }
    return productsDocument;
}
```

There are a few remarkable things about this example:

- It periodically reloads the list of products.

- It can download the list of products from a Web site, such as the XML
  servlet from Emailaholic. However, it can also load the document from
  a file, such as the file created by XMLi.

- It breaks the list of products in the Product object. Each product object
  is responsible for one product. Product objects are used for URLs of
  the form /shop/xmli/1.

In most cases, the shop ends up applying XSL style sheets to the XML document, such as

```
public void doGet(HttpServletRequest request,
                  HttpServletResponse response)
   throws IOException, ServletException
{
   XMLUtil.transform(getDocument(),
                  getXSL(),
                  response.getWriter(),
                  response.getCharacterEncoding());
}
```

The one exception is the checkout. When the user buys a product, the shop loads an HTML form to collect the buyer's name and address. The form is directly created in HTML.

When the user has provided the relevant data, the shop creates an XML file with the order. The order is posted automatically to the Web site of Emailaholic. For XMLi, the order is saved in a local file. As explained previously, Emailaholic imports the orders in a database whereas XMLi views them online with a style sheet.

The following example shows how to generate the XML order:

```
public void doSaveOrder(HttpServletRequest request,
                  HttpServletResponse response)
   throws ServletException, IOException
{
   String productid = request.getParameter("product"),
          merchantid = request.getParameter("merchant");
   Product product = getProduct(merchantid,productid);
   if(null == product)
   {
      response.sendError(HttpServletResponse.SC_NOT_FOUND);
      return;
   }
   Merchant merchant = product.getMerchant();
   String postURL = merchant.getPostURL();
   Writer writer = null;
   if(null != postURL)
      writer = new StringWriter();
```

```
else
{
    String directory = getInitParameter(merchant.getID()
                                          + ".orders"),
            // should be enough to avoid duplicates
            fname = String.valueOf(System.currentTimeMillis())
                                      + ".xml";
    File file = new File(directory,fname);
    writer = new FileWriter(file);
}
writer.write("<?xml version=\"1.0\"?>");
writer.write("<order>");
writer.write("<buyer");
writeAttribute("name",request,writer);
writeAttribute("street",request,writer);
writeAttribute("region",request,writer);
writeAttribute("postal-code",request,writer);
writeAttribute("locality",request,writer);
writeAttribute("country",request,writer);
writeAttribute("email",request,writer);
writer.write("/>");
writer.write("<product");
writeAttribute("quantity",request,writer);
writer.write(" id=\"");
writer.write(product.getID());
writer.write("\" name=\"");
writer.write(product.getName());
writer.write("\" price=\"");
writer.write(product.getPrice());
writer.write("\"/></order>");
writer.close();
if(null != postURL)
{
    Dictionary parameters = new Hashtable();
    String user = merchant.getPostUser(),
            password = merchant.getPostPassword(),
            xmlData = writer.toString();
    parameters.put("user",user);
```

```
        parameters.put("password",password);
        parameters.put("xmldata",xmlData);
        HTTPPost post = new HTTPPost(postURL,parameters);
        post.doRequest();
    }
    writer = response.getWriter();
    writer.write("<HTML><HEAD><TITLE>Checkout</TITLE></HEAD>");
    writer.write("<BODY><P>Thank you for shopping with us!");
    writer.write("<BR><A HREF=\"");
    writer.write(request.getServletPath());
    writer.write("\">Return to the shop</A>");
    writer.write("</BODY></HTML>");
    writer.flush();
}
```

XML Server

EXAMPLE

The data tier is a servlet that generates lists of products in XML from a database. This is very similar to generating the order in the previous example. The servlet also accepts orders in XML and stores them in the database. This is easily done with DOM, as you can see:

```
protected void doPost(HttpServletRequest request,
                       HttpServletResponse response)
    throws ServletException, IOException
{
    String sqlDriver = getInitParameter("sql.driver"),
           sqlURL = getInitParameter("sql.url"),
           sqlUser = request.getParameter("user"),
           sqlPassword = request.getParameter("password"),
           xmlData = request.getParameter("xmldata");

    Reader reader = new StringReader(xmlData);
    Document orderDocument = XMLUtil.parse(reader);
    Element orderElement = orderDocument.getDocumentElement(),
            buyerElement =
                XMLUtil.extractFirst(orderElement,"buyer"),
            productElement =
                XMLUtil.extractFirst(orderElement,"product");
    String name = buyerElement.getAttribute("name"),
```

```
                    street = buyerElement.getAttribute("street"),

                    region = buyerElement.getAttribute("region"),

                    postal_code = buyerElement.getAttribute("postal-code"),

                    locality = buyerElement.getAttribute("locality"),

                    country = buyerElement.getAttribute("country"),

                    email = buyerElement.getAttribute("email"),

                    productid = productElement.getAttribute("id"),

                    productname = productElement.getAttribute("name"),

                    productprice = productElement.getAttribute("price"),

                    productquantity =

                        productElement.getAttribute("quantity");


        try

        {

            Class.forName(sqlDriver);

            Connection connection =

                DriverManager.getConnection(sqlURL,

                                                sqlUser,

                                                sqlPassword);

            connection.setAutoCommit(false);

            try

            {

                PreparedStatement stmt =

                    connection.prepareStatement(

                    "insert into orders (name,street,region," +

                    "postal_code,locality,country,email," +

                    "productid,productname,productprice," +

                    "productquantity) " +

                    "values(?,?,?,?,?,?,?,?,?,?,?)");

                try

                {

                    stmt.setString(1,name);

                    stmt.setString(2,street);

                    stmt.setString(3,region);

                    stmt.setString(4,postal_code);

                    stmt.setString(5,locality);

                    stmt.setString(6,country);

                    stmt.setString(7,email);
```

```
                    stmt.setString(8,productid);
                    stmt.setString(9,productname);
                    stmt.setDouble(10,
                        formatter.parse(productprice).doubleValue());
                    stmt.setString(11,productquantity);
                    stmt.executeUpdate();
                    connection.commit();
                }
                finally
                {
                    stmt.close();
                }
            }
            finally
            {
                connection.close();
            }
        }
        catch(ClassNotFoundException e)
        {
            throw new ServletException(e);
        }
        catch(SQLException e)
        {
            throw new ServletException(e);
        }
        catch(ParseException e)
        {
            throw new ServletException(e);
        }
        response.setStatus(HttpServletResponse.SC_OK);
        response.setContentType("text/xml");
        Writer writer = response.getWriter();
        writer.write("<?xml version=\"1.0\"?>");
        writer.write("<status>200</status>");
        writer.flush();
    }
```

How XML Helps

As soon as there are two or more parties, they need to communicate. Currently, two approaches are particularly popular for client/server applications:

- middleware such as CORBA (Common Object Request Broker Architecture), DCOM (Distributed Component Object Model), or RPC (Remote Procedure Call)

- exchange formats such as HTML or XML

Middleware

I won't cover middleware in great detail (this is an XML book, not a middleware book), but I want to provide you with enough information for a comparison.

The basic idea behind middleware is to reduce the effort required to write distributed applications. Networks are not always safe, reliable, and dependable. In fact, one could argue that they are exactly the opposite. To work around these limitations, programmers have to implement specific protocols.

It is not uncommon for network-specific code to amount to more than 10 times the business code. This process takes time and is not very productive. Indeed, the time spent wrestling with the network and its security is not spent solving actual business problems.

Middleware includes tools that deal with the network. For example, a network might fail but middleware has logic to gracefully recover from these failures. Also, on a network several computers need to collaborate. Middleware offers tools to manage the interaction between these computers.

Middleware is based on specific protocols but, instead of overwhelming programmers with details, it hides them. Programmers are free to concentrate on business issues and, therefore, be more productive.

Listing 11.1 illustrates this. This is a simple CORBA client that appends one line to an order and confirms it. A server maintains the order.

Listing 11.1: Small CORBA Example

EXAMPLE

```
import org.omg.CORBA.*;


public class StockExchangeClient
{
    static public void main(String[] args)
```

```
    {
        String order = args[0],
                product = args[1];
        int quantity = Integer.parseInt(args[2]);
        ORB orb = ORB.init(args,null);
        Order remoteOrder = OrderHelper.bind(orb,order);
        remoteOrder.appendLine(product,quantity);
        remoteOrder.confirm();
    }
}
```

Listing 11.1 is interesting because you can hardly tell it is a distributed application. The only lines that explicitly deal with networks are these two:

```
ORB orb = ORB.init(args,null);
Order remoteOrder = OrderHelper.bind(orb,order);
```

and they are not very difficult. Without going into any details, they connect to an order on the server. More interestingly, the application can manipulate the order, which is a server object, just as if it were a client object:

```
remoteOrder.appendLine(product,quantity);
remoteOrder.confirm();
```

That's the power of middleware; it completely hides the distributed aspect.

Experience shows that middleware works better on LANs or intranets than on cross-enterprise applications. This is because, with middleware, the client directly manipulates objects on the server. This leads to a very tight coupling between the client and the server. It is therefore simpler if both parties are controlled by the same organization.

NOTE

Middleware gurus are quick to point out that it doesn't have to be that way. Indeed there are several mechanisms, including dynamic invocation, that support very flexible coupling with middleware.

While it is correct technically, in practice, experience shows that most solutions based on middleware are relatively inflexible and are therefore best suited for internal use.

Common Format

For applications that work across several organizations, it is easier to exchange documents in a common format. This is how the Web works: A Web server requests HMTL documents from a Web browser. This process has proved to scale well to millions of users.

EXAMPLE

HTML is a good format but it is intended for human consumption only. XML, as you have seen, is similar but can be manipulated by applications. XCommerce illustrates how it works (see Figure 11.5).

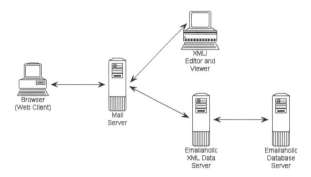

Figure 11.5: The Web mall, XCommerce

As you can see, this is an n-tiered application: The client converses with the mall server. The mall server converses with the XML data server. The data server itself may be connected to a database server.

XML has many strong points for this setup:

- XML is extensible, which allows the different partners to build on commonalities while retaining the option to extend the basic services where appropriate.

- XML is structure-rich, which allows the middle server to process product information (such as extracting prices).

- XML is versatile, therefore most data in the application are stored in XML. In particular, XML is used for configuration information (the list of merchants), for product information, and to store the orders themselves.

- XML scales well. Small merchants can prepare product lists manually with an editor while larger merchants can generate the list from a database.

- As a secondary benefit of scalability, XML gives the merchants lots of flexibility in deploying their solutions. A merchant can start with a simple solution and upgrade as the business expands.

- XML is based on the Web; therefore, it is often possible to reuse HTML investments.

- XML is textual, which simplifies testing and debugging (this should not be neglected because very few applications work flawlessly the first time).

- XML is cost effective to deploy because many vendors support it; companion standards are also available.

XML for the Data Tiers

XML brings its emphasis on structure, its extensibility, its scalability, and its versatility to the data tiers. This chapter has discussed the structure aspect at length already, so let's review the other features.

Extensibility

Figure 11.6 is the structure for the list of products. Listing 11.2 is an example of a list of products.

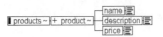

Figure 11.6: *Structure for the list of products*

Listing 11.2: Product List in XML

```
<?xml version="1.0"?>
<products merchant="emailaholic">
<product id="0">
<name>Ultra Word Processor</name>
<description>More words per minute than
the competition.</description>
<price>$799.99</price>
</product>
<product id="1">
<name>Super Calculator</name>
<description>Cheap and reliable with power saving.</description>
<price>$5.99</price>
</product>
```

continues

Listing 11.2: continued

```
<product id="2">
<name>Safest Safe</name>
<description>Choose the authentic Safest Safe.</description>
<price>$1,999.00</price>
</product>
</products>
```

> ✔ Obviously, some merchants will want to provide more information than is supported in the list of products. For example, they will want to add images, manufacturer information, and more. This is possible using the technique introduced in the section "Building on XML Extensibility" in Chapter 10 (page 312).

Listing 11.3 illustrates how one merchant can publish additional product information. The merchant has to provide a style sheet to display the extra information to the buyer.

Listing 11.3: Extending the Core Format

```
<?xml version="1.0"?>
<products merchant="emailaholic"
          xmlns:em="http://www.emailaholic.com/xt/1.0">
<product id="0">
<name>Ultra Word Processor</name>
<em:manufacturer>Ultra Word Inc.</em:manufacturer>
<em:image>wordprocessor.jpg</em:image>
<em:warranty>1 month</em:warranty>
<description>More words per minute than
the competition.</description>
<price>$799.99</price>
</product>
<product id="1">
<name>Super Calculator</name>
<em:manufacturer>United Calculators Corp.</em:manufacturer>
<em:image>calculator.jpg</em:image>
<em:warranty>6 months</em:warranty>
<description>Cheap and reliable with power saving.</description>
<price>$5.99</price>
</product>
<product id="2">
<name>Safest Safe</name>
```

```
<em:manufacturer>Safe Safe Inc.</em:manufacturer>

<em:image>safe.jpg</em:image>

<em:warranty>lifetime</em:warranty>

<description>Choose the authentic Safest Safe.</description>

<price>$1,999.00</price>

</product>

</products>
```

Scalability

EXAMPLE

1. Currently, XCommerce has two merchants. Emailaholic, the first merchant, is a large company. It has a Web site with a database of products available online. It dynamically generates XML documents from its database.

Listing 11.4 is an extract from a servlet that generates the XML document for Emailaholic. The complete listing is in Chapter 12, "Putting It All Together: An e-Commerce Example." Listing 11.5 is a server that Emailaholic uses to manage its database; again, the complete listing is in Chapter 12. Listing 11.4 generates XML; Listing 11.5 generates HTML for a similar document.

Compare both listings and see how similar they are. Both are based on the same Web technology and both are based on very similar markup languages. For Emailaholic, it is not much more difficult to write Listing 11.4, which uses the newer XML, than to write Listing 11.5, which uses the well-known HTML technology. In practice, it means that Emailaholic can reuse its HTML experience with XML.

What does it all mean? It means that adding XML in a Web project is easy. XML is popular because it is that simple.

It is also popular because it is based on many techniques that are already well known through HTML; therefore, people are rapidly productive with HTML. I have seen projects where people would take their HTML-based application and turn it into an XML application in a matter of days, not weeks.

Listing 11.4: Writing an XML Document

```
protected void doGet(HttpServletRequest request,

                     HttpServletResponse response)

    throws ServletException, IOException

{

    response.setContentType("application/xml");
```

continues

Listing 11.4: continued

```
Writer writer = response.getWriter();
String sqlDriver = getInitParameter("sql.driver"),
        sqlURL = getInitParameter("sql.url"),
        sqlUser = getInitParameter("sql.user"),
        sqlPassword = getInitParameter("sql.password"),
        merchant = getInitParameter("merchant");
writer.write("<?xml version=\"1.0\"?>");
writer.write("<products merchant=\"");
writer.write(merchant);
writer.write("\" xmlns:em=\"http://www.emailaholic");
writer.write(".com/xt/1.0\">");
try
{
    Class.forName(sqlDriver);
    Connection connection =
        DriverManager.getConnection(sqlURL,
                                    sqlUser,
                                    sqlPassword);
    try
    {
        Statement stmt = connection.createStatement();
        try
        {
            ResultSet rs =
                stmt.executeQuery("select id, name, " +
                    "manufacturer, image, warranty, " +
                    "description, price from products");
            while(rs.next())
            {
                writer.write("<product id=\"");
                writer.write(String.valueOf(rs.getInt(1)));
                writer.write("\"><name>");
                writer.write(rs.getString(2));
                writer.write("</name><em:manufacturer>");
                writer.write(rs.getString(3));
                writer.write("</em:manufacturer><em:image>");
                writer.write(rs.getString(4));
```

```
                    writer.write("</em:image><em:warranty>");

                    writer.write(rs.getString(5));

                    writer.write("</em:warranty><description>");

                    writer.write(rs.getString(6));

                    writer.write("</description><price>");

                    writer.write(formatter.format(rs.getDouble(7)));

                    writer.write("</price></product>");

                }

            }

            finally

            {

                stmt.close();

            }

        }

        finally

        {

            connection.close();

        }

    }

    catch(ClassNotFoundException e)

    {

        throw new ServletException;

    }

    catch(SQLException e)

    {

        throw new ServletException(e);

    }

    writer.write("</products>");

    writer.flush();

}
```

Listing 11.5: Writing an HTML Document

```
protected void doPage(HttpServletRequest request,

                      HttpServletResponse response,

                      Connection connection)

    throws SQLException, IOException

{

    Writer writer = response.getWriter();
```

continues

Listing 11.4: continued

```
writer.write("<HTML><HEAD><TITLE>XML Server Console" +
    "</TITLE></HEAD><BODY>");
Statement stmt = connection.createStatement();
try
{
    // ... deleted, see chapter 12 for complete listing
    ResultSet rs =
        stmt.executeQuery("select id, name from products");
    writer.write("<TABLE>");
    while(rs.next())
    {
        writer.write("<TR><TD>");
        writer.write(rs.getString(2));
        writer.write("</TD><TD><FORM ACTION=\"");
        writer.write(request.getServletPath());
        writer.write("\" METHOD=\"POST\">");
        writer.write(" <INPUT TYPE=\"SUBMIT\"");
        writer.write(" VALUE=\"Delete\">");
        writer.write("<INPUT TYPE=\"HIDDEN\"");
        writer.write(" NAME=\"action\" VALUE=\"delete\">");
        writer.write("</FORM></TD></TR>");
    }
    writer.write("</TABLE>");
    // ... deleted, see chapter 12 for complete listing
}
finally
{
    stmt.close();
}
writer.write("</BODY></HTML>");
writer.flush();
}
```

2. XMLi is the second merchant. XMLi is a smaller company and it
   doesn't have a Web site. Fortunately, there is more than one way to
   generate XML documents. A small merchant, like XMLi, can prepare
   its list of products (in XML) manually and upload the list to the mall
   site. Figure 11.7 shows the editor XMLi uses.

✔ This editor is nothing more than a style sheet and JavaScript so it is very simple to deploy. The source code is in the section "Viewer and Editor" in Chapter 12 (page 444).

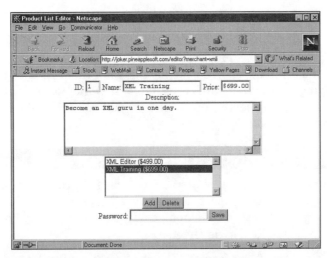

Figure 11.7: Editing the list of products

Versatility

EXAMPLE

The Web mall needs to forward the orders to the merchants. When a visitor buys from the Web site, the order is also represented as an XML document. So, XML serves all of the data exchange needs. Listing 11.6 shows a sample order.

Listing 11.6: An Order in XML

```
<?xml version="1.0"?>

<order>

<buyer name="John Doe"
        street="34 Fountain Square Plaza"
        region="OH"
        postal-code="45202"
        locality="Cincinnati"
        country="US"
        email="jdoe@emailaholic.com"/>

<product quantity="1"
        id="xmli"
        name="XML Book"
        price="$19.99"/>

</order>
```

The order benefits from all the other qualities of XML. In particular, the middle tier posts the order to the Emailaholic site, where it is automatically parsed and loaded into a database.

Orders for XMLi are not posted to a Web site because XMLi has no Web site. Instead, the orders are saved in files. To review its order, XMLi applies a style sheet to them.

Again, the complete source code for this is in the next chapter. However, the underlying idea is that XML is scalable: It works for Emailaholic, which built a specialized server, but it also works for XMLi, which needs a simple, browser-based tool.

XML on the Middle Tier

On the middle tier, XML is attractive because of the large range of tools and standards that support it—mainly XML parsers and XSL processors. Tools reduce the cost of development. In fact, many operations can be implemented as XSL style sheets.

EXAMPLE

1. A style sheet can format the list of products for the end user. By bundling an inexpensive XSL processor on the middle tier, the interface with the buyers is built in no time.

Listing 11.7 shows the style sheet that formats the list of products seen previously in Listing 11.2. Figure 11.8 is the result in a browser.

✔ The section "The Middle Tier" in Chapter 12 (page 386) presents the servlet that applies these style sheets.

Listing 11.7: Formatting the List of Products

```
<?xml version="1.0" encoding="ISO-8859-1"?>
<xsl:stylesheet xmlns:xsl="http://www.w3.org/1999/XSL/Transform/"
                xmlns="http://www.w3.org/TR/REC-html40">

<xsl:output method="html"/>

<xsl:template match="/">
   <HTML>
   <HEAD>
      <TITLE>Online Shop</TITLE>
   </HEAD>
   <BODY>
      <TABLE BORDER="0"><xsl:for-each select="products/product">
      <TR><TD><B><A><xsl:attribute name="HREF">/shop/<xsl:value-of
```

```
        select="/products/@merchant"/>/<xsl:value-of
        select="@id"/></xsl:attribute><xsl:value-of
        select="name"/></A></B><BR/>
        <xsl:value-of select="price"/></TD>
        <TD><FORM ACTION="/shop/checkout" METHOD="POST">
           <INPUT TYPE="HIDDEN" NAME="merchant">
              <xsl:attribute name="value"><xsl:value-of
                 select="/products/@merchant"/></xsl:attribute>
           </INPUT>
           <INPUT TYPE="HIDDEN" NAME="product">
              <xsl:attribute name="value"><xsl:value-of
                 select="@id"/></xsl:attribute>
           </INPUT>
           <INPUT TYPE="HIDDEN" NAME="quantity" VALUE="1"/>
           <INPUT TYPE="SUBMIT" VALUE="Buy"/>
        </FORM></TD>
     </TR></xsl:for-each></TABLE>
  </BODY>
  </HTML>
</xsl:template>


</xsl:stylesheet>
```

OUTPUT

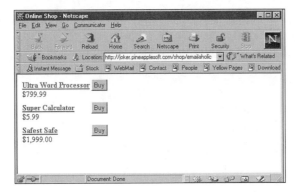

Figure 11.8: *The list of products in a browser*

2. Thanks to style sheets, merchants can customize the presentation of their sites. Emailaholic is not happy with the standard style sheet, and it provides its own style sheet (see Listing 11.8). This style sheet works with documents such as the one in Listing 11.3.

Again, this style sheet will work with the servlet in Chapter 12. The important thing to remember is that each merchant can add tags to the product description and provide a style sheet that takes advantage of the new tags.

Listing 11.8: The Emailaholic Style Sheet

```
<?xml version="1.0" encoding="ISO-8859-1"?>
<xsl:stylesheet xmlns:xsl="http://www.w3.org/1999/XSL/Transform/"
                xmlns:em="http://www.emailaholic.com/xt/1.0"
                xmlns="http://www.w3.org/TR/REC-html40">


<xsl:output method="html"/>


<xsl:template match="/">
    <HTML>
    <HEAD>
       <TITLE>Emailaholic.com</TITLE>
    </HEAD>
    <BODY BGCOLOR="orange">
       <CENTER><TABLE BGCOLOR="white" WIDTH="50%"><TR><TD><CENTER>
          <TABLE BORDER="0"><xsl:for-each
             select="products/product"><TR>
             <TD><B><A><xsl:attribute
                name="HREF">/shop/emailaholic/<xsl:value-of
                select="@id"/></xsl:attribute><xsl:value-of
                select="name"/></A></B><BR/>
             by <xsl:value-of select="em:manufacturer"/><BR/>
             <xsl:value-of select="price"/></TD>
             <TD><FORM ACTION="/shop/checkout" METHOD="POST">
                <INPUT TYPE="HIDDEN" NAME="merchant"
                   VALUE="emailaholic"/>
                <INPUT TYPE="HIDDEN" NAME="product">
                   <xsl:attribute name="value"><xsl:value-of
                      select="@id"/></xsl:attribute>
                </INPUT>
                <INPUT TYPE="HIDDEN" NAME="quantity" VALUE="1"/>
                <INPUT TYPE="SUBMIT" VALUE="Buy"/>
             </FORM></TD>
          </TR></xsl:for-each></TABLE>
       </CENTER></TD></TR></TABLE></CENTER>
```

```
        </BODY>
      </HTML>
</xsl:template>


</xsl:stylesheet>
```

This style sheet differs from Listing 11.7 because it uses the information in the `http://www.emailaholic.com/xt/1.0` namespace. It also adopts a different presentation; see Figure 11.9 for the result in a browser.

OUTPUT

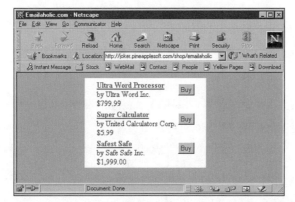

Figure 11.9: Emailaholic style sheet in a browser

EXAMPLE

3. Finally, style sheets are useful for filtering information. The style sheets in Listings 11.7 and 11.8 do not present all the information from Listings 11.2 and 11.3. They both ignore the description. Listing 11.8 ignores most of Emailaholic-specific information. This keeps the list of products small and quicker to download.

Style sheets in Listings 11.9 and 11.10 provide more details. They use all the information available in the original document, but they present one product only. Listing 11.9 is the standard mall style sheet whereas Listing 11.10 is specific to Emailaholic.

These style sheets also work with the servlet introduced in Chapter 12. The idea, however, is that the style sheet is used to present more or less detailed information to the user.

Listing 11.9: Product.xsl

```
<?xml version="1.0" encoding="ISO-8859-1"?>
<xsl:stylesheet xmlns:xsl="http://www.w3.org/1999/XSL/Transform/"
                xmlns="http://www.w3.org/TR/REC-html40">


<xsl:output method="html"/>


<xsl:template match="/">
    <HTML>
    <HEAD>
        <TITLE>Online Shop</TITLE>
    </HEAD>
    <BODY>
        <P><B><xsl:value-of select="product/name"/></B><BR/>
            <xsl:value-of select="product/description"/><BR/>
            <xsl:value-of select="product/price"/>
            <FORM ACTION="/shop/checkout" METHOD="POST">
                <INPUT TYPE="TEXT" SIZE="3" NAME="quantity" VALUE="1"/>
                <INPUT TYPE="SUBMIT" VALUE="Buy"/>
                <INPUT TYPE="HIDDEN" NAME="merchant">
                    <xsl:attribute name="value"><xsl:value-of
                        select="product/@merchant"/></xsl:attribute>
                </INPUT>
                <INPUT TYPE="HIDDEN" NAME="product">
                    <xsl:attribute name="value"><xsl:value-of
                        select="product/@id"/></xsl:attribute>
                </INPUT>
            </FORM></P>
    </BODY>
    </HTML>
</xsl:template>


</xsl:stylesheet>
```

Listing 11.10: Emailaholic Style Sheet for Product

```
<?xml version="1.0" encoding="ISO-8859-1"?>
<xsl:stylesheet xmlns:xsl="http://www.w3.org/1999/XSL/Transform/"
                xmlns:em="http://www.emailaholic.com/xt/1.0"
                xmlns="http://www.w3.org/TR/REC-html40">
```

```
<xsl:output method="html"/>

<xsl:template match="/">
   <HTML>
   <HEAD>
      <TITLE>Emailaholic.com</TITLE>
   </HEAD>
   <BODY BGCOLOR="orange">
      <CENTER><TABLE BGCOLOR="white" WIDTH="50%"><TR><TD><CENTER>
         <IMG ALIGN="RIGHT"><xsl:attribute
    name="SRC">http://catwoman.pineapplesoft.com:81/<xsl:value-of
            select="product/em:image"/></xsl:attribute></IMG>
         <B><xsl:value-of select="product/name"/></B><BR/>
         by <I><xsl:value-of
            select="product/em:manufacturer"/></I><BR/>
         <xsl:value-of select="product/description"/><BR/>
         <SMALL>Warranty: <xsl:value-of
            select="product/em:warranty"/></SMALL><BR/>
         <xsl:value-of select="product/price"/>
         <FORM ACTION="/shop/checkout" METHOD="POST">
            <INPUT TYPE="TEXT" SIZE="3" NAME="quantity" VALUE="1"/>
            <INPUT TYPE="SUBMIT" VALUE="Buy"/>
            <INPUT TYPE="HIDDEN" NAME="merchant"
                   VALUE="emailaholic"/>
            <INPUT TYPE="HIDDEN" NAME="product">
               <xsl:attribute name="value"><xsl:value-of
                  select="product/@id"/></xsl:attribute>
            </INPUT>
         </FORM>
      </CENTER></TD></TR></TABLE></CENTER>
   </BODY>
   </HTML>
</xsl:template>

</xsl:stylesheet>
```

OUTPUT

Figure 11.10 shows the result in a browser. Notice that more information is available than shown in Figure 11.9.

Figure 11.10: *Product information in a browser*

Client

The last tier is the client. Ultimately, it will be possible to send XML to the client and apply style sheets on the client. Currently, I would advise against sending any XML to the client. It makes more sense to convert to HTML on the server.

There are several problems with XML on the client:

- Currently, XML is supported only by the latest generation of browsers. Studies show that surfers are less likely to update their browsers than they were in the past, so implementation might take a while.

- Even if your target audience has XML-capable browsers, not all browsers were born equal. There are important differences between version 4.0 and version 5.0 of Internet Explorer and Mozilla, for example.

- XSL implementations are particularly unstable. Internet Explorer 4.0 supported a very early version of XSL. Internet Explorer 5.0 is closer to the standard, but will need changes. Currently, no browser has a complete implementation of XSL.

In conclusion, it will probably take more than two years before XML will be common. Currently converting XML to HTML on the server is the safe solution. It buys you the best of both worlds: It works with older browsers but it still allows you to take advantage of XML in your applications.

In the previous chapters, you saw many examples that performed lots of processing on the client side. However, in each case, I warned that it would work only with specific browsers. XCommerce relies heavily on server-side conversion because it is a more realistic example.

EXAMPLE

If you need special processing on the client, you can always resort to JavaScript. It is even possible to combine XSL and JavaScript. Listing 11.11 demonstrates how to generate client-side JavaScript from a server-side XSL style sheet.

Listing 11.11: Generating JavaScript from XSL

```
<?xml version="1.0" encoding="ISO-8859-1"?>
<xsl:stylesheet xmlns:xsl="http://www.w3.org/1999/XSL/Transform/"
                xmlns="http://www.w3.org/TR/REC-html40">


<xsl:output method="html"/>


<xsl:template match="/">
   <HTML><HEAD><TITLE>Product List Editor</TITLE>
      <SCRIPT LANGUAGE="JavaScript" SRC="editor.js">
      <xsl:text> </xsl:text></SCRIPT>
      <SCRIPT LANGUAGE="JavaScript"><xsl:comment>
      function load(form)
      {
      <xsl:for-each select="products/product">
         doAddProduct(form,
                       "<xsl:value-of select="@id"/>",
                       "<xsl:value-of select="name"/>",
                       "<xsl:value-of select="price"/>",
                       "<xsl:value-of select="description"/>");
      </xsl:for-each>
      }
      // </xsl:comment>
      </SCRIPT>
      </HEAD>
      <BODY ONLOAD="load(document.controls)">
         <CENTER>
            <FORM NAME="controls" METHOD="POST"
                  ACTION="editor">
               ID: <INPUT TYPE="TEXT" NAME="id" SIZE="3"/>
               Name: <INPUT TYPE="TEXT" NAME="name"/>
               Price: <INPUT TYPE="TEXT" NAME="price"
                           SIZE="7"/><BR/>
               Description:<BR/>
```

continues

Listing 11.11: continued

```
                <TEXTAREA NAME="description" ROWS="5"
                        COLS="50"/><BR/>
                <SELECT NAME="productlist" SIZE="5"
                        WIDTH="250"/><BR/>
                <INPUT TYPE="BUTTON" VALUE="Add"
                        ONCLICK="addProduct(controls)"/>
                <INPUT TYPE="BUTTON" VALUE="Delete"
                        ONCLICK="deleteProduct(controls)"/><BR/>
                Password: <INPUT TYPE="PASSWORD" NAME="pwd"/>
                <INPUT TYPE="SUBMIT" VALUE="Save"
                        ONCLICK="exportProduct(controls)"/>
                <INPUT TYPE="HIDDEN" NAME="xmldata"/>
                <INPUT TYPE="HIDDEN" NAME="merchant">
                    <xsl:attribute name="VALUE">
                        <xsl:value-of select="products/@merchant"/>
                    </xsl:attribute>
                </INPUT>
            </FORM>
        </CENTER>
    </BODY>
  </HTML>
</xsl:template>


</xsl:stylesheet>
```

This is useful because the style sheet populates a list and data structure for
the JavaScript application. The following extract (taken from Listing 11.11)
is used to generate the JavaScript code based on the XML document:

```
function load(form)
{
<xsl:for-each select="products/product">
    doAddProduct(form,
                "<xsl:value-of select="@id"/>",
                "<xsl:value-of select="name"/>",
                "<xsl:value-of select="price"/>",
                "<xsl:value-of select="description"/>");
</xsl:for-each>
}
```

Applying the style sheet in Listing 11.11 to the XML document in Listing 11.3 generates the following JavaScript code. Note that this JavaScript code reflects the products in the XML document. If you used a different XML document for the list of products, the JavaScript would reflect that

```
doAddProduct("0",

             "Ultra Word Processor",

             "More words per minute than the competition.",

             "$799.99");

doAddProduct("1",

             "Super Calculator",

             "Cheap and reliable with power saving.",

             "$5.99");

doAddProduct("2",

             "Safest Safe",

             "Choose the authentic Safest Safe.",

             "$1,999.00");
```

CAUTION

Note that the JavaScript code is generated on the server but it is executed on the client.

NOTE

I advise against sending XML to the client because there are not enough XML-capable browsers.

This might not be true on an intranet. An intranet is a controlled environment; therefore, you might be able to control which browser is being used. Moreover, you can tailor your documents to the appropriate browsers.

If, however, the intranet is large, stick to server-side conversion of XML. In a large intranet, it is difficult to upgrade all the users simultaneously. If your appplication depends on Internet Explorer 5.0 and 500 users out there are still using Internet Explorer 4.0, it might not be possible to upgrade them.

Server-Side Programming Language

XCommerce relies extensively on XSL. From a certain point of view, XSL is used as a scripting language for XML documents.

However, there are features that are not possible with XSL. For example, there is no standard mechanism to split a document. This would be useful for separating the list of products in a number of product documents.

Therefore, XSL is not enough. A medium-sized XML application needs code to compare documents, compile new documents, handle user authentication, and more. All these features are not being covered, or not properly covered, by XSL.

The main options for server-side programming languages that work well with XML are Perl, JavaScript, Python, Omnimark, and Java.

Perl

Perl is a scripting language. It is popular for CGI scripting because it offers superior text manipulation. However, with XML, you'd rather manipulate the text with XSL, so many of the features in Perl are not as important with XML as with raw text.

JavaScript

JavaScript is also a scripting language. It is particularly popular for browsers. Many examples in this book rely on JavaScript. There are server-side versions of JavaScript from Microsoft and Netscape. Microsoft offers Active Server Page (ASP). Netscape supports Server-Side JavaScript (SSJS).

EXAMPLE

Although ASP and SSJS are very similar, they are incompatible. ASP and SSJS encourage you to mix JavaScript statements in an HTML or an XML page. The server, not the browser, executes the script to generate the final page. Listing 11.12 shows you how to use SSJS to create an XML document with product information.

Listing 11.12: Creating XML with SSJS

```
<SERVER>
deleteResponseHeader("content-type")
addResponseHeader("content-type","application/xml")
database.connect("ODBC","products","SYSDBA","masterkey","")
product = database.cursor("select * from products where id = '" + request.id + "'")
product.next()
</SERVER><product>
<name><SERVER>write(product.name)</SERVER></name>
<description><SERVER>write(product.description)</SERVER></description>
<price><SERVER>write(product.price);product.close()</SERVER></price>
</product>
```

The first few lines change the type of the document to XML. Next, it connects to the database. Finally, it reads various information from the database and inserts it into an XML document.

The major problem with JavaScript is that it is not portable. An application developed with Microsoft's ASP does not work on Netscape servers and vice versa. Obviously, ASP is available only on Windows Web servers. Using JavaScript with Apache on Linux is simply not an option.

Python

Python is an object-oriented scripting language with a very pleasant syntax. Python offers an XML parser. Although Python is rapidly gaining in popularity, it is yet not as popular as Perl and JavaScript.

There is a Java implementation of Python which gives you access to all the Java tools.

Omnimark

Omnimark is another scripting language that was developed specifically to process SGML documents. It was later extended to support XML. If you need a scripting language to manipulate XML documents, Omnimark is a very good choice.

The major advantages of Omnimark are that it is available free of charge from www.omnimark.com, it runs on many platforms, it has built-in support for text manipulation and XML, and it has a compiler.

However, Omnimark is not well known outside of SGML circles and it is a proprietary language.

Java

The last option is Java. This is the language I have used for most of XCommerce (there is some client-side JavaScript as well). Keep in mind that these are not client-side applets, but Java applications running on the server.

Java has many strong points for XML development:

- Many XML tools are available in Java. Indeed, most of the XML tools (parser, XSL processor, XQL engine, and so on) were first made available for Java.

- Java is highly portable. There are versions of Java for all the major Web servers and then some.

- Java is a typed language and it is compiled. The compiler catches many errors. This is important for server-side programming because a faulty script can crash your server.

- There are several high-quality development environments available, so you can choose the one that works best for you.

- Many vendors support Java. You have an ample supply of books, components, and services.

If you are familiar with JavaScript but you think Java is too complex, think twice. With XML, you will write more XSL code than Java or JavaScript code, anyway. You really need not worry about complex concepts in Java.

✔ If you are not familiar with Java but you would like to learn enough Java to run the examples, turn to Appendix A, "Crash Course on Java," (page 457).

What's Next

The next chapter contains the entire source code for XCommerce. It provides a good illustration of what is possible with XML.

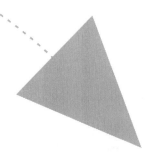

Putting It All Together:
An e-Commerce Example

This chapter contains the commented source code for XCommerce. In this chapter, you learn

- how to use XML in a medium-sized application

- how XSL and DOM make it easy to build sophisticated applications

- how to build and install a complete application

Building XCommerce

CAUTION
This example relies heavily on XSL. However, XSL was not final at the time of this writing. It is likely that the proposed standard will have changed by the time you read this book. Some of these changes may create incompatibilities. If you experience problems running this example, I invite you to check www.quecorp.com/series/by_example/ for an update.

This section explains how to build and compile the application and where to copy the various files.

Classpath

XCommerce uses several libraries in addition to its own classes. Therefore, you need to be sure all the pieces are included; otherwise, it won't run. Specifically, you will need the following libraries:

- XML for Java, the XML parser from IBM or another DOM parser. You download XML for Java from www.alphaworks.ibm.com.

- LotusXSL, the XSL processor or another XSL processor. You download LotusXSL from www.alphaworks.ibm.com.

- Jetty or another servlet engine. You download Jetty from www.mortbay.com.

- a JDBC-compliant database. Under Windows, the easiest solution is to use an ODBC database. JDBC is Java API to interface with a database. It is similar to ODBC and indeed, ODBC databases are also JDBC-compliant.

You need to tell the Java environment where to find these files. As explained in Appendix A, this is done through the classpath. The classpath looks like

```
-classpath c:\jetty\lib\javax.servlet.jar;
➥c:\lotusxsl\lotusxsl.jar;c:\xml4j\xml4j.jar;.
```

Obviously, you have to adapt these paths to your machine.

Configuration File

EXAMPLE

In order to set up the XCommerce configuration files, you need a servlet engine; see Appendix A.

You also need to define properties similar to those in Listings 12.1, 12.2, 12.3, and 12.4. These listings show Jetty configuration files. Even though other servlet engines use different formats for configuration, the same properties must be defined.

Listing 12.1: jetty.prp

```
# configuration for the online shop
shop./.InetAddrPort      : 0.0.0.0:80
shop./.Directory./       : ./docs
shop./.Servlet./shop%    : shop=com.psol.xcommerce.Shop?
➥./properties/shop.prp
shop./.Servlet./editor$ : editor=com.psol.xcommerce.Editor?
➥./properties/viewedit.prp
shop./.Servlet./viewer$ : viewer=com.psol.xcommerce.Viewer?
➥./properties/viewedit.prp
# configuration for the Emailaholic data server
emailaholic./.InetAddrPort      : 0.0.0.0:81
emailaholic./.Directory./       : ./emailaholic
emailaholic./.Servlet./xml      : xml=com.psol.xcommerce.XMLServer?
➥./properties/xmlserver.prp
emailaholic./.Servlet./console : console=com.psol.xcommerce.
➥XMLServerConsole?./properties/xmlserver.prp
```

Listing 12.2: shop.prp

```
merchants.xml=./data/merchants.xml
merchants.xsl=./xsl/merchants.xsl
xmli.orders=./xmli
```

Listing 12.3: xmlserver.prp

```
merchant=emailaholic
sql.driver=sun.jdbc.odbc.JdbcOdbcDriver
sql.url=jdbc:odbc:XCommerce
# sql.user=SYSDBA
# sql.password=masterkey
```

Listing 12.4: viewedit.prp

```
editor.xsl=./xsl/editor.xsl
viewer.xsl=./xsl/viewer.xsl
# XMLi products
xmli.xml=./data/xmli.xml
xmli.pwd=xmli
xmli.orders=./xmli
```

Directories

The configuration files require that the files be organized in the following directories:

- data contains the list of merchants and an XMLi product list.
- xsl contains the style sheet for the shop, with the exception of Emailaholic-specific style sheets.
- properties contains all of the property files.
- docs is the document directory for the shop. It contains the JavaScript editor.js.
- emailaholic is the document directory for Emailaholic. It contains Emailaholic XSL files and images.
- xmli is an empty directory where XMLi orders are stored.

Compiling and Running

Before running this application, you must compile all the Java files. Use the Java compiler such as:

```
javac -classpath c:\jetty\lib\javax.servlet.jar;
➥c:\lotusxsl\lotusxsl.jar;c:\xml4j\xml4j.jar;. -sourcepath .
➥ Shop.java
```

It does not matter in which order you compile the files but you need to compile them all. It may be convenient to create a batch file to automate compiling.

Now you are ready to start your Web server. If you use Jetty, use the following command line:

```
java -classpath c:\jetty\lib\javax.servlet.jar;
➥c:\lotusxsl\lotusxsl.jar;c:\xml4j\xml4j.jar;.
➥com.mortbay.Jetty.Server21 properties\jetty.prp
```

CAUTION

Before you attempt to run the application, make sure that your *classpath* contains all the libraries that you need. These libraries include the servlet classes, the database driver, LotusXSL, IBM XML for Java, and the class to the XCommerce servlets themselves.

Also be sure you have created the database. This requires creating the Data Source in ODBC and entering product information with the console servlet.

URLs

Here are the URLs for the application. You may have to substitute the name of your computer in place of localhost:

- localhost/shop is the entry point for the shop.

- localhost/editor?merchant=xmli for the product editor.

- localhost/viewer?merchant=xmli for the order viewer.

- localhost:81/console for the console for Emailaholic data server.

Database

Emailaholic needs a database. Any JDBC-compliant database will do. The easiest solution, when running Windows, is probably to use an ODBC-compliant database. First, you need to create a blank database. The exact procedure depends on the database you use.

Next, you must create a Data Source with ODBC. In the Control Panel, double-click the ODBC icon. Select either User DSN or System DSN and click the Add button. Enter the XCommerce as Data Source name and the parameters to connect to the blank database you have just created. See Figure 12.1.

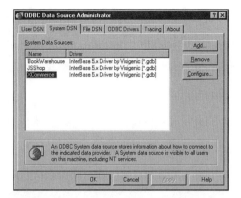

Figure 12.1: *Creating the Data Source in ODBC*

Before you can use the XML server, you need to create the database schema and insert a few products in the database. This is what `XMLServerConsole` is for. Point your browser to `localhost:81/console`. First click Create Tables, (see Figure 12.2). Enter the product information, as shown in Figure 12.3.

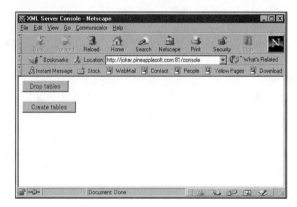

Figure 12.2: *Creating the database schema*

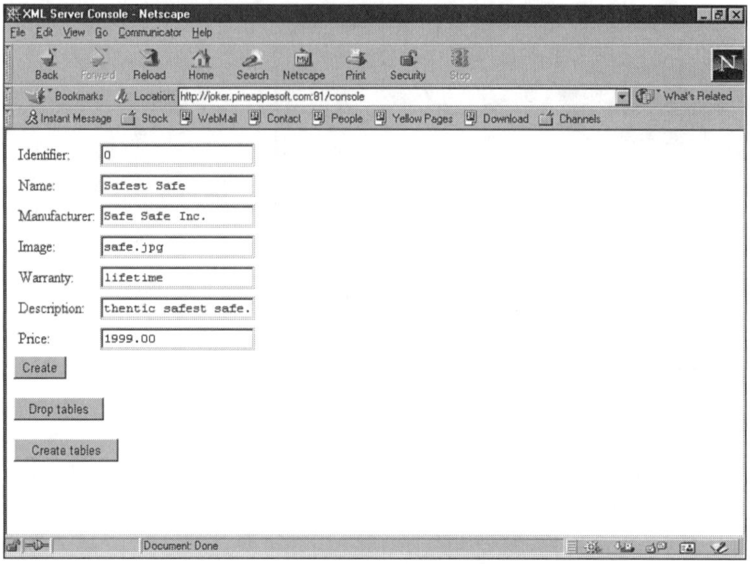

Figure 12.3: *Creating products in the database*

The Middle Tier

As explained in Chapter 11, "N-Tiered Architecture and XML," the middle tier server is a servlet that manages various XML documents. There is a document for the list of merchants or another for the list of products, and more. The servlet applies style sheets to them.

The middle tier server is made of the Shop class, shown in Listing 12.5. Shop decodes the URL and routes the requests to the appropriate object.

Listing 12.5: Shop.java

```
package com.psol.xcommerce;

import java.io.*;
import java.util.*;
import org.w3c.dom.*;
import javax.servlet.*;
import javax.servlet.http.*;

/**
 * Shop manages the shop, using XSL for any output.
 *
 * @version Sep 10, 1999
```

```
 * @author Benoît Marchal <bmarchal@pineapplesoft.com>
 */

public class Shop
    extends HttpServlet
{
    /**
     * the merchant list and the shopping cart
     */
    protected MerchantCollection merchants;
    protected Comlet checkout;

    /**
     * return the list of merchants
     */
    public MerchantCollection getMerchants()
    {
        return merchants;
    }

    /**
     * initializes the servlet
     */
    public void init()
        throws ServletException
    {
        merchants = new MerchantCollection(this);
        checkout = new Checkout(this);
    }

    /**
     * handle GET request
     * @param request the request received from the client
     * @param response interface to the client
     * @exception IOException error writing the reply
     * @exception ServletException error in processing the request
     */
```

continues

Listing 12.5: continued

```java
protected void doGet(HttpServletRequest request,
                     HttpServletResponse response)
   throws IOException, ServletException
{
   Comlet comlet = translateURL(request);
   if(null != comlet)
      comlet.doGet(request,response);
   else
      response.sendError(HttpServletResponse.SC_NOT_FOUND);
}

/**
 * handle POST request
 * @param request the request received from the client
 * @param response interface to the client
 * @exception IOException error writing the reply
 * @exception ServletException error in processing the request
 */
protected void doPost(HttpServletRequest request,
                      HttpServletResponse response)
   throws IOException, ServletException
{
   Comlet comlet = translateURL(request);
   if(null != comlet)
      comlet.doPost(request,response);
   else
      response.sendError(HttpServletResponse.SC_NOT_FOUND);
}

/**
 * Returns the time it was last modified.
 * @param request the request received from the client
 * @return time in milliseconds since January 1, 1970 midnight
 */
protected long getLastModified(HttpServletRequest request)
{
   try
```

```
    {
        Comlet comlet = translateURL(request);
        if(null != comlet)
            return comlet.getLastModified();
        else
            return -1;
    }
    catch(ServletException e)
    {
        return -1;
    }
}


/**
 * decode the URL and select the Comlet that will
 * handle the request
 * @param request the request received from the client
 * @return the Comlet identified in the request
 * @exception problem loading one of the object
 */
protected Comlet translateURL(HttpServletRequest request)
    throws ServletException
{
    String merchantID = null,
           pathInfo = request.getPathInfo();
    StringTokenizer tokenizer = null;
    if(null != pathInfo)
    {
        tokenizer = new StringTokenizer(pathInfo,"/");
        if(tokenizer.hasMoreTokens())
            merchantID = tokenizer.nextToken();
    }
    if(null == merchantID)
        return merchants;
    if(merchantID.equals("checkout"))
        return checkout;
    Merchant merchant = merchants.getMerchant(merchantID);
```

continues

Listing 12.5: continued

```
    String productID = null;
    if(tokenizer.hasMoreTokens())
        productID = tokenizer.nextToken();
    if(null == merchant || null == productID)
        return merchant;
    else
        return merchant.getProduct(productID);
}
}
```

The objects that really handle the request are derived from `Comlet`, defined in Listing 12.6. `Comlet` defines methods for the `GET` and `POST` requests.

Listing 12.6: Comlet.java

```java
package com.psol.xcommerce;

import java.io.*;
import java.util.*;
import javax.servlet.*;
import javax.servlet.http.*;

/**
 * Comlet is a subset of the servlet interface, Shop
 * delegates HTTP requests to Comlet descendants.
 *
 * @version Sep 10, 1999
 * @author Benoît Marchal <bmarchal@pineapplesoft.com>
 */

public class Comlet
    implements ServletConfig
{
    /**
     * properties
     */
    protected ServletConfig servletConfig;
    protected long lastModified = -1;
    protected Shop shop;
```

```
/**
 * creates a new Comlet
 * @param shop the shop it is part of
 */
public Comlet(Shop shop)
{
    this.shop = shop;
}

/**
 * return the servlet config
 */
public ServletConfig getServletConfig()
{
    return shop.getServletConfig();
}

/**
 * return the shop it is part of
 */
public Shop getShop()
{
    return shop;
}

/**
 * convenience: implements ServletConfig
 * @param name the parameter whose value is requested
 * @return the parameter value
 */
public String getInitParameter(String name)
{
    return shop.getInitParameter(name);
}

/**
```

continues

Listing 12.6: continued

```
 * convenience: implements ServletConfig
 * @return an enumeration of names
 */
public Enumeration getInitParameterNames()
{
    return shop.getInitParameterNames();
}


/**
 * convenience: implements ServletConfig
 * @return the config object
 */
public ServletContext getServletContext()
{
    return shop.getServletContext();
}


/**
 * handle GET request
 * @param request the request received from the client
 * @param response interface to the client
 * @exception IOException error writing the reply
 * @exception ServletException error in processing the request
 */
public void doGet(HttpServletRequest request,
                  HttpServletResponse response)
    throws IOException, ServletException
{
    response.sendError(HttpServletResponse.SC_BAD_REQUEST);
}


/**
 * handle POST request
 * @param request the request received from the client
 * @param response interface to the client
 * @exception IOException error writing the reply
 * @exception ServletException error in processing the request
```

```
     */
    public void doPost(HttpServletRequest request,
                        HttpServletResponse response)
        throws IOException, ServletException
    {
        response.sendError(HttpServletResponse.SC_BAD_REQUEST);
    }


    /**
     * return the time the data was last modified
     */
    public long getLastModified()
    {
        return lastModified;
    }


    /**
     * data has changed, update lastModified
     */
    public void freshened()
    {
        lastModified = System.currentTimeMillis();
    }
}
```

MerchantCollection

URLs in the form /shop are handled by MerchantCollection, which manages a list of merchants in XML. See Listing 12.7. Listing 12.8 is the list of merchants and Listing 12.9 is the style sheet.

EXAMPLE

Listing 12.7: MerchantCollection.java

```
package com.psol.xcommerce;

import java.io.*;
import java.util.*;
import org.w3c.dom.*;
import javax.servlet.*;
import javax.servlet.http.*;
```

continues

Listing 12.7: continued

```
/**
 * represents a list of merchants
 *
 * @version Sep 10, 1999
 * @author Benoît Marchal <bmarchal@pineapplesoft.com>
 */

public class MerchantCollection
    extends Comlet
{
    /**
     * properties
     */
    protected Dictionary merchants = new Hashtable();
    protected Document merchantsDocument = null,
                       merchantsXSL = null;

    /**
     * creates a new Merchant object
     * @param shop the shop it is part of
     * @param ServletException error reading the merchant list
     */
    public MerchantCollection(Shop shop)
        throws ServletException
    {
        super(shop);
        String fname = getInitParameter("merchants.xml");
        if(null != fname)
            merchantsDocument = XMLUtil.parse(fname);
        if(null == merchantsDocument)
            throw new UnavailableException(shop,"merchants.xml");
        freshened();
        Element topLevel = merchantsDocument.getDocumentElement();
        Enumeration enumeration =
            XMLUtil.extract(topLevel,"merchant");
        while(enumeration.hasMoreElements())
        {
```

```
        Element element =
            (Element)enumeration.nextElement();
        Merchant merchant =
            new Merchant(element,shop);
        merchants.put(merchant.getID(),merchant);
    }
}


/**
 * return a document with the list of merchants
 */
protected Document getDocument()
{
    return merchantsDocument;
}


/**
 * return the style sheet for the list of merchants
 * @exception ServletException error reading the document
 */
protected Document getXSL()
    throws ServletException
{
    if(null == merchantsXSL)
    {
        String fname = getInitParameter("merchants.xsl");
        if(null != fname)
            merchantsXSL = XMLUtil.parse(fname);
    }
    return merchantsXSL;
}


/**
 * return a given merchant.
 * @param id merchant id
 */
public Merchant getMerchant(String id)
```

continues

Listing 12.7: continued

```java
{
    return (Merchant)merchants.get(id);
}


/**
 * handle GET request
 * @param request the request received from the client
 * @param response interface to the client
 * @exception IOException error writing the reply
 * @exception ServletException error in processing the request
 */
public void doGet(HttpServletRequest request,
                  HttpServletResponse response)
    throws IOException, ServletException
{
    XMLUtil.transform(getDocument(),
                      getXSL(),
                      response.getWriter(),
                      response.getCharacterEncoding());
}
}
```

Listing 12.8: Merchants.xml

```xml
<?xml version="1.0"?>
<merchants>
    <merchant id="xmli">
        <name>XMLi</name>
        <description>Your specialist for XML products!</description>
        <products href="./data/xmli.xml"/>
        <stylesheet-all href="./xsl/products.xsl"/>
        <stylesheet href="./xsl/product.xsl"/>
    </merchant>
    <merchant id="emailaholic">
        <name>Emailaholic.com</name>
        <description>The largest electronic shop.
        All products delivered via email!</description>
        <products update="3600"
            href="http://localhost:81/xml"/>
```

```
    <stylesheet-all
        href="http://localhost:81/products.xsl"/>
    <stylesheet
        href="http://localhost:81/product.xsl"/>
    <post href="http://localhost:81/xml"
        user="SYSDBA" password="masterkey"/>
    </merchant>
</merchants>
```

Listing 12.9: Merchants.xsl

```
<?xml version="1.0" encoding="ISO-8859-1"?>
<xsl:stylesheet xmlns:xsl="http://www.w3.org/1999/XSL/Transform/"
                xmlns="http://www.w3.org/TR/REC-html40">


<xsl:output method="html"/>


<xsl:template match="/">
    <HTML>
    <HEAD>
        <TITLE>Online Shop</TITLE>
    </HEAD>
    <BODY>
        <P>Visit one of the following prestigious merchants:</P>
        <xsl:for-each select="merchants/merchant">
            <P><B><A><xsl:attribute name="HREF">shop/<xsl:value-of
                select="@id"/></xsl:attribute><xsl:value-of
                select="name"/></A></B><BR/>
                <xsl:value-of select="description"/><BR/></P>
        </xsl:for-each>
    </BODY>
    </HTML>
</xsl:template>


</xsl:stylesheet>
```

Merchant

EXAMPLE

Requests to /shop/emailaholic are forwarded to Merchant objects. Listing 12.10 is the Merchant class. It uses style sheets similar to Listings 12.11 and 12.12.

Listing 12.10: Merchant.java

```java
package com.psol.xcommerce;

import java.io.*;
import java.util.*;
import org.w3c.dom.*;
import javax.servlet.*;
import javax.servlet.http.*;

/**
 * a merchant is a collection of products
 *
 * @version Sep 10, 1999
 * @author Benoît Marchal <bmarchal@pineapplesoft.com>
 */

public class Merchant
    extends Comlet
{
    /**
     * properties
     */
    protected Element merchantElement;
    protected Dictionary products = null;
    protected Document productsDocument = null,
                       productsXSL = null,
                       productXSL = null;
    protected String id;
    protected long expire = Long.MAX_VALUE;

    /**
     * creates a new Merchant object
     * @param element the merchant element
     * @param shop the shop it is part of
     */
    public Merchant(Element element,Shop shop)
    {
        super(shop);
```

```
        merchantElement = element;
    }


    /**
     * return the element id
     */
    public String getID()
    {
        return merchantElement.getAttribute("id");
    }


    /**
     * return the post URL
     */
    public String getPostURL()
    {
        Element postElement =
            XMLUtil.extractFirst(merchantElement,"post");
        if(null != postElement)
            return postElement.getAttribute("href");
        else
            return null;
    }


    /**
     * return the post user
     */
    public String getPostUser()
    {
        Element postElement =
            XMLUtil.extractFirst(merchantElement,"post");
        if(null != postElement)
            return postElement.getAttribute("user");
        else
            return null;
    }
```

continues

Listing 12.10: continued

```
/**
 * return the post password
 */
public String getPostPassword()
{
    Element postElement =
        XMLUtil.extractFirst(merchantElement,"post");
    if(null != postElement)
        return postElement.getAttribute("password");
    else
        return null;
}


/**
 * return the list of products
 * @exception ServletException error reading the document
 */
protected Document getDocument()
    throws ServletException
{
    if(null == productsDocument ||
        expire < System.currentTimeMillis())
    {
        Element productsElement =
            XMLUtil.extractFirst(merchantElement,"products");
        if(null != productsElement)
        {
            String fname =
                productsElement.getAttribute("href");
            String update =
                productsElement.getAttribute("update");
            if(!XMLUtil.isEmpty(fname))
            {
                productsDocument = XMLUtil.parse(fname);
                freshened();
                productXSL = null;
                productsXSL = null;
```

```
            }
            if(!XMLUtil.isEmpty(update))
            {
                long u = Long.parseLong(update) * 1000;
                expire = System.currentTimeMillis() + u;
            }
        }
    }
    return productsDocument;
}


/**
 * return the style sheet for a list of products
 * @exception ServletException error reading the document
 */
protected Document getXSL()
    throws ServletException
{
    if(null == productsXSL)
    {
        Element productsXSLElement =
            XMLUtil.extractFirst(merchantElement,
                                 "stylesheet-all");
        if(null != productsXSLElement)
        {
            String fname =
                productsXSLElement.getAttribute("href");
            if(!XMLUtil.isEmpty(fname))
                productsXSL = XMLUtil.parse(fname);
        }
    }
    return productsXSL;
}


/**
 * return the style sheet for one product
 * @exception ServletException error reading the document
```

continues

Listing 12.10: continued

```
   */
   public Document getProductXSL()
      throws ServletException
   {
      if(null == productXSL)
      {
         Element productXSLElement =
            XMLUtil.extractFirst(merchantElement,"stylesheet");
         if(null != productXSLElement)
         {
            String fname =
               productXSLElement.getAttribute("href");
            if(!XMLUtil.isEmpty(fname))
               productXSL = XMLUtil.parse(fname);
         }
      }
      return productXSL;
   }


   /**
    * return a given product
    * @param id product index
    */
   public Product getProduct(String id)
      throws ServletException
   {
      if(null == products ||
         expire < System.currentTimeMillis())
      {
         Document productsDocument = getDocument();
         if(null != productsDocument)
         {
            Element topLevel =
               productsDocument.getDocumentElement();
            Enumeration enumeration =
               XMLUtil.extract(topLevel,"product");
            products = new Hashtable();
```

```
            while(enumeration.hasMoreElements())
            {
                Element element =
                    (Element)enumeration.nextElement();
                Product product =
                    new Product(element,this,shop);
                products.put(product.getID(),product);
            }
        }
    }
    // re-test: reading the product may fail
    if(null != products)
        return (Product)products.get(id);
    else
        return null;
}


/**
 * handle GET request
 * @param request the request received from the client
 * @param response interface to the client
 * @exception IOException error writing the reply
 * @exception ServletException error in processing the request
 */
public void doGet(HttpServletRequest request,
                    HttpServletResponse response)
    throws IOException, ServletException
{
    XMLUtil.transform(getDocument(),
                        getXSL(),
                        response.getWriter(),
                        response.getCharacterEncoding());
}
}
```

Product

Requests for a specific product take the form `/shop/xmli/1`. They are forwarded to `Product` objects, as shown in Listing 12.11.

Listing 12.11: Product.java

```java
package com.psol.xcommerce;

import java.io.*;
import java.text.*;
import org.w3c.dom.*;
import javax.servlet.*;
import javax.servlet.http.*;

/**
 * a product is various information like price
 *
 * @version Sep 10, 1999
 * @author Benoît Marchal <bmarchal@pineapplesoft.com>
 */

public class Product
    extends Comlet
{
    /**
     * properties
     */
    protected Element productElement;
    protected Document productDocument;
    protected Merchant merchant;

    /**
     * creates a new product
     * @param element XML description of the product
     * @param merchant merchant owning this product
     * @param shop the shop it is part of
     */
    public Product(Element element,
                   Merchant merchant,
                   Shop shop)
    {
```

```
    super(shop);
    productElement = element;
    this.merchant = merchant;
}

/**
 * returns the DOM Element
 */
public Element getElement()
{
    return productElement;
}

/**
 * returns the merchant
 */
public Merchant getMerchant()
{
    return merchant;
}

/**
 * return the product id
 */
public String getID()
{
    return productElement.getAttribute("id");
}

/**
 * return the product name
 */
public String getName()
{
    Element nameElement =
        XMLUtil.extractFirst(productElement,"name");
    return XMLUtil.getText(nameElement);
```

continues

Listing 12.11: continued

```
    }

    /**
     * return the product price
     */
    public String getPrice()
    {
        Element priceElement =
            XMLUtil.extractFirst(productElement,"price");
        return XMLUtil.getText(priceElement);
    }

    /**
     * return a document around the product
     */
    protected Document getDocument()
    {
        if(null == productDocument)
        {
            productDocument = XMLUtil.createDocument(productElement);
            Element element = productDocument.getDocumentElement();
            element.setAttribute("merchant",merchant.getID());
        }
        return productDocument;
    }

    /**
     * handle GET request
     * @param request the request received from the client
     * @param response interface to the client
     * @exception IOException error writing the reply
     * @exception ServletException error in processing the request
     */
    public void doGet(HttpServletRequest request,
                      HttpServletResponse response)
        throws IOException, ServletException
    {
```

```
    XMLUtil.transform(getDocument(),
                        merchant.getProductXSL(),
                        response.getWriter(),
                        response.getCharacterEncoding());
  }


  /**
   * return the time the data was last modified
   */
  public long getLastModified()
  {
      return merchant.getLastModified();
  }
}
```

Checkout

Listing 12.12 handles requests to check out of the shop, which is used for purchases. Checkout collects information about the buyer and creates an order in XML. The order is either saved as a local file or posted to the merchant Web server. Posting to a remote site is done through HTTPPost, defined in Listing 12.13.

Listing 12.12: Checkout.java

```
package com.psol.xcommerce;


import java.io.*;
import java.text.*;
import java.util.*;
import org.w3c.dom.*;
import javax.servlet.*;
import javax.servlet.http.*;


/**
 * presents the invoice and emails it
 *
 * @version Sep 10, 1999
 * @author Benoît Marchal <bmarchal@pineapplesoft.com>
 */
```

continues

Listing 12.12: continued

```
public class Checkout
    extends Comlet
{
    /**
     * creates a new Checkout object
     * @param shop the shop it is part of
     */
    public Checkout(Shop shop)
    {
        super(shop);
    }


    /**
     * handle POST request
     * @param request the request received from the client
     * @param response interface to the client
     * @exception IOException error writing the reply
     * @exception ServletException error in processing the request
     */
    public void doPost(HttpServletRequest request,
                        HttpServletResponse response)
        throws ServletException, IOException
    {
        if(isAddressComplete(request))
            doSaveOrder(request,response);
        else
            doCollectData(request,response);
    }


    /**
     * return true if the address is complete
     * @param request client request
     */
    protected boolean isAddressComplete(HttpServletRequest request)
    {
        // region is not mandatory
        String[] fields =
```

```
    {
        "name", "street", "postal-code",
        "locality", "country", "email"
    };
    int found = 0;
    for(int i = 0;i < fields.length;i++)
    {
        String value = request.getParameter(fields[i]);
        if(!XMLUtil.isEmpty(value))
            found++;
    }
    return found == fields.length;
}


/**
 * save the order
 * @param request the request received from the client
 * @param response interface to the client
 * @exception IOException error writing the reply
 * @exception ServletException error in processing the request
 */
public void doSaveOrder(HttpServletRequest request,
                        HttpServletResponse response)
    throws ServletException, IOException
{
    String productid = request.getParameter("product"),
           merchantid = request.getParameter("merchant");
    Product product = getProduct(merchantid,productid);
    if(null == product)
    {
        response.sendError(HttpServletResponse.SC_NOT_FOUND);
        return;
    }
    Merchant merchant = product.getMerchant();
    String postURL = merchant.getPostURL();
    Writer writer = null;
    if(null != postURL)
```

continues

Listing 12.12: continued

```
          writer = new StringWriter();
      else
      {
          String directory = getInitParameter(merchant.getID()
                                            + ".orders"),
                  // should be enough to avoid duplicates
                  fname = String.valueOf(System.currentTimeMillis())
                                    + ".xml";
          File file = new File(directory,fname);
          writer = new FileWriter(file);
      }
      writer.write("<?xml version=\"1.0\"?>");
      writer.write("<order>");
      writer.write("<buyer");
      writeAttribute("name",request,writer);
      writeAttribute("street",request,writer);
      writeAttribute("region",request,writer);
      writeAttribute("postal-code",request,writer);
      writeAttribute("locality",request,writer);
      writeAttribute("country",request,writer);
      writeAttribute("email",request,writer);
      writer.write("/>");
      writer.write("<product");
      writeAttribute("quantity",request,writer);
      writer.write(" id=\"");
      writer.write(product.getID());
      writer.write("\" name=\"");
      writer.write(product.getName());
      writer.write("\" price=\"");
      writer.write(product.getPrice());
      writer.write("\"/></order>");
      writer.close();
      if(null != postURL)
      {
          Dictionary parameters = new Hashtable();
          String user = merchant.getPostUser(),
                  password = merchant.getPostPassword(),
```

```
                        xmlData = writer.toString();
        parameters.put("user",user);
        parameters.put("password",password);
        parameters.put("xmldata",xmlData);
        HTTPPost post = new HTTPPost(postURL,parameters);
        post.doRequest();
    }
    writer = response.getWriter();
    writer.write("<HTML><HEAD><TITLE>Checkout</TITLE></HEAD>");
    writer.write("<BODY><P>Thank you for shopping with us!");
    writer.write("<BR><A HREF=\"");
    writer.write(request.getServletPath());
    writer.write("\">Return to the shop</A>");
    writer.write("</BODY></HTML>");
    writer.flush();
}


/**
 * helper method: return the product
 */
protected Product getProduct(String merchantid,
                                String productid)
    throws ServletException
{
    MerchantCollection merchants = shop.getMerchants();
    Merchant merchant = merchants.getMerchant(merchantid);
    if(null != merchant)
        return merchant.getProduct(productid);
    else
        return null;
}


/**
 * helper method: write one attribute
 */
protected void writeAttribute(String id,
                                HttpServletRequest request,
```

continues

Listing 12.12: continued

```
                                    Writer writer)
    throws IOException
{
    String value = request.getParameter(id);
    if(!XMLUtil.isEmpty(value))
    {
       writer.write(" ");
       writer.write(id);
       writer.write("=\"");
       writer.write(value);
       writer.write("\"");
    }
}


/**
 * collect buyer data
 * @param request the request received from the client
 * @param response interface to the client
 * @exception IOException error writing the reply
 * @exception ServletException error in processing the request
 */
public void doCollectData(HttpServletRequest request,
                          HttpServletResponse response)
    throws ServletException, IOException
{
    String productid = request.getParameter("product"),
           merchantid = request.getParameter("merchant"),
           quantity = request.getParameter("quantity");
    Product product = getProduct(merchantid,productid);
    if(null == product)
    {
       response.sendError(HttpServletResponse.SC_NOT_FOUND);
       return;
    }
    Writer writer = response.getWriter();
    writer.write("<HTML><HEAD><TITLE>Checkout</TITLE></HEAD>");
    writer.write("<BODY><P>Enter your name and address:");
```

```
        writer.write("<FORM METHOD=\"POST\" ACTION=\"");
        writer.write(request.getServletPath() + "/checkout");
        writer.write("\"><TABLE BORDER=\"0\">");
        writeRow("Name *:","name",request,writer);
        writeRow("Street *:","street",request,writer);
        writeRow("Region:","region",request,writer);
        writeRow("ZIP or postal-code *:","postal-code",request,writer);
        writeRow("Locality *:","locality",request,writer);
        writeRow("Country *:","country",request,writer);
        writeRow("Email *:","email",request,writer);
        writer.write("</TABLE>");
        writer.write("Your order: ");
        writer.write(quantity);
        writer.write(" * ");
        writer.write(product.getName());
        writer.write(" at ");
        writer.write(product.getPrice());
        writer.write(" each<BR>");
        writer.write("<INPUT TYPE=\"HIDDEN\" NAME=\"product\"");
        writer.write(" VALUE=\"");
        writer.write(productid);
        writer.write("\">");
        writer.write("<INPUT TYPE=\"HIDDEN\" NAME=\"merchant\"");
        writer.write(" VALUE=\"");
        writer.write(merchantid);
        writer.write("\">");
        writer.write("<INPUT TYPE=\"HIDDEN\" NAME=\"quantity\"");
        writer.write(" VALUE=\"");
        writer.write(quantity);
        writer.write("\">");
        writer.write("<INPUT TYPE=\"SUBMIT\" VALUE=\"Order\">");
        writer.write("</FORM></HTML>");
        writer.flush();
    }

    /**
     * helper method: write one row
```

continues

Listing 12.12: continued

```
      */
    protected void writeRow(String label,
                            String id,
                            HttpServletRequest request,
                            Writer writer)
       throws IOException
    {
      writer.write("<TR><TD>");
      writer.write(label);
      writer.write("</TD><TD>");
      writer.write("<INPUT TYPE=\"TEXT\" NAME=\"");
      writer.write(id);
      writer.write("\"");
      String value = request.getParameter(id);
      if(!XMLUtil.isEmpty(value))
      {
         writer.write(" VALUE=\"");
         writer.write(value);
         writer.write("\"");
      }
      writer.write("></TD></TR>");
   }
}
```

Listing 12.13: HTTPPost.java

```
package com.psol.xcommerce;

import java.io.*;
import java.net.*;
import java.util.*;

/**
 * Does an HTTP POST.
 *
 * @version Sep 10, 1999
 * @author Benoît Marchal <bmarchal@pineapplesoft.com>
 */
```

```java
public class HTTPPost
{
    /**
     * properties
     */
    protected URL url;
    protected String query;

    /**
     * Creates a new HTTPPost.
     * @param url URL to connect to
     * @parameters POST request parameter
     */
    public HTTPPost(URL url,Dictionary parameters)
    {
        this.url = url;
        query = buildQuery(parameters);
    }

    /**
     * Creates a new HTTPPost.
     * @param url URL to connect to
     * @parameters POST request parameter
     * @exception MalformedURLException if the URL is invalid
     */
    public HTTPPost(String url,Dictionary parameters)
        throws MalformedURLException
    {
        this(new URL(url),parameters);
    }

    /**
     * executes the post request
     * @exception IOException error posting the data
     */
    public void doRequest()
        throws IOException
```

continues

Listing 12.13: continued

```
{
    // this stupid thing does not default to 80...
    int port = url.getPort();
    if(port == -1)
        port = 80;
    Socket s = new Socket(url.getHost(),port);
    PrintStream o = new PrintStream(s.getOutputStream());
    o.print("POST "); o.print(url.getFile());
    o.print(" HTTP/1.0\r\n");
    o.print("Accept: text/html text/xml\r\n");
    o.print("Host: "); o.print(url.getHost()); o.print("\r\n");
    o.print("Content-type: ");
    o.print("application/x-www-form-urlencoded\r\n");
    o.print("Content-length: "); o.print(query.length());
    o.print("\r\n\r\n");
    o.print(query);
    o.print("\r\n");
    InputStream i = s.getInputStream();
    StringBuffer reply = new StringBuffer();
    int c = i.read();
    boolean firstLine = true;
    while(c != -1)
    {
        if(firstLine)
            if(c == '\r' || c == '\n')
                firstLine = false;
            else
                reply.append((char)c);
        c = i.read();
    }
    String stReply = reply.toString();
    int returnCode = Integer.parseInt(stReply.substring(9,12));
    if(!(returnCode >= 200 && returnCode < 300))
        throw new ProtocolException(stReply.substring(13));
}

/**
```

```
 * format the request according to the proper encoding
 * @param parameters query parameters
 * @return string with the query properly formatted
 */
protected String buildQuery(Dictionary parameters)
{
    StringBuffer request = new StringBuffer();
    Enumeration keys = parameters.keys();
    String key = null;
    boolean first = true;
    while(keys.hasMoreElements())
    {
        if(!first)
            request.append('&');
        else
            first = false;
        key = (String)keys.nextElement();
        request.append(key);
        request.append('=');
        request.append(
            URLEncoder.encode((String)parameters.get(key)));
        // request.append("\r\n");
    }
    return request.toString();
}
}
```

Encapsulating XML Tools

EXAMPLE

You use the DOM interface to encapsulate tools in XCommerce; however, there are holes in DOM. In particular, there is no standard way to create or parse XML documents. The XSL processor is even worse because it has no API at all.

The class XMLUtil encapsulates the vendor-specific part in the XML parser and XSL processor. If you later decide to use another XML parser, XMLUtil is the only class that needs updating. XMLUtil is defined in Listing 12.14.

Listing 12.14: XMLUtil.java

```
package com.psol.xcommerce;

import java.io.*;
import java.util.*;
import org.xml.sax.*;
import org.w3c.dom.*;
import com.lotus.xsl.*;
import javax.servlet.*;
import com.ibm.xml.dom.*;
import com.ibm.xml.parsers.*;
import com.lotus.xml.*;
import com.lotus.xml.xml4j2dom.*;

/**
 * XMLUtil isolates non-portable aspects of DOM, calling
 * XSL processor and some utility functions.<BR>
 * This version is for IBM's XML for Java, to use another
 * processor this is the only class to change.
 *
 * @version Sep 10, 1999
 * @author Benoît Marchal <bmarchal@pineapplesoft.com>
 */

class XMLUtil
{
    /**
     * the HTML doctype
     */
    protected static final String DOCTYPE =
        "<!DOCTYPE HTML PUBLIC \"-//W3C//DTD HTML 4.0 " +
        "Transitional//EN\">";

    /**
     * parses a document with DOM
     * @param systemID system id (URL) for the document
     * @return DOM Document
     * @exception ServletException error parsing the document
```

```java
     */
    public static Document parse(String systemID)
        throws ServletException
    {
        try
        {
            DOMParser parser = new DOMParser();
            parser.parse(systemID);
            return parser.getDocument();
        }
        catch(SAXException e)
        {
            throw new ServletException(e);
        }
        catch(IOException e)
        {
            throw new ServletException(e);
        }
    }


    /**
     * parses a document with DOM
     * @param reader reader for the document
     * @return DOM Document
     * @exception ServletException error parsing the document
     */
    public static Document parse(Reader reader)
        throws ServletException
    {
        try
        {
            InputSource inputSource = new InputSource(reader);
            DOMParser parser = new DOMParser();
            parser.parse(inputSource);
            return parser.getDocument();
        }
        catch(SAXException e)
```

continues

Listing 12.14: continued

```
    {
        throw new ServletException(e);
    }
    catch(IOException e)
    {
        throw new ServletException(e);
    }
}

/**
 * turns DOM tree in a string
 * @param node root of the tree
 */
public static String toString(Node node)
{
    // IBM parser has no "saveAs" method or we would use it
    // this version does not handle all node types
    StringBuffer buffer = new StringBuffer();
    switch(node.getNodeType())
    {
        case Node.ATTRIBUTE_NODE:
        {
            Attr attr = (Attr)node;
            buffer.append(' ');
            buffer.append(attr.getName());
            buffer.append("=\"");
            buffer.append(attr.getValue());
            buffer.append('\"');
            break;
        }
        case Node.DOCUMENT_NODE:
        {
            Document document = (Document)node;
            Element topLevel = document.getDocumentElement();
            buffer.append("<?xml version=\"1.0\"?>");
            buffer.append(toString(topLevel));
            break;
```

```
        }
        case Node.ELEMENT_NODE:
        {
            Element element = (Element)node;
            buffer.append("<");
            buffer.append(element.getTagName());
            NamedNodeMap attrs = element.getAttributes();
            for(int i = 0;i < attrs.getLength();i++)
                buffer.append(toString(attrs.item(i)));
            NodeList children = node.getChildNodes();
            if(children.getLength() == 0)
                // shorthand for empty element
                buffer.append("/>");
            else
            {
                buffer.append(">");
                for(int i = 0;i < children.getLength();i++)
                    buffer.append(toString(children.item(i)));
                buffer.append("</");
                buffer.append(element.getTagName());
                buffer.append(">");
            }
            break;
        }
        case Node.TEXT_NODE:
        {
            Text text = (Text)node;
            buffer.append(text.getData());
            break;
        }
        default:
            throw new NotImplementedError();
    }
    return buffer.toString();
}

/**
```

Listing 12.14: continued

```
 * creates an empty DOM document
 * @return DOM document
 */
public static Document createDocument()
{
   Document document = new DocumentImpl();
   return document;
}


/**
 * creates a DOM document with a top-level element
 * @param element top-level element
 * @return DOM document
 */
public static Document createDocument(Element element)
{
   Document document = createDocument();
   Node celement = cloneNode(document,element);
   document.appendChild(celement);
   return document;
}


/**
 * clone a DOM Node in the context of a Document<BR>
 * Element.cloneNode() does not work when copying elements
 * from one document to another, the clone remains attached
 * to original document
 * @param document document to attach the clone to
 * @param node node to clone
 * @return the clone
 */
public static Node cloneNode(Document document,
                                       Node node)
{
   // o = original
   // c = clone
   switch(node.getNodeType())
```

```
        {
            case Node.ATTRIBUTE_NODE:
            {
                Attr o = (Attr)node,
                    c = document.createAttribute(o.getName());
                c.setValue(o.getValue());
                return c;
            }
            case Node.ELEMENT_NODE:
            {
                Element o = (Element)node,
                        c = document.createElement(o.getTagName());
                NodeList children = o.getChildNodes();
                for(int i = 0;i < children.getLength();i++)
                {
                    Node n = cloneNode(document,children.item(i));
                    c.appendChild(n);
                }
                NamedNodeMap attrs = o.getAttributes();
                for(int i = 0;i < attrs.getLength();i++)
                {
                    Attr a = (Attr)cloneNode(document,attrs.item(i));
                    c.setAttributeNode(a);
                }
                return c;
            }
            case Node.TEXT_NODE:
            {
                Text o = (Text)node,
                    c = document.createTextNode(o.getData());
                return c;
            }
            default:
                throw new NotImplementedError();
        }
    }
```

continues

Listing 12.14: continued

```
/**
 * apply a style sheet and prints the result
 * @param document original document
 * @param xsl style sheet
 * @param writer output writer
 * @param encoding character encoding
 */
public static void transform(Document document,
                             Document xsl,
                             PrintWriter writer,
                             String encoding)
   throws ServletException
{
   XML4JLiaison4dom liaison = new XML4JLiaison4dom();
   XSLTInputSource documentIn = new XSLTInputSource(document),
                   xslIn = new XSLTInputSource(xsl);
   XSLTResultTarget result = new XSLTResultTarget(writer);
   try
   {
      XSLProcessor xslProcessor = new XSLProcessor(liaison);
      xslProcessor.process(documentIn,xslIn,result);
   }
   catch(Exception e)
   {
      throw new ServletException(e);
   }
}


/**
 * retrieve elements in the children of a node<BR>
 * it assumes no recursive structure, in other
 * word in products/product/related/product,
 * it would NOT find the second product
 * @param element top of tree
```

```
 * @param name element we are looking for
 * @return an enumeration of the elements found
 */
public static Enumeration extract(Element element,String name)
{
    // ultimately replace with a XQL engine
    Vector vector = new Vector();
    extract(element,name,vector);
    return vector.elements();
}


/**
 * retrieve the first element in the children of a node
 * @param element top of tree
 * @param name element we are looking for
 * @return an enumeration of the elements found
 */
public static Element extractFirst(Element element,
                                   String name)
{
    Vector vector = new Vector();
    extract(element,name,vector);   // not optimized
    if(vector.size() > 0)
        return (Element)vector.firstElement();
    else
        return null;
}


/**
 * helper method for extract
 * @param node top of tree
 * @param name element we are looking for
 * @return an enumeration of the elements found
 */
protected static void extract(Node node,
                              String name,
                              Vector vector)
```

continues

Listing 12.14: continued

```
{
    if(node.getNodeType() == Node.ELEMENT_NODE)
    {
        if(node.getNodeName().equals(name))
            // we stop, so it does not work with
            // recursive structures
            vector.addElement(node);
        else
        {
            NodeList children = node.getChildNodes();
            for(int i = 0;i < children.getLength();i++)
                extract(children.item(i),name,vector);
        }
    }
}


/**
 * returns the text in the node
 * @param node the node to read from
 * @return the text in the node
 */
public static String getText(Node node)
{
    StringBuffer text = new StringBuffer();
    if(node.getNodeType() == Node.ELEMENT_NODE)
    {
        NodeList children = node.getChildNodes();
        for(int i = 0;i < children.getLength();i++)
        {
            Node n = children.item(i);
            if(n.getNodeType() == Node.TEXT_NODE)
            {
                Text t = (Text)n;
                text.append(t.getData());
            }
        }
    }
```

```java
        return text.toString();
   }


   /**
    * check if a string is empty
    * @param string string to test
    * @return true if empty, false otherwise
    */
   public static boolean isEmpty(String string)
   {
      if(null != string)
         return string.trim().length() == 0;
      else
         return true;
   }


   /**
    * Write the input in XML (or HTML) by escaping what
    * must be escaped.
    * @param writer write on this
    * @param string string to write
    * @exception IOException error writing
    */
   public static void writeInXML(Writer writer,String string)
      throws IOException
   {
      for(int i = 0;i < string.length();i++)
      {
         char c = string.charAt(i);
         if(c == '<')
            writer.write("&lt;");
         else if(c == '&')
            writer.write("&amp;");
         else
            writer.write(c);
      }
   }
}
```

XMLUtil throws a NotImplementedError exception when it hits something that is currently not implemented. It is better to debug applications that clearly report their limits. NotImplementedError is defined in Listing 12.15.

Listing 12.15: NotImplementedError.java

```java
package com.psol.xcommerce;


/**

 * As the name implies, it signals that something is not yet

 * implemented. It is cleaner than hijacking some other error

 * core. In particular, it saves on debugging! No trying to

 * figure out why something failed when it's not there yet.

 *

 * @version Sep 10, 1999

 * @author Benoît Marchal <bmarchal@pineapplesoft.com>

 */


public class NotImplementedError

   extends Error

{

   /**

    * constructs a NotImplementedError with no specified detail message

    */

   public NotImplementedError()

   {

      super();

   }


   /**

    * constructs a NotImplementedError with a detail message

    * @param st detail message

    */

   public NotImplementedError(String st)

   {

      super(st);

   }

}
```

The Data Tier

EXAMPLE

Listing 12.16 shows the data tier for `Emailaholic`. This data tier can generate a list of products in response to `GET` requests. It also accepts orders sent with `POST` requests. For security purposes, the database username and password must be provided.

Listing 12.16: XMLServer.java

```java
package com.psol.xcommerce;

import java.io.*;
import java.sql.*;
import java.text.*;
import org.w3c.dom.*;
import javax.servlet.*;
import javax.servlet.http.*;

/**
 * XMLServer returns database records in XML.
 *
 * @version Dec 23, 1999
 * @author Benoît Marchal <bmarchal@pineapplesoft.com>
 */

public class XMLServer
    extends HttpServlet
{
   /**
    * currency formater for numbers
    */
   protected NumberFormat formatter =
      NumberFormat.getCurrencyInstance();


   /**
    * process GET request
    * @param request HTTP request
    * @param response hold the response
    * @exception ServletException error processing the request
    * @exception IOException error writing the result
```

continues

Listing 12.16: continued

```
    */
    protected void doGet(HttpServletRequest request,
                          HttpServletResponse response)
      throws ServletException, IOException
    {

        response.setContentType("application/xml");
        Writer writer = response.getWriter();
        String sqlDriver = getInitParameter("sql.driver"),
               sqlURL = getInitParameter("sql.url"),
               sqlUser = getInitParameter("sql.user"),
               sqlPassword = getInitParameter("sql.password"),
               merchant = getInitParameter("merchant");
        writer.write("<?xml version=\"1.0\"?>");
        writer.write("<products merchant=\"");
        writer.write(merchant);
        writer.write("\">");
        try
        {

            Class.forName(sqlDriver);
            Connection connection =
                DriverManager.getConnection(sqlURL,
                                            sqlUser,
                                            sqlPassword);
            try
            {

                Statement stmt = connection.createStatement();
                try
                {

                    ResultSet rs =
                        stmt.executeQuery("select id, name, " +
                            "manufacturer, img, warranty, " +
                            "description, price from products");
                    while(rs.next())
                    {

                        writer.write("<product id=\"");
                        writer.write(String.valueOf(rs.getInt(1)));
                        writer.write("\" xmlns:em=\"http://www.emailaholic");
```

```
                        writer.write(".com/xt/1.0\"><name>");
                        writer.write(rs.getString(2));
                        writer.write("</name><em:manufacturer>");
                        writer.write(rs.getString(3));
                        writer.write("</em:manufacturer><em:image>");
                        writer.write(rs.getString(4));
                        writer.write("</em:image><em:warranty>");
                        writer.write(rs.getString(5));
                        writer.write("</em:warranty><description>");
                        writer.write(rs.getString(6));
                        writer.write("</description><price>");
                        writer.write(formatter.format(rs.getDouble(7)));
                        writer.write("</price></product>");
                    }
                }
                finally
                {
                    stmt.close();
                }
            }
            finally
            {
                connection.close();
            }
        }
        catch(ClassNotFoundException e)
        {
            throw new ServletException(e);
        }
        catch(SQLException e)
        {
            throw new ServletException(e);
        }
        writer.write("</products>");
        writer.flush();
    }
```

continues

Listing 12.16: continued

```
/**
 * process POST request
 * @param request HTTP request
 * @param response hold the response
 * @exception ServletException error processing the request
 * @exception IOException error writing the result
 */
protected void doPost(HttpServletRequest request,
                      HttpServletResponse response)
    throws ServletException, IOException
{
    // there is no error checking at all
    // if incorrect, throws an exception:
    // it goes to a computer so it's for technicians anyway
    String sqlDriver = getInitParameter("sql.driver"),
           sqlURL = getInitParameter("sql.url"),
           sqlUser = request.getParameter("user"),
           sqlPassword = request.getParameter("password"),
           xmlData = request.getParameter("xmldata");

    Reader reader = new StringReader(xmlData);
    Document orderDocument = XMLUtil.parse(reader);
    Element orderElement = orderDocument.getDocumentElement(),
            buyerElement =
                XMLUtil.extractFirst(orderElement,"buyer"),
            productElement =
                XMLUtil.extractFirst(orderElement,"product");
    String name = buyerElement.getAttribute("name"),
           street = buyerElement.getAttribute("street"),
           region = buyerElement.getAttribute("region"),
           postal_code =
               buyerElement.getAttribute("postal-code"),
           locality = buyerElement.getAttribute("locality"),
           country = buyerElement.getAttribute("country"),
           email = buyerElement.getAttribute("email"),
           productid = productElement.getAttribute("id"),
           productname = productElement.getAttribute("name"),
```

```
            productprice = productElement.getAttribute("price"),
            productquantity =
                productElement.getAttribute("quantity");


try
{
    Class.forName(sqlDriver);
    Connection connection =
        DriverManager.getConnection(sqlURL,
                                        sqlUser,
                                        sqlPassword);
    try
    {
        PreparedStatement stmt =
            connection.prepareStatement(
            "insert into orders (name,street,region," +
            "postal_code,locality,country,email," +
            "productid,productname,productprice," +
            "productquantity) " +
            "values(?,?,?,?,?,?,?,?,?,?,?)");
        try
        {
            stmt.setString(1,name);
            stmt.setString(2,street);
            stmt.setString(3,region);
            stmt.setString(4,postal_code);
            stmt.setString(5,locality);
            stmt.setString(6,country);
            stmt.setString(7,email);
            stmt.setString(8,productid);
            stmt.setString(9,productname);
            stmt.setDouble(10,
                formatter.parse(productprice).doubleValue());
            stmt.setString(11,productquantity);
            stmt.executeUpdate();
            connection.commit();
```

continues

Listing 12.16: continued

```
            }
            finally
            {
                stmt.close();
            }
        }
        finally
        {
            connection.close();
        }
    }
    catch(ClassNotFoundException e)
    {
        throw new ServletException(e);
    }
    catch(SQLException e)
    {
        throw new ServletException(e);
    }
    catch(ParseException e)
    {
        throw new ServletException(e);
    }
    response.setStatus(HttpServletResponse.SC_OK);
    response.setContentType("text/xml");
    Writer writer = response.getWriter();
    writer.write("<?xml version=\"1.0\"?>");
    writer.write("<status>200</status>");
    writer.flush();
    }
}
```

Listing 12.17 is XMLServerConsole, a simple management interface for the database.

Listing 12.17: XMLServerConsole.java

```java
package com.psol.xcommerce;

import java.io.*;
import java.sql.*;
import javax.servlet.*;
import javax.servlet.http.*;

/**
 * Simple console to create database and enter data in
 * the SQL database.
 *
 * @version Dec 23, 1999
 * @author Benoît Marchal <bmarchal@pineapplesoft.com>
 */

public class XMLServerConsole
    extends HttpServlet
{
    /**
     * handles GET request
     * @param request HTTP request
     * @param response hold the response
     * @exception SerlvetException error handling the request
     * @exception IOException error writing the reply
     */
    protected void doGet(HttpServletRequest request,
                         HttpServletResponse response)
        throws ServletException, IOException
    {
        doProcess(request,response);
    }

    /**
     * handles GET request
     * @param request HTTP request
     * @param response hold the response
     * @exception SerlvetException error handling the request
```

continues

Listing 12.17: continued

```java
 * @exception IOException error writing the reply
 */
protected void doPost(HttpServletRequest request,
                      HttpServletResponse response)
    throws ServletException, IOException
{
    doProcess(request,response);
}


/**
 * GET and POST requests are forwarded here
 * @param request HTTP request
 * @param response hold the response
 * @exception SerlvetException error handling the request
 * @exception IOException error writing the reply
 */
protected void doProcess(HttpServletRequest request,
                         HttpServletResponse response)
    throws ServletException, IOException
{
    String sqlDriver = getInitParameter("sql.driver"),
           sqlURL = getInitParameter("sql.url"),
           sqlUser = getInitParameter("sql.user"),
           sqlPassword = getInitParameter("sql.password");
    try
    {
        Class.forName(sqlDriver);
        Connection connection =
            DriverManager.getConnection(sqlURL,
                                        sqlUser,
                                        sqlPassword);
        try
        {
            String action = request.getParameter("action");
            if(null != action)
            {
                if(action.equalsIgnoreCase("create"))
                    doUpdates(request,connection,createStatements);
```

```
                    else if(action.equalsIgnoreCase("drop"))
                        doUpdates(request,connection,dropStatements);
                    else if(action.equalsIgnoreCase("delete"))
                        doDelete(request,connection);
                    else if(action.equalsIgnoreCase("insert"))
                        doInsert(request,connection);
                }
                doPage(request,response,connection);
            }
            finally
            {
                connection.close();
            }
        }
        catch(Exception e)
        {
            throw new ServletException(e);
        }
    }


    /**
     * drop and create statements to delete/create the database
     */
    private static final String[] dropStatements =
    {
        "drop table products",
        "drop table orders",
    };
    private static final String[] createStatements =
    {
        "create table products (id integer not null constraint idconstraint pri-
mary key," +
        "name varchar(50),manufacturer varchar(50)," +
        "img varchar(30),warranty varchar(20)," +
        "description varchar(150),price real)",
        "create table orders (name varchar(50)," +
        "street varchar(100),region varchar(50)," +
        "postal_code varchar(15),locality varchar(50)," +
```

continues

Listing 12.17: continued

```
           "country varchar(25),email varchar(50)," +
           "productid integer,productname varchar(50)," +
           "productprice real,productquantity integer)"
   };


   /**
    * execute a number of updates on the database
    * (typically to create schema)
    * @param request HTTP request
    * @param connection database connection
    * @param statements statements to execute
    * @throw SQLException one statement throw an exception
    */
   protected void doUpdates(HttpServletRequest request,
                            Connection connection,
                            String[] statements)
      throws SQLException
   {
      Statement stmt = connection.createStatement();
      SQLException e = null;
      try
      {
         for(int i = 0;i < statements.length;i++)
            try
               { stmt.executeUpdate(statements[i]); }
            catch(SQLException x)
               { e = e != null ? e : x; }
         if(null != e)
         {
            throw e;
         }
      }
      finally
      {
         stmt.close();
      }
   }
```

```
/**
 * delete one product from the database
 * @param request HTTP request
 * @param connection database connection
 * @return the form to display (the result screen if you like)
 */
protected void doDelete(HttpServletRequest request,
                        Connection connection)
    throws SQLException
{
    PreparedStatement stmt =
        connection.prepareStatement(
            "delete from products where id = ?");
    try
    {
        String id = request.getParameter("id");
        stmt.setInt(1,Integer.parseInt(id));
        stmt.executeUpdate();
    }
    finally
    {
        stmt.close();
    }
}


/**
 * create a new product in the database
 * @param request HTTP request
 * @param connection database connection
 * @return the form to display (the result screen if you like)
 */
protected void doInsert(HttpServletRequest request,
                        Connection connection)
    throws SQLException, Exception
{
    String id = request.getParameter("id"),
           name = request.getParameter("name"),
```

continues

Listing 12.17: continued

```
            manufacturer = request.getParameter("manufacturer"),
            image = request.getParameter("image"),
            warranty = request.getParameter("warranty"),
            description = request.getParameter("description"),
            price = request.getParameter("price");
    PreparedStatement stmt =
        connection.prepareStatement(
            "insert into products (id,name,manufacturer,img," +
            "warranty,description,price) values(?,?,?,?,?,?,?)");
    try
    {
        stmt.setString(1,id);
        stmt.setString(2,name);
        stmt.setString(3,manufacturer);
        stmt.setString(4,image);
        stmt.setString(5,warranty);
        stmt.setString(6,description);
        stmt.setString(7,price);
        stmt.executeUpdate();
    }
    finally
    {
        stmt.close();
    }
}


/**
 * check whether the schema has been created
 * @return true if the schema is complete, false otherwise
 */
protected boolean isSchemaCreated(Connection connection)
    throws SQLException
{
    // ask the name of all the tables in the database
    // check if one of them is "products"
    DatabaseMetaData meta = connection.getMetaData();
    ResultSet rs =
        meta.getTables(null,null,null,new String[] { "TABLE" });
```

```
    int found = 0;
    while(rs.next())
    {
        String tableName = rs.getString("TABLE_NAME");
        if(tableName.equalsIgnoreCase("products")
            || tableName.equalsIgnoreCase("orders"))
            found++;
    }
    rs.close();
    return 2 == found;
}


/**
 * display the page, etc.
 * @param request HTTP request
 * @param connection database connection
 */
protected void doPage(HttpServletRequest request,
                      HttpServletResponse response,
                      Connection connection)
    throws SQLException, IOException
{
    Writer writer = response.getWriter();
    writer.write("<HTML><HEAD><TITLE>XML Server Console" +
        "</TITLE></HEAD><BODY>");
    Statement stmt = connection.createStatement();
    try
    {

        if(isSchemaCreated(connection))
        {
            writer.write("<P><FORM ACTION=\"");
            writer.write(request.getServletPath());
            writer.write("\" METHOD=\"POST\"><TABLE>");
            writer.write("<TR><TD>Identifier:</TD>");
            writer.write("<TD><INPUT TYPE=\"TEXT\"");
            writer.write(" NAME=\"id\"></TD></TR>");
```

continues

Listing 12.17: continued

```
            writer.write("<TR><TD>Name:</TD>");
            writer.write("<TD><INPUT TYPE=\"TEXT\"");
            writer.write(" NAME=\"name\"></TD></TR>");
            writer.write("<TR><TD>Manufacturer:</TD>");
            writer.write("<TD><INPUT TYPE=\"TEXT\"");
            writer.write(" NAME=\"manufacturer\"></TD></TR>");
            writer.write("<TR><TD>Image:</TD>");
            writer.write("<TD><INPUT TYPE=\"TEXT\"");
            writer.write(" NAME=\"image\"></TD></TR>");
            writer.write("<TR><TD>Warranty:</TD>");
            writer.write("<TD><INPUT TYPE=\"TEXT\"");
            writer.write(" NAME=\"warranty\"></TD></TR>");
            writer.write("<TR><TD>Description:</TD>");
            writer.write("<TD><INPUT TYPE=\"TEXT\"");
            writer.write(" NAME=\"description\"></TD></TR>");
            writer.write("<TR><TD>Price:</TD>");
            writer.write("<TD><INPUT TYPE=\"TEXT\"");
            writer.write(" NAME=\"price\"></TD></TR>");
            writer.write("</TABLE><INPUT TYPE=\"SUBMIT\"");
            writer.write(" VALUE=\"Create\">");
            writer.write("<INPUT TYPE=\"HIDDEN\"");
            writer.write(" NAME=\"action\" VALUE=\"insert\">");
            writer.write("</FORM><P>");
            ResultSet rs =
                stmt.executeQuery("select id, name from products");
            writer.write("<TABLE>");
            while(rs.next())
            {
                writer.write("<TR><TD>");
                writer.write(rs.getString(2));
                writer.write("</TD><TD><FORM ACTION=\"");
                writer.write(request.getServletPath());
                writer.write("\" METHOD=\"POST\">");
                writer.write(" <INPUT TYPE=\"SUBMIT\"");
                writer.write(" VALUE=\"Delete\">");
                writer.write("<INPUT TYPE=\"HIDDEN\"");
                writer.write(" NAME=\"action\" VALUE=\"delete\">");
```

```
                    writer.write("<INPUT TYPE=\"HIDDEN\"");
                    writer.write(" NAME=\"id\" VALUE=\"");
                    writer.write(rs.getString(1));
                    writer.write("\">");
                    writer.write("</FORM></TD></TR>");
                }
                writer.write("</TABLE>");
                rs = stmt.executeQuery("select name, " +
                        "productname from orders");
                writer.write("<TABLE>");
                while(rs.next())
                {
                    writer.write("<TR><TD>");
                    writer.write(rs.getString(1));
                    writer.write("</TD><TD>");
                    writer.write(rs.getString(2));
                    writer.write("</TD></TR>");
                }
                writer.write("</TABLE>");
            }
            writer.write("<P><FORM ACTION=\"");
            writer.write(request.getServletPath());
            writer.write("\" METHOD=\"POST\">");
            writer.write("<INPUT TYPE=\"SUBMIT\"");
            writer.write(" VALUE=\"Drop tables\">");
            writer.write("<INPUT TYPE=\"HIDDEN\"");
            writer.write(" NAME=\"action\" VALUE=\"drop\">");
            writer.write("</FORM>");
            writer.write("<FORM ACTION=\"");
            writer.write(request.getServletPath());
            writer.write("\" METHOD=\"POST\">");
            writer.write("<INPUT TYPE=\"SUBMIT\"");
            writer.write(" VALUE=\"Create tables\">");
            writer.write("<INPUT TYPE=\"HIDDEN\"");
            writer.write(" NAME=\"action\" VALUE=\"create\">");
            writer.write("</FORM>");
        }
        finally
```

continues

Listing 12.17: continued

```
    {
        stmt.close();
    }
    writer.write("</BODY></HTML>");
    writer.flush();
  }
}
```

Viewer and Editor

EXAMPLE

XMLi is a smaller merchant. It doesn't have a Web site or a database. XMLi creates its list of products manually with the editor shown in Listings 12.18, 12.19, and 12.20. Listing 12.18 is the Java servlet, Listing 12.19 is the JavaScript file, and Listing 12.20 is the XSL style sheet. You edit a list of products through a URL like `http://localhost/editor?merchant=xmli`.

Listing 12.18: Editor.java

```
package com.psol.xcommerce;

import java.io.*;
import org.w3c.dom.*;
import javax.servlet.*;
import javax.servlet.http.*;

/**
 * Editor is a web-tool to create product lists
 * for smaller merchants.
 *
 * @version Sep 10, 1999
 * @author Benoît Marchal <bmarchal@pineapplesoft.com>
 */

public class Editor
    extends HttpServlet
{
    /**
     * the editor's style sheet
     */
    protected Document styleSheet;
```

```
/**
 * initializes the servlet, read the style sheet
 * @exception could not read the style sheet
 */
public void init()
    throws ServletException
{
    String fname = getInitParameter("editor.xsl");
    styleSheet = XMLUtil.parse(fname);
}


/**
 * process GET requests
 * @param request request received from the client
 * @param response response to the client
 */
protected void doGet(HttpServletRequest request,
                     HttpServletResponse response)
    throws IOException, ServletException
{
    String merchant = request.getParameter("merchant"),
           fname = getInitParameter(merchant + ".xml");
    if(null == merchant ¦¦ null == fname)
    {
        response.sendError(HttpServletResponse.SC_NOT_FOUND);
        return;
    }
    Document document = XMLUtil.parse(fname);
    XMLUtil.transform(document,
                      styleSheet,
                      response.getWriter(),
                      response.getCharacterEncoding());
}


/**
 * handle POST method, HttpServlet forward POST request from service()
```

continues

Listing 12.18: continued

```
     * to this method
     * @param request the request received from the client
     * @param response interface to the client
     */
    protected void doPost(HttpServletRequest request,
                          HttpServletResponse response)
       throws IOException, ServletException
    {
       String merchant = request.getParameter("merchant"),
              fname = getInitParameter(merchant + ".xml");
       if(null == merchant || null == fname)
       {
          response.sendError(HttpServletResponse.SC_NOT_FOUND);
          return;
       }
       String pwdRequest = request.getParameter("pwd"),
              pwdCheck = getInitParameter(merchant + ".pwd"),
              xml = request.getParameter("xmldata");
       if(null != pwdCheck && !pwdCheck.equals(pwdRequest))
       {
          response.sendError(HttpServletResponse.SC_FORBIDDEN);
          return;
       }
       Writer writer = new FileWriter(fname);
       writer.write(xml);
       writer.close();
       writer = response.getWriter();
       writer.write("<HTML><HEAD><TITLE>Confirmation");
       writer.write("</TITLE></HEAD><BODY><P>");
       writer.write("Your changes were saved as follow:<PRE>");
       XMLUtil.writeInXML(writer,xml);
       writer.write("<PRE></BODY></HTML>");
       writer.flush();
    }
}
```

Listing 12.19: Editor.js

```
// editor.js, common code for Editor


var products = new Array();


function addProduct(form)
{
    // collects data from the form
    var id = form.id.value,
        name = form.name.value,
        price = form.price.value,
        description = form.description.value;


    doAddProduct(form,id,name,price,description);
}


function doAddProduct(form,id,name,price,description)
{
    var productList = form.productlist,
        product = new Product(id,name,price,description);


    // arrays are zero-based so products.length points
    // to one past the latest product
    // JavaScript automatically allocates memory
    var pos = products.length;
    products[pos] = product;


    var option = new Option(name + " (" + price + ")",pos);


    productList.options[productList.length] = option;
}


function deleteProduct(form)
{
    var productList = form.productlist,
        pos = productList.selectedIndex;


    if(pos != -1)
```

continues

Listing 12.19: continued

```
    {
        var product = productList.options[pos].value;
        productList.options[pos] = null;
        products[product] = null;
    }
}


function exportProduct(form)
{
    var xmlCode = "",
        merchant = form.merchant.value,
        attribute = "merchant='" + merchant + "'";


    var i;
    for(i = 0;i < products.length;i++)
        if(products[i] != null)
            xmlCode += products[i].toXML();


    xmlCode = element("products",attribute,xmlCode);


    form.xmldata.value = "<?xml version='1.0'?>" + xmlCode;
}


function resetAll(form,document)
{
    priceList = null;
    form.output.value = "";
}


function element(name,attributes,content)
{
    var result = "<" + name;
    if(attributes != "")
        result += " " + attributes;
    result += ">";
    result += content;
    result += "</" + name + ">\r";
```

```
        return result;
    }


    function escapeXML(string)
    {
        var result = "",
            i,
            c;
        for(i = 0;i < string.length;i++)
        {
            c = string.charAt(i);
            if(c == '<')
                result += "&lt;";
            else if(c == '&')
                result += "&amp;";
            else
                result += c;
        }
        return result;
    }


    // declares product object

    function Product(id,name,price,description)
    {
        this.id = id;
        this.name = name;
        this.price = price;
        this.description = description;
        this.toXML = product_toXML;
    }


    function product_toXML()
    {
        var attrs = "id='" + this.id + "'",
            result = element("name","",escapeXML(this.name));
        result += element("price","",escapeXML(this.price));
```

continues

Listing 12.19: continued

```
result += element("description","",
                    escapeXML(this.description));
return element("product",attrs,result);
}
```

Listing 12.20: editor.xsl

```
<?xml version="1.0" encoding="ISO-8859-1"?>
<xsl:stylesheet xmlns:xsl="http://www.w3.org/1999/XSL/Transform/"
                 xmlns="http://www.w3.org/TR/REC-html40">


<xsl:output method="html"/>


<xsl:template match="/">
    <HTML><HEAD><TITLE>Product List Editor</TITLE>
        <SCRIPT LANGUAGE="JavaScript" SRC="editor.js">
        <xsl:text> </xsl:text></SCRIPT>
        <SCRIPT LANGUAGE="JavaScript"><xsl:comment>
        function load(form)
        {
        <xsl:for-each select="products/product">
            doAddProduct(form,
                        "<xsl:value-of select="@id"/>",
                        "<xsl:value-of select="name"/>",
                        "<xsl:value-of select="price"/>",
                        "<xsl:value-of select="description"/>");
        </xsl:for-each>
        }
        // </xsl:comment>
        </SCRIPT>
        </HEAD>
        <BODY ONLOAD="load(document.controls)">
            <CENTER>
                <FORM NAME="controls" METHOD="POST"
                    ACTION="editor">
                    ID: <INPUT TYPE="TEXT" NAME="id" SIZE="3"/>
                    Name: <INPUT TYPE="TEXT" NAME="name"/>
                    Price: <INPUT TYPE="TEXT" NAME="price"
                            SIZE="7"/><BR/>
```

```
                Description:<BR/>
                <TEXTAREA NAME="description" ROWS="5"
                          COLS="50"/><BR/>
                <SELECT NAME="productlist" SIZE="5"
                          WIDTH="250"/><BR/>
                <INPUT TYPE="BUTTON" VALUE="Add"
                       ONCLICK="addProduct(controls)"/>
                <INPUT TYPE="BUTTON" VALUE="Delete"
                       ONCLICK="deleteProduct(controls)"/><BR/>
                Password: <INPUT TYPE="PASSWORD" NAME="pwd"/>
                <INPUT TYPE="SUBMIT" VALUE="Save"
                       ONCLICK="exportProduct(controls)"/>
                <INPUT TYPE="HIDDEN" NAME="xmldata"/>
                <INPUT TYPE="HIDDEN" NAME="merchant">
                    <xsl:attribute name="VALUE">
                        <xsl:value-of select="products/@merchant"/>
                    </xsl:attribute>
                </INPUT>
            </FORM>
          </CENTER>
        </BODY>
      </HTML>
  </xsl:template>


</xsl:stylesheet>
```

Note that this editor cannot start from an empty file because it needs the merchant name in the style sheet. When creating a new merchant, you must also create the following file (an empty list of products):

```
<?xml version='1.0'?><products merchant='xmli'/>
```

Listing 12.21 and the accompanying style sheet in Listing 12.22 display the orders for XMLi.

Listing 12.21: Viewer.java

```java
package com.psol.xcommerce;


import java.io.*;
import org.w3c.dom.*;
```

continues

Listing 12.21: continued

```java
import javax.servlet.*;
import javax.servlet.http.*;

/**
 * Viewer is a web-tool to view orders
 * for smaller merchants.
 *
 * @version Sep 10, 19999
 * @author Benoît Marchal <bmarchal@pineapplesoft.com>
 */

public class Viewer
    extends HttpServlet
{
    /**
     * the viewer's style sheet
     */
    protected Document styleSheet;

    /**
     * initializes the servlet, read the style sheet
     * @exception could not read the style sheet
     */
    public void init()
        throws ServletException
    {
        String fname = getInitParameter("viewer.xsl");
        styleSheet = XMLUtil.parse(fname);
    }

    /**
     * process GET requests
     * @param request request received from the client
     * @param response response to the client
     */
    protected void doGet(HttpServletRequest request,
                         HttpServletResponse response)
```

```
    throws IOException, ServletException
{

    String merchant = request.getParameter("merchant"),
            path = getInitParameter(merchant + ".orders"),
            fname = request.getParameter("fname");
    if(null == merchant || null == path)
    {
        response.sendError(HttpServletResponse.SC_NOT_FOUND);
        return;
    }
    if(null == fname)
    {
        File file = new File(path);
        String[] files = file.list();
        Writer writer = response.getWriter();
        writer.write("<HTML><HEAD><TITLE>Order list</TITLE>");
        writer.write("</HEAD><BODY><UL>");
        for(int i = 0;i < files.length;i++)
        {
            writer.write("<LI><A HREF=\"");
            writer.write(request.getServletPath());
            writer.write("?merchant=");
            writer.write(merchant);
            writer.write("&fname=");
            writer.write(files[i]);
            writer.write("\">");
            writer.write(files[i]);
            writer.write("</A></LI>");
        }
        writer.write("</UL></BODY></HTML>");
        writer.flush();
    }
    else
    {
        File file = new File(path,fname);
        Document document = XMLUtil.parse(file.getPath());
        XMLUtil.transform(document,
```

continues

Listing 12.21: continued

```
                            styleSheet,
                            response.getWriter(),
                            response.getCharacterEncoding());
    }
  }
}
```

Listing 12.22: viewing.xsl

```xml
<?xml version="1.0" encoding="ISO-8859-1"?>
<xsl:stylesheet xmlns:xsl="http://www.w3.org/1999/XSL/Transform/"
                xmlns="http://www.w3.org/TR/REC-html40">

<xsl:output method="html"/>

<xsl:template match="/">
   <HTML>
   <HEAD>
      <TITLE>Order</TITLE>
   </HEAD>
   <BODY>
      <P>You have received the following order from:</P>
      <TABLE BORDER="0">
        <TR><TD>Name:</TD>
        <TD><xsl:value-of
           select="order/buyer/@name"/></TD></TR>
        <TR><TD>Street:</TD>
        <TD><xsl:value-of
           select="order/buyer/@street"/></TD></TR>
        <TR><TD>Region:</TD>
        <TD><xsl:value-of
           select="order/buyer/@region"/></TD></TR>
        <TR><TD>ZIP or postal code:</TD>
        <TD><xsl:value-of
           select="order/buyer/@postal-code"/></TD></TR>
        <TR><TD>Locality:</TD>
        <TD><xsl:value-of
           select="order/buyer/@locality"/></TD></TR>
        <TR><TD>Country:</TD>
```

```
            <TD><xsl:value-of
               select="order/buyer/@country"/></TD></TR>
            <TR><TD>E-mail:</TD>
            <TD><xsl:value-of
               select="order/buyer/@email"/></TD></TR>
        </TABLE>
        <P>The order is for the following item:</P>
        <TABLE BORDER="0">
         <TR><TD><B>ID</B></TD><TD><B>Name</B></TD>
               <TD ALIGN="RIGHT"><B>Price</B></TD>
               <TD ALIGN="RIGHT"><B>Quantity</B></TD></TR>
            <xsl:for-each select="order/product">
               <TR>
                  <TD><xsl:value-of select="@id"/></TD>
                  <TD><xsl:value-of select="@name"/></TD>
                  <TD ALIGN="RIGHT"><xsl:value-of
                     select="@price"/></TD>
                  <TD ALIGN="RIGHT"><xsl:value-of
                     select="@quantity"/></TD>
               </TR>
            </xsl:for-each>
        </TABLE>
      </BODY>
      </HTML>
  </xsl:template>

</xsl:stylesheet>
```

The scalability of XML should not be underestimated. The same document works for Emailaholic (which needs integration) as for XMLi (which prefers to view the orders online).

What's Next

What's next? Your turn. See where XML makes sense in your environment and start your first application today. XML is versatile and flexible, so it's ideal when starting small. You can gain experience and grow as you become more confident.

I hope you enjoyed reading this book as much as I enjoyed writing it.

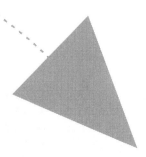

Appendix A

Crash Course on Java

If you are a JavaScript, Perl, or C++ programmer and you are not familiar with Java, this appendix is for you. Java is a natural companion to XML. This appendix teaches you just enough Java to be able use it with XML.

In this appendix, you learn

- how Java compares to JavaScript and other programming languages
- why Java is important for XML
- how to install a Java runtime environment and run Java applications
- enough Java to read and write simple programs

You don't have to become a super-trooper in Java programming, but some familiarity with "the other Web language" is required for serious fun with XML. If anything, there are more XML tools available in Java than in any other language.

✔ If you want to quickly learn how to run the Java package introduced in Chapter 3, turn to the section "Downloading Java Tools," on page 459, and the section "Understanding the Classpath,"on page 480.

Java in Perspective

There is lot of discussion about the relative importance of Java and XML. In my experience, they are complementary. Admittedly, I am somewhat biased in favor of Java. I formed my company, Pineapplesoft, with a focus on Java development. At the time, I bet on the importance of cross-platform applications.

I believed (and still do) that a low level object-oriented programming language for the Internet is required. C++ is low-level but is not portable enough (you can't run the same program unmodified on different machines).

XML is not a programming language, just as HTML is not a programming language. XML is a language to encode information. That is useful but you also need programming to manipulate the information in XML documents.

One of the major misconceptions is that Java equals applets. Applets might have been popular in the early days of Java but they never had a fighting chance against Macromedia Flash or Dynamic HTML. For simple animation, JavaScript is simpler than Java. For complex animation, Flash is more efficient.

The value of Java lies elsewhere. In combination with XML, Java is particularly relevant for

- heavy-duty server-side applications
- components for scripting languages

Server-Side Applications

As you will see, Java combines a high-performance server environment with portability.

Portability is essential on the server side because there is more diversity in that space than on the desktop. Windows clearly rules the desktop but there is no clear winner among servers: UNIX, Windows NT, and AS/400 are all major platforms.

Furthermore, a typical organization might have all of these platforms running at once, and your application might have to run on both UNIX and Windows servers.

Finally, for servers, portability equates with scalability: When new hardware is introduced to boost the performance, existing software must still run on it. As an added bonus, software can be developed on cheap machines and deployed on high-end servers.

Components of the Server-Side Applications

Increasingly, we rely on scripting languages—such as JavaScript, Perl, Python, or ColdFusion—to combine components such as an XSL Processor or database access.

Scripting languages are high-level programming languages. They are usually interpreted and typeless. This makes them able to create applications quickly. These languages are at their best when they are gluing components together.

XML fits well with this style of programming. The numerous companion standards (DOM, SAX, XSL, CSS, X-Schema, RDF, and so on) are being made available as components.

Scripting languages are not the best tool for writing components. For one thing, it is difficult to integrate scripting languages with one another. Furthermore, because scripting languages are high level, they are less efficient.

Java is well adapted to write these components because it is a compiled, low-level programming language. Additionally, most scripting languages can interface with Java components. Java portability means that the components are available on a large number of platforms. In Java, components are called *JavaBeans*.

As has already been noted, there are more XML components (parsers, XSL processors, conversion, and so on) written in Java than in any other language.

Downloading Java Tools

This section lists the various pieces you need to run the examples in this book. I have chosen software that is available free of charge when possible.

If you find yourself doing lots of Java development, however, you will want to buy an integrated development environment such as Café (www.symantec.com), Visual Age (www.software.ibm.com), or JBuilder (www.inprise.com).

Java Environment

The trick behind Java portability is the *Java Virtual Machine* or JVM. Java programs are compiled to a portable binary format, called the *class files*. To execute the binaries, you need a JVM.

The JVM is available on most platforms. You can download a JVM for your platform from java.sun.com. It comes in one of two versions:

- Java Runtime Environment (JRE) is a naked JVM. It can run existing Java applications but lacks the tools to develop new ones.

- Java Development Kit (JDK) offers everything in the JRE as well as development tools such as the compiler.

If you plan to run the examples in this book, you need a JDK to compile them. If you are interested in running only existing packages (such as LotusXSL), a JRE is enough.

At the time of this writing, there are three major generations of JVMs:

- JDK 1.0 is the original version. Seldom used anymore, it was slow and limited.

- JDK 1.1 is the most common version. It is a mature product that greatly improved the usability of JDK 1.0.x.

- Java 2 (also known as JDK 1.2) is the newest version. It is not available on every platform yet. It adds many bells and whistles to Java—not all of them useful. The graphical component is not as stable as its JDK 1.1 equivalent. However, you don't need the graphical component in this book.

Which version you choose depends on the components you want to use. Most components require at least JDK 1.1. If available on your platform, I advise you to download Java 2. The examples in this book have been developed on Java 2, but they should run unmodified on JDK 1.1.

XML Components

The examples in this book have been tested with IBM's XML for Java (version 2.0.9) and LotusXSL (version 0.17). XML for Java is a parser that supports both the SAX and DOM interfaces. LotusXSL is an implementation of XSLT.

At the time of this writing, both are available free of charge from `www.alphaworks.ibm.com`. If this changes, I will post an update at `www.mcp.com`.

There are several other parsers and XSL processors for Java:

- Sun's ProjectX is another parser that supports DOM and SAX. It is available from `java.sun.com`.

- Microsoft has a DOM parser available from `msdn.microsoft.com`. The Microsoft parser is also available as a COM component.

- The DataChannel parser, XJParse (available from `www.datachannel.com`), integrates XSL support.

- Microstar's Ælfred (available from `www.microstar.com`) is a SAX-only parser that boasts a very small memory footprint.

- James Clark has written a SAX-compliant parser (XP) and an XSL processor (XT). Both are available from `www.jclark.com`.

Servlet Engine

Servlets are Java's version of CGI scripts. Servlets include a standard API in order to interface Java with Web servers. The e-commerce example in Chapter 12, "Putting It All Together: An e-Commerce Example," is based on servlets. You need a servlet-enabled Web server.

If your Web server is Apache, Netscape, IIS, or WebSTAR, you can add servlet support through one of the following three products:

- JRun is available from www.jrun.com. It supports the major Web servers and then some.

- ServletExec is available from www.newatlanta.com. It supports the major Web servers.

- Locomotive is available from www.locomotive.org. It supports fewer servers than the other two but it is an open-source project.

Alternatively, you can turn to a Web server that natively support servlets. These include

- WebSTAR, which is available from www.ora.com.

- Java Web Server, which is available from jserv.javasoft.com. As the name implies, it is written in Java.

- Jetty, which is available from www.mortbay.com, is also written in Java but it is an open-source product.

I strongly recommend Jetty. It is a full-featured Web server (it even supports proxy) with a small memory footprint. It is also fast to download. The only limitation is that the user interface is old-fashioned: You must edit text files. Finally, I use Jetty throughout the book which is another good reason to give it a try.

If you want ease of use, WebSTAR is a good choice. In addition to servlets, it also supports ASP and iHTML.

NOTE

Open-source software means that the source code for the software is freely available. Users are encouraged to download the source code and modify it as appropriate (for example, to fix bugs or add new features).

You are encouraged to contribute your modifications to the community. This approach leads to the development of software by volunteers.

The most famous open-source software are Linux and GNU (two UNIX variants), Apache (a Web server), and Mozilla (Netscape Web browser).

Your First Java Application

Enough talk, let's code. This section shows you how to write, compile, and run your first Java application.

Listing A.1 is a Java application that converts a text file to your platform end-of-line convention.

Listing A.1: Java Application

EXAMPLE

```java
package com.psol.lel;

import java.io.*;

/**
 * Rewrite a text file with system-specific end of lines.<BR>
 * Useful for text files downloaded from the Net.
 *
 * @author Benoît Marchal
 * @version 28 August 1999
 */

public class LeL
{
    /**
     * Entry-point for the program.<BR>
     * Expect two filenames on the command-line: input and output.
     *
     * @param args command-line parameters
     */
    public static void main(String[] args)
    {
        if(args.length < 2)
            System.err.println("Usage is: java com.psol.lel.LeL
 input output");
        // we don't want to overwrite a file by mistake
        else if(new File(args[1]).exists())
            System.err.println("Error: output file already exists!");
        else
            try
            {
                BufferedReader reader =
                    new BufferedReader(new FileReader(args[0]));
                PrintWriter writer =
                    new PrintWriter(new FileWriter(args[1]));
```

```
                    // the try/finally guarantees the writer is closed
                    try
                    {
                        for(String line = reader.readLine();
                            null != line;
                            line = reader.readLine())
                            writer.println(line);
                    }
                    finally
                    {
                        writer.close();
                    }
                }
                catch(IOException e)
                {
                    System.err.println("Error: " + e.getMessage());
                }
            }
        }
```

UNIX uses an LF character to signal end of lines, the Mac uses the CR character, and Windows uses a combination of CR/LF. Needless to say, text files (such as XML documents) saved on one platform are not easy to manipulate on another platform. This application rewrites the file to your platform convention.

You must save this program in a file called LeL.java. Java is picky about filenames. To compile, issue this command:

```
javac -d . LeL.java
```

CAUTION
This assumes the Java compiler is in your path. If not, you will have to prefix the `javac` command with the path to the compiler, as in

```
c:\java\javac -d . LeL.java
```

OUTPUT

You can run it with

```
java com.psol.lel.LeL unixfile.txt windowsfile.txt
```

Figures A.1 and A.2 illustrate how the LeL program reorganizes the file. Notice that in Figure A.1 the lines are all wrong.

Figure A.1: A UNIX *file under Windows*

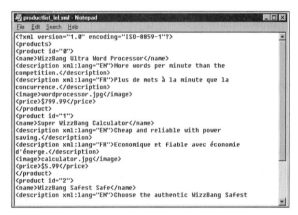

Figure A.2: The same file after *LeL rewrote it*

Flow of Control

Java has all the usual statements for tests and loops: if/else, switch/case, for, while, and do/while. Multiple statements are grouped with the { and } characters. Java also supports exceptions to report error conditions (see the section entitled "Exceptions").

EXAMPLE

1. The following example loops through the lines in the input file and prints them in the output file:

```java
for(String line = reader.readLine();
    null != line;
    line = reader.readLine())
   writer.println(line);
```

2. The following example tests the value of args.length to print an error message:

```
if(args.length < 2)
        System.err.println("Usage is: java com.psol.lel.LeL
➥ input output");
```

Variables

Of course, Java has variables. Variables in Java must be declared before being used. Furthermore, Java is a typed language so every variable must have a type.

1. The following example declares one variable, line. The declaration must include the type. The type precedes the name of the variable in the declaration. Variables can be initialized with the = operator.

```
String line = reader.readLine();
```

Java supports the following primitive types:

- boolean: true or false
- char: Unicode character
- byte: 8-bit signed integer
- short: 16-bit signed integer
- int: 32-bit signed integer
- long: 64-bit signed integer
- float: 32-bit floating-point
- double: 64-bit floating-point

Object variables are implemented as references to objects. In the example, String declares a variable line as a reference to a String object.

2. To declare arrays, append the [] characters to the type, as in

```
int[] arrayOfInteger = new int[6];
```

Class

Because Java is an object-oriented language, it supports the notions of classes and objects. An *object* is an instance of a class. A *class* is a type for a category of objects. In Java, with the exception of the primitive types, everything is an object.

The following example declares a class LeL:

```
public class LeL
{
```

```
    // ...
}
```

Creating Objects

Every object in Java is allocated on the heap. To create objects in Java, you use the new operator.

EXAMPLE

1. The following example creates a `BufferedReader` object:

```
BufferedReader reader =
    new BufferedReader(new FileReader(args[0]));
```

EXAMPLE

2. Objects are typically assigned to variables, but they need not be. It is also very common to create anonymous objects that are used and discarded in one sequence. The following example creates a `File` object, calls its `exists()` method, and then discards it. The object is immediately discarded because it is never assigned to a variable:

```
if(new File(args[1]).exists())
    System.err.println("Error: output file already exists!");
```

You don't have to explicitly destroy objects in Java. When an object is no longer in use, it is automatically reclaimed by the garbage collector.

Accessing Fields and Methods

A class contains fields or data variables that are attached to objects. It also contains methods with the executable code of the class.

EXAMPLE

To access a field or a method of an object, you separate its name from the object reference with a dot, as in

```
writer.close();
```

Static

By default, the variables or methods declared in a class are attached to objects of that class. However, it is possible to declare variables or methods attached to the class.

EXAMPLE

1. The following example declares a class with two fields: x and y. Every `Point` object has the two fields:

```
class Point
{
    public int x, y;
}
```

EXAMPLE

2. However, it is possible to attach methods or fields to the class itself. These are declared with the `static` modifier. This is useful, for example, for keeping track of how many `Point` objects have been created:

```java
class Point
{
    public int x, y;
    public static int numberOfPoints = 0;
}
```

Method and Parameters

In Java, the code is contained in methods. Note that there are no stand-alone methods. Every method must be attached to a class.

EXAMPLE

The following example declares the `main()` method. A method accepts parameters that are declared, like variables, in parentheses.

```java
public static void main(String[] args)
{
    // ...
}
```

Methods may return a value. The type of the return value is declared before the method name. If the method returns no value, its type is `void`.

`main()` is a special method that serves as the entry point for the application.

Constructors

A class can have special methods, known as *constructors*. The constructors are called when the object is created with the `new` operator. Constructors are used to initialize the fields in a class. Constructors are declared like methods but without a return value.

EXAMPLE

The `Point` class now has a constructor to initializes its fields:

```java
public class Point
{
    public int x, y;
    public Point(int x1,int y1)
    {
        x = x1;
        y = y1;
    }
}
```

Package

Java programs are organized in packages. Java packages play a role similar to XML namespaces: They prevent naming conflicts.

EXAMPLE

Packages are declared with the `package` statement, as in the following example:

```
package com.psol.lel;
```

A package is also a logical unit that groups related classes. Therefore, you can place all the classes of one application in a single package. In this case, the `lel` package stands for "local end of line." Large applications may be split over several packages.

To avoid conflicts in the name of packages, their names should always start with your domain name in reverse order.

Imports

The name of a class is its package name followed by the class name. In other words, the name of the class `LeL` that's in the package `com.psol.lel` is `com.psol.lel.LeL`.

EXAMPLE

To save some typing, you can import classes or packages with the `import` statement. The following line imports classes from the `java.io` package. Thanks to the import, the class `java.io.IOException` is available as simply `IOException`.

```
import java.io.*;
```

Packages whose names start with `java` are part of the core API. The core API is the standard Java library.

Access Control

Classes, methods, and fields have *access control*, which limits how classes can access other classes or methods on other classes.

EXAMPLE

Classes can be either `package` or `public`. Fields and methods can be `package`, `public`, `protected`, or `private`. These different options are declared with modifiers. The following class is `public` but its fields are `protected`:

```
public class Length
{
    protected int length;
    protected String unit;
}
```

These options are defined as follows:

- public is accessible from anywhere. Public access is declared with the public modifier.

- package is accessible from the current package only. Package access is declared with no modifier. It is the default.

- protected is accessible to the class descendant only. Protected access is declared with the protected modifier.

- private is accessible to the class only. Private access is declared with the private modifier.

Comments and Javadoc

Java has a special form of comments that you can use to automatically generate documentation for your application.

EXAMPLE

1. Like C++ or JavaScript, comments are enclosed in /* and */.

```
/**
* Rewrite a text file with system-specific end of lines.<BR>
* Useful for text files downloaded from the Net.
*
* @author Benoît Marchal
* @version 28 August 1999
*/
```

This comment is known as a *javadoc comment*. Javadoc comments are enclosed in /** and */. They should be used for the class documentation. The javadoc program can extract these comments from the source code and automatically generate an HTML file with the class documentation.

As you can see, I can include HTML tags (like <BR>) in the javadoc comments. They eventually end up in the documentation.

The main advantage to placing the class documentation in the source code is that it minimizes the chances that the documentation is out-of-date.

To generate the documentation, issue the following command. This creates several HTML files with the documentation. The documentation is very complete and includes index, table of contents, and more.

OUTPUT

Figure A.3 shows the documentation page that is being generated.

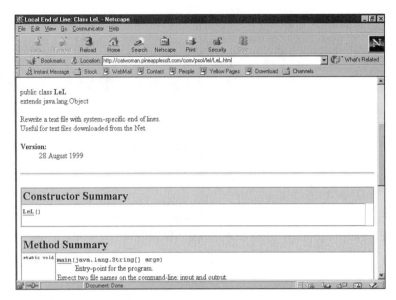

Figure A.3: *Javadoc documentation*

Javadoc recognizes paragraphs starting with the @ character as special paragraphs. The most common ones are

- `@version`   States the application version

- `@author`   States the name of the author (you can have multiple `@author` paragraphs)

- `@param`   Documents a method parameter (you can have multiple `@param` paragraphs)

- `@return`   Documents the value returned by a method

- `@exception`   Documents the exception that a method can throw

EXAMPLE

2. There is an alternative form for short comments, also derived from C++. Anything after the `//` characters until the end of the line is a comment, as in

```
// we don't want to overwrite a file by mistake
```

Exception

Like other object-oriented programming languages, Java uses exceptions to signal errors. An exception is an object that describes the error.

1. To throw an exception, use the keyword `throw`:

```
throw new ServletException("Error: invalid parameter");
```

2. To report on exceptions, you must catch them with a `try`/`catch` statement. If an exception is thrown in the `try` statement, control goes to the `catch` statement, as in

```
try
{
    // ...
    // can throw an IOException
}
catch(IOException e)
{
    System.err.println("Error: " + e.getMessage());
}
```

3. An optional `finally` statement can be attached to a `try`. The `finally` statement is always executed, whether an exception is thrown or not. A `finally` statement is ideal for cleanup code that must be executed, as in

```
try
{
    // ...
    // can throw an exception
}
finally
{
    writer.close();
}
```

4. Exceptions that are not caught in a method must be declared in the `throws` statement of the method. The compiler won't allow a method to throw exceptions if the exceptions are not declared, as in

```
protected void doGet(HttpServletRequest request,
                     HttpServletResponse response)
    throws IOException
{
    // ...
    // can throw an IOException
}
```

Servlets

The first Web servers were simply file servers. As illustrated in Figure A.4, a browser would request a file from the server and the server would return it. The browser would render the file onscreen. If the file included hyperlinks, the user could point and click to request more files.

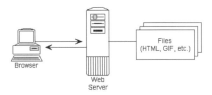

Figure A.4: *Serving files*

Most Web sites are still being developed according to this model, which has the advantage of simplicity.

The major limitation to this model, however, is that these Web sites are static. For the user, interaction is limited to following hyperlinks. A user cannot query a Web site and receive an answer based on that query.

Also, the information must be made available in HTML files. This is not appropriate for information that changes rapidly. For example, stock quotes change several times a day and it is not practical to continuously update the files.

Instead, it makes more sense to dynamically create an HTML page in response to user requests. The data in the page can come from a querying database or from an XML document.

As illustrated in Figure A.5, an application is required to generate the page based on the user's request.

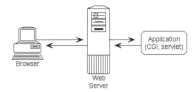

Figure A.5: *Serving applications*

The Web server is now an application server because it serves both files and applications. The standard API for a Web server is the *Common Gateway Interface* or CGI. Applications that need to interface with the server must follow CGI.

CGI is a very simple API. It specifies how the Web server invokes the application, how it passes the parameters it received from the user, and how the application must return the page.

CGI is a very popular interface that is supported by all the major Web servers. However, CGI has proven to be relatively inefficient. In particular, with CGI, the Web server must invoke a new instance of the application for each request. This alone invokes a huge overhead. Web sites that relied heavily on CGI were slow.

In response, server vendors developed more efficient APIs (NSAPI and WAI for Netscape, ISAPI for Microsoft). These alternative APIs are very similar in scope to CGI but are more efficient. Unfortunately, unlike CGI, which is common to most servers, the alternative APIs are vendor specific. An application developed for Netscape's Web servers won't work with a Microsoft server.

The Java community proposed servlets as a standard replacement for CGI. Servlets are efficient because they are loaded once when the server starts. The Web server can reuse the servlet for multiple requests. Furthermore, servlets are portable and they work with all the major Web servers.

The e-commerce example in Chapter 12 uses servlets extensively. The next section explains how to write servlets.

Your First Servlet

It's time to put this in practice with a simple servlet example.

Listing A.2 is the XDic servlet. This servlet returns the definition of terms entered in a form on a Web browser.

Listing A.2: The Servlet

EXAMPLE

```
package com.psol.xdic;

import java.io.*;
import java.net.*;
import java.util.*;
import javax.servlet.*;
import javax.servlet.http.*;

/**
```

continues

Listing A.2: continued

```
 * XDic is a simple servlet that "plays the dictionary".
 *
 * @version Aug 28, 1999
 * @author Benoît Marchal <bmarchal@pineapplesoft.com>
 */

public class XDic
    extends HttpServlet
{
    /**
     * handle GET method, HttpServlet forward GET request from service()
     * to this method
     * @param request the request received from the client
     * @param response interface to the client
     */
    protected void doGet(HttpServletRequest request,
                         HttpServletResponse response)
        throws IOException
    {
        response.setContentType("text/html");
        Writer w = response.getWriter();
        w.write("<HTML>");
        w.write("<HEAD><TITLE>XDic</TITLE></HEAD>\n");
        w.write("<BODY>\n");
        String word = request.getParameter("word");
        if(null != word)
        {
            w.write("<P><B>"); w.write(word); w.write(":</B> ");
            String lowCaseWord = word.toLowerCase();
            String definition = getInitParameter(lowCaseWord);
            if(null == definition)
                w.write("unknown, sorry");
            else
                w.write(definition);
            w.write("\n<HR>\n");
        }
        w.write("<FORM ACTION=\"");
```

```
        w.write(request.getRequestURI());

        w.write("\">\n");

        w.write("<INPUT NAME=\"word\">\n");

        w.write("<INPUT TYPE=\"SUBMIT\">\n");

        w.write("</BODY>\n");

        w.write("</HTML>");


        w.flush();

    }

}
```

You need to compile the servlet with the following command:

```
javac -classpath c:\jetty\lib\javax.servlet.jar -d . XDic.java
```

Depending on which servlet engine you use and where it is installed on your system, you need to adapt the classpath parameter so it uses the correct path. See the section entitled "Understanding the Classpath" that follows.

CAUTION

If there is an error message similar to "`Package javax.servlet not found in import.`", it means that the `classpath` is incorrect (be sure it points to the right file).

To run the example with Jetty, you need the two configuration files in Listings A.3 and A.4. Other servlet engines will need similar configuration. Check the user manual of your servlet engine for more specific information.

Listing A.3: jetty.prp, the Server Configuration File

```
# configuration for the XDic servlet

xdic./.InetAddrPort     : 0.0.0.0:80

xdic./.Log./            : err

xdic./.Servlet./xdic$   : xdic=com.psol.xdic.XDic?./XDic.prp
```

The properties are as follows:

- `xdic./.InetAddrPort` is the address the Web server should listen to. `0.0.0.0` means accept all connection. `80` is the port; you will have to select another port if you already have a Web server on your machine.

- `xdic./.Log./` select how to print error messages. It takes either a filename or `err`, which stands for the console.

- xdic./.Servlet./xdic$ installs the xdic servlet. It takes the servlet's class name as a parameter. The class name may be followed by a question mark and a filename for the servlet's properties.

Listing A.4: XDic.prp, the Servlet Configuration File

```
xml=eXtensible Markup Language
xsl=XML Stylesheet Language
xslt=XSL Transformation
xslfo=XSL Formatting Objects
dtd=Document Type Definition
dcd=Document Content Description
xql=XML Query Language
sax=Simple API for XML
sox=Schema for Object-Oriented XML
ddml=Document Definition Markup Language
dom=Document Object Model
rdf=Resource Description Framework
css=Cascading Style Sheet
```

If using Jetty, save Listings A.3 and A.4 in the directory where you compiled the servlet. Be sure you use the correct filenames (jetty.prp and XDic.prp).

Go to the command line and change to the servlet's directory. The following commands launch the server. You might have to adapt the classpath to point to your copy of Jetty:

```
set classpath=c:\jetty\lib\javax.servlet.jar;
➥c:\jetty\lib\com.mortbay.Jetty.jar;.
java com.mortbay.Jetty.Server jetty.prp
```

OUTPUT

The last argument on this command is the filename for Listing A.3. Jetty comes with a default jetty.prp file but you must use the one in Listing A.3.

Figure A.6 shows the result in a Web browser. The servlet generates a page that contains the definition of the term and a form to issue another query.

Inheritance

The servlet introduces one new Java construct: *inheritance*. Like any object-oriented language, Java allows classes to inherit characteristics from other classes. A class that inherits from another class is said to be a *descendant*. The class it inherits from is its *ancestor*.

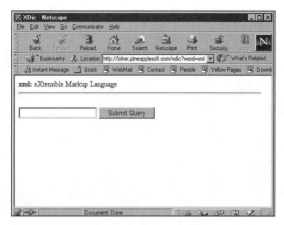

Figure A.6: *The servlet in a Web browser*

The descendant has all the methods and fields defined in its ancestor, plus any new fields or method it decides to implement.

EXAMPLE

Inheritance is indicated with the `extends` keyword followed by the ancestor name. In Java, a class cannot inherit from more than one class (single inheritance). In the following example, `XDic` inherits from `HttpServlet`:

```
public class XDic
    extends HttpServlet
{
    // ...
}
```

doGet()

Java servlets must inherit from `HttpServlet` and overwrite one or more methods among `doGet()`, `doPost()`, and `doPut()`. Each of these methods corresponds to an HTTP command. In Listing A.2, the servlet overwrites `doGet()` to handle `GET` requests.

When the user fills in a form and presses the submit button, the browser prepares a request with the form data. It calls the Web server and passes it the request.

The Web server recognizes this is a servlet request so it invokes the servlet to prepare a response. The servlet analyses the request, computes a result, and formats it as an HTML page. It returns the HTML page to the Web server, which forwards it to the browser. You can follow the different steps on Figure A.5.

If you are not familiar with this style of programming, it is important to remember that the servlet is invoked to answer a request from the browser. The servlet must collect all the information from the browser and prepare an HTML page with the result.

1. The servlet can access parameters sent by the browser through the HttpRequest object. For example, the method getParameter() returns the value of a form field:

EXAMPLE

```
String word = request.getParameter("word");
```

2. To generate an answer, the servlet uses the HttpResponse object. In the following example, the servlet sets the MIME type of the result to text/html (meaning HTML) and it starts printing the page on a Writer:

EXAMPLE

```
response.setContentType("text/html");
Writer w = response.getWriter();
w.write("<HTML>");
w.write("<HEAD><TITLE>XDic</TITLE></HEAD>\n");
w.write("<BODY>\n");
```

3. Finally, the servlet can access configuration information through the getInitParameter(). In the following example, the servlet looks up the definition of a word from the configuration file:

EXAMPLE

```
String definition = getInitParameter(lowCaseWord);
```

The configuration file is in Listing A.4.

More Java Language Concepts

You now have enough background on Java to be able to read and follow the various examples introduced in the book. There are, however, three important aspects of the Java language that have not been covered—this section will introduce them.

This and Super

Java also declares two keywords: this and super. They are used like ordinary variables but this refers to the current object whereas super refers to the ancestor of the current object.

In the following example, the object invokes a method on its ancestor:

```
super.init(config);
```

EXAMPLE

Interfaces and Multiple Inheritance

You have seen that Java supports only single inheritance: A class cannot have more than one ancestor. Multiple inheritance in Java is based on interfaces.

An interface is the skeleton of a class; it declares the methods that a class must support but it does not provide the implementation. Implementation of the methods must be provided in a class.

EXAMPLE

1. Many Java APIs are defined in terms of interfaces. Listing A.5 is one of the interfaces defined by SAX.

Listing A.5: A SAX Interface

```java
package org.xml.sax;


/**

 * Receive notification of general document events.

 * Most comments removed to simplify the listing.

 *

 * @author David Megginson (ak117@freenet.carleton.ca)

 * @version 1.0

 */
public interface DocumentHandler {
  public abstract void setDocumentLocator (Locator locator);
  public abstract void startDocument ()
    throws SAXException;
  public abstract void endDocument ()
    throws SAXException;
  public abstract void startElement (String name,
                                        AttributeList atts)
    throws SAXException;
  public abstract void endElement (String name)
    throws SAXException;
  public abstract void characters (char ch[],
                                    int start,
                                    int length)
    throws SAXException;
  public abstract void ignorableWhitespace (char ch[],
                                              int start,
                                              int length)
```

continues

Listing A.5: continued

```
        throws SAXException;

    public abstract void processingInstruction (String target,
                                                       String data)

        throws SAXException;

}
```

EXAMPLE

2. A class can implement more than one interface, which is how multiple inheritance is supported in Java. In the following example, SAXServlet inherits from HttpServlet and implements two interfaces: DocumentHandler and EntityResolver.

```
public class SAXServlet

    extends HttpServlet

    implements DocumentHandler, EntityResolver

{

    // ...

}
```

Understanding the Classpath

One of the most confusing aspects of Java is probably the *classpath*. Most of the problems when running Java applications are related to the classpath.

The JVM loads Java classes as needed. If your application uses the HttpServlet class, the JVM will load it. However, the JVM needs to know where the class is located. To find classes, the JVM looks in the classpath.

The classpath contains a list of directories or JAR files (more on JAR files in the next section) that the JVM searches. If the JVM cannot find a class in the classpath, it reports a java.lang.ClassNotFoundException error.

EXAMPLE

1. You can set the classpath for a given application with the classpath parameter, as in

```
javac -classpath c:\jetty\lib\javax.servlet.jar -d . XDic.java
```

EXAMPLE

2. Alternatively, you can set a global classpath as an environment variable, as in

```
set classpath=c:\jetty\lib\javax.servlet.jar;
➥c:\jetty\lib\com.mortbay.Jetty.jar;.
```

EXAMPLE

3. It is easy to make spelling errors in classpath. For example, in the following command, the path to the servlet JAR is incorrect:

```
javac -classpath c:\jetti\lib\javax.servlet.jar -d . XDic.java
```

EXAMPLE The compiler reports the following error:

```
XDic.java:6: Package javax.servlet not found in import.
import javax.servlet.*;
```

However, it is easy to recognize that this error is linked to an incorrect classpath: If the compiler cannot find a package, it's a sure sign that the classpath is incorrect.

CAUTION

Neither the compiler nor the JVM will issue a warning if there are invalid directories in the classpath.

Invalid directories are ignored but, of course, these invalid directories still cause problems because the JVM cannot find your classes.

EXAMPLE

4. In the following example, because the classpath does not contain a reference to the current path , the JVM cannot find the classes:

```
set classpath=c:\jetty\lib\javax.servlet.jar;
➥c:\jetty\lib\com.mortbay.Jetty.jar
```

The JVM will complain that

```
Cannot find servlet class com.psol.xdic.XDic
java.lang.ClassNotFoundException: com.psol.xdic.Xdic
```

Again, it is easy to link this problem to a classpath problem. Don't forget that the classpath must contain not only the different components your application uses (servlet, Java parser, and so on), but also the classes for your application.

CAUTION

The behavior of the classpath has changed between JDK 1.1 and Java 2. With Java 2, the JVM always appends the path of its runtime libraries to the classpath.

With JDK 1.1 however, you have to include the runtime libraries. In other words, you must be sure that the classpath contains a reference to the JVM's runtime libraries.

JAR Files

As you have seen, when you compile Java applications, the compiler generates several directories and subdirectories. There is one directory for every word in the package name. The com.psol.lel package, for example, creates three directories: com, psol, and lel.

This makes it difficult to deploy applications because you must not only copy the class files but also make sure you create all the right directories and copy the files to the right places.

Java Archive (JAR) files were introduced to solve this problem. A JAR file groups all the classes in an application and it ensures that the paths are also preserved.

Internally, JAR files are zip files so you can create them with WinZIP or another zip tool. In practice, however, it is easier to use the JAR application included in the JDK.

EXAMPLE

You create a JAR file with the following command:

```
jar cvf xdic.jar com\psol\xdic\XDic.class
```

If everything goes well, this command creates a new file xdir.jar. You can use this file in a classpath instead of your application directory, as in

```
set classpath=c:\jetty\lib\javax.servlet.jar;
➥c:\jetty\lib\com.mortbay.Jetty.jar;xdir.jar
```

Java Core API

Java comes with an extensive library that covers many needs. The standard library or core API is available in the java packages. The main packages are as follows:

- java.applet defines the API for applets.

- java.awt is the library for graphical user interface development. AWT supports buttons, menus, list boxes, and more.

- java.beans provides services for Java components or JavaBeans.

- java.io provides services to read and write data streams (mainly from files).

- java.lang provides core objects such as exceptions. You do not need to import this package; it is always imported.

- java.net provides network services.

- java.sql provides access to SQL databases through an interface similar to ODBC.

- java.util provides utility classes such as Vector, Hashtable, and Calendar.

Obviously, you are not limited to the packages in the core API. You can download more packages such as IBM's XML for Java and use them in your application.

What's Next

Study the examples in Chapter 12 to improve your mastery of Java. With the combination of Java and XML, you are limited only by your imagination.

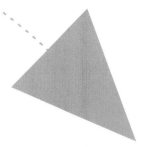

Glossary

API—Application Programming Interface.

attribute—A name/value pair attached to an element.

CORBA—Common Object Request Broker Architecture, an object-oriented middleware.

CSS—Cascading Style Sheet, a style sheet language originally developed for HTML. See also *XSL*.

DCD—Document Content Description, a proposed replacement for DTD. See also *DDML*, *DTD*, *SOX*, *XML-Data*, and *X-Schema*.

DDML—Document Definition Markup Language, a proposed replacement for *DTD*. See also *DCD*, *DTD*, *SOX*, *XML-Data*, and *X-Schema*.

document—Unit of control in XML.

DOM—Document Object Model, an API for XML parsers. See also *SAX*.

DTD—Document Type Definition, the model of an XML document. See also *DCD*, *DDML*, *SOX*, *XML-Data*, and *X-Schema*.

EDI—Electronic Data Interchange, a technology used to electronically exchange business documents such as invoices and orders.

element—Logical unit of information in XML.

entity—Physical unit of storage in XML.

HTML—Hypertext Markup Language, the format of Web pages.

HTTP—Hypertext Transport Protocol, the protocol spoken by Web servers and browsers.

ISO—International Standards Organization, an official organization that publishes standards.

markup—Structural information or formatting instructions added to the content of an electronic document.

middleware—Technology that simplifies the building of distributed applications.

namespace—A mechanism used to identify the owner of XML elements. The namespace enables XML to combine elements from different sources.

notation—Format of an external entity in XML.

parser—Software library in charge of reading and writing XML documents.

PI—Processing Instruction, a mechanism for including non-XML instructions in an XML document.

RDF—Resource Description Framework, a proposed W3C recommendation to carry metadata.

SAX—Simple API for XML. See also *DOM*.

SGML—Standard Generalized Markup Language, the ancestor of both HTML and XML.

SOX—Schema for object-oriented XML, a proposed replacement for DTD. See also *DCD*, *DDML*, *DTD*, *XML-Data*, and *X-Schema*.

tag—Element of markup in XML.

URL—Uniform Resource Locator, the address of a resource on the Web.

W3C—World Wide Web Consortium, the body in charge of Web standardization.

XLink—A mechanism for establishing links in XML documents.

XML—eXtensible Markup Language, a new markup language published by the W3C to address the limitations of HTML.

XML-Data—A proposed replacement for DTD. See also *DCD*, *DDML*, *DTD*, *SOX*, and *X-Schema*.

XQL—XML Query Language, a proposed language for extracting data from XML documents.

XSL—XML Stylesheet Language, a style sheet language developed specifically for XML. See also *CSS*.

X-Schema—A generic name for proposed replacement of the DTD. See also *DCD*, *DDML*, *DTD*, *SOX*, and *XML-Data*.

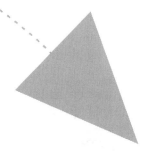

Index

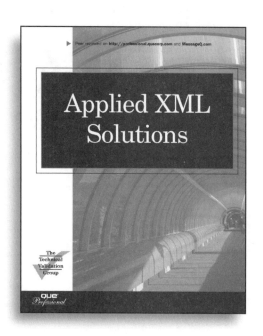